THE SAGA OF TANYA THE EVIL

18

ORIGINAL STORY: Carlo Zen
ART: Chika Tojo
CHARACTER DESIGN: Shinobu Shinotsuki

EMPIRE (including occupied territory)
COUNTRIES AT WAR
REGIONS OF CONFLICT
NEUTRAL COUNTRIES
100 0 100 200 300
REGADONIA ENTENTE ALLIANCE
RUSSY FEDERATION
IMPERIAL NORDEN
ALBION COMMONWEALTH
IMPERIAL OSTLAND (POTENTIAL DISPUTE)
EMPIRE
UNIFIED STATES
IMPERIAL DACIA
PRINCIPALITY OF DACIA
FRANÇOIS REPUBLIC
KINGDOM OF ILDOA
WALDSTÄTTE CONFEDERACY
ISPAGNA COLLECTIVE
UNREDEEMED ILDOA (POTENTIAL DISPUTE)

Die Zeiten

DIE KRIEGSGESCHICHTE EINES KLEINEN MÄDCHEN No.018

The battle log so far...

Our protagonist, a coolheaded salaryman in contemporary Japan, dies after being pushed off a train platform by a resentful man he fired.

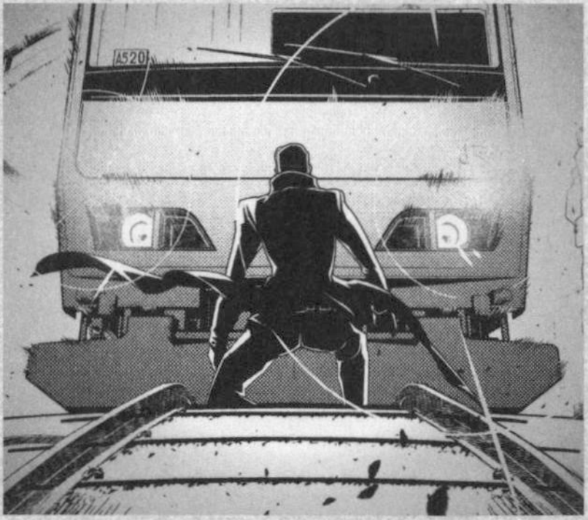
A520

In the world beyond death, he encounters Being X, who claims to be the Creator. His lack of faith angers the being, and he is reborn in another world where gunfire and magic intermingle in combat. "You will be born into an unscientific world as a woman, come to know war, and be driven to your limits!"
In the other world, he is reincarnated as Tanya Degurechaff. Upon recognition of her magic aptitude, she is sent to the battlefield at the age of nine.

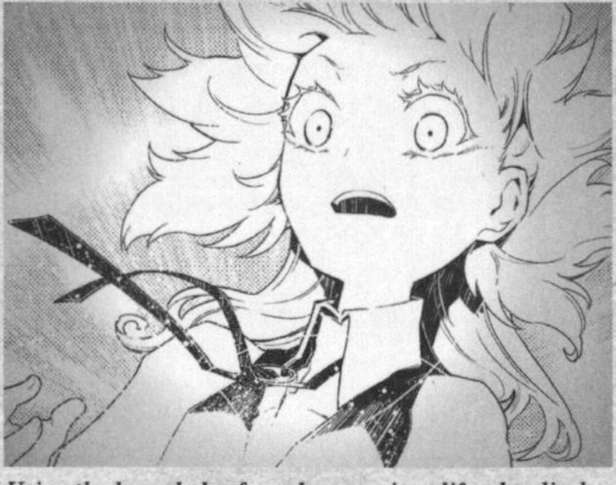

Using the knowledge from her previous life, she climbs the ranks, aiming for a safe position in the rear, but her outstanding achievements and bravery make such a good impression on her superiors that she is, on the contrary, repeatedly sent to the front lines...

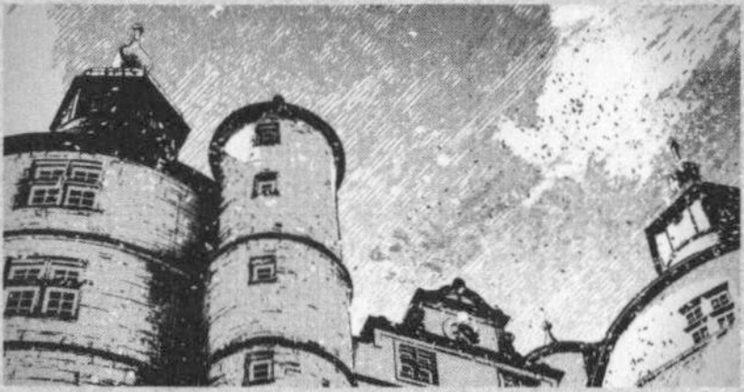

Tanya has become the leader of the 203rd Aerial Mage Battalion and, after many hardships along the way, been stationed on the fiercely contested Rhine lines in recognition of her achievements in Dacia and Norden. Despite her best efforts, the war refused to turn in the Empire's favor, and the battle of attrition on the Rhine became an utter quagmire.
In response, General von Zettour devised and executed a new plan—Operation Shock and Awe. The Empire would give up its own territory in order to create an axis of advance spanning much of the continent, enabling them to carry out the largest encirclement in recorded history.
After drawing in and overstretching the Republican Army in the first stage of the plan, the General Staff gave the command to attack the François Republic's now defenseless headquarters. Tanya and the 203rd were charged with accomplishing this mission and ordered to fly across the continent on long-range missiles, code-named V-1s, that should have been impossible to create with this era's technology.

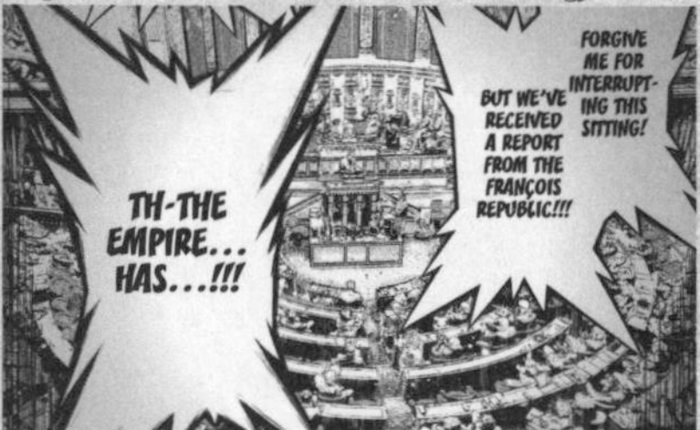
FORGIVE ME FOR INTERRUPTING THIS SITTING!
BUT WE'VE RECEIVED A REPORT FROM THE FRANÇOIS REPUBLIC!!!
TH-THE EMPIRE... HAS...!!!

After making it through this flight, Tanya and her team successfully completed their assault on the HQ. The unprepared Republican soldiers guarding the headquarters were helpless to stop these hardened aerial mages from laying waste to the base, and the Commonwealth spies hiding there died, impotently lamenting the failure of their mission in the process.
Meanwhile, few members of the ruling class of the Commonwealth are aware they are in such dire straits. With the Republican Army seemingly advancing into imperial territory uncontested, the Empire appears to already have one foot in the grave. Little do they realize that a portal to hell yawns open below their own feet even as they speak...

THE SAGA OF TANYA THE EVI

Character Introductions

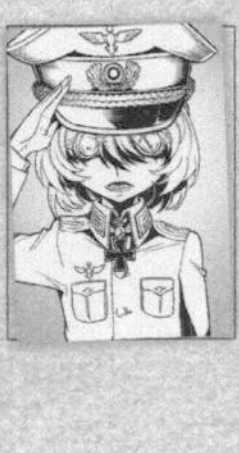

Name des Paßinhabers

Tanya von Degurechaff

(Rufname, Familienname)

Dienstgrad	Dienststellung
MAJOR	AERIAL MAGIC OFFICER

An extremely rational little girl who was a salaryman in her previous life. Joins the army to escape life in the orphanage. Becomes a mage after her talent for magic is recognized. She couldn't care less about national defense and simply wants to live a quiet life safe in the rear. Unfortunately, misunderstanding after misunderstanding causes others to think she is a patriot full of fighting spirit.

(Angaben zur Person)

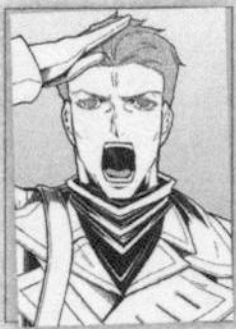

Name des Paßinhabers

Johann-Mattäus Weiss

(Rufname, Familienname)

Dienstgrad	Dienststellung
FIRST LIEUTENANT	AERIAL MAGIC OFFICER

A mage in the Imperial Army and a member of Major Degurechaff's 203rd Aerial Mage Battalion. He's an earnest, outstanding soldier, but because he doesn't have much combat experience, most of his knowledge comes from textbooks. Having made it through the hellish training, it's clear his skills and fighting spirit are impeccable. That plus his talent for unit management means the army has high expectations of him.

(Angaben zur Person)

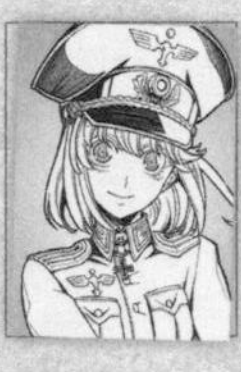

Name des Paßinhabers

Viktoriya Ivanovna Serebryakov

(Rufname, Familienname)

Dienstgrad	Dienststellung
SECOND LIEUTENANT	AERIAL MAGIC OFFICER

A mage in the Imperial Army. After being practically forcec to enlist in the cadet corps due to her magic abilities, she is stationed in a unit on the front lines. Having proven herself capable in combat, she is recommended for the officer track. She sees Major Degurechaff as a kind, peace-loving individual and respects and supports her as her outstanding adjutant.

(Angaben zur Person)

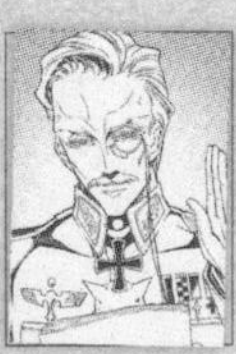

Name des Paßinhabers

Hans von Zettour

(Rufname, Familienname)

Dienstgrad	Dienststellung
MAJOR GENERAL	DEPUTY DIRECTOR OF THE SERVICE CORPS IN THE GENERAL STAFF

Employing his clear thinking and wealth of knowledge, he works on logistics and plans operations with his friend and colleague Major General Rudersdorf, the Deputy Director of Operations. He has a very high opinion of Major Degurechaff and does what he can to take her wishes into account. He's so far learned that in war college, evaluators had concerns that he was "too scholarly and thus not suited to becoming a general."

(Angaben zur Person)

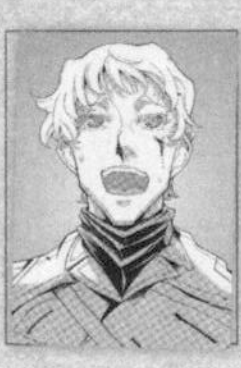

Name des Paßinhabers

Warren Grantz

(Rufname, Familienname)

Dienstgrad	Dienststellung
SECOND LIEUTENANT	AERIAL MAGIC OFFICER

A newly commissioned officer joining the 203rd Aerial Mage Battalion as a replenishment. A fresh grad from the academy, he dreams of fighting heroically to defend his country. He's still quite green as both an officer and a mage but he has a lot of potential, so his future seems bright.

(Angaben zur Person)

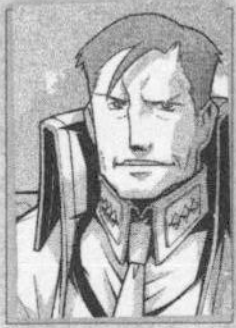

Name des Paßinhabers

Sir Isaac Dustin Drake

(Rufname, Familienname)

Dienstgrad	Dienststellung
COLONEL	ALBION COMMONWEALTH MARINE MAGIC OFFICER

A Commonwealth colonel, an aerial mage who has become an Ace of Aces, and the head of the Drake family, which has produced powerful mages for generations. Amid the general atmosphere of optimism pervading the Commonwealth, he is one of the few people still conscious of the threat posed by the Empire. On First Lord Marlborough's orders, he has led two battalions across the Dodobird Strait to assault the Imperial Army's headquarters.

(Angaben zur Person)

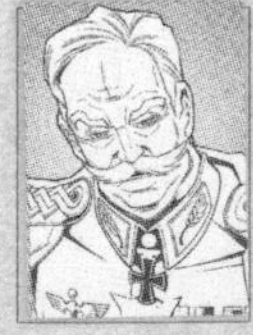

Name des Paßinhabers

Kurt von Rudersdorf

(Rufname, Familienname)

Dienstgrad	Dienststellung
MAJOR GENERAL	DEPUTY DIRECTOR OF OPERATIONS IN THE GENERAL STAFF

One of the geniuses who bears the weight of the Empire's future on his shoulders. Generally speaking, he draws up the entire Empire's battle plans and has a hand in most orders issued to the Imperial Army. Unlike his friend Major General Zettour, the Deputy Director of the Service Corps, he is the spitting image of a military man, and his own war college evaluation said that he was "both sharp and dynamic, though he has a tendency to daydream."

(Angaben zur Person)

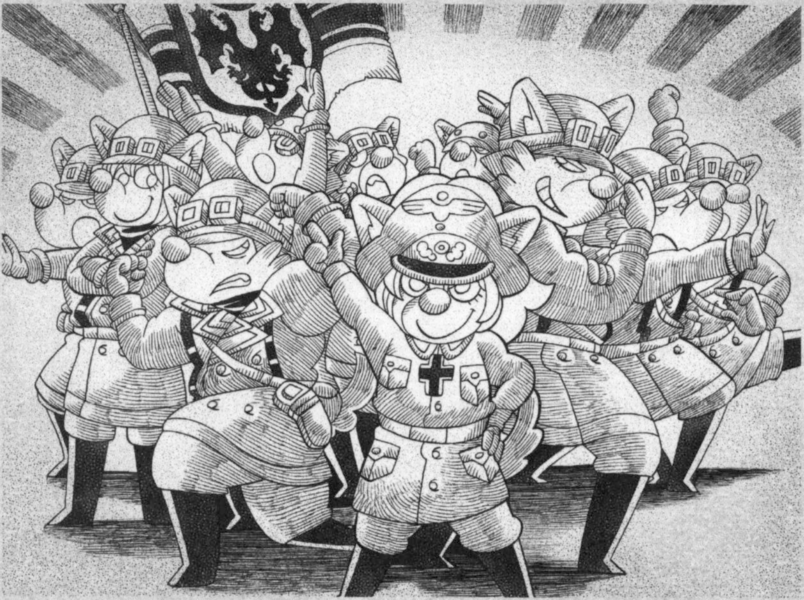

REPORTING DIRECTLY TO THE IMPERIAL ARMY GENERAL STAFF AT CENTRAL

THE 203RD AERIAL MAGE BATTALION

PERSONNEL

48 WITH FULL HEAD COUNT (1 COMMAND COMPANY, 3 WORKING COMPANIES; TOTAL OF 4 COMPANIES MAKES AN AUGMENTED BATTALION)

EQUIPMENT

IMPERIAL ARMY TYPE 97 ASSAULT COMPUTATION ORB (PREPRODUCTION RUN) / IMPERIAL ARMY AERIAL MAGE RIFLE / MACHINE GUNS / HAND GRENADES, ETC.

This unit is an aerial mage battalion commanded by the youngest recipient of the Silver Wings Assault Badge, Major Tanya "White Silver" von Degurechaff. Screened using the harshest tactics upon formation and put through training of unparalleled difficulty, its members are true elites. Thanks to their strong solidarity, they possess excellent morale, and having achieved significant results in a number of fierce battles, each of them has attained ace status. Thus, the 203rd is a "Named Unit" that sets both friend and foe trembling.

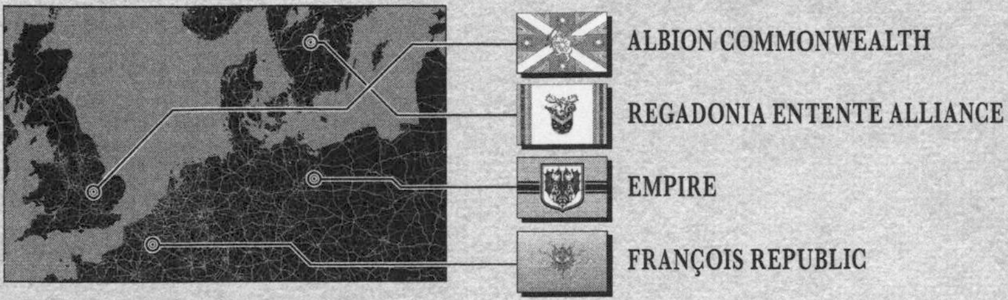
ALBION COMMONWEALTH
REGADONIA ENTENTE ALLIANCE
EMPIRE
FRANÇOIS REPUBLIC

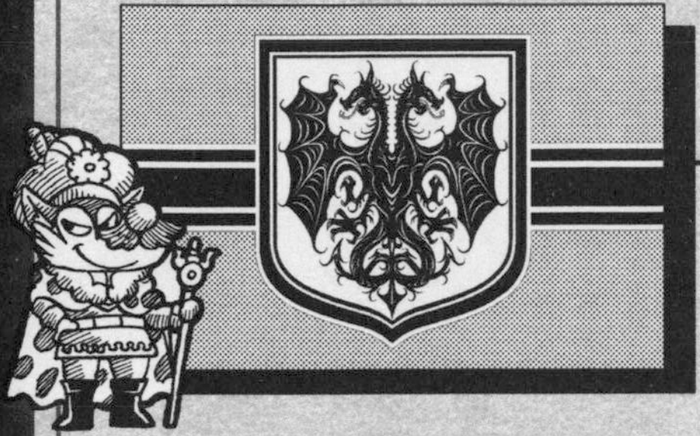

EMPIRE

Also known as the Reich, it is a country with vast territory. As an emerging power, it has an efficient economic system and a traditional government, as well as a lack of discrimination based on race or sex, so it considers itself an ideal state. Geographically enclosed by major powers, it views its surrounding neighbors as potential enemies.

REGADONIA ENTENTE ALLIANCE

A northern country with an economically driven government that is ruled by ten councilors. In response to the stagnant domestic situation, it performed exercises in contested territory in order to display its power, which in turn ruffled the Empire's feathers and sparked the current war.

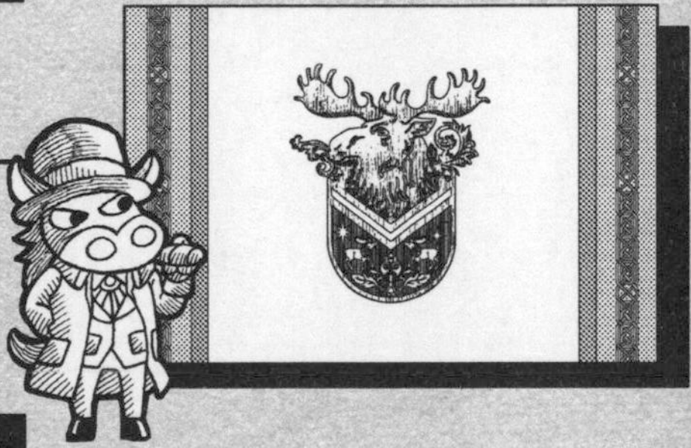

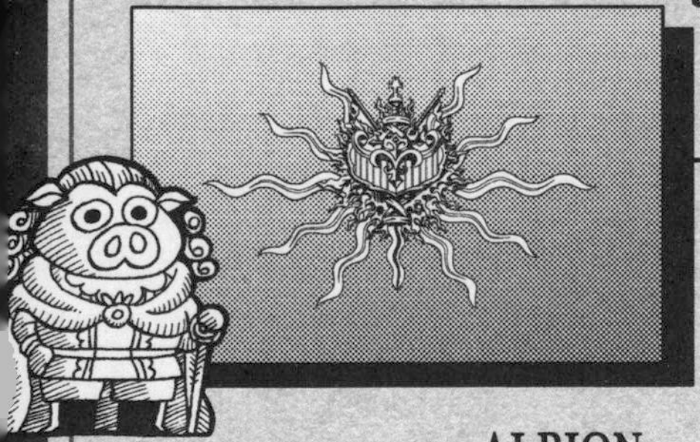

FRANÇOIS REPUBLIC

A large country that continues to have pride in its history but has switched to republican government. Though primarily an agricultural nation, its trade system and colonies contribute to its solid economic foundation. Since its national security plan was dependent on the Regadonia Entente Alliance's fighting power, it has been roped into the fight against the Empire.

ALBION COMMONWEALTH

A kingdom that has succeeded in modernizing while maintaining its old way of governance. There is a long history of shadowy political warfare within its royal court, and its venerable intelligence service has become quite skilled at preserving the nation by manipulating other countries from behind the scenes. In the current war, it's outwardly neutral.

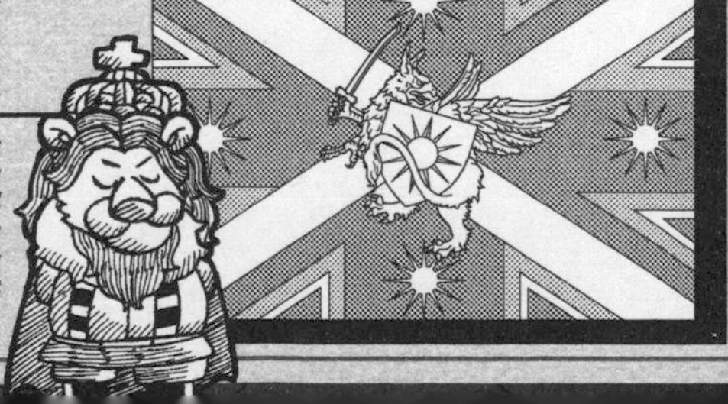

The Saga of Tanya the Evil

18

Original Story: Carlo Zen   Art: Chika Tojo
Character Design: Shinobu Shinotsuki

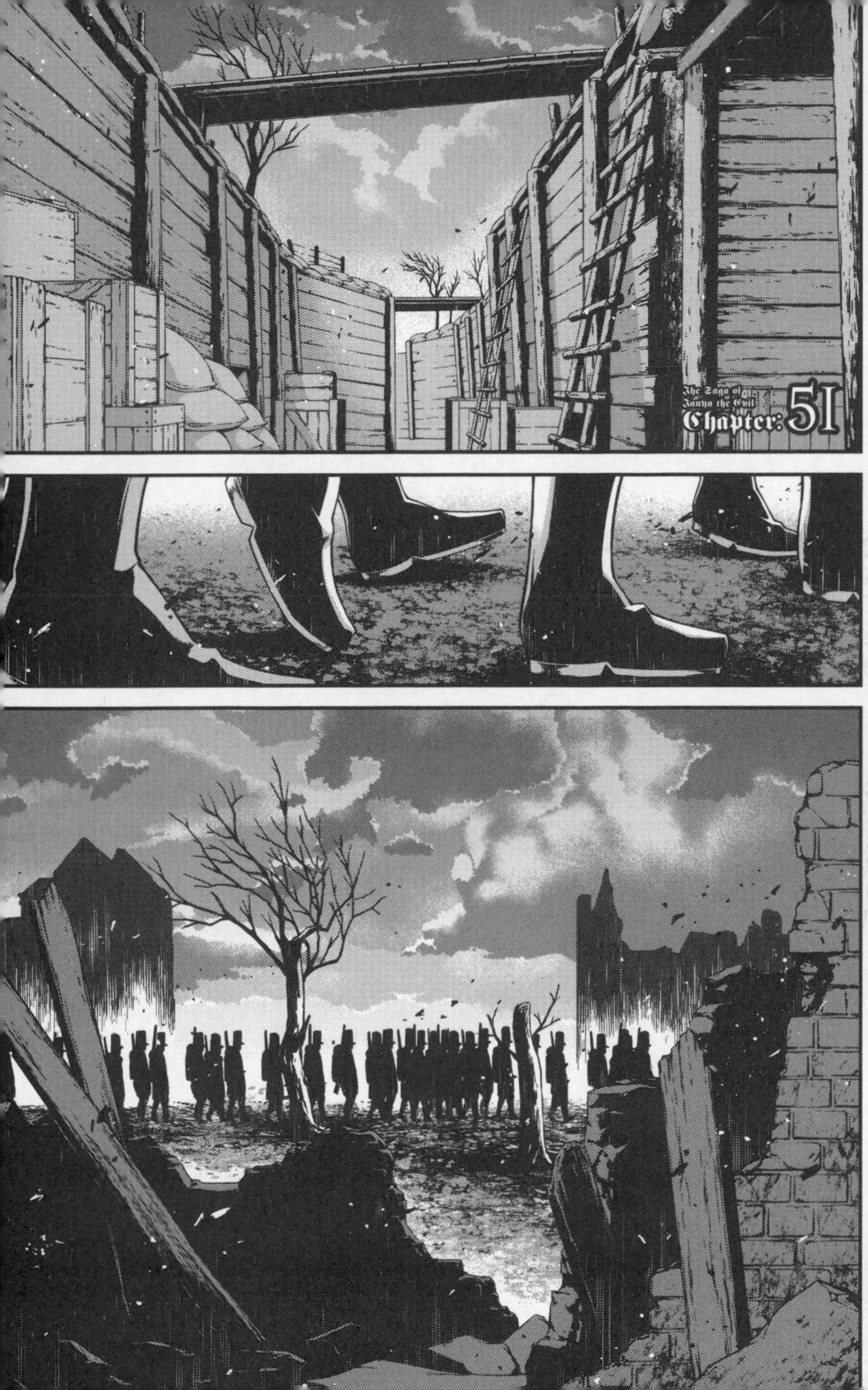
The Saga of Tanya the Evil
Chapter: 51

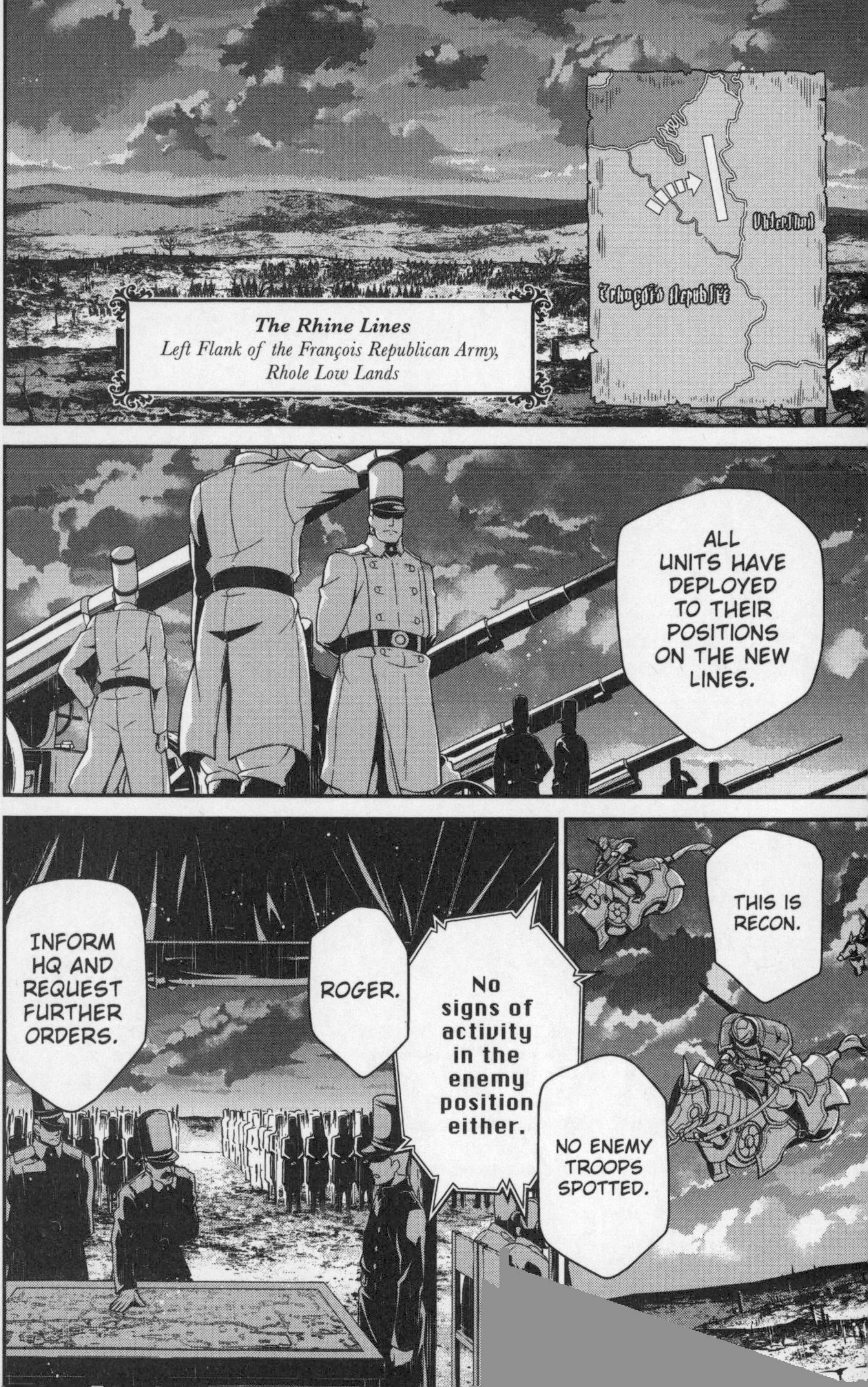
The Rhine Lines
Left Flank of the François Republican Army, Rhole Low Lands
ALL UNITS HAVE DEPLOYED TO THEIR POSITIONS ON THE NEW LINES.
THIS IS RECON.
NO ENEMY TROOPS SPOTTED.
No signs of activity in the enemy position either.
ROGER.
INFORM HQ AND REQUEST FURTHER ORDERS.

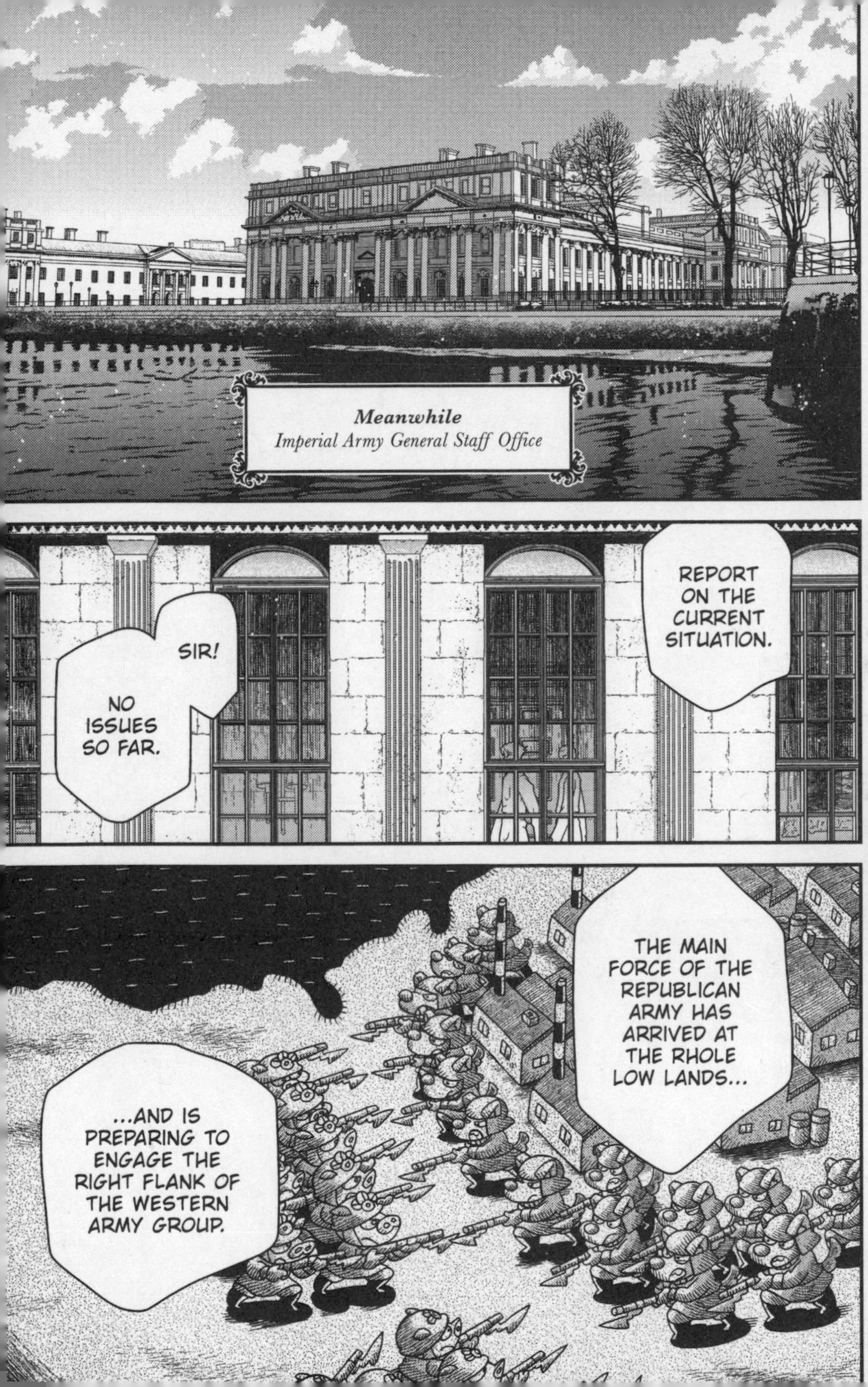
Meanwhile
Imperial Army General Staff Office
REPORT ON THE CURRENT SITUATION.
SIR!
NO ISSUES SO FAR.
THE MAIN FORCE OF THE REPUBLICAN ARMY HAS ARRIVED AT THE RHOLE LOW LANDS...
...AND IS PREPARING TO ENGAGE THE RIGHT FLANK OF THE WESTERN ARMY GROUP.

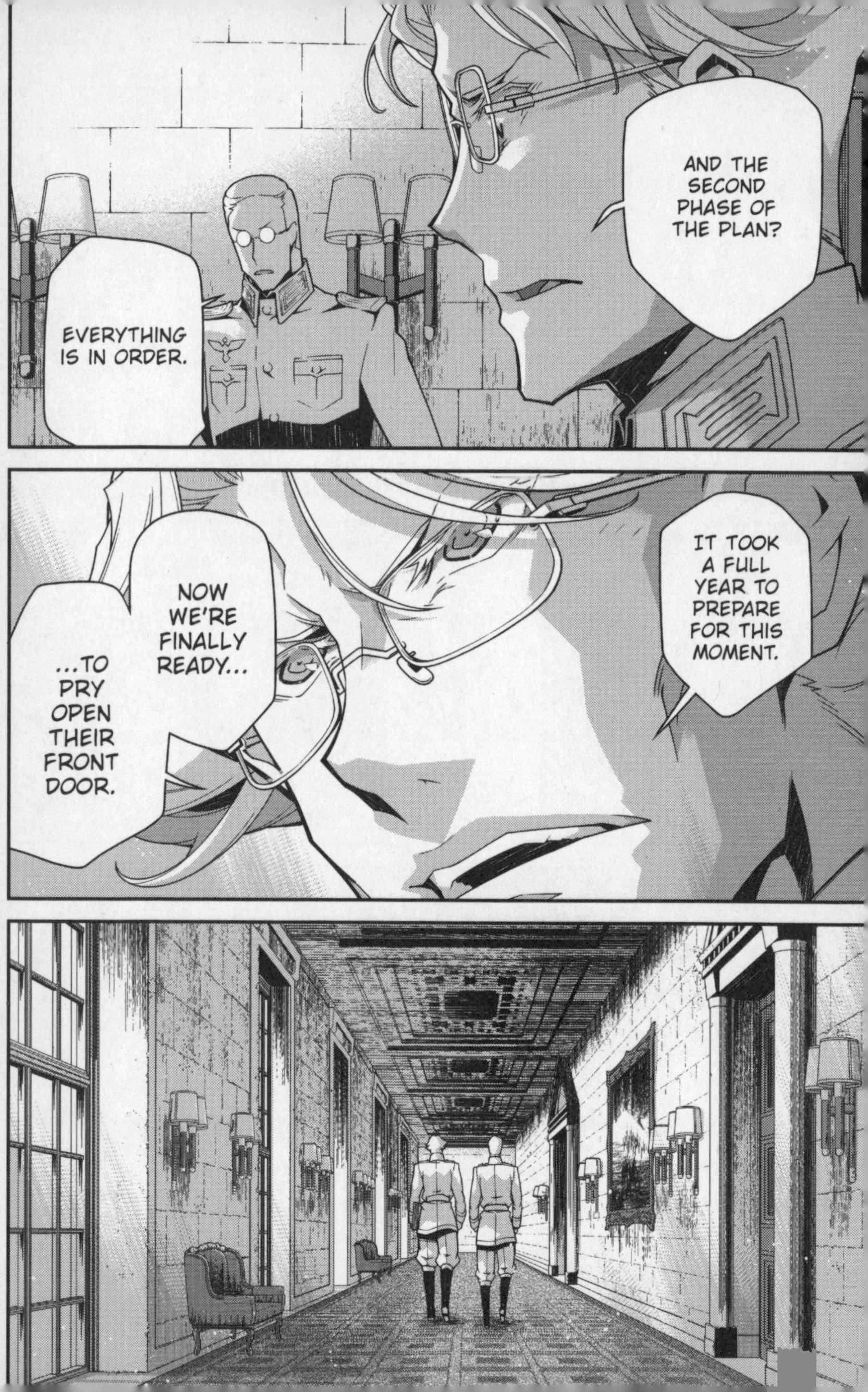
AND THE SECOND PHASE OF THE PLAN?
EVERYTHING IS IN ORDER.
IT TOOK A FULL YEAR TO PREPARE FOR THIS MOMENT.
NOW WE'RE FINALLY READY...
...TO PRY OPEN THEIR FRONT DOOR.

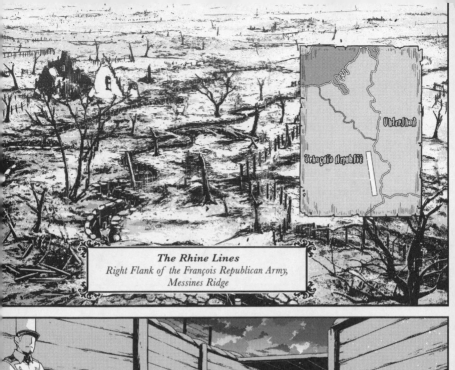

The Rhine Lines
Right Flank of the François Republican Army,
Messines Ridge

UGH... THERE'S NOTHING TO DO HERE ON THE RIGHT FLANK.

I'M ACTUALLY JEALOUS OF THOSE GUYS ON THE LEFT.

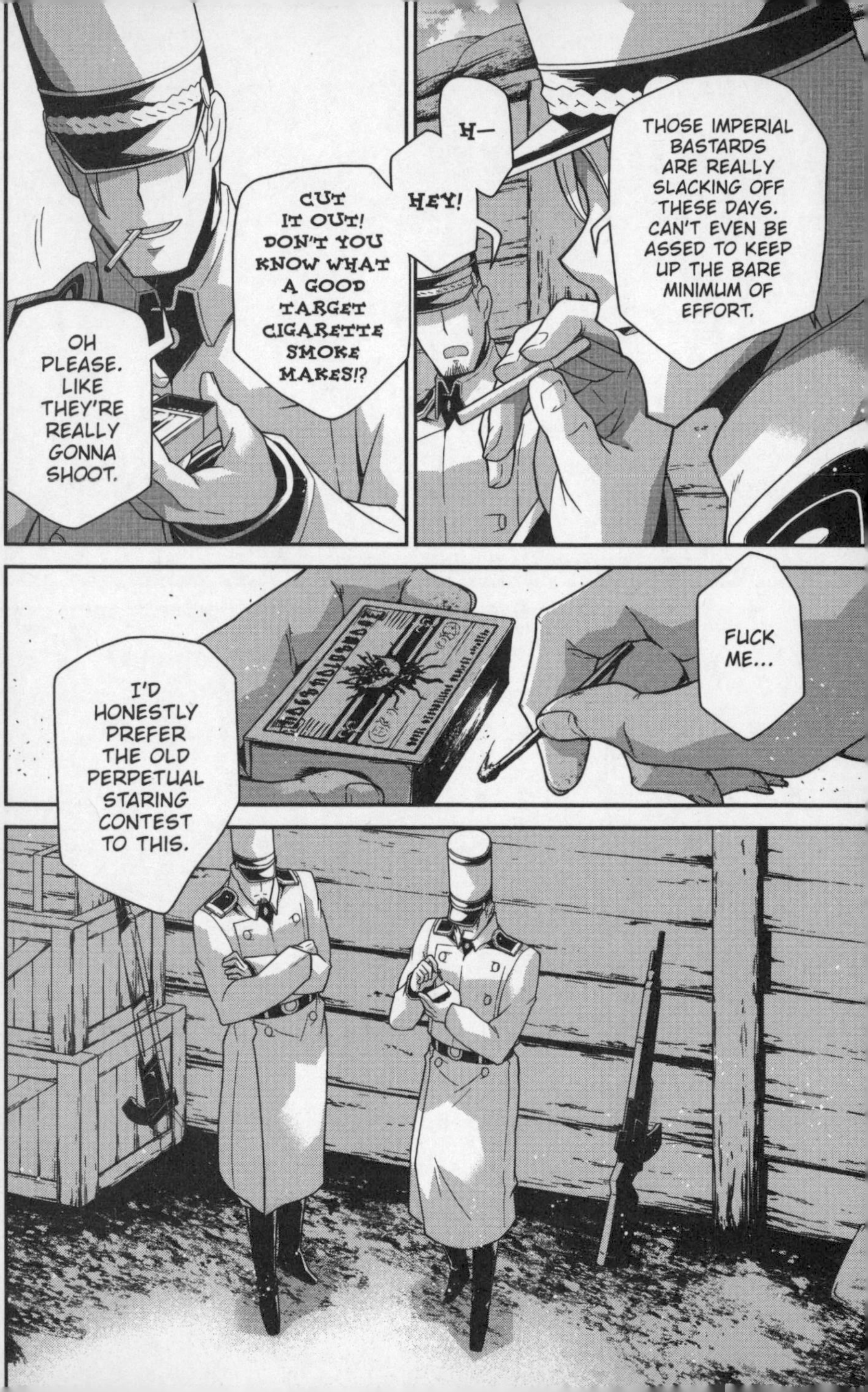
THOSE IMPERIAL BASTARDS ARE REALLY SLACKING OFF THESE DAYS. CAN'T EVEN BE ASSED TO KEEP UP THE BARE MINIMUM OF EFFORT.
H—
HEY!
CUT IT OUT! DON'T YOU KNOW WHAT A GOOD TARGET CIGARETTE SMOKE MAKES!?
OH PLEASE. LIKE THEY'RE REALLY GONNA SHOOT.
FUCK ME...
I'D HONESTLY PREFER THE OLD PERPETUAL STARING CONTEST TO THIS.

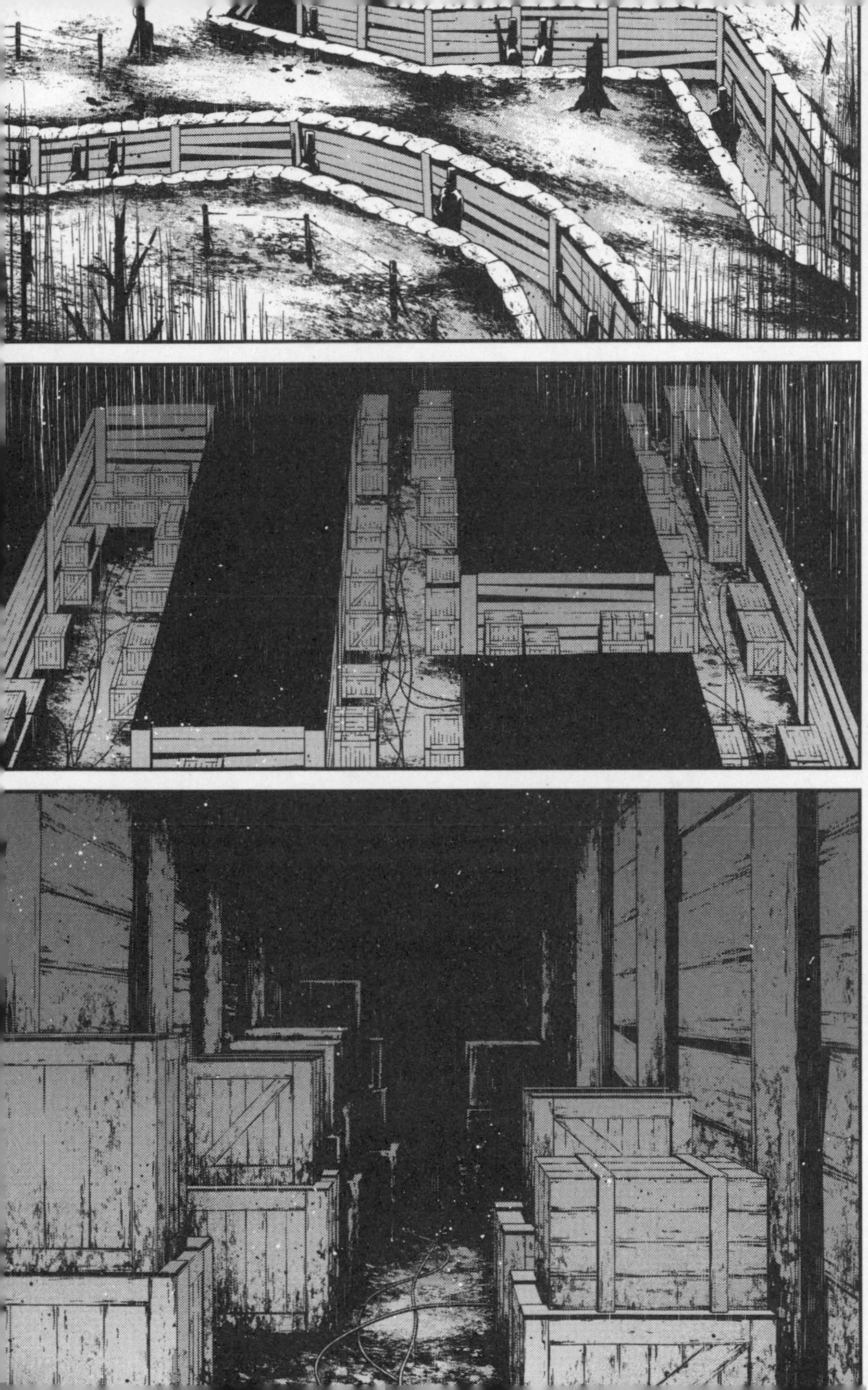

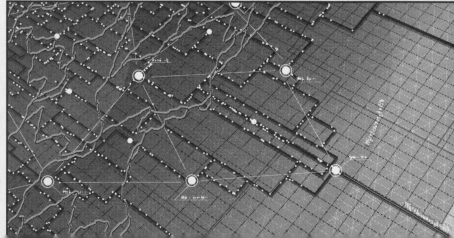

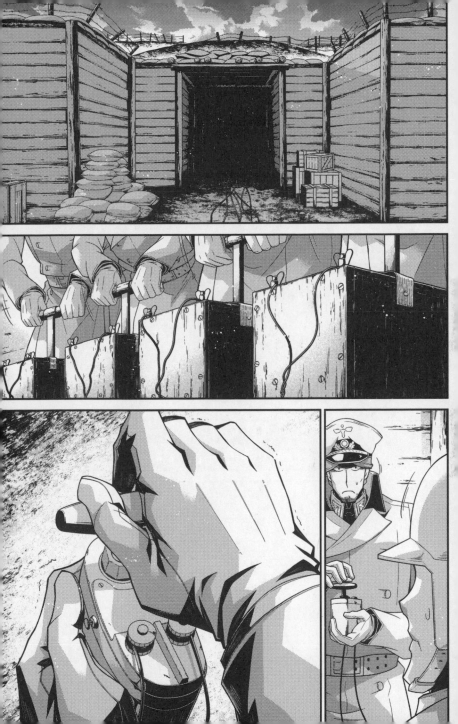

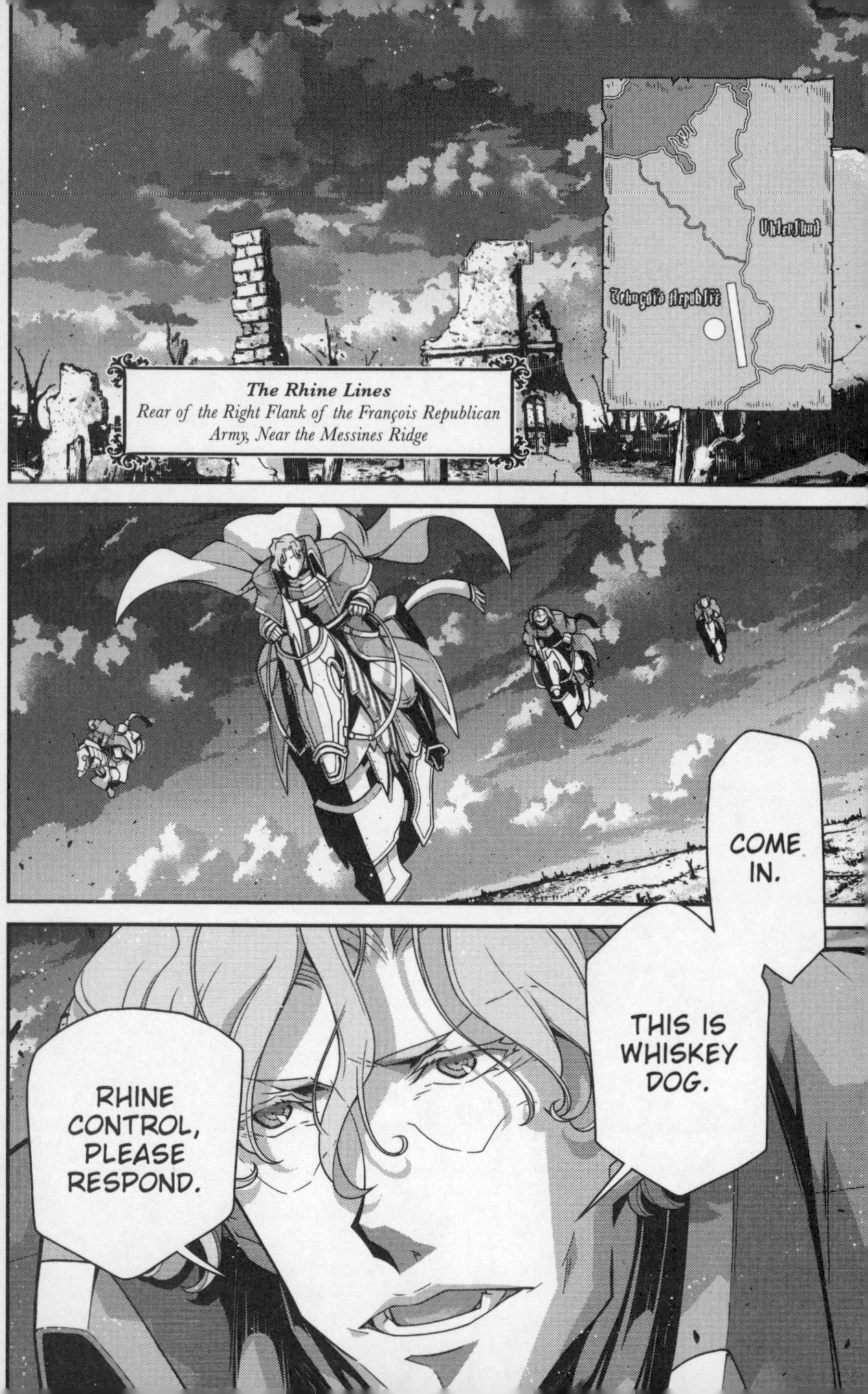
The Rhine Lines
Rear of the Right Flank of the François Republican Army, Near the Messines Ridge
COME IN.
THIS IS WHISKEY DOG.
RHINE CONTROL, PLEASE RESPOND.

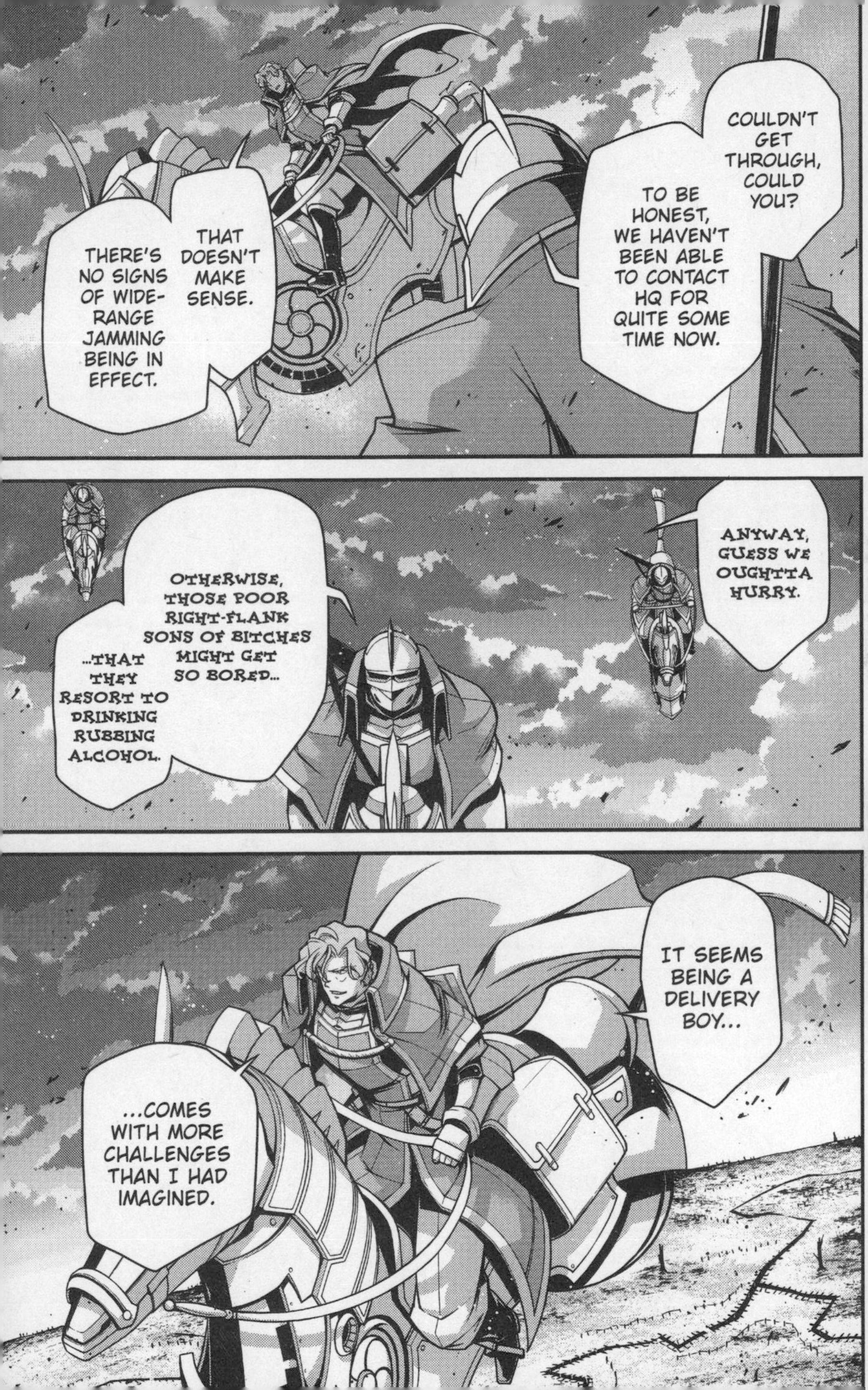
COULDN'T GET THROUGH, COULD YOU?
TO BE HONEST, WE HAVEN'T BEEN ABLE TO CONTACT HQ FOR QUITE SOME TIME NOW.
THAT DOESN'T MAKE SENSE.
THERE'S NO SIGNS OF WIDE-RANGE JAMMING BEING IN EFFECT.
ANYWAY, GUESS WE OUGHTTA HURRY.
OTHERWISE, THOSE POOR RIGHT-FLANK SONS OF BITCHES MIGHT GET SO BORED...
...THAT THEY RESORT TO DRINKING RUBBING ALCOHOL.
IT SEEMS BEING A DELIVERY BOY...
...COMES WITH MORE CHALLENGES THAN I HAD IMAGINED.

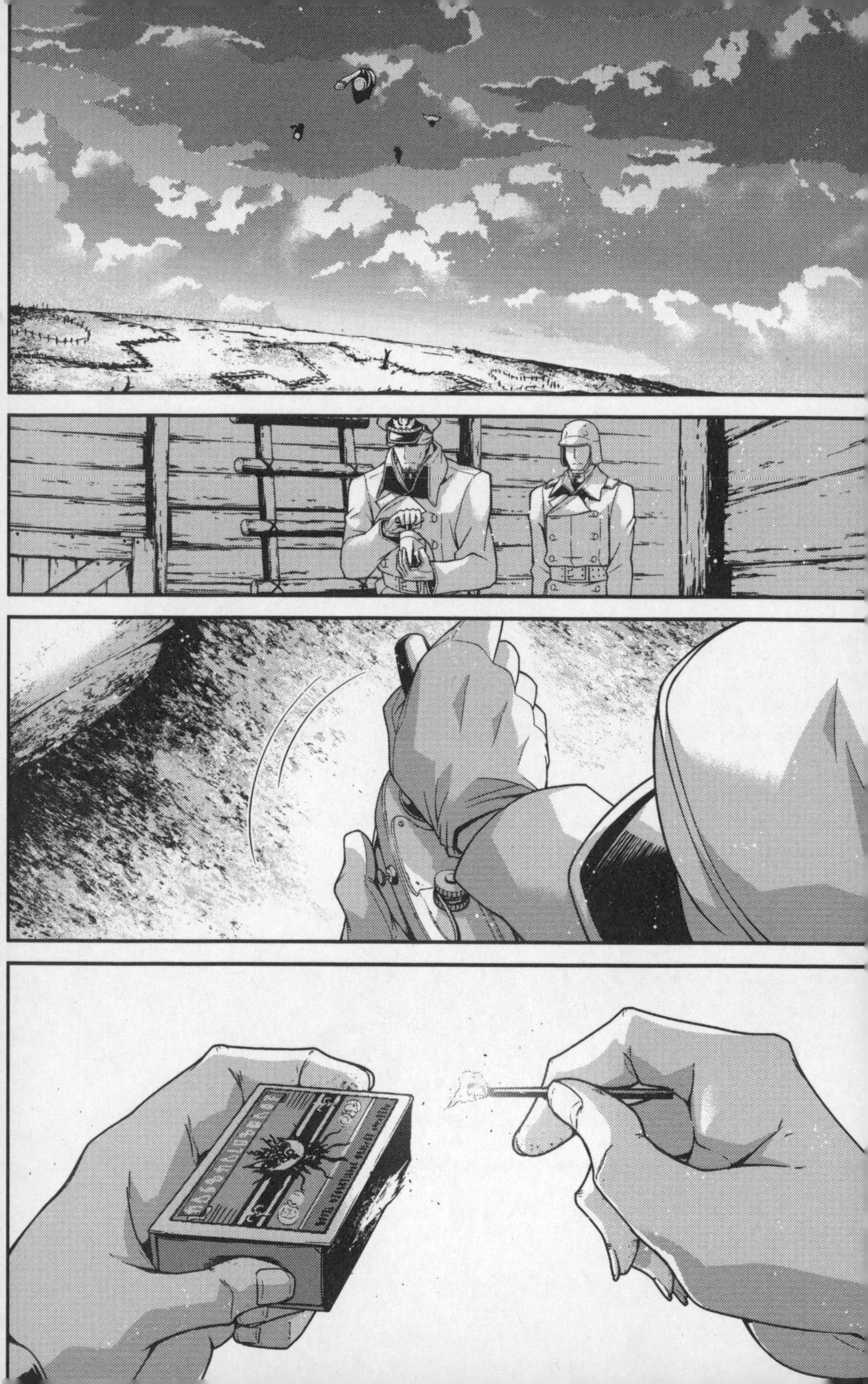

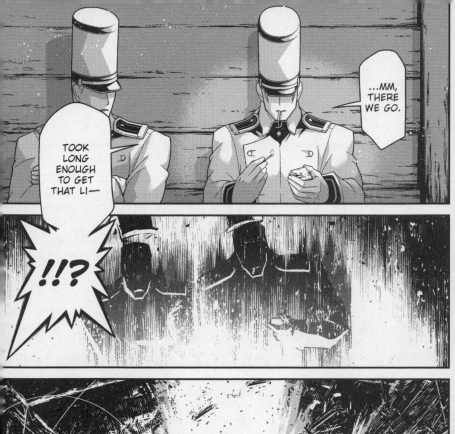

...MM, THERE WE GO.

TOOK LONG ENOUGH TO GET THAT LI—

!!?

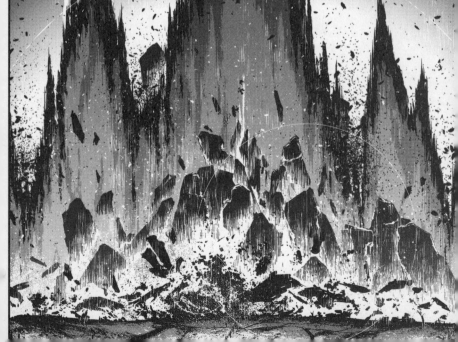

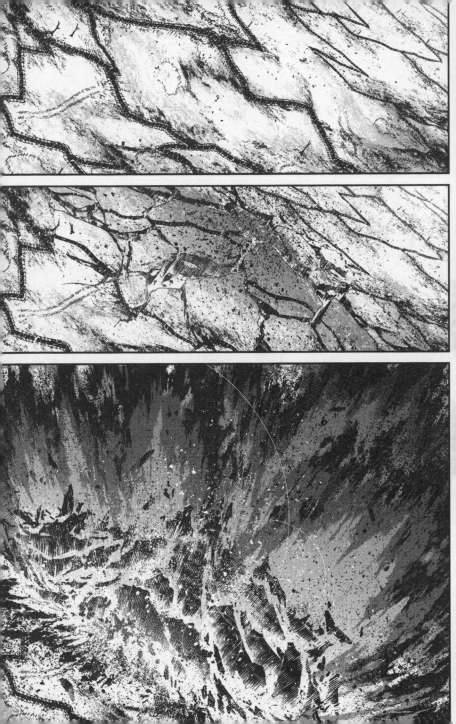

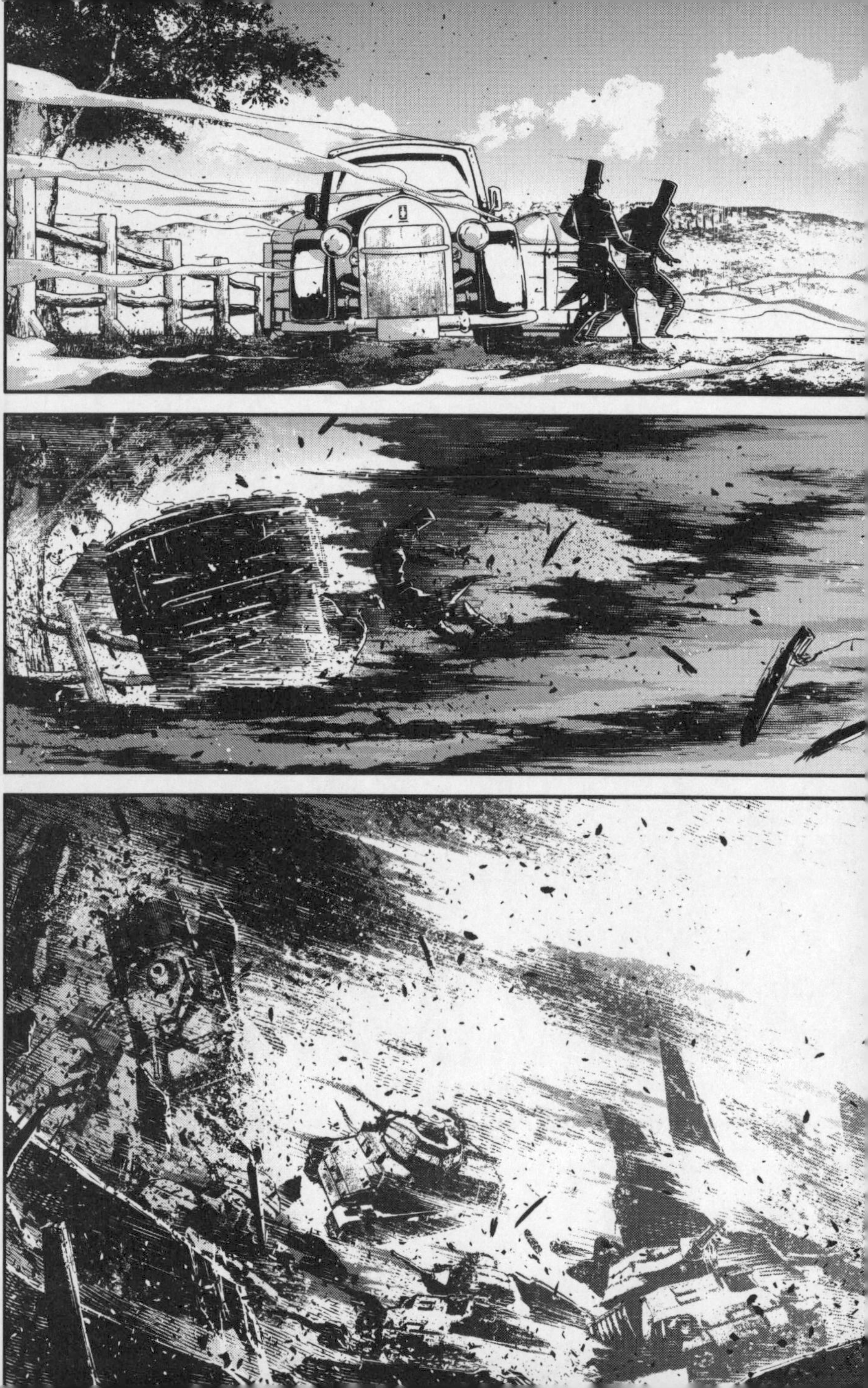

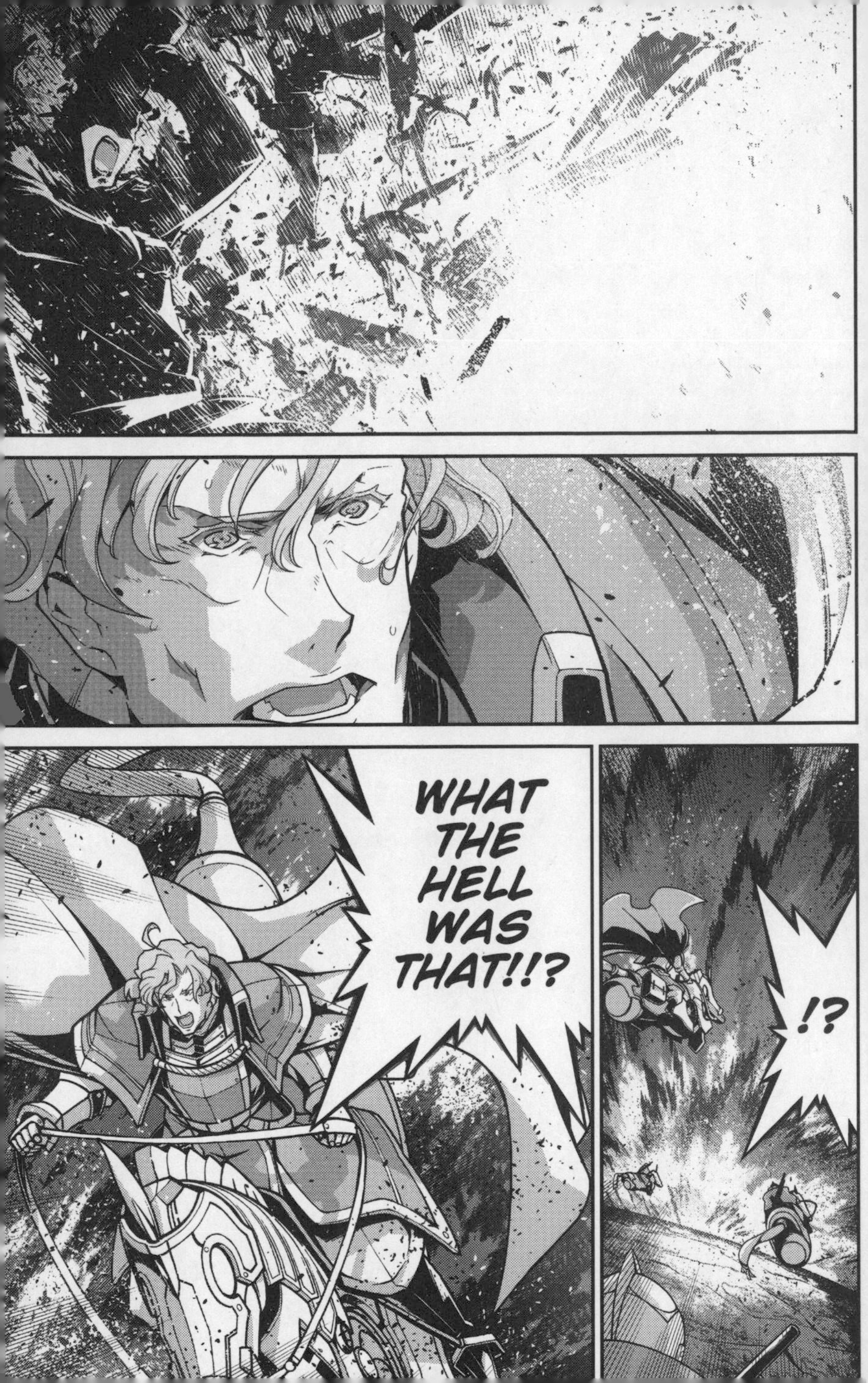
!?
WHAT THE HELL WAS THAT!!?

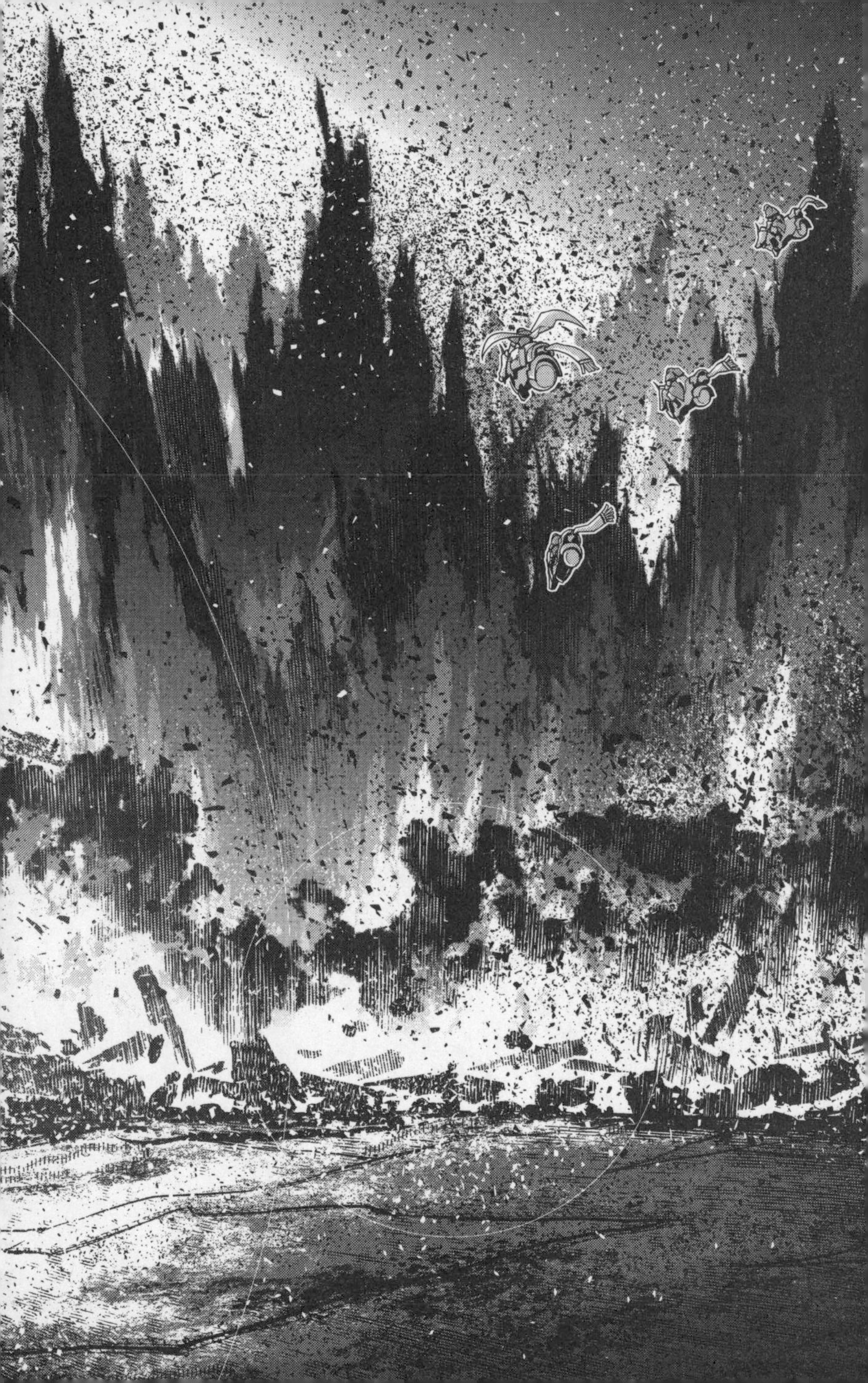

Chapter 51

The Intervention, Which Was Too Late II

The Saga of Tanya the Evil

Chapter: 51

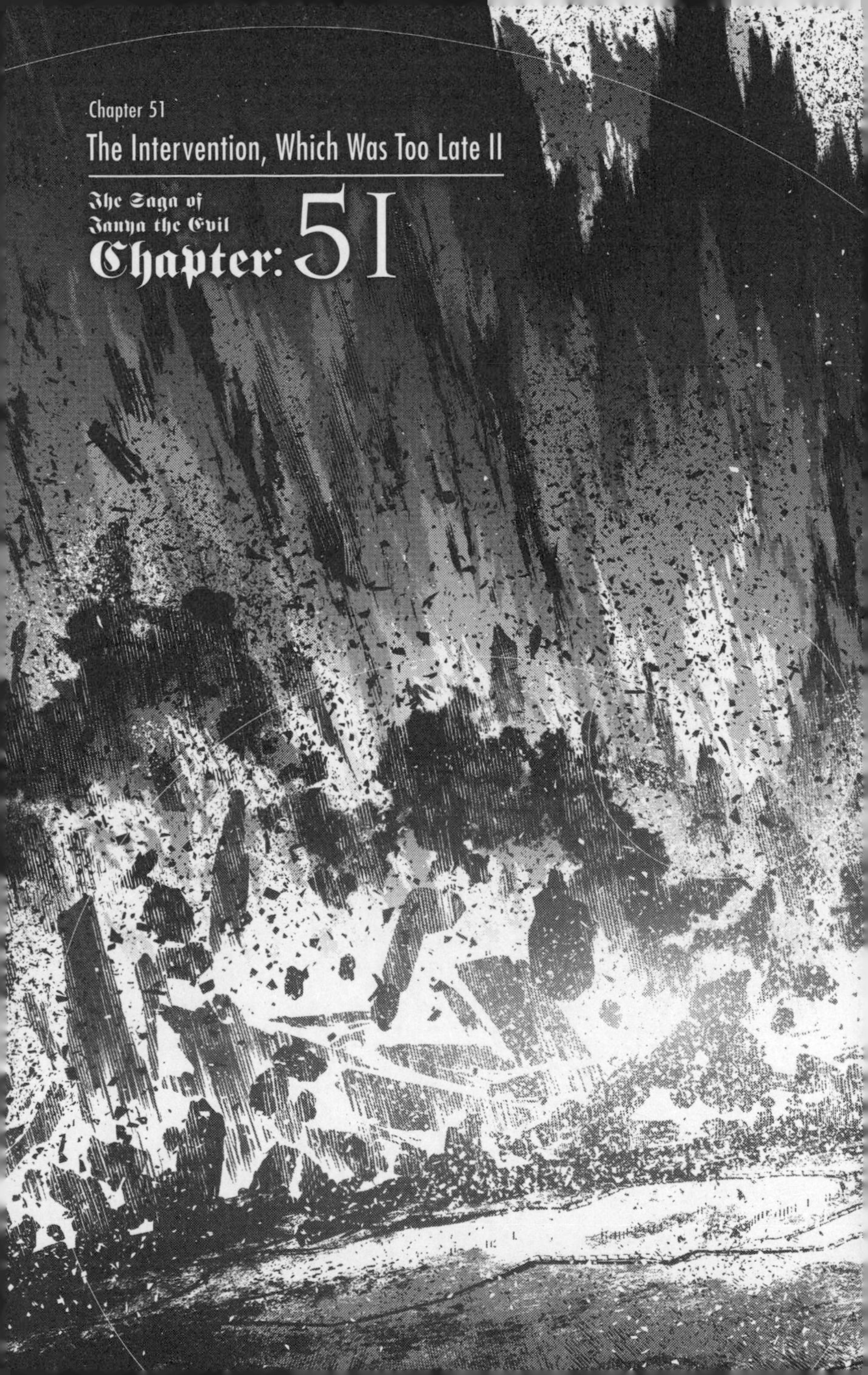

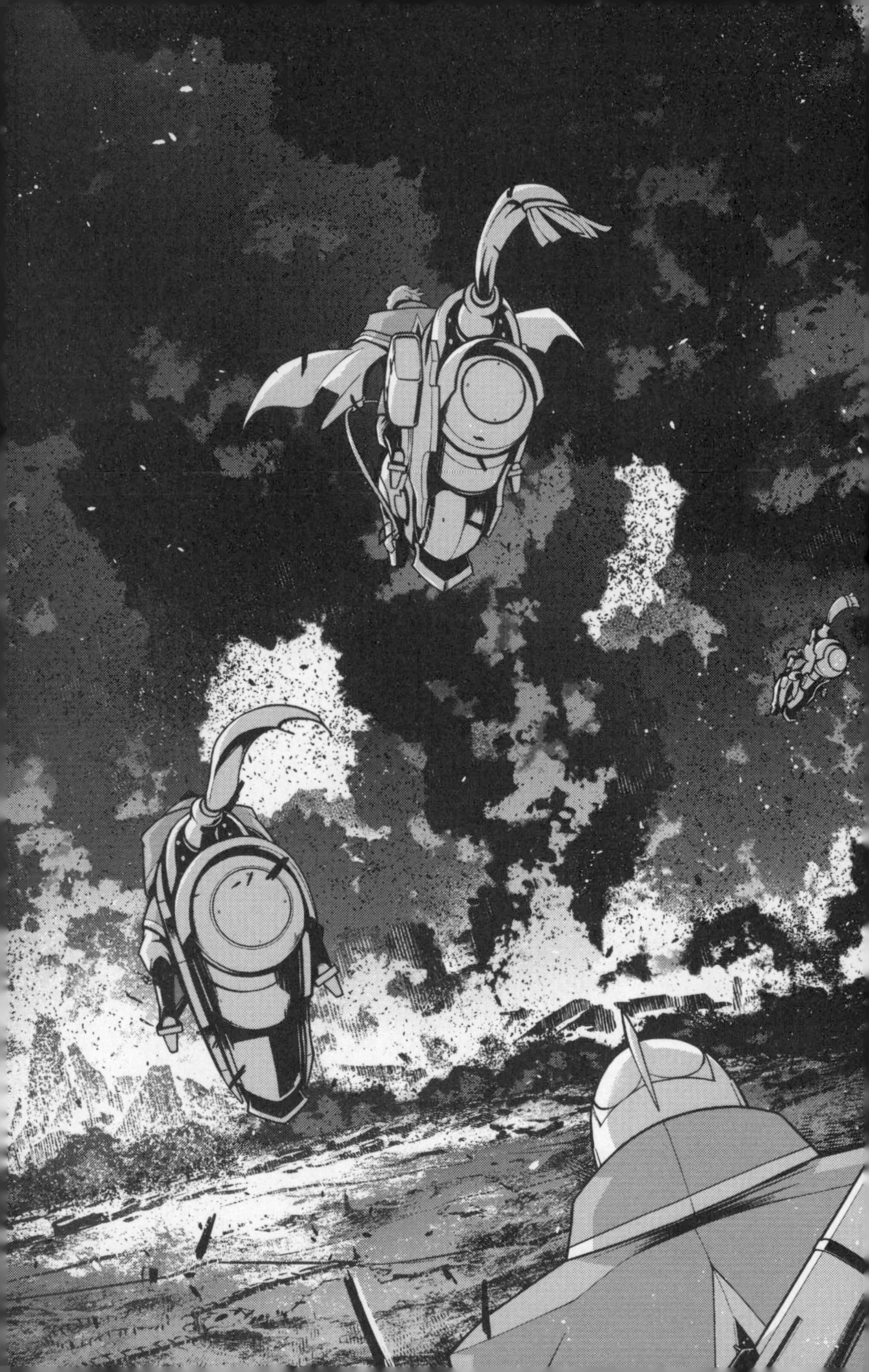

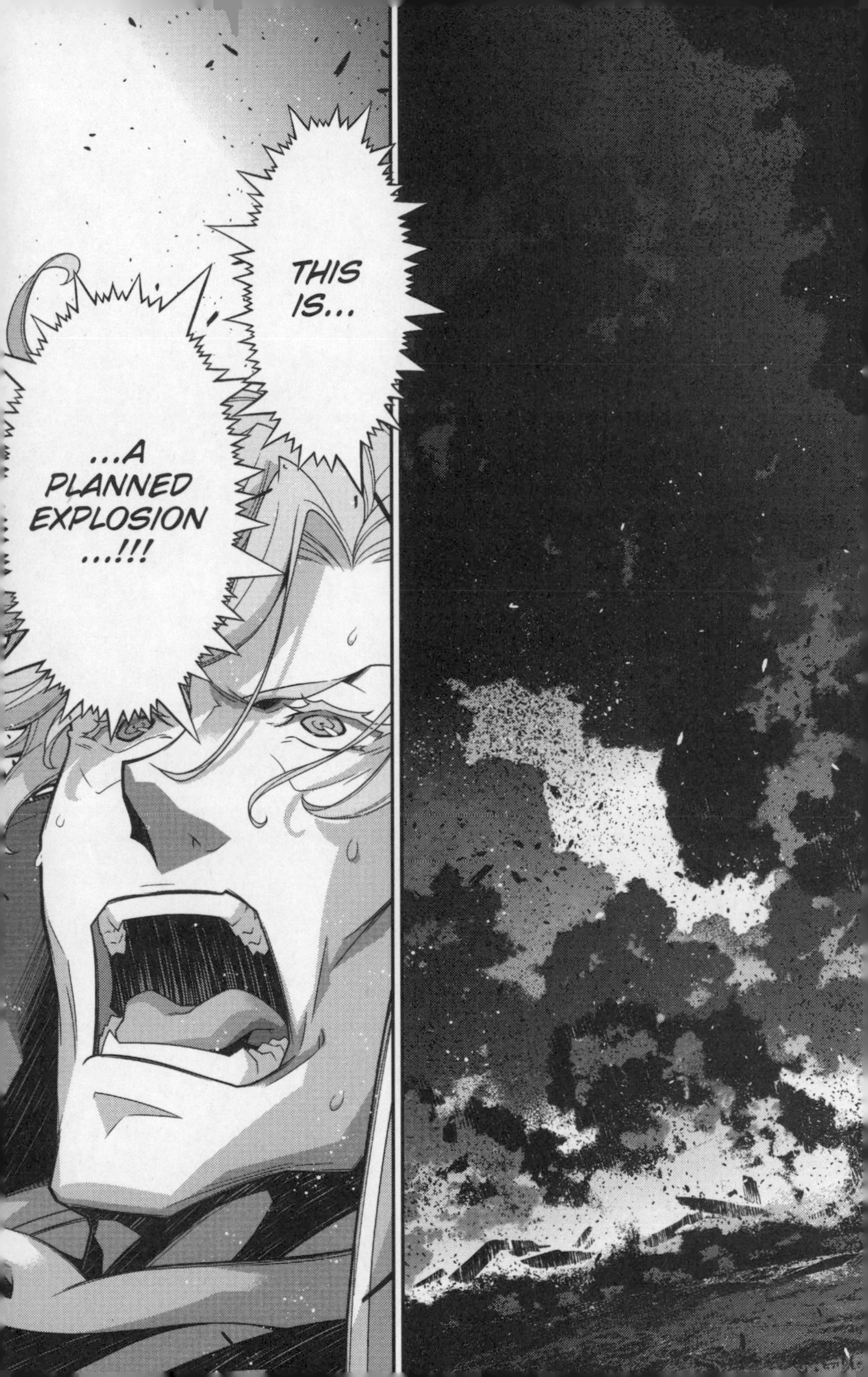
THIS IS...
...A PLANNED EXPLOSION ...!!!

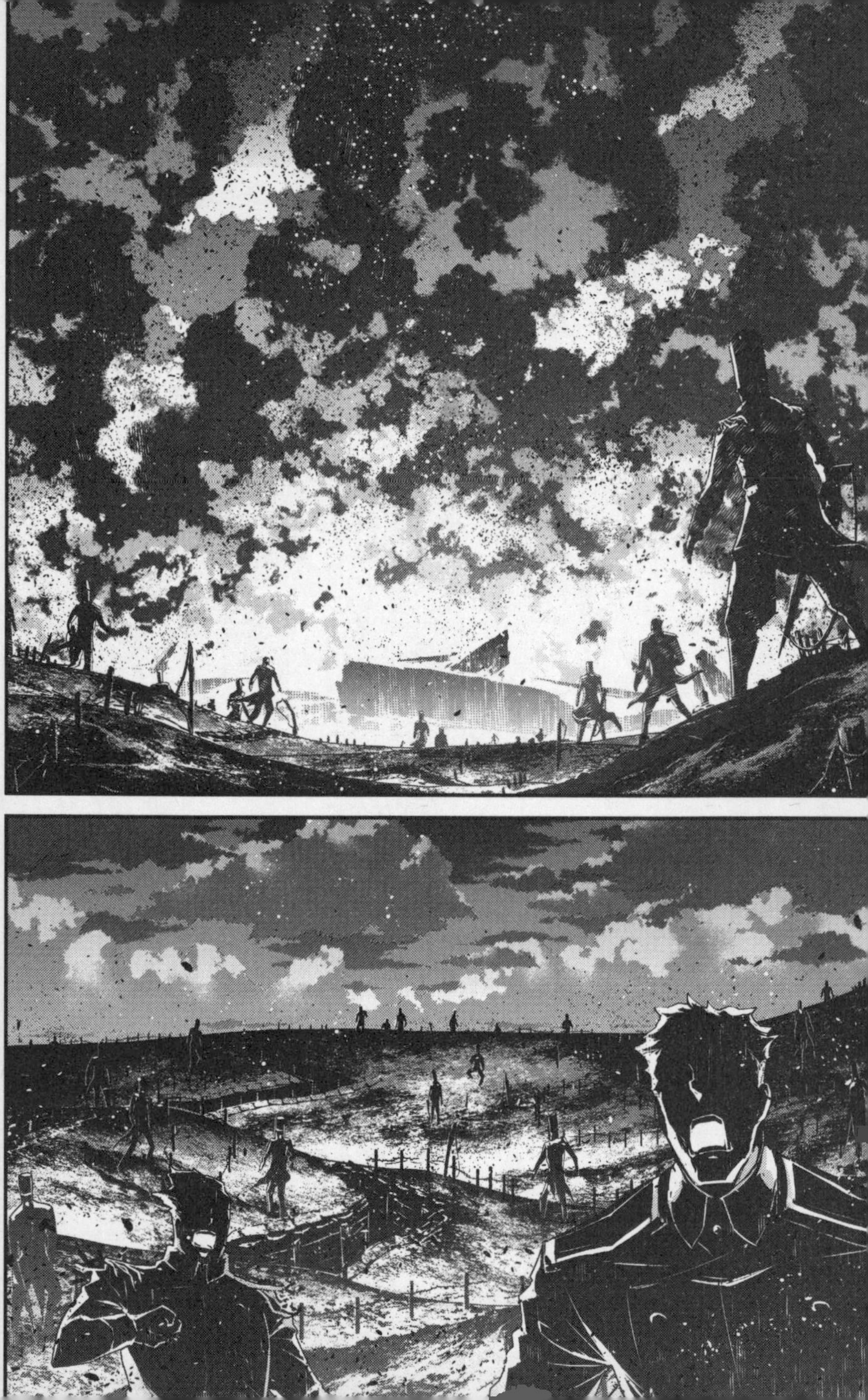

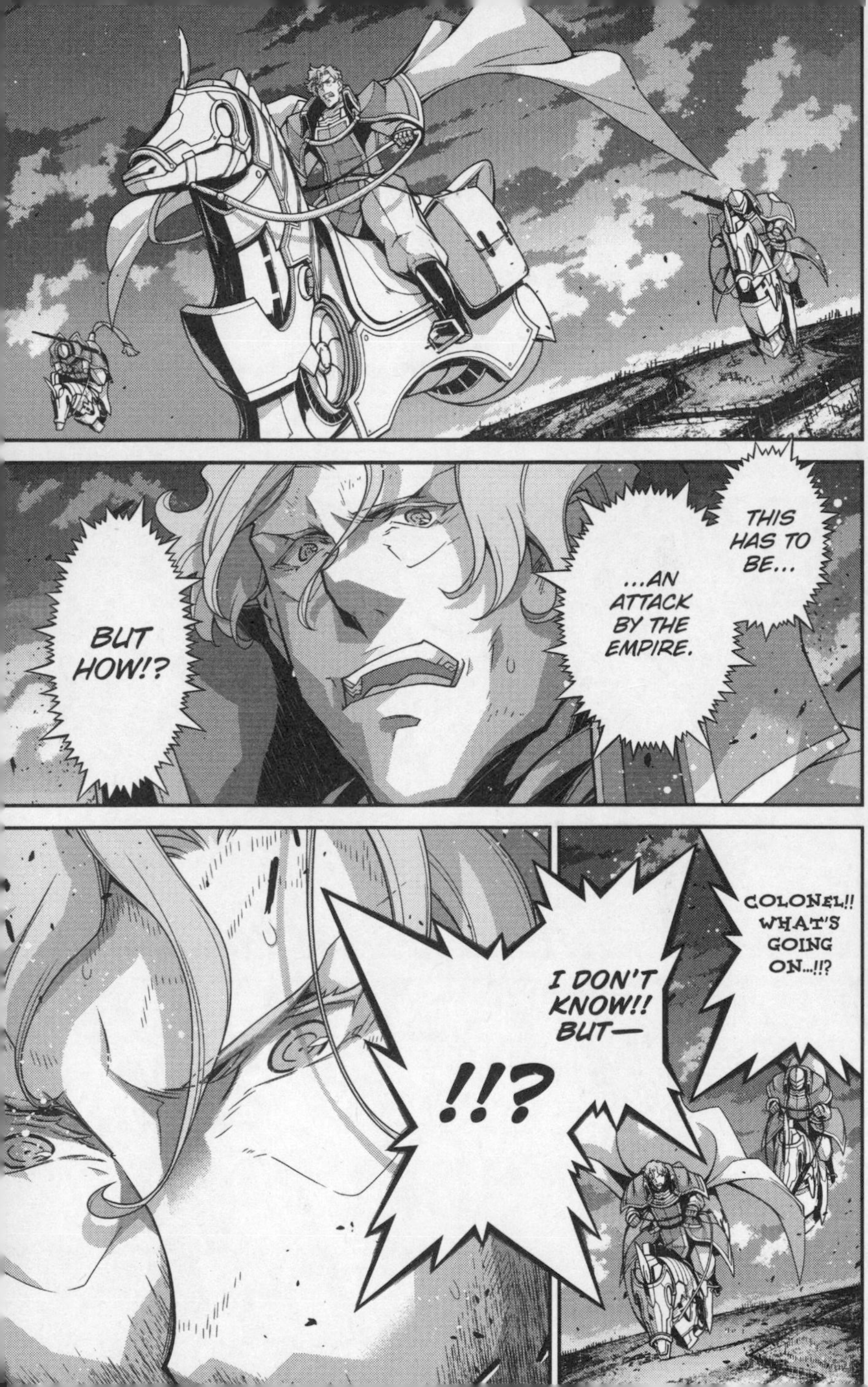
THIS HAS TO BE...
...AN ATTACK BY THE EMPIRE.
BUT HOW!?
COLONEL!! WHAT'S GOING ON...!?
I DON'T KNOW!! BUT—
!!?

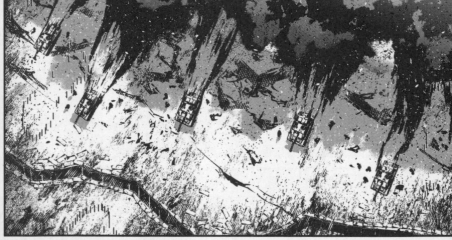

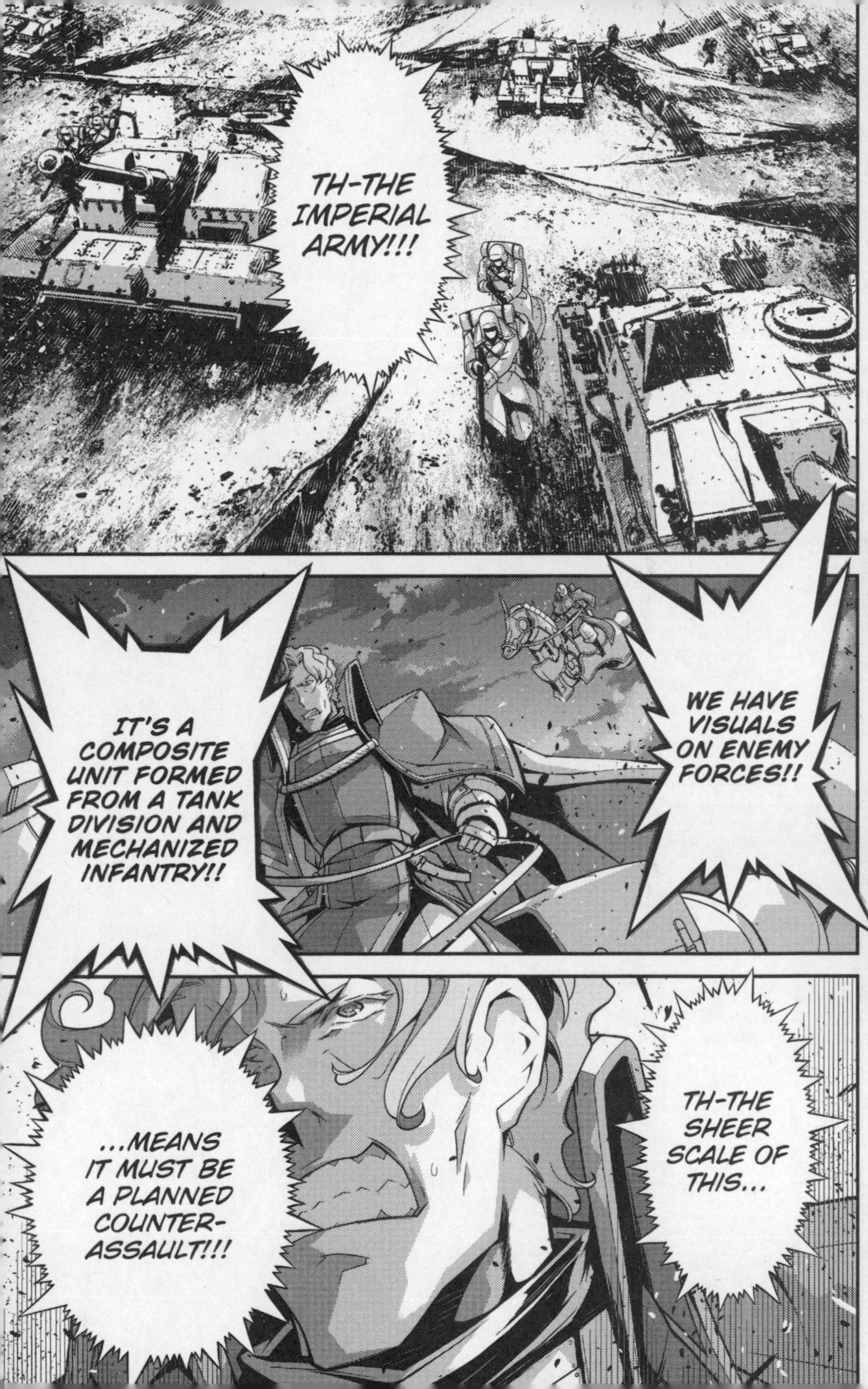
TH-THE IMPERIAL ARMY!!!
WE HAVE VISUALS ON ENEMY FORCES!!
IT'S A COMPOSITE UNIT FORMED FROM A TANK DIVISION AND MECHANIZED INFANTRY!!
TH-THE SHEER SCALE OF THIS...
...MEANS IT MUST BE A PLANNED COUNTER-ASSAULT!!!

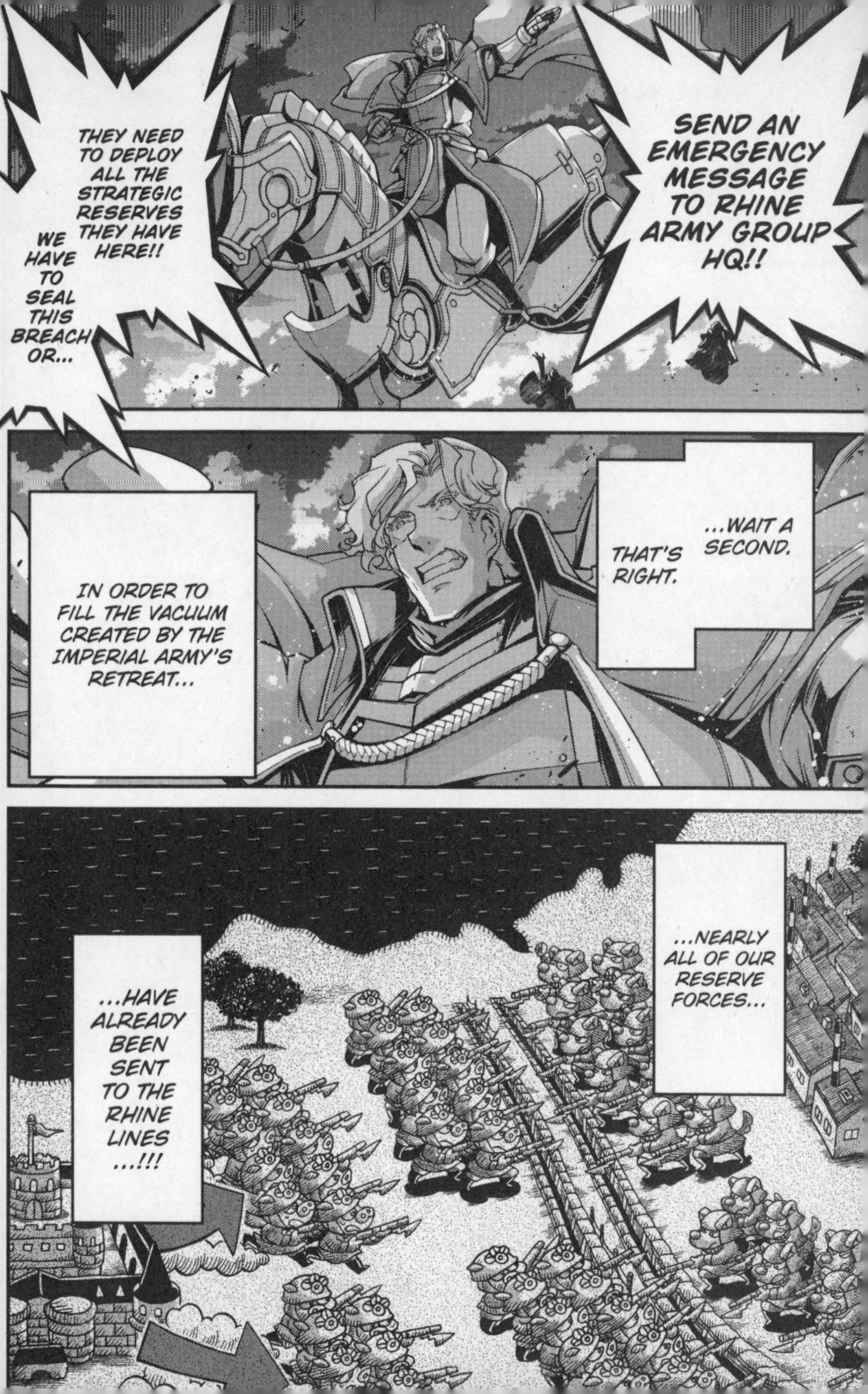
SEND AN EMERGENCY MESSAGE TO RHINE ARMY GROUP HQ!!
THEY NEED TO DEPLOY ALL THE STRATEGIC RESERVES THEY HAVE HERE!!
WE HAVE TO SEAL THIS BREACH OR...
...WAIT A SECOND.
THAT'S RIGHT.
IN ORDER TO FILL THE VACUUM CREATED BY THE IMPERIAL ARMY'S RETREAT...
...NEARLY ALL OF OUR RESERVE FORCES...
...HAVE ALREADY BEEN SENT TO THE RHINE LINES ...!!!

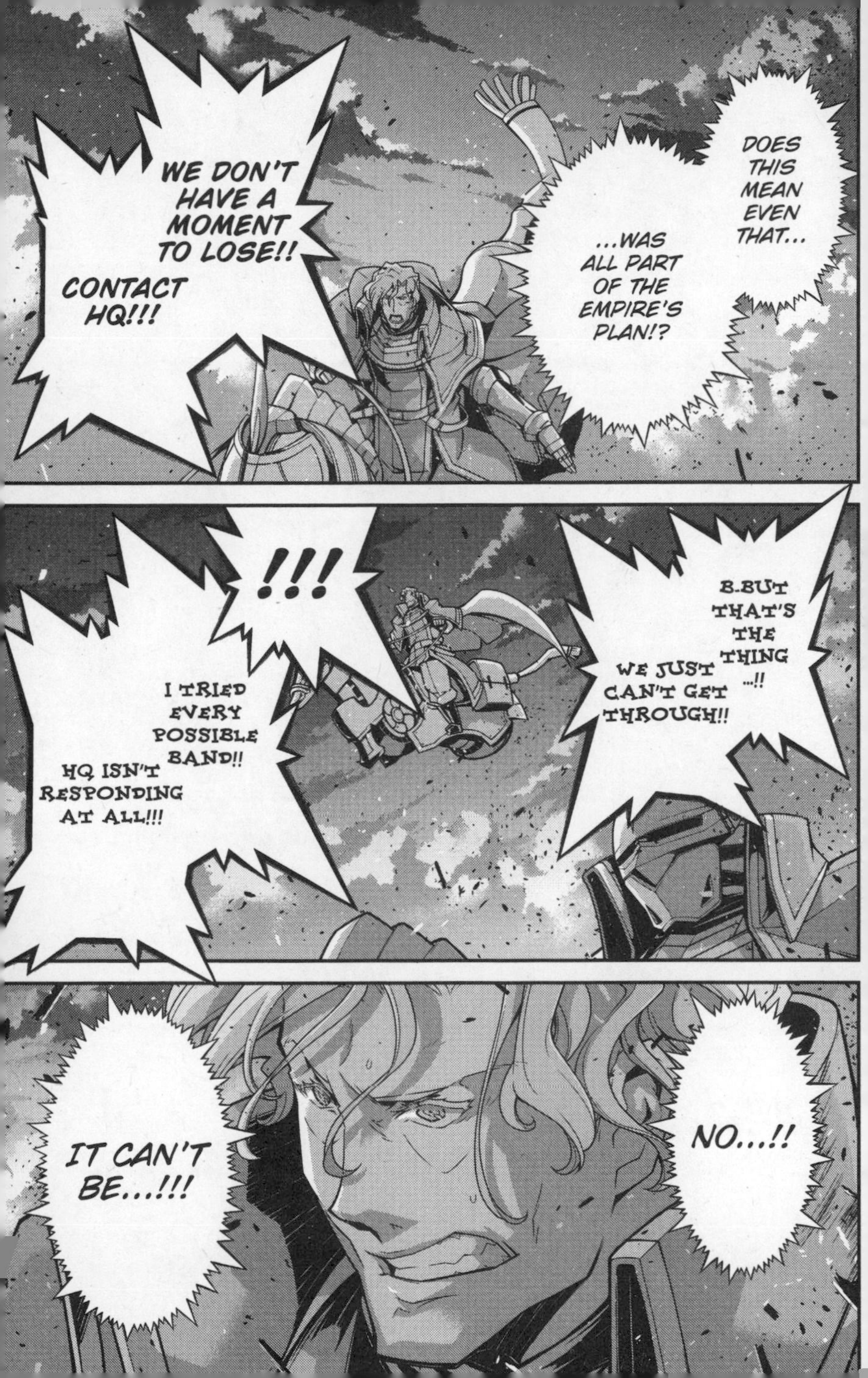
DOES THIS MEAN EVEN THAT...
...WAS ALL PART OF THE EMPIRE'S PLAN!?
WE DON'T HAVE A MOMENT TO LOSE!!
CONTACT HQ!!!
B-BUT THAT'S THE THING ...!!
WE JUST CAN'T GET THROUGH!!
!!!
I TRIED EVERY POSSIBLE BAND!!
HQ ISN'T RESPONDING AT ALL!!!
NO...!!
IT CAN'T BE...!!!

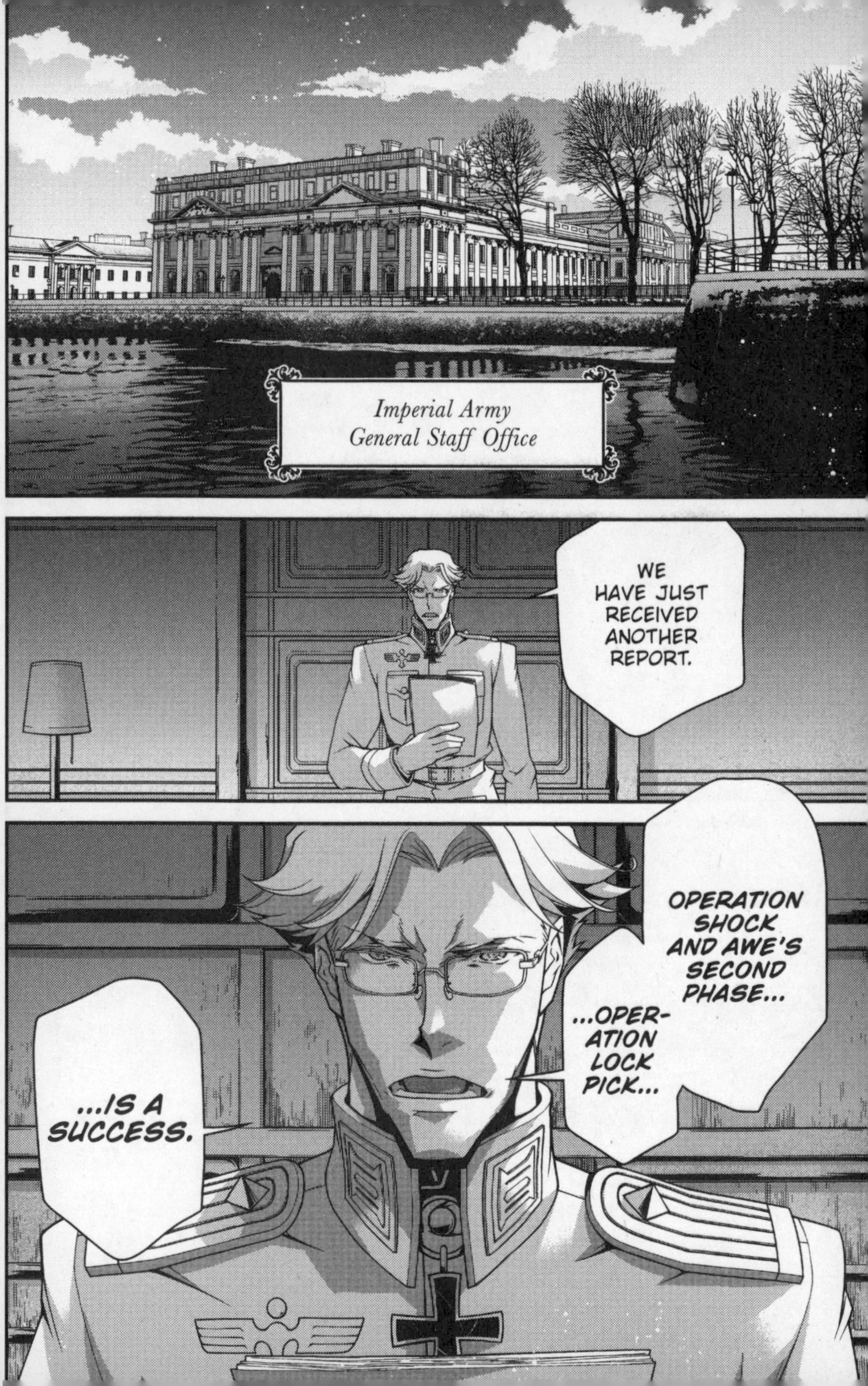
Imperial Army General Staff Office
WE HAVE JUST RECEIVED ANOTHER REPORT.
OPERATION SHOCK AND AWE'S SECOND PHASE...
...OPER-ATION LOCK PICK...
...IS A SUCCESS.

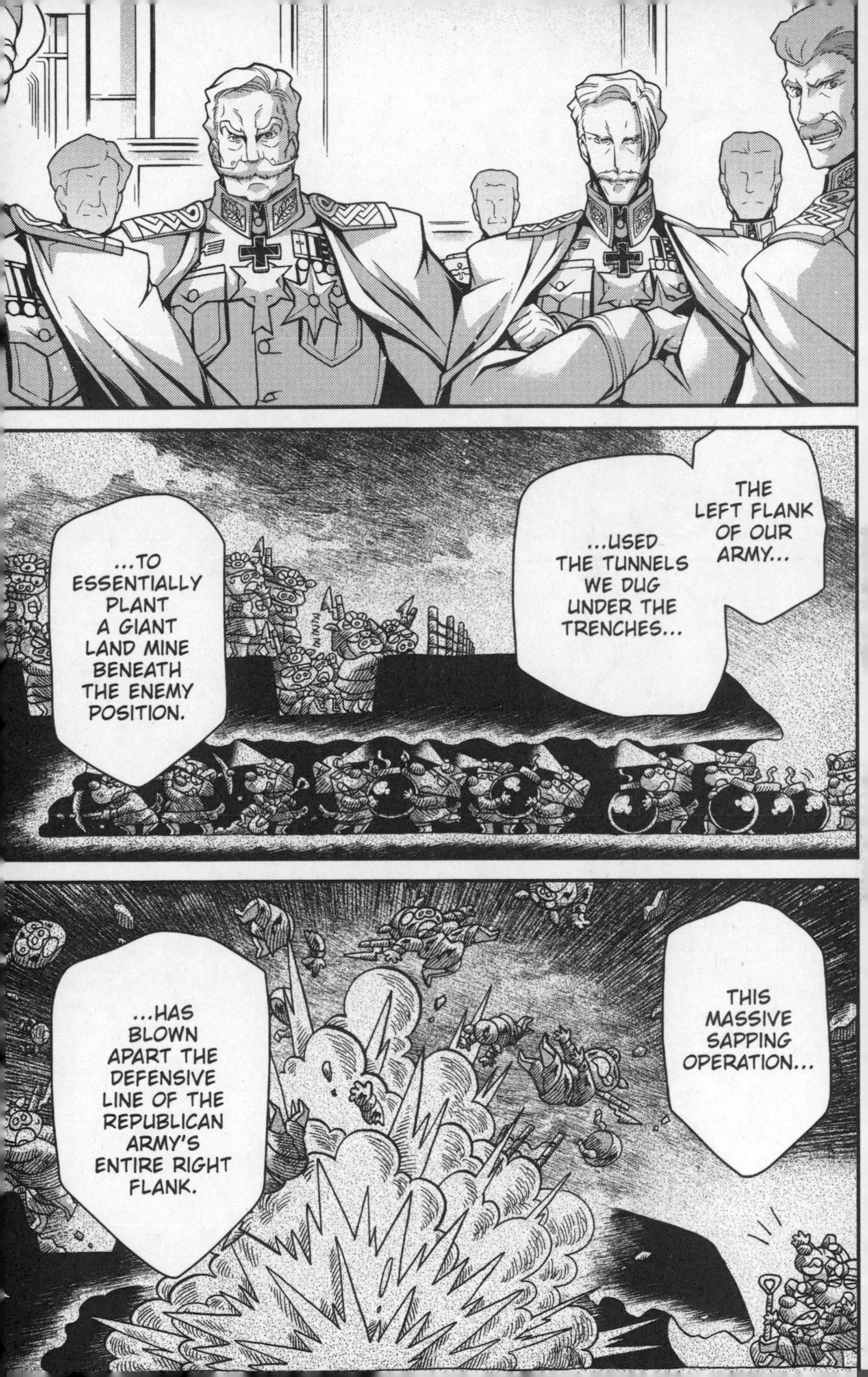
THE LEFT FLANK OF OUR ARMY...
...USED THE TUNNELS WE DUG UNDER THE TRENCHES...
...TO ESSENTIALLY PLANT A GIANT LAND MINE BENEATH THE ENEMY POSITION.
THIS MASSIVE SAPPING OPERATION...
...HAS BLOWN APART THE DEFENSIVE LINE OF THE REPUBLICAN ARMY'S ENTIRE RIGHT FLANK.

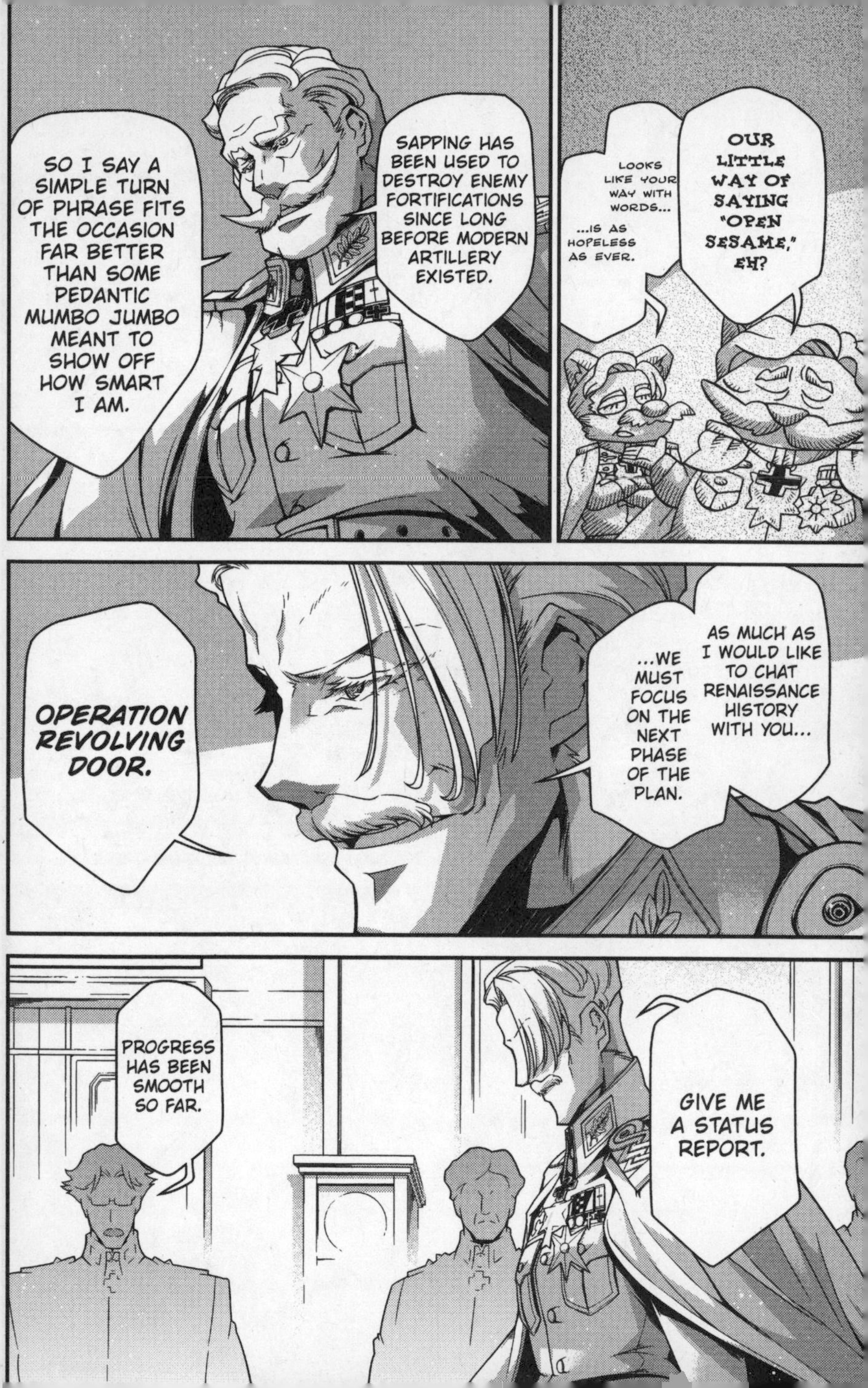
OUR LITTLE WAY OF SAYING "OPEN SESAME," EH?
LOOKS LIKE YOUR WAY WITH WORDS...
...IS AS HOPELESS AS EVER.
SAPPING HAS BEEN USED TO DESTROY ENEMY FORTIFICATIONS SINCE LONG BEFORE MODERN ARTILLERY EXISTED.
SO I SAY A SIMPLE TURN OF PHRASE FITS THE OCCASION FAR BETTER THAN SOME PEDANTIC MUMBO JUMBO MEANT TO SHOW OFF HOW SMART I AM.
AS MUCH AS I WOULD LIKE TO CHAT RENAISSANCE HISTORY WITH YOU...
...WE MUST FOCUS ON THE NEXT PHASE OF THE PLAN.
OPERATION REVOLVING DOOR.
GIVE ME A STATUS REPORT.
PROGRESS HAS BEEN SMOOTH SO FAR.

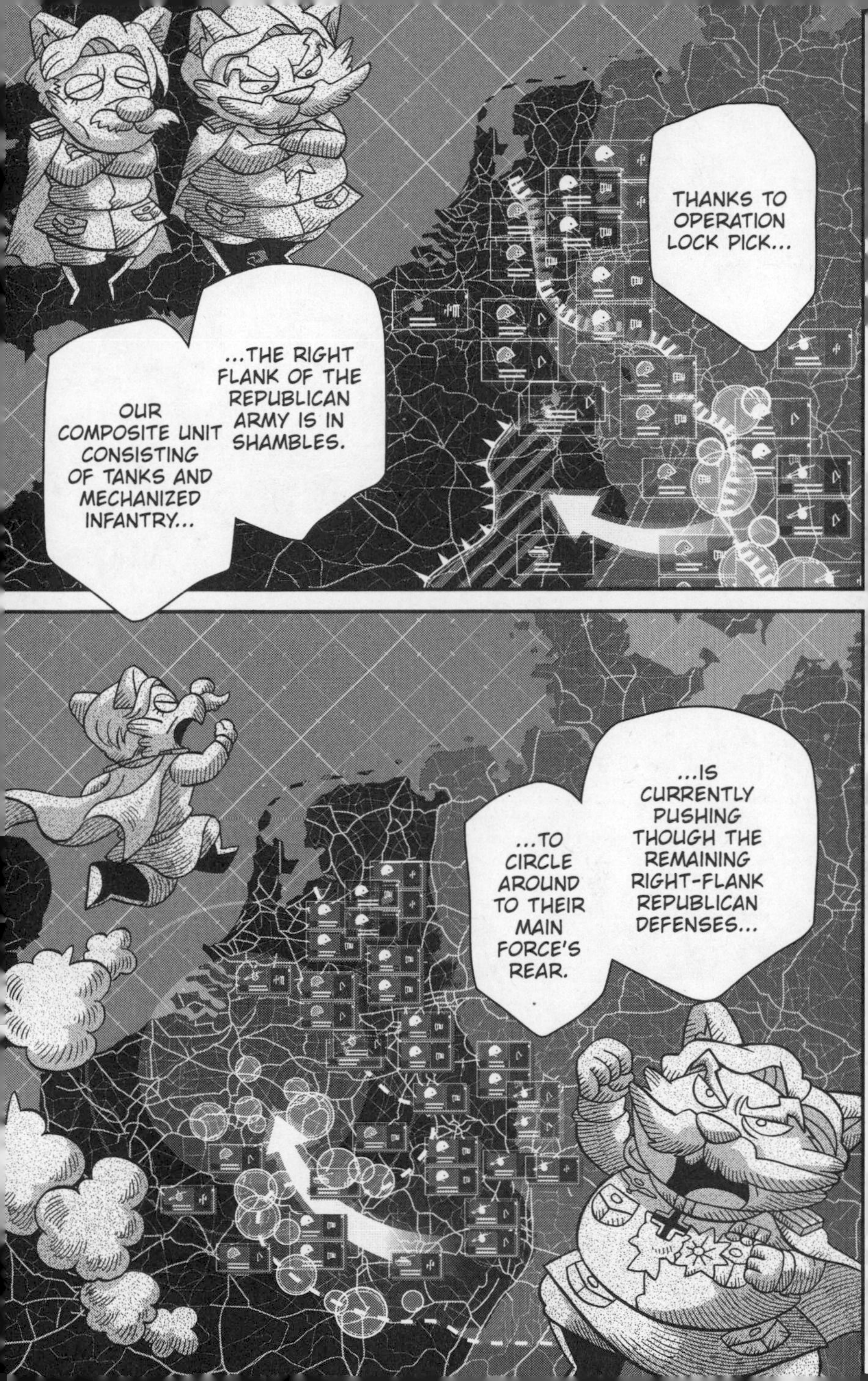

THANKS TO OPERATION LOCK PICK...
...THE RIGHT FLANK OF THE REPUBLICAN ARMY IS IN SHAMBLES.
OUR COMPOSITE UNIT CONSISTING OF TANKS AND MECHANIZED INFANTRY...
...IS CURRENTLY PUSHING THOUGH THE REMAINING RIGHT-FLANK REPUBLICAN DEFENSES...
...TO CIRCLE AROUND TO THEIR MAIN FORCE'S REAR.

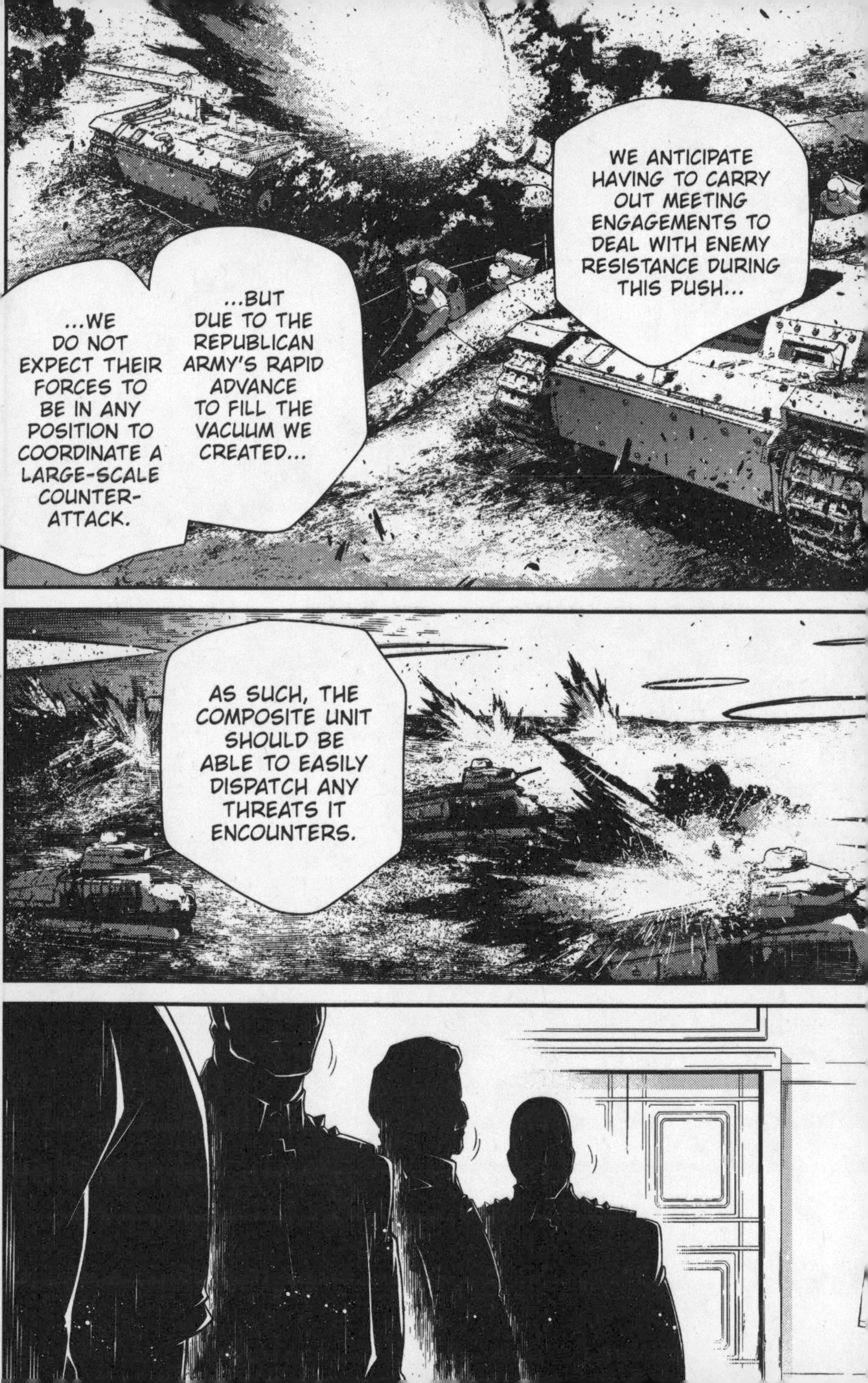
WE ANTICIPATE HAVING TO CARRY OUT MEETING ENGAGEMENTS TO DEAL WITH ENEMY RESISTANCE DURING THIS PUSH...
...BUT DUE TO THE REPUBLICAN ARMY'S RAPID ADVANCE TO FILL THE VACUUM WE CREATED...
...WE DO NOT EXPECT THEIR FORCES TO BE IN ANY POSITION TO COORDINATE A LARGE-SCALE COUNTER-ATTACK.
AS SUCH, THE COMPOSITE UNIT SHOULD BE ABLE TO EASILY DISPATCH ANY THREATS IT ENCOUNTERS.

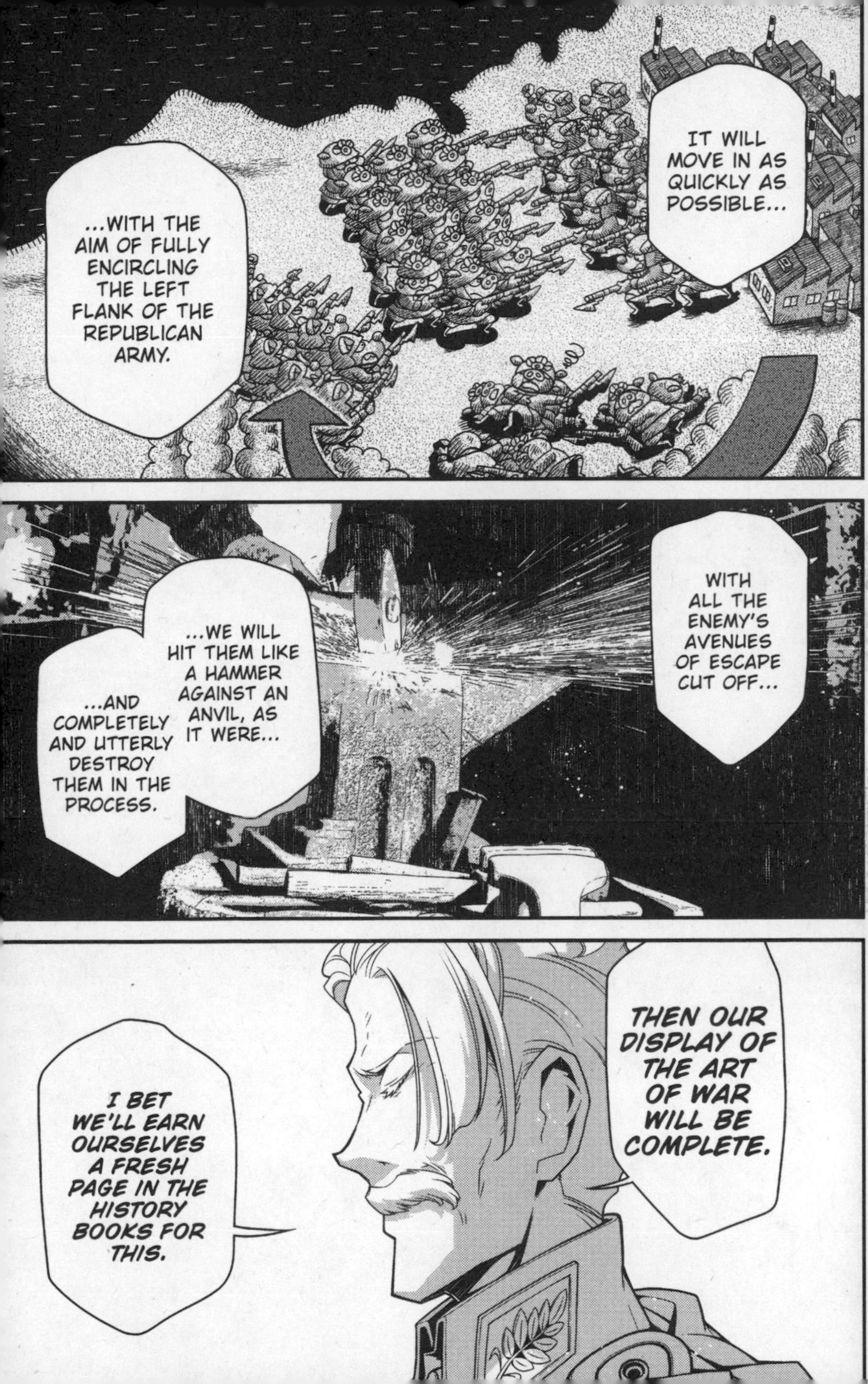
IT WILL MOVE IN AS QUICKLY AS POSSIBLE...
...WITH THE AIM OF FULLY ENCIRCLING THE LEFT FLANK OF THE REPUBLICAN ARMY.
WITH ALL THE ENEMY'S AVENUES OF ESCAPE CUT OFF...
...WE WILL HIT THEM LIKE A HAMMER AGAINST AN ANVIL, AS IT WERE...
...AND COMPLETELY AND UTTERLY DESTROY THEM IN THE PROCESS.
THEN OUR DISPLAY OF THE ART OF WAR WILL BE COMPLETE.
I BET WE'LL EARN OURSELVES A FRESH PAGE IN THE HISTORY BOOKS FOR THIS.

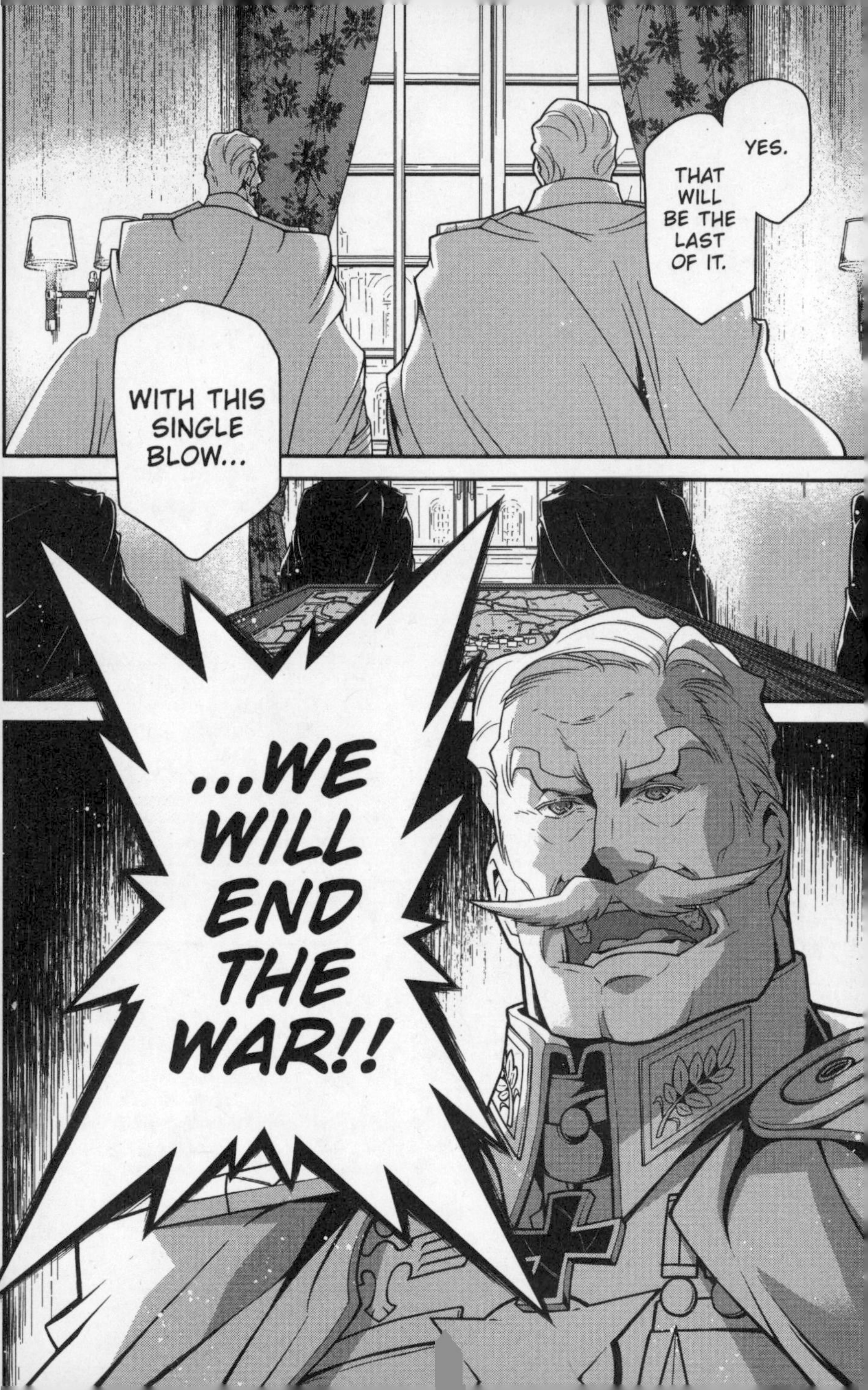
YES. THAT WILL BE THE LAST OF IT.
WITH THIS SINGLE BLOW...
...WE WILL END THE WAR!!

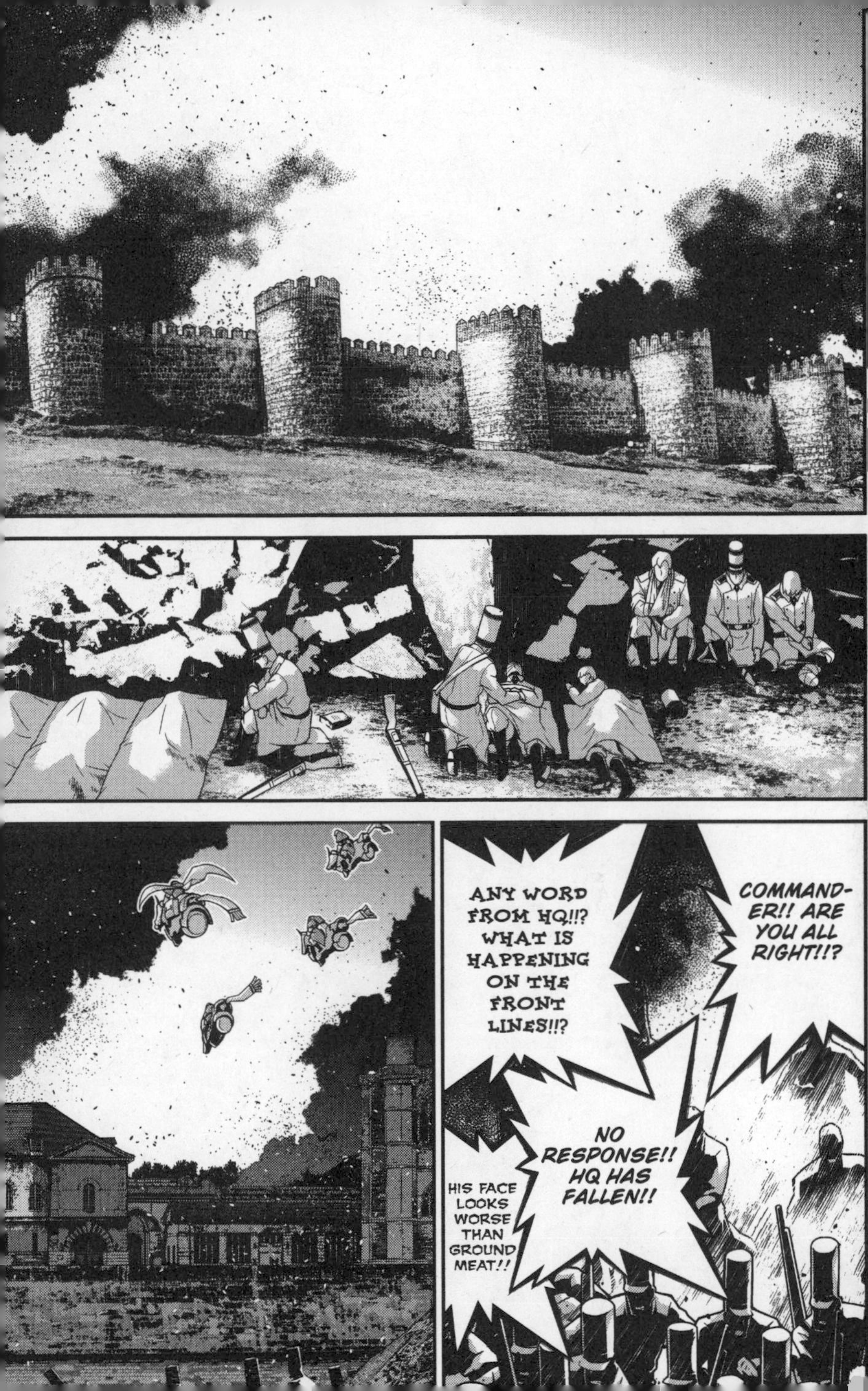
COMMANDER!! ARE YOU ALL RIGHT!!?
ANY WORD FROM HQ!!? WHAT IS HAPPENING ON THE FRONT LINES!!?
NO RESPONSE!! HQ HAS FALLEN!!
HIS FACE LOOKS WORSE THAN GROUND MEAT!!

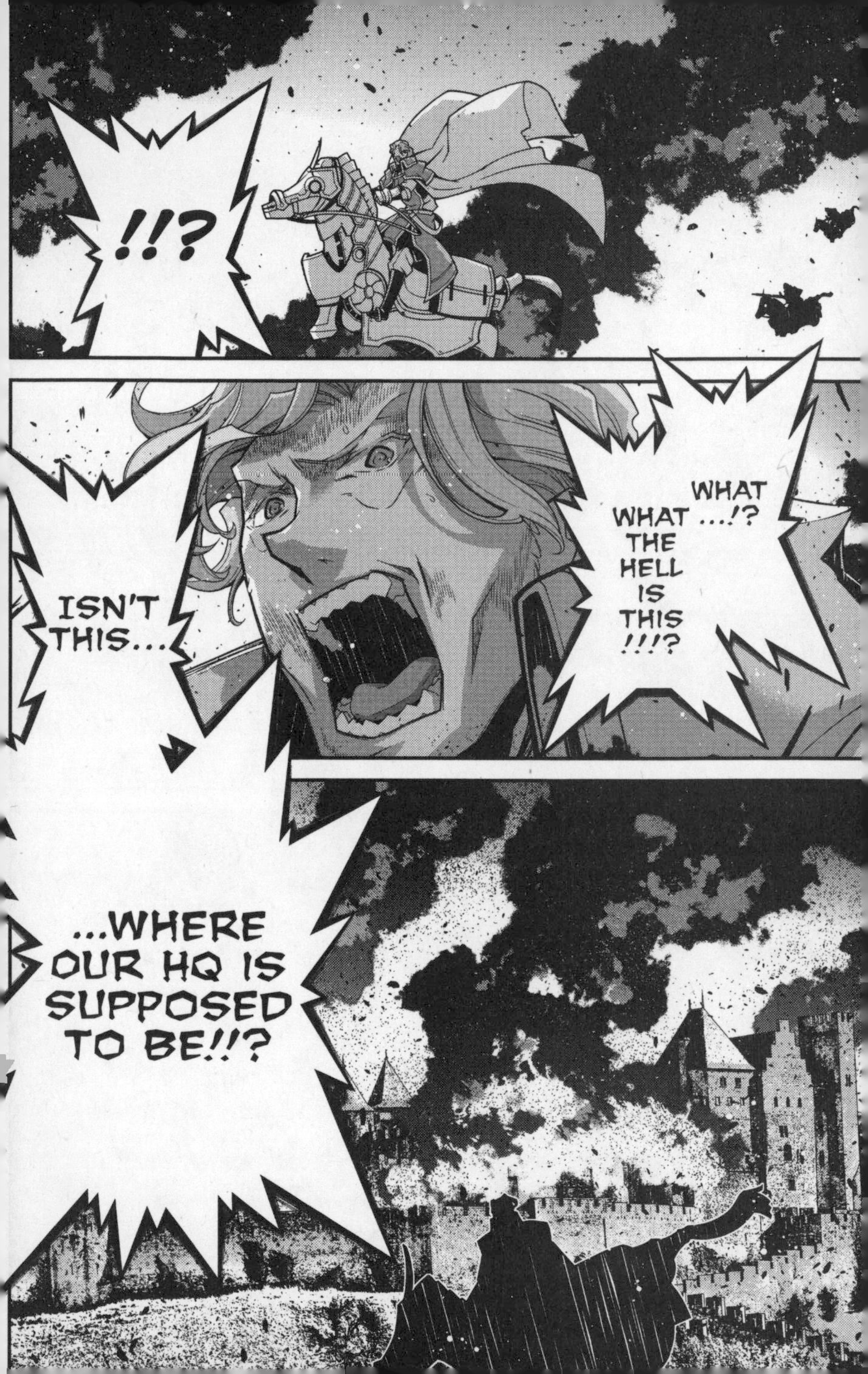
!!?
WHAT ...!?
WHAT THE HELL IS THIS!!!?
ISN'T THIS...
...WHERE OUR HQ IS SUPPOSED TO BE!!?

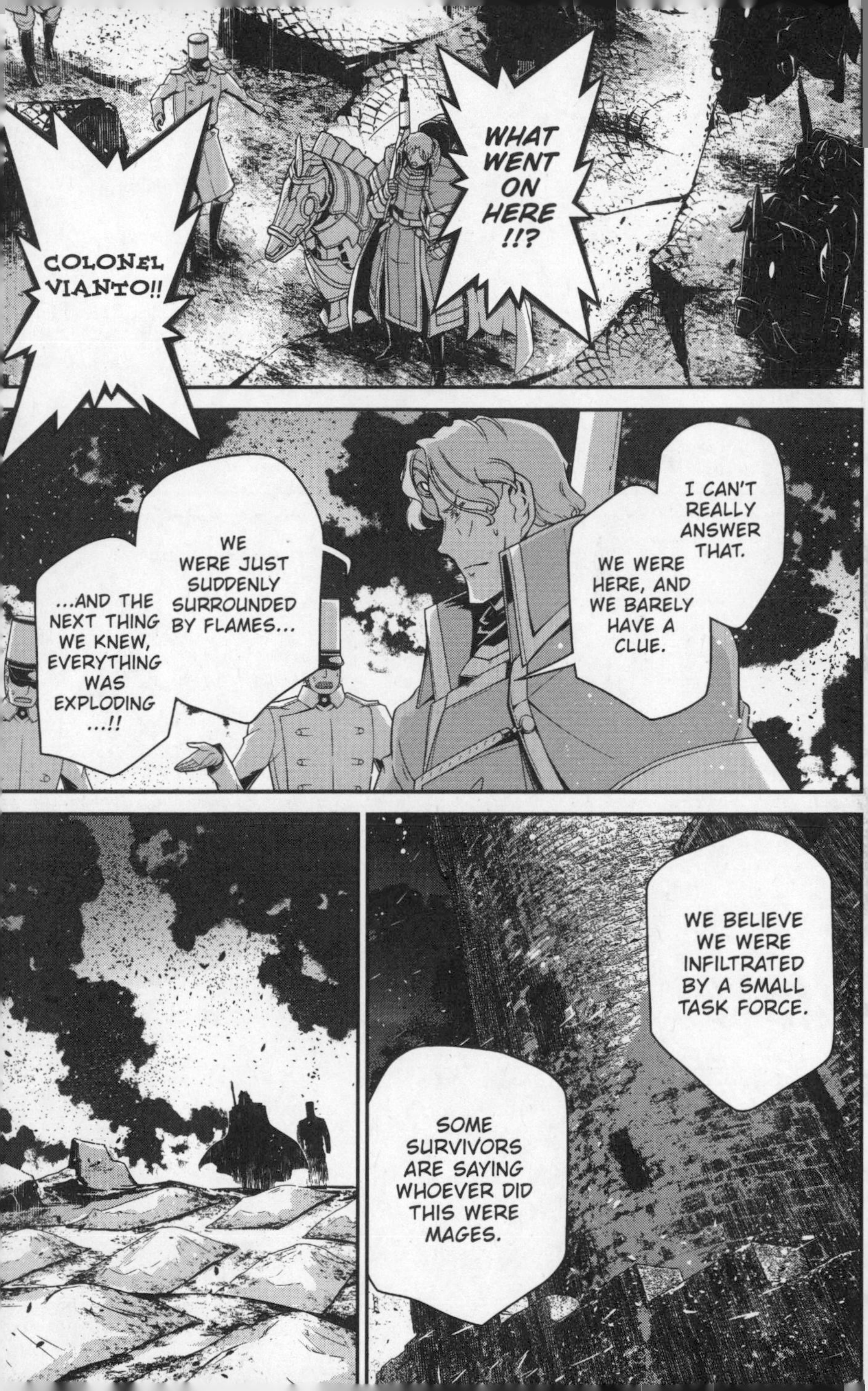
WHAT WENT ON HERE!!?
COLONEL VIANTO!!
I CAN'T REALLY ANSWER THAT.
WE WERE HERE, AND WE BARELY HAVE A CLUE.
WE WERE JUST SUDDENLY SURROUNDED BY FLAMES...
...AND THE NEXT THING WE KNEW, EVERYTHING WAS EXPLODING...!!
WE BELIEVE WE WERE INFILTRATED BY A SMALL TASK FORCE.
SOME SURVIVORS ARE SAYING WHOEVER DID THIS WERE MAGES.

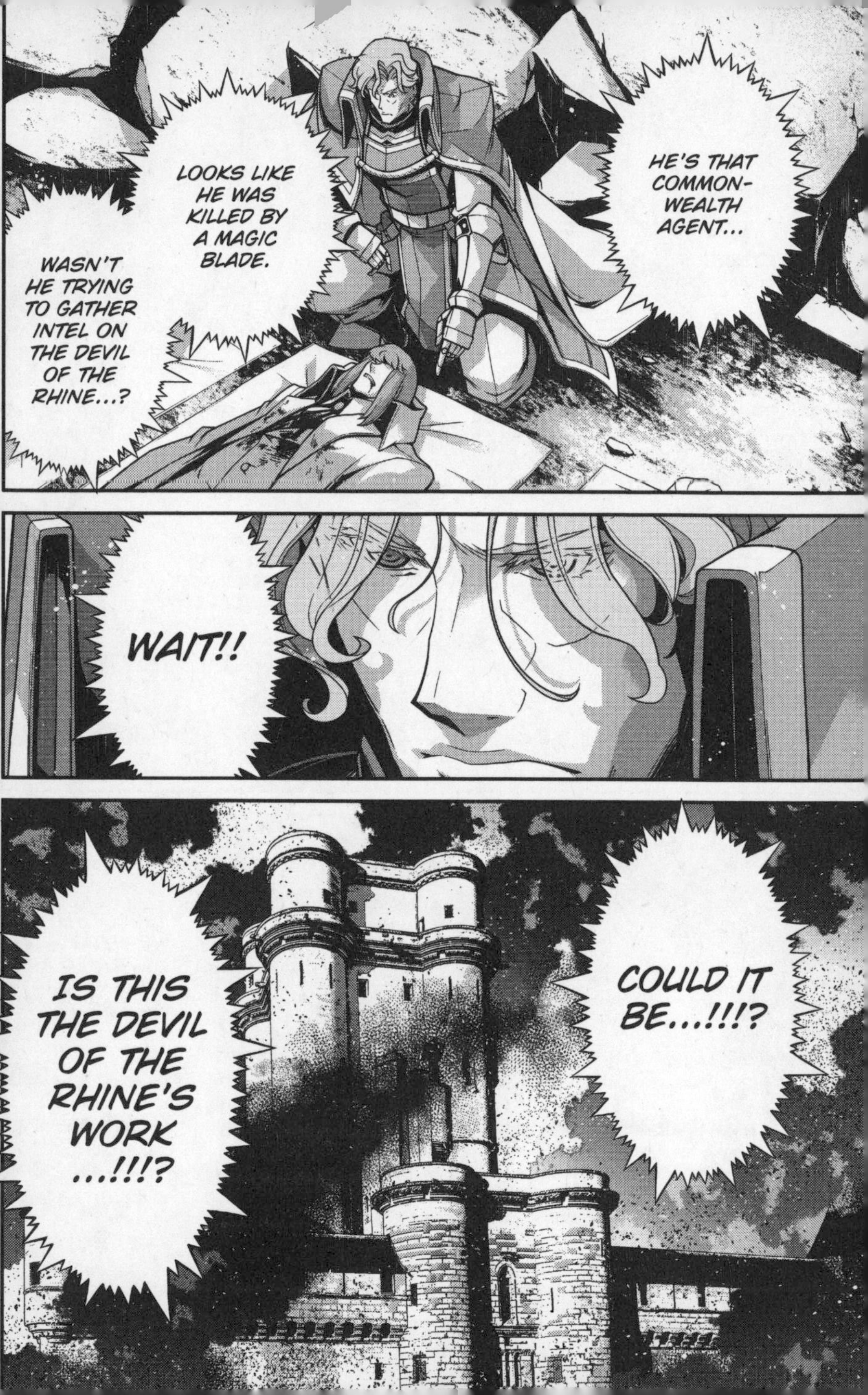
HE'S THAT COMMON-WEALTH AGENT...
LOOKS LIKE HE WAS KILLED BY A MAGIC BLADE.
WASN'T HE TRYING TO GATHER INTEL ON THE DEVIL OF THE RHINE...?
WAIT!!
COULD IT BE...!!!?
IS THIS THE DEVIL OF THE RHINE'S WORK ...!!!?

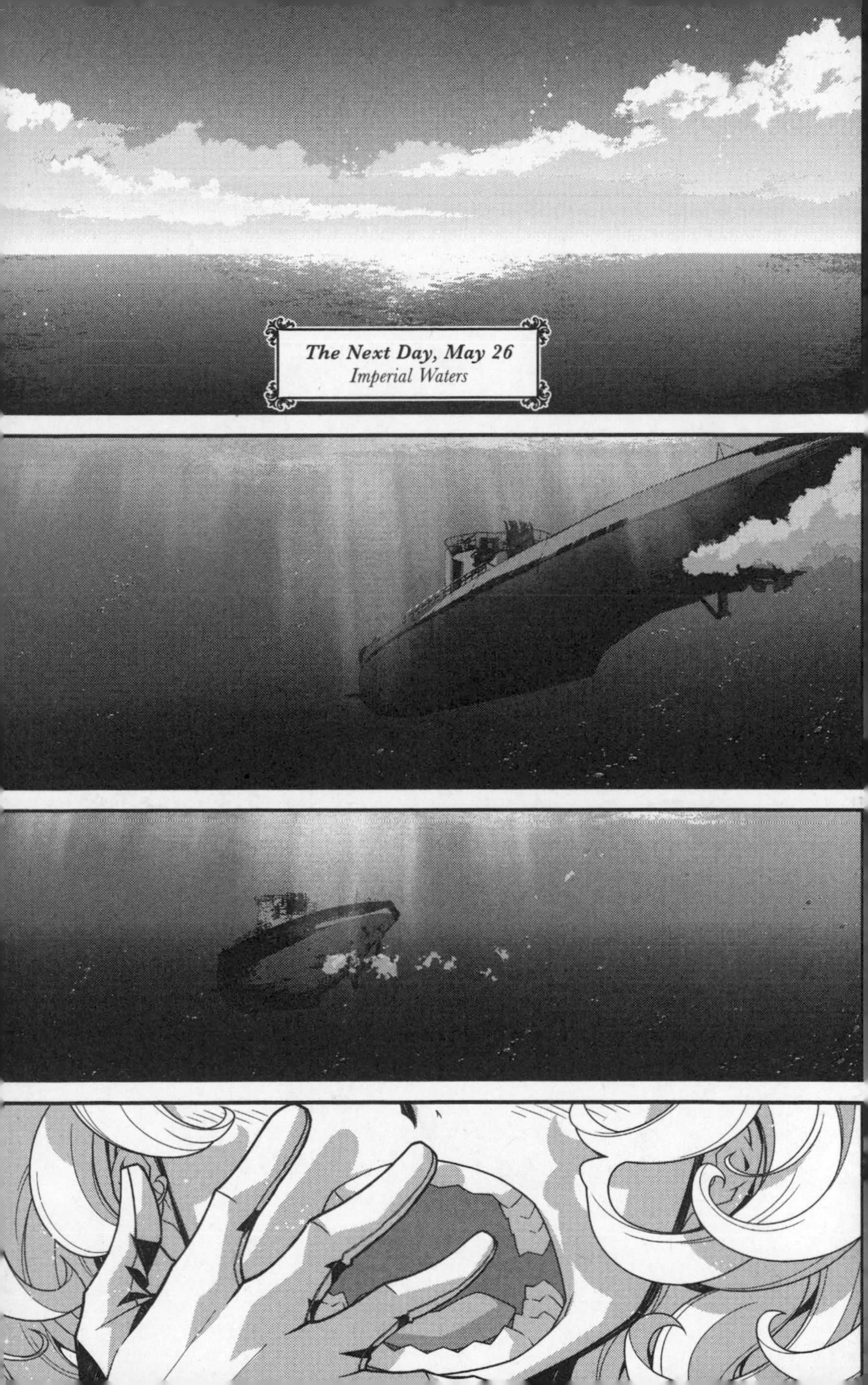
The Next Day, May 26
Imperial Waters

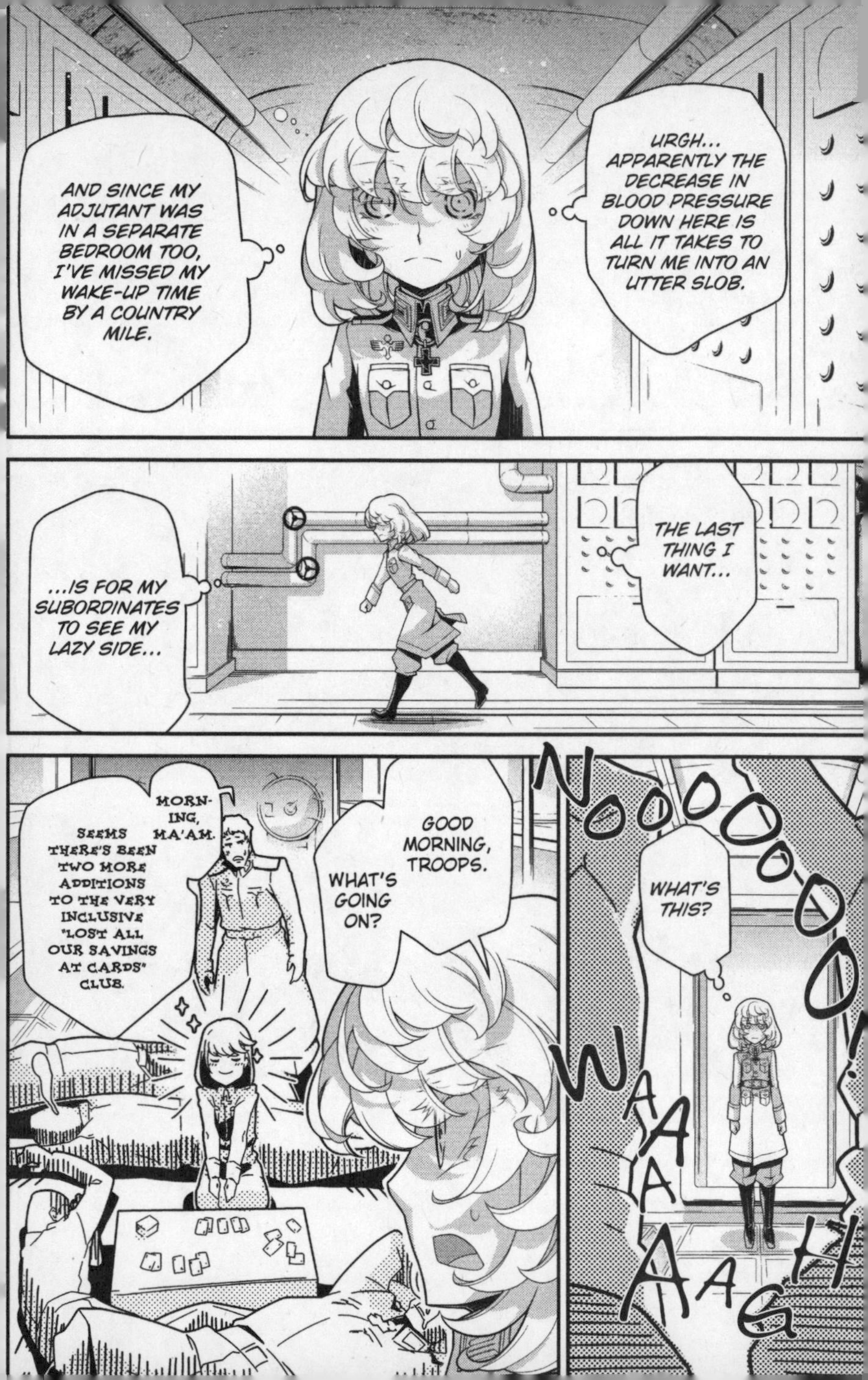
URGH... APPARENTLY THE DECREASE IN BLOOD PRESSURE DOWN HERE IS ALL IT TAKES TO TURN ME INTO AN UTTER SLOB.
AND SINCE MY ADJUTANT WAS IN A SEPARATE BEDROOM TOO, I'VE MISSED MY WAKE-UP TIME BY A COUNTRY MILE.
THE LAST THING I WANT...
...IS FOR MY SUBORDINATES TO SEE MY LAZY SIDE...
NOOOOOOOO! WAAAAAAGH
WHAT'S THIS?
GOOD MORNING, TROOPS.
WHAT'S GOING ON?
MORNING, MA'AM.
SEEMS THERE'S BEEN TWO MORE ADDITIONS TO THE VERY INCLUSIVE "LOST ALL OUR SAVINGS AT CARDS" CLUB.

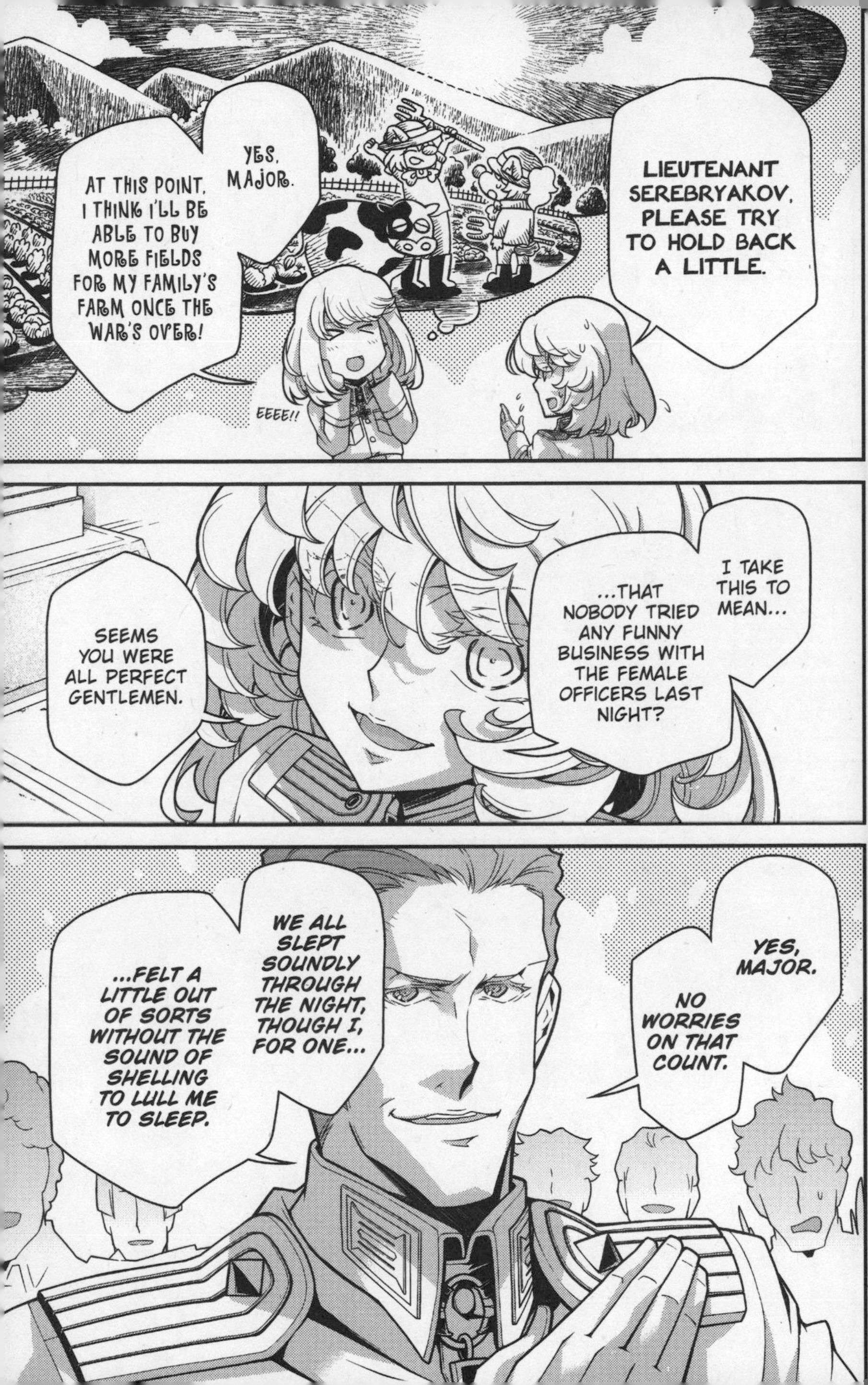
LIEUTENANT SEREBRYAKOV, PLEASE TRY TO HOLD BACK A LITTLE.
YES, MAJOR.
AT THIS POINT, I THINK I'LL BE ABLE TO BUY MORE FIELDS FOR MY FAMILY'S FARM ONCE THE WAR'S OVER!
EEEE!!
I TAKE THIS TO MEAN...
...THAT NOBODY TRIED ANY FUNNY BUSINESS WITH THE FEMALE OFFICERS LAST NIGHT?
SEEMS YOU WERE ALL PERFECT GENTLEMEN.
YES, MAJOR.
NO WORRIES ON THAT COUNT.
WE ALL SLEPT SOUNDLY THROUGH THE NIGHT, THOUGH I, FOR ONE...
...FELT A LITTLE OUT OF SORTS WITHOUT THE SOUND OF SHELLING TO LULL ME TO SLEEP.

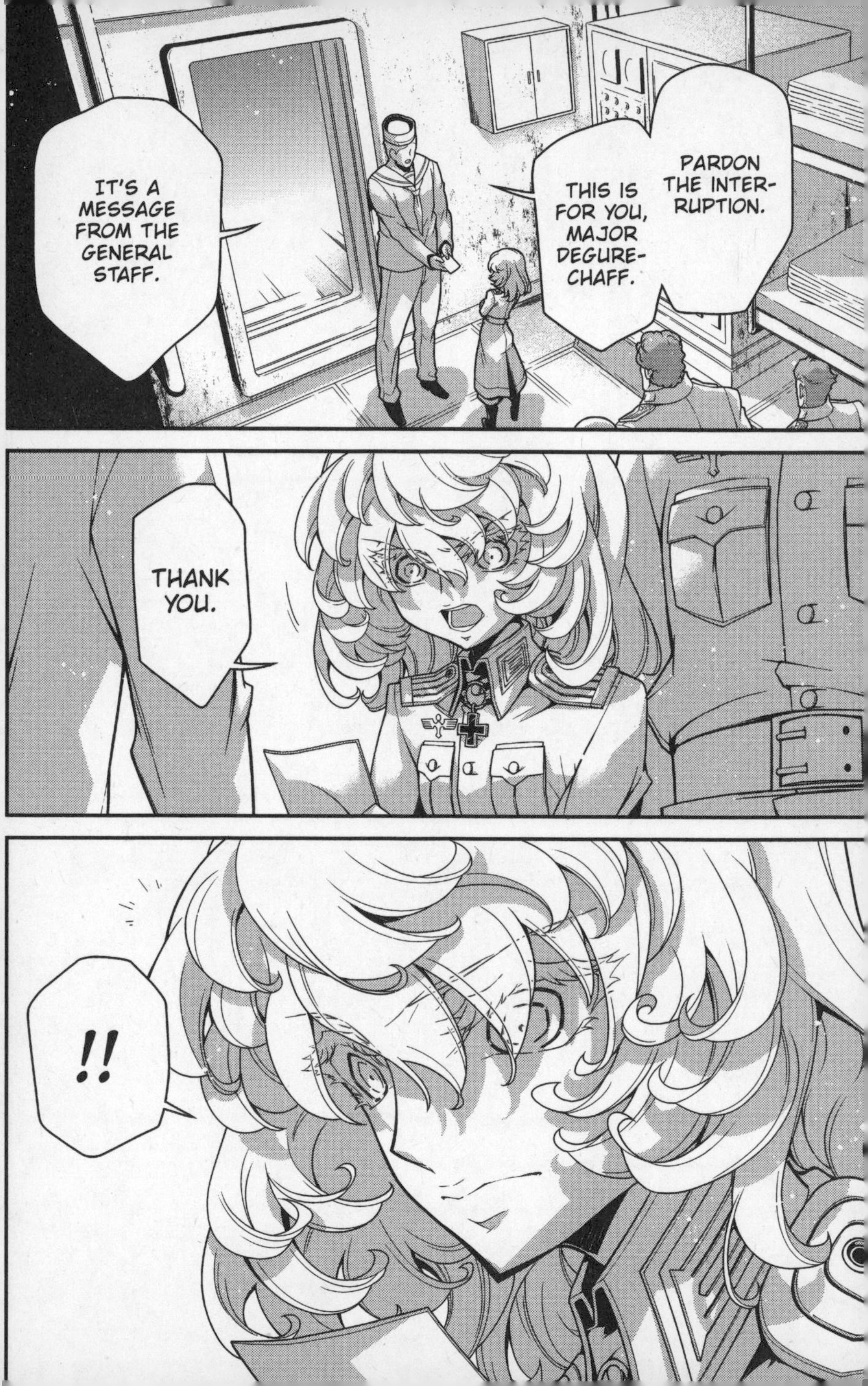
PARDON THE INTER-RUPTION.
THIS IS FOR YOU, MAJOR DEGURE-CHAFF.
IT'S A MESSAGE FROM THE GENERAL STAFF.
THANK YOU.
!!

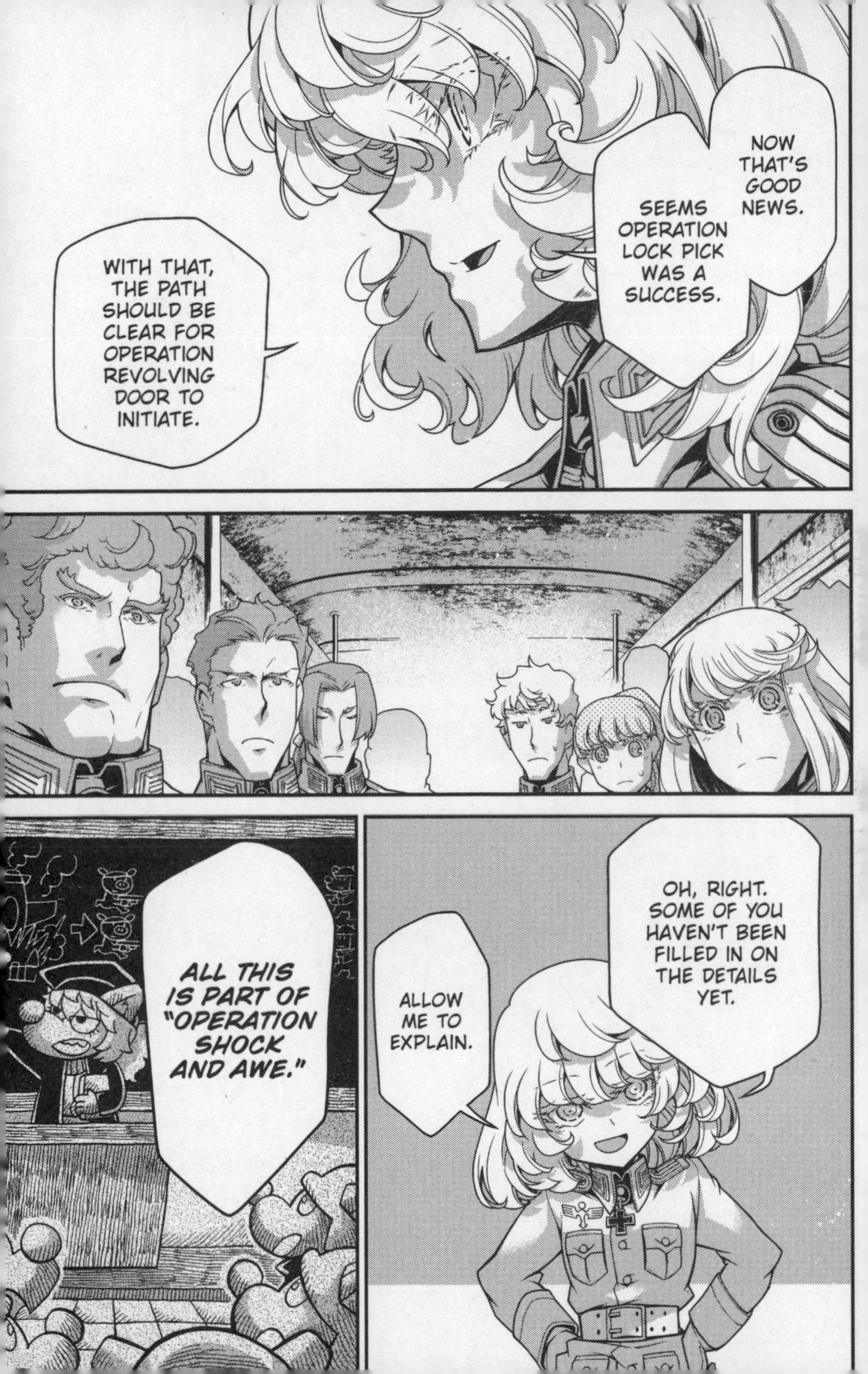
NOW THAT'S GOOD NEWS.
SEEMS OPERATION LOCK PICK WAS A SUCCESS.
WITH THAT, THE PATH SHOULD BE CLEAR FOR OPERATION REVOLVING DOOR TO INITIATE.
OH, RIGHT. SOME OF YOU HAVEN'T BEEN FILLED IN ON THE DETAILS YET.
ALLOW ME TO EXPLAIN.
ALL THIS IS PART OF "OPERATION SHOCK AND AWE."

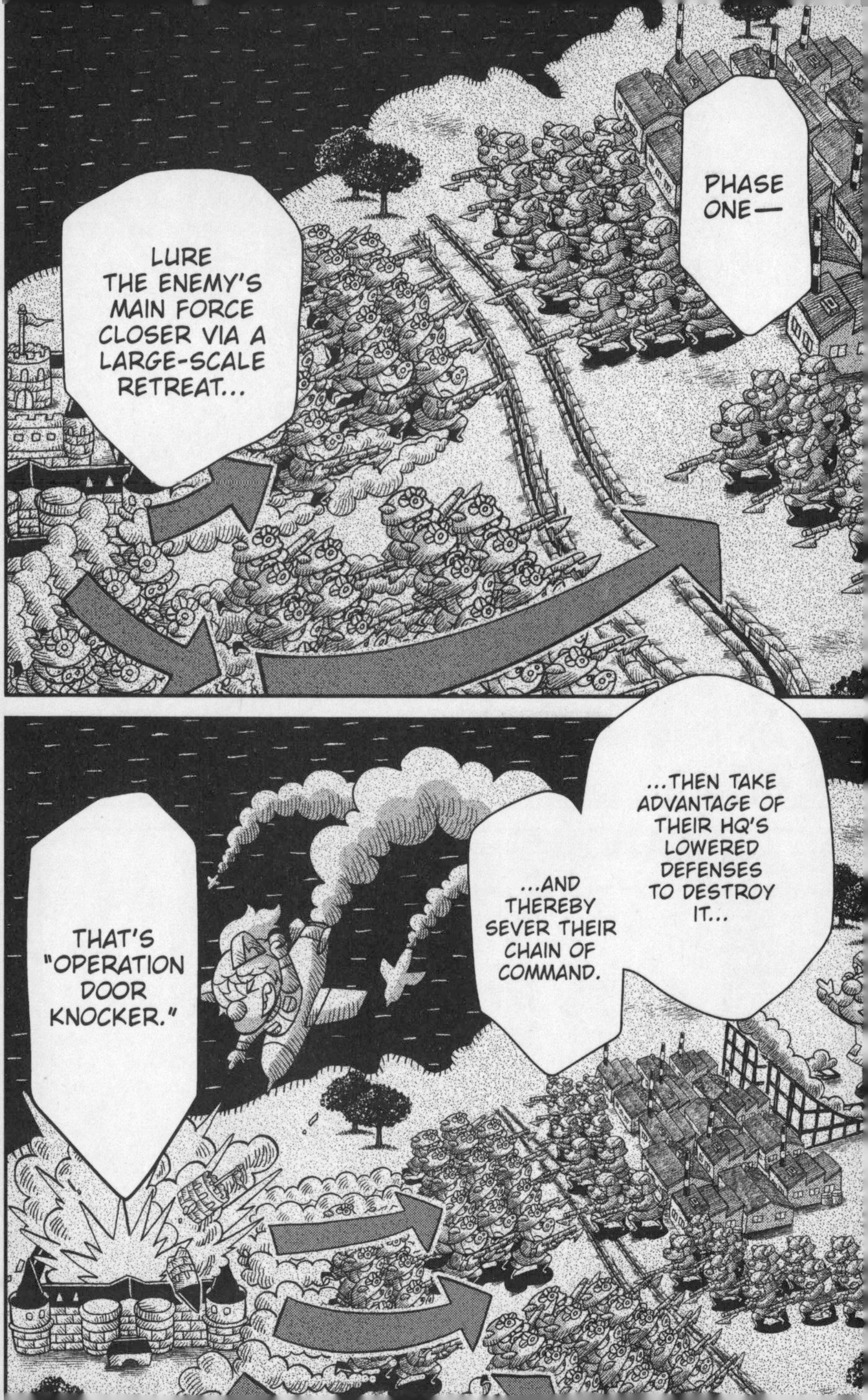
PHASE ONE—
LURE THE ENEMY'S MAIN FORCE CLOSER VIA A LARGE-SCALE RETREAT...
...THEN TAKE ADVANTAGE OF THEIR HQ'S LOWERED DEFENSES TO DESTROY IT...
...AND THEREBY SEVER THEIR CHAIN OF COMMAND.
THAT'S "OPERATION DOOR KNOCKER."

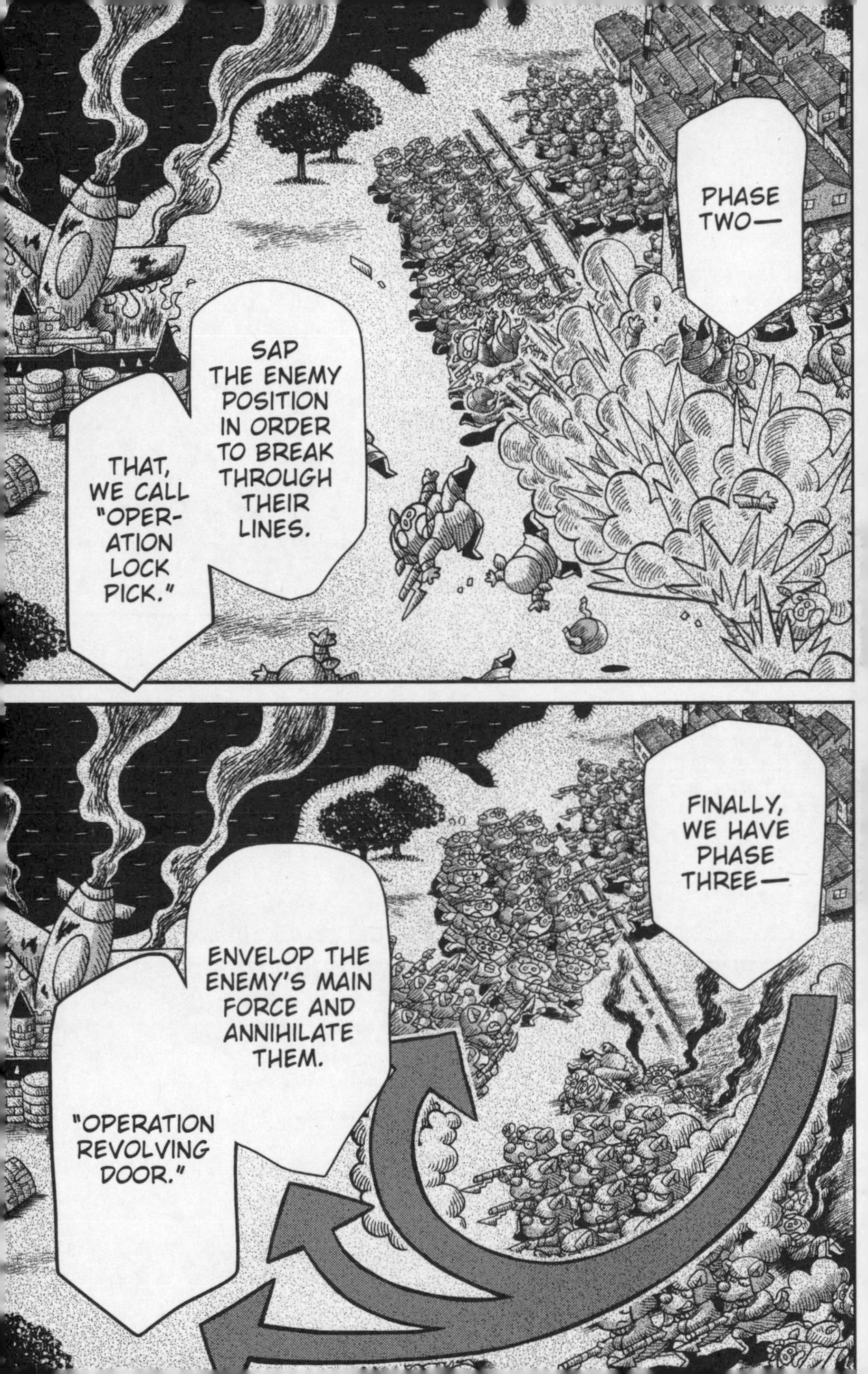
PHASE TWO—
SAP THE ENEMY POSITION IN ORDER TO BREAK THROUGH THEIR LINES.
THAT, WE CALL "OPER-ATION LOCK PICK."
FINALLY, WE HAVE PHASE THREE—
ENVELOP THE ENEMY'S MAIN FORCE AND ANNIHILATE THEM.
"OPERATION REVOLVING DOOR."

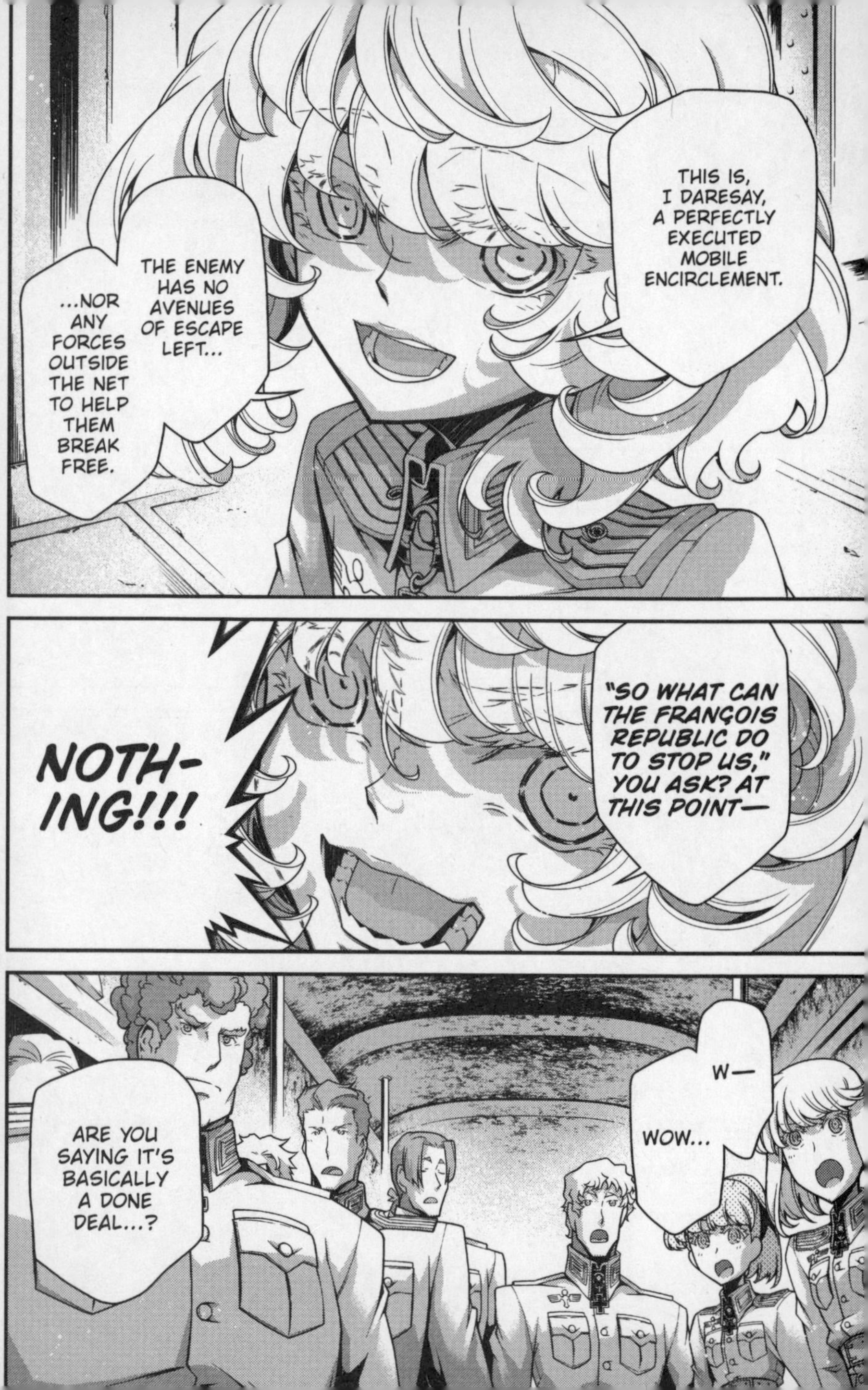

THIS IS, I DARESAY, A PERFECTLY EXECUTED MOBILE ENCIRCLEMENT.
THE ENEMY HAS NO AVENUES OF ESCAPE LEFT...
...NOR ANY FORCES OUTSIDE THE NET TO HELP THEM BREAK FREE.
"SO WHAT CAN THE FRANÇOIS REPUBLIC DO TO STOP US," YOU ASK? AT THIS POINT—
NOTH-ING!!!
W—
WOW...
ARE YOU SAYING IT'S BASICALLY A DONE DEAL...?

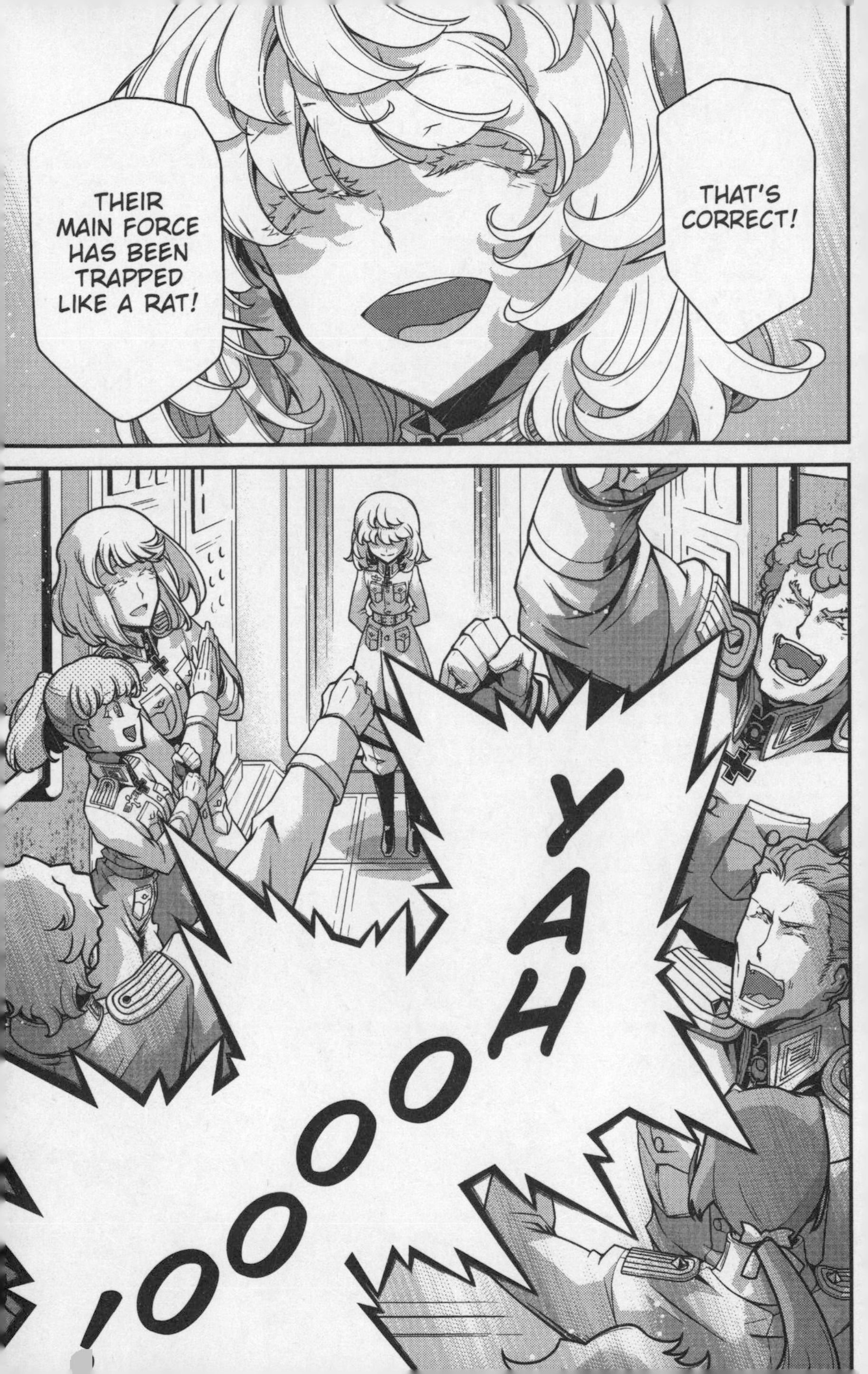
THAT'S CORRECT!
THEIR MAIN FORCE HAS BEEN TRAPPED LIKE A RAT!
YAHOOOO!

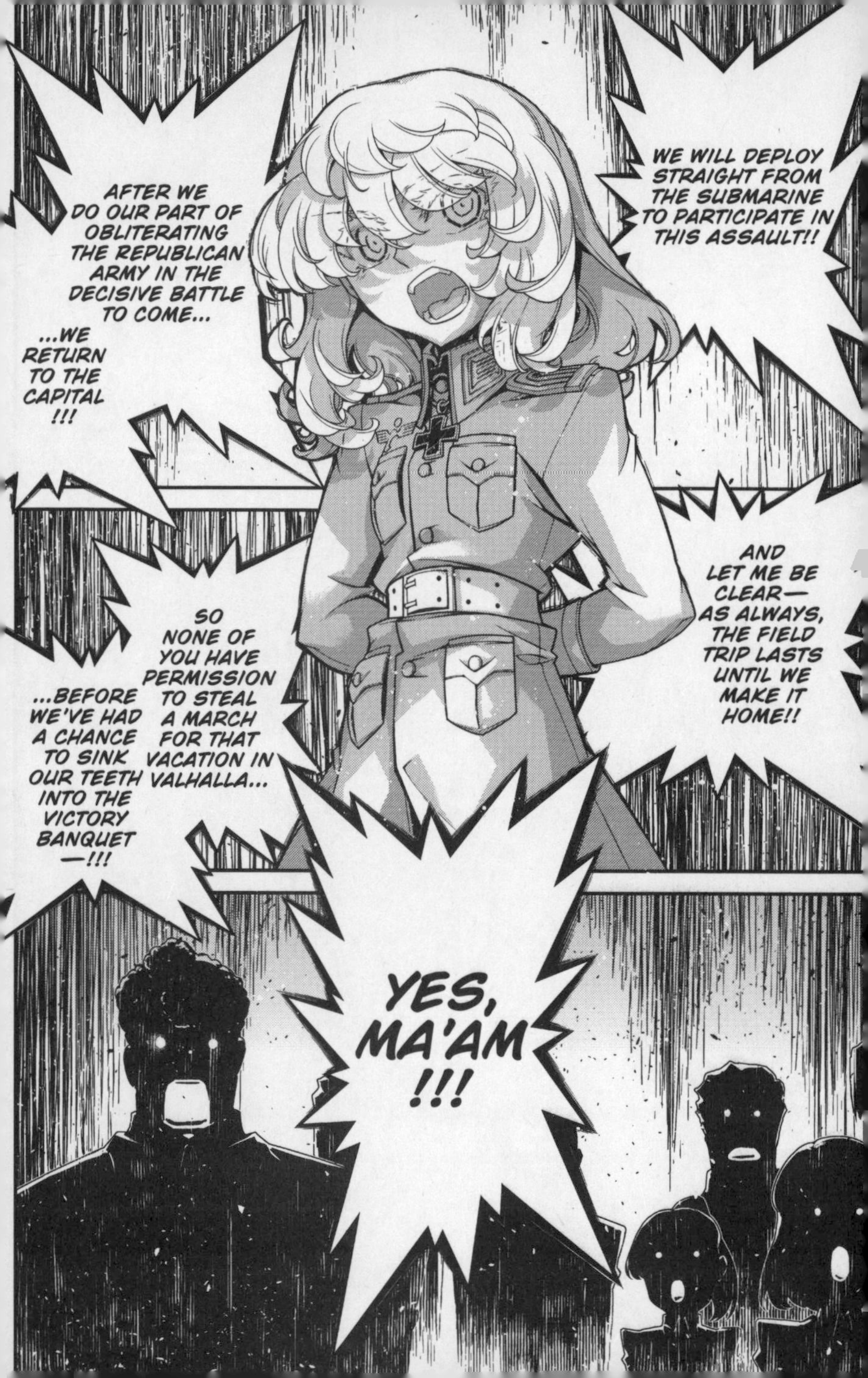
WE WILL DEPLOY STRAIGHT FROM THE SUBMARINE TO PARTICIPATE IN THIS ASSAULT!!
AFTER WE DO OUR PART OF OBLITERATING THE REPUBLICAN ARMY IN THE DECISIVE BATTLE TO COME...
...WE RETURN TO THE CAPITAL!!!
AND LET ME BE CLEAR— AS ALWAYS, THE FIELD TRIP LASTS UNTIL WE MAKE IT HOME!!
SO NONE OF YOU HAVE PERMISSION TO STEAL A MARCH FOR THAT VACATION IN VALHALLA...
...BEFORE WE'VE HAD A CHANCE TO SINK OUR TEETH INTO THE VICTORY BANQUET—!!!
YES, MA'AM!!!

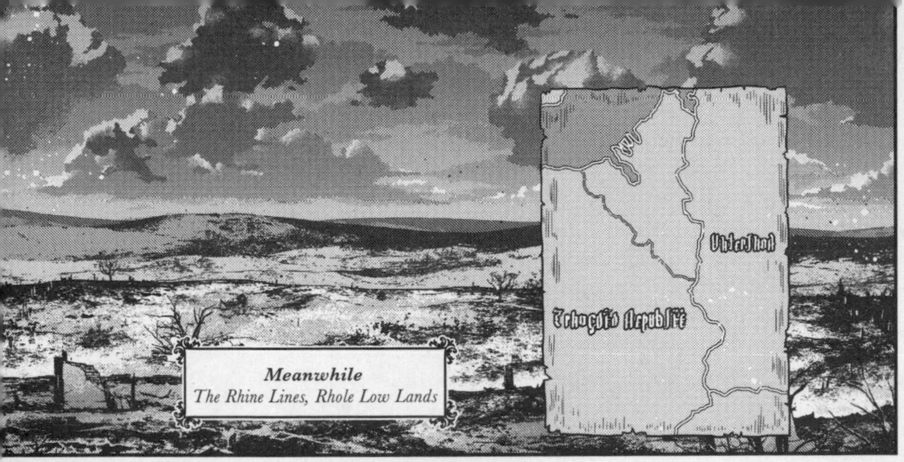
Meanwhile
The Rhine Lines, Rhole Low Lands
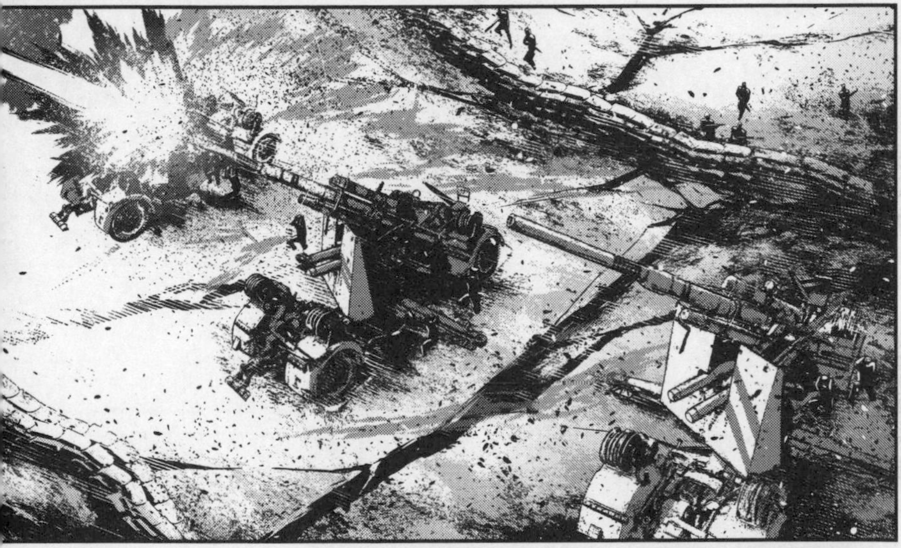
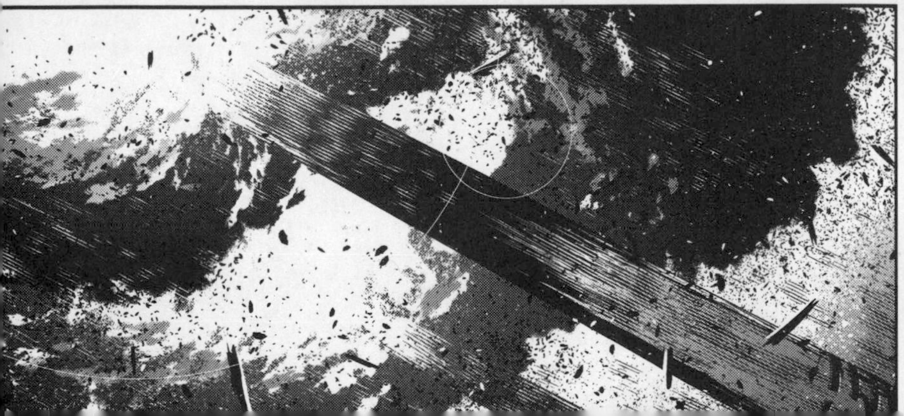

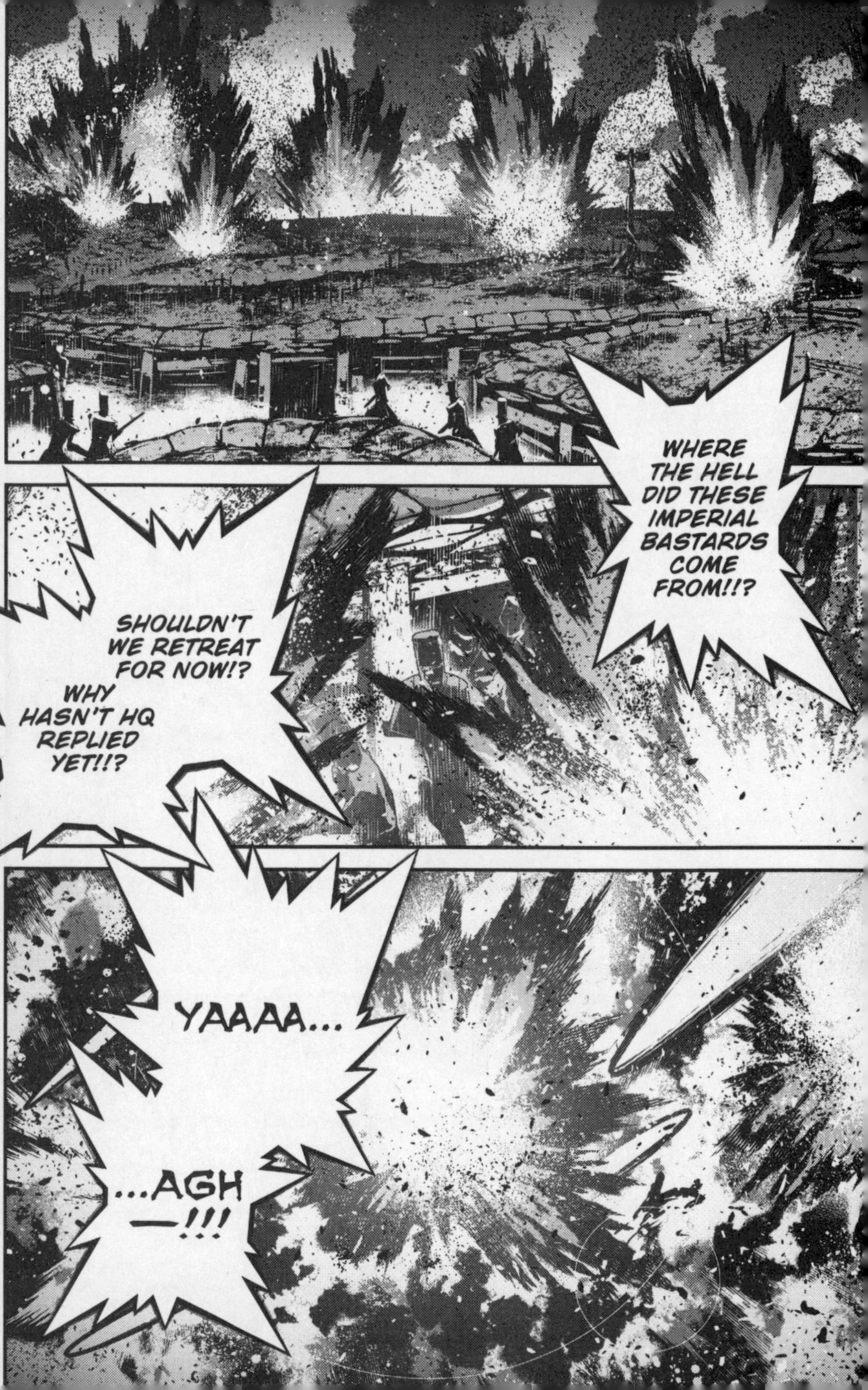
WHERE THE HELL DID THESE IMPERIAL BASTARDS COME FROM!!?
SHOULDN'T WE RETREAT FOR NOW!?
WHY HASN'T HQ REPLIED YET!!?
YAAAA...
...AGH—!!!

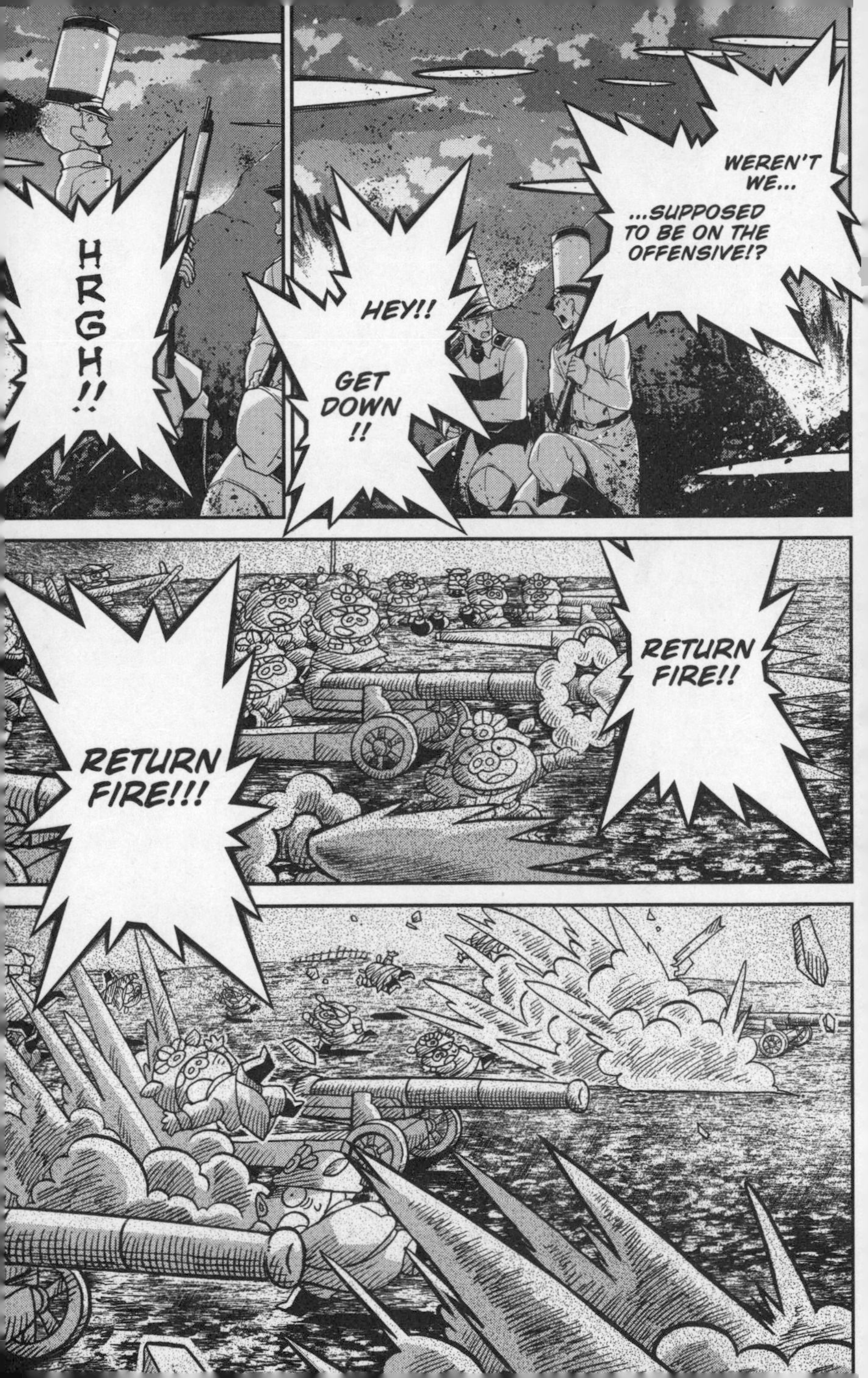
WEREN'T WE...
...SUPPOSED TO BE ON THE OFFENSIVE!?
HEY!!
GET DOWN!!
HRGH!!
RETURN FIRE!!
RETURN FIRE!!!

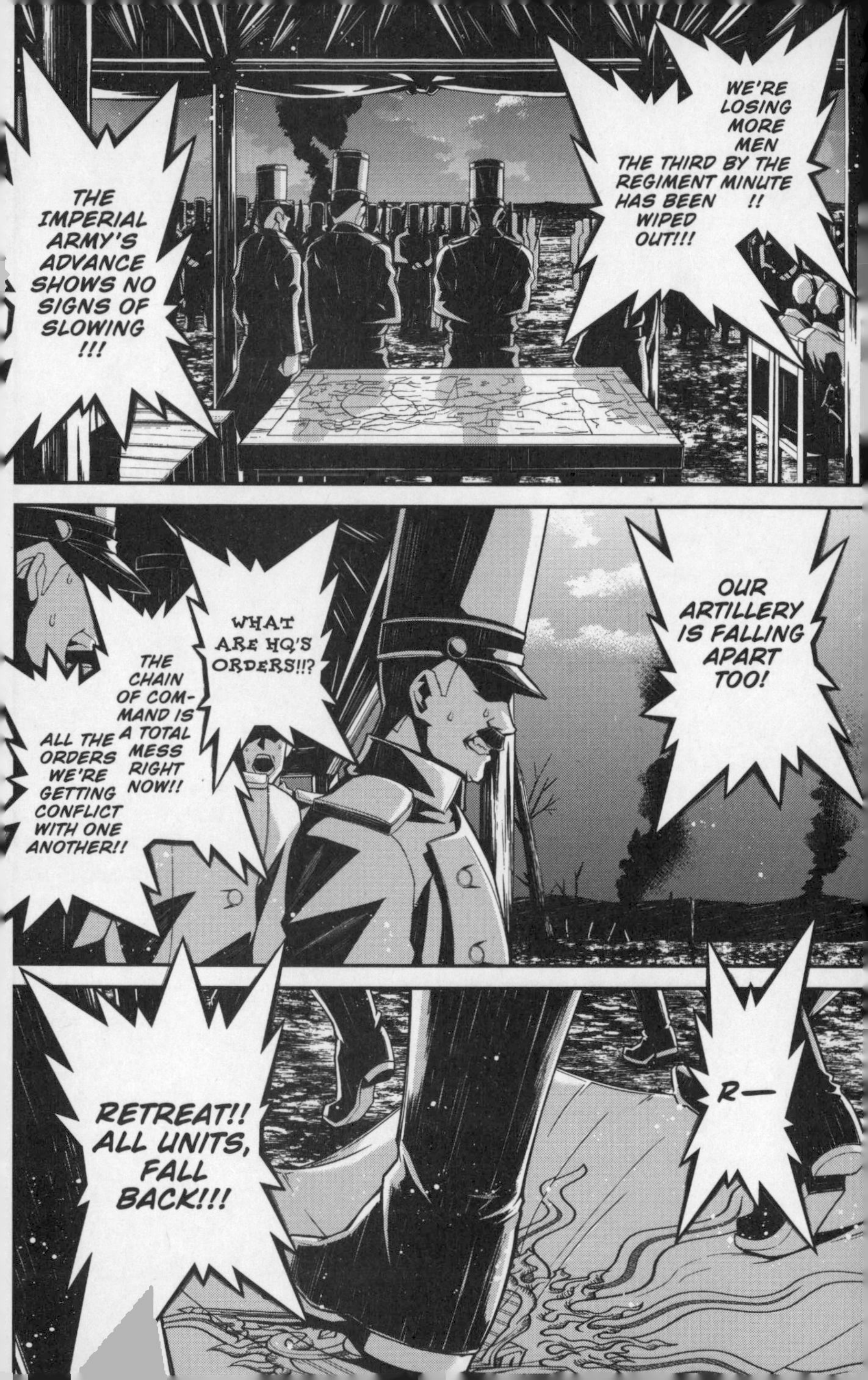
WE'RE LOSING MORE MEN BY THE MINUTE !!
THE THIRD REGIMENT HAS BEEN WIPED OUT!!!
THE IMPERIAL ARMY'S ADVANCE SHOWS NO SIGNS OF SLOWING !!!
OUR ARTILLERY IS FALLING APART TOO!
WHAT ARE HQ'S ORDERS!!?
THE CHAIN OF COM-MAND IS A TOTAL MESS RIGHT NOW!!
ALL THE ORDERS WE'RE GETTING CONFLICT WITH ONE ANOTHER!!
R—
RETREAT!! ALL UNITS, FALL BACK!!!

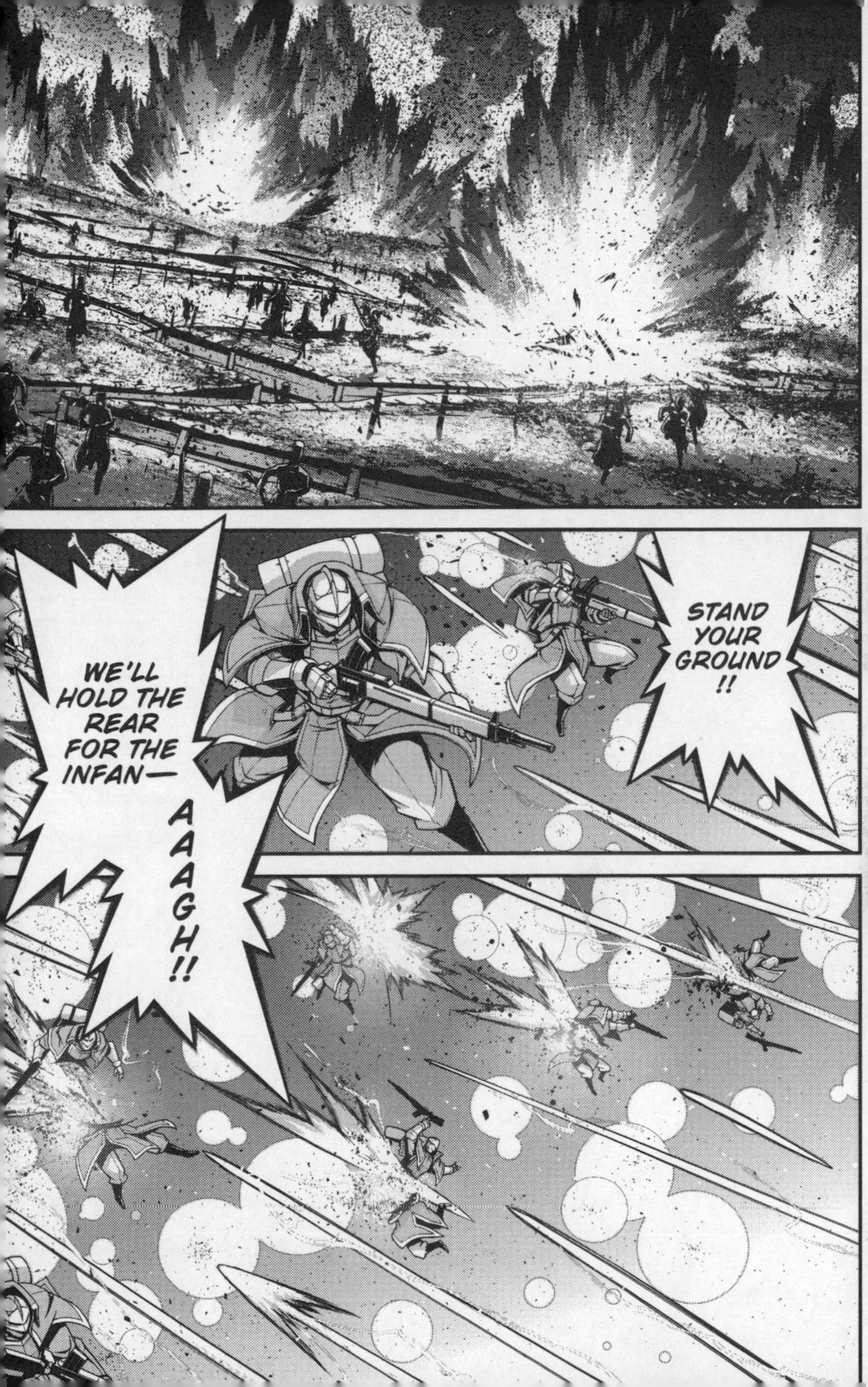
STAND YOUR GROUND!!
WE'LL HOLD THE REAR FOR THE INFAN—
AAAAGH!!

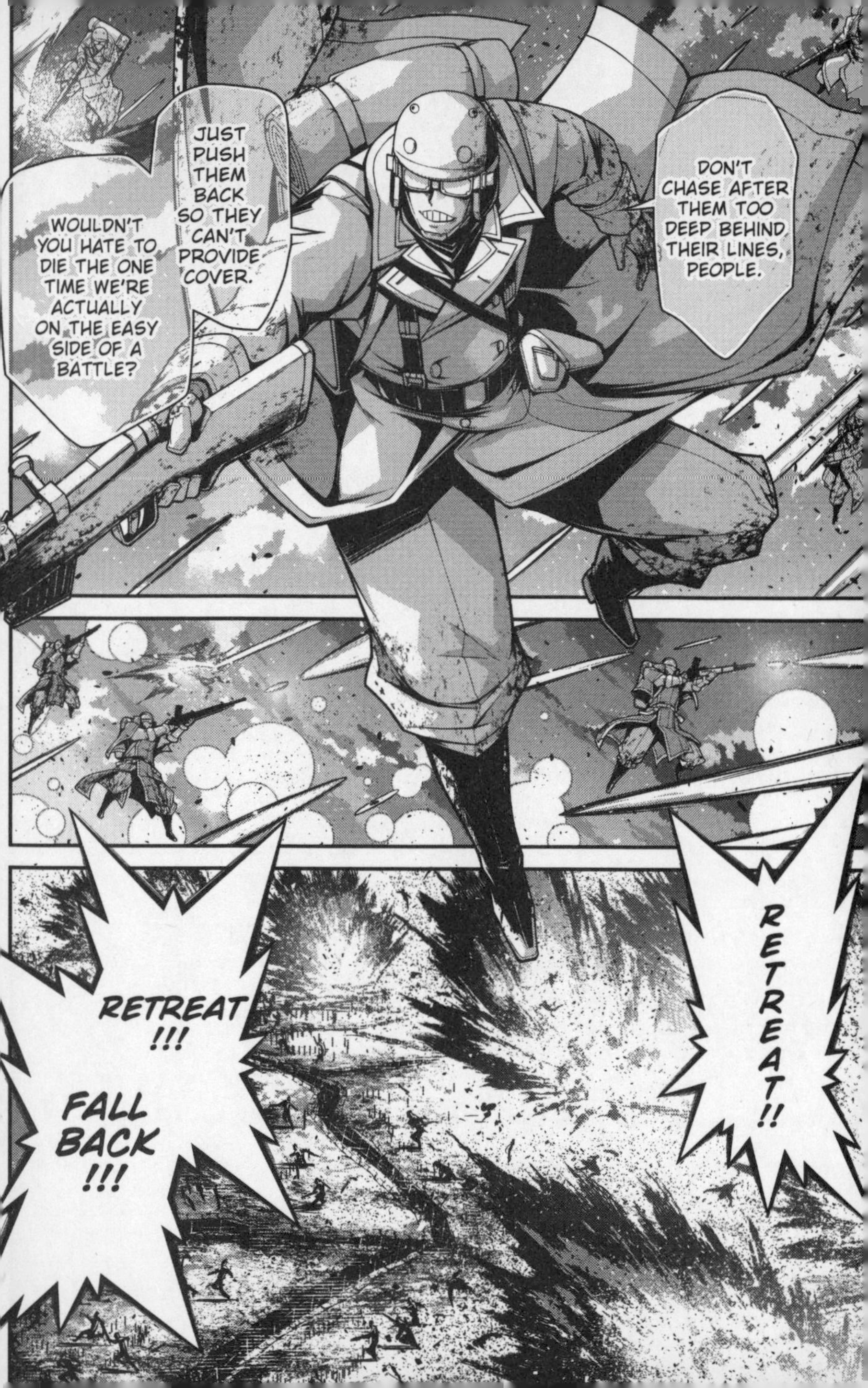
DON'T CHASE AFTER THEM TOO DEEP BEHIND THEIR LINES, PEOPLE.
JUST PUSH THEM BACK SO THEY CAN'T PROVIDE COVER.
WOULDN'T YOU HATE TO DIE THE ONE TIME WE'RE ACTUALLY ON THE EASY SIDE OF A BATTLE?
RETREAT!!
RETREAT!!!
FALL BACK!!!

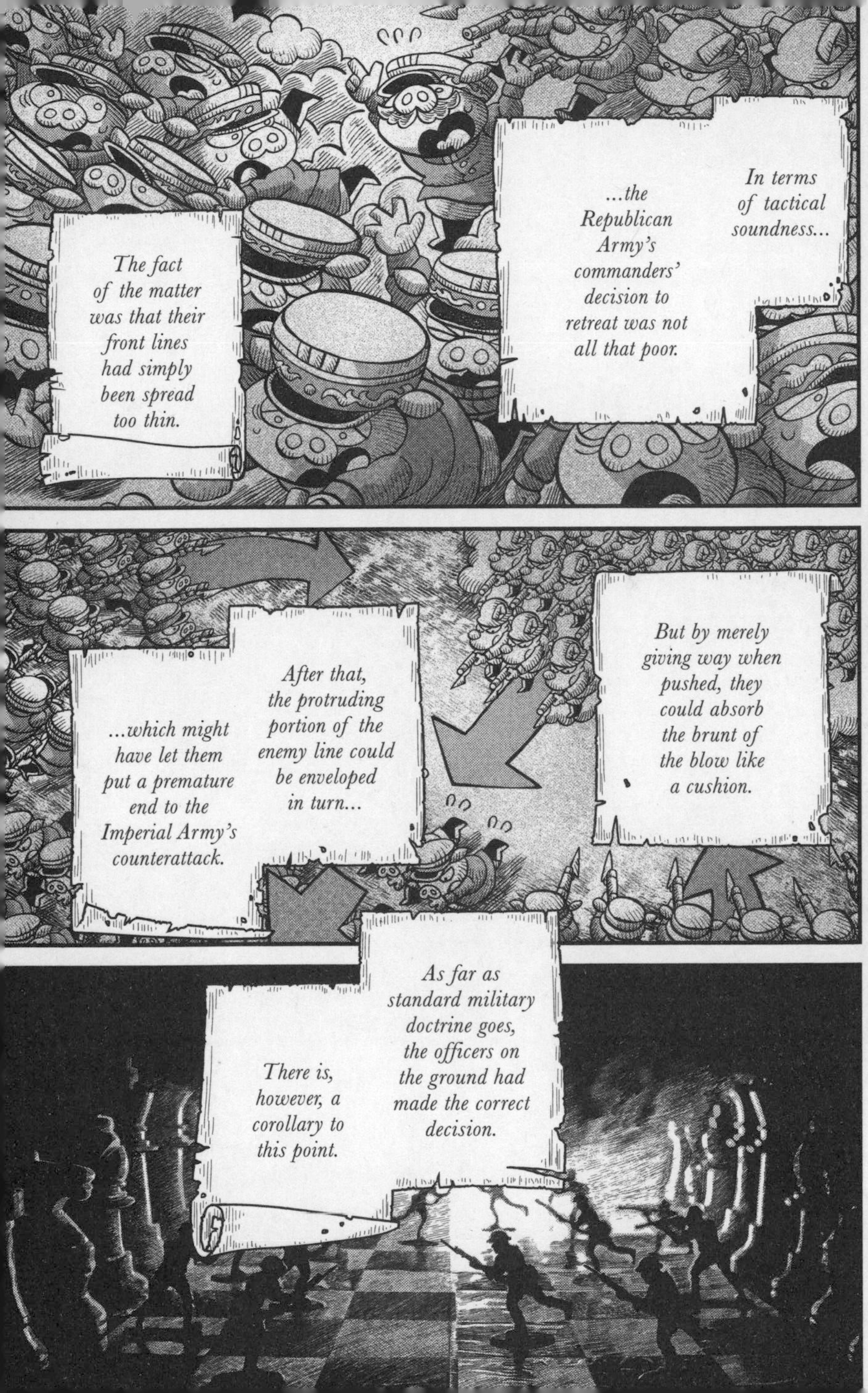
In terms of tactical soundness...
...the Republican Army's commanders' decision to retreat was not all that poor.
The fact of the matter was that their front lines had simply been spread too thin.
But by merely giving way when pushed, they could absorb the brunt of the blow like a cushion.
After that, the protruding portion of the enemy line could be enveloped in turn...
...which might have let them put a premature end to the Imperial Army's counterattack.
As far as standard military doctrine goes, the officers on the ground had made the correct decision.
There is, however, a corollary to this point.

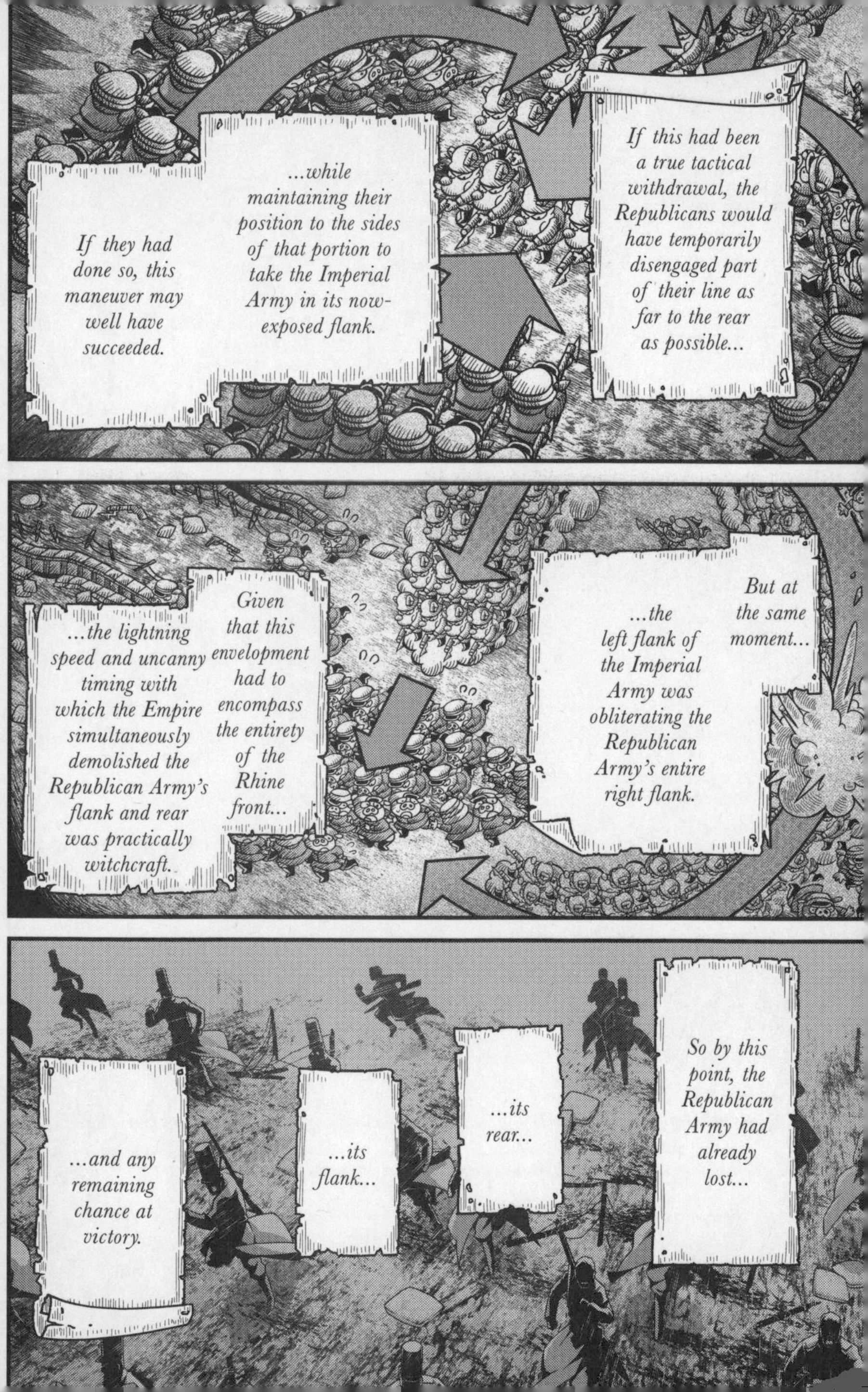
If this had been a true tactical withdrawal, the Republicans would have temporarily disengaged part of their line as far to the rear as possible...
...while maintaining their position to the sides of that portion to take the Imperial Army in its now-exposed flank.
If they had done so, this maneuver may well have succeeded.
But at the same moment...
...the left flank of the Imperial Army was obliterating the Republican Army's entire right flank.
Given that this envelopment had to encompass the entirety of the Rhine front...
...the lightning speed and uncanny timing with which the Empire simultaneously demolished the Republican Army's flank and rear was practically witchcraft.
So by this point, the Republican Army had already lost...
...its rear...
...its flank...
...and any remaining chance at victory.

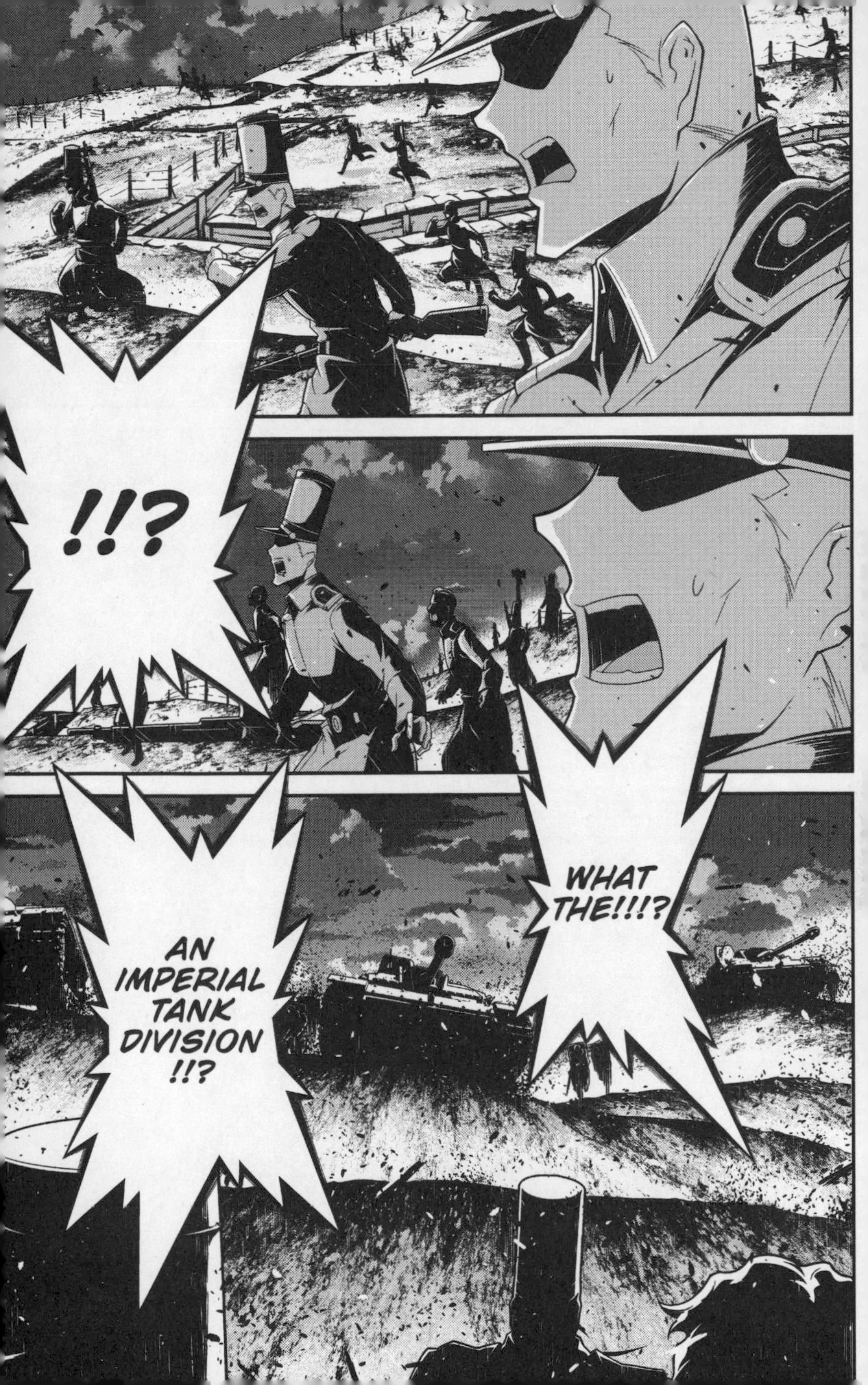
!!?
WHAT THE!!!?
AN IMPERIAL TANK DIVISION!!?

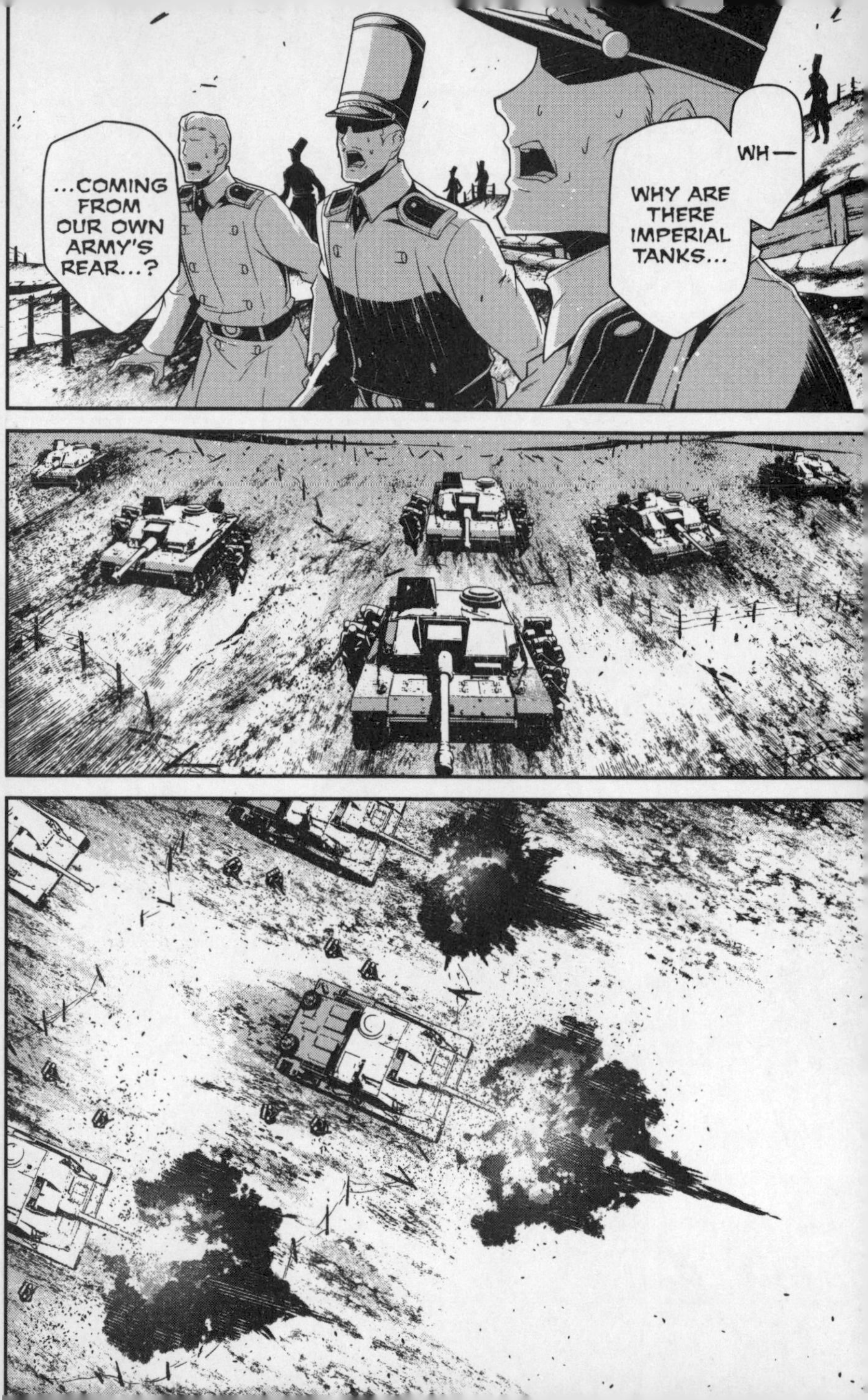
WH—
WHY ARE THERE IMPERIAL TANKS...
...COMING FROM OUR OWN ARMY'S REAR...?

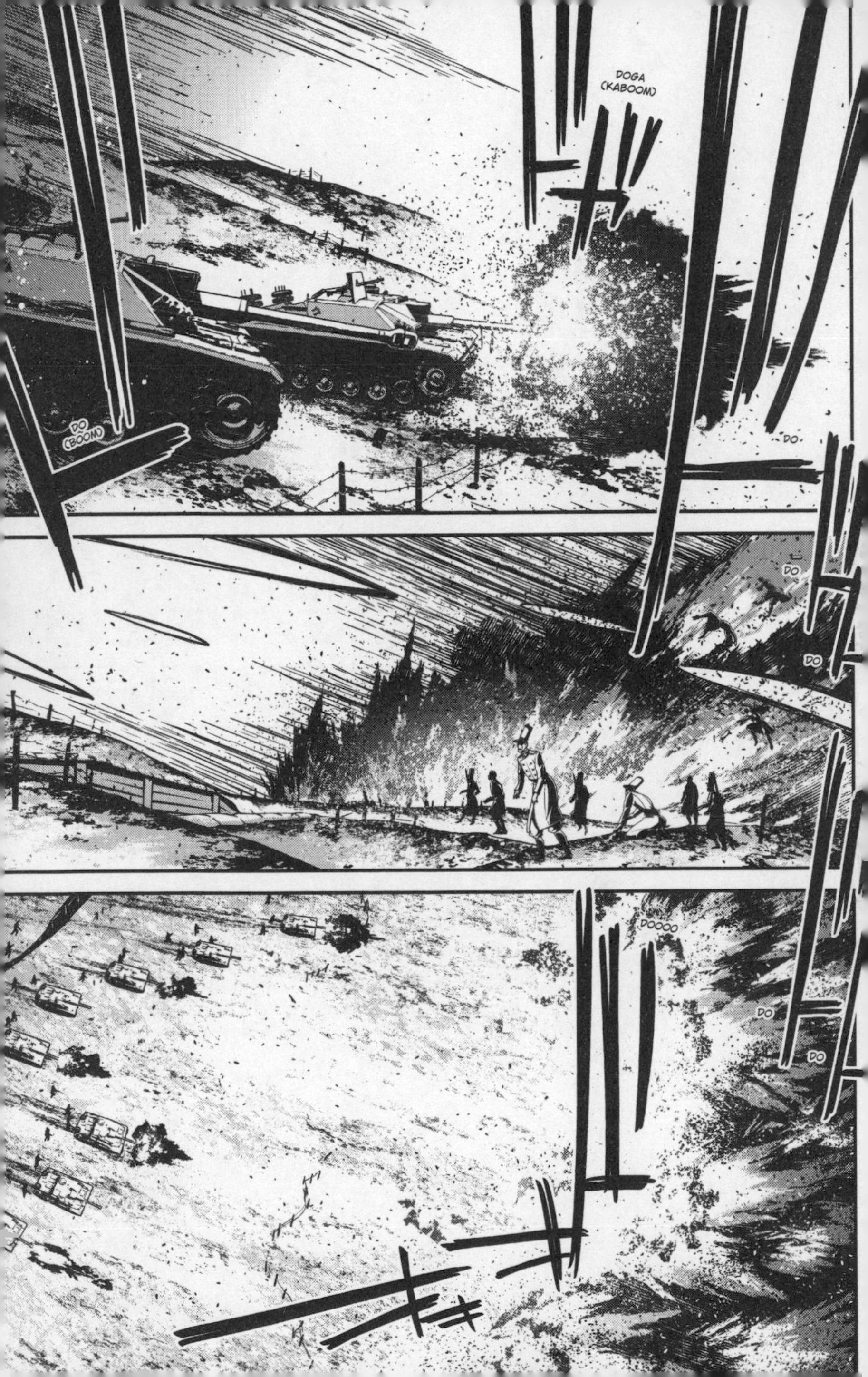
DOGA
(KABOOM)
DO
DO
(BOOM)
DO
DO
DOOOO
DO
DO

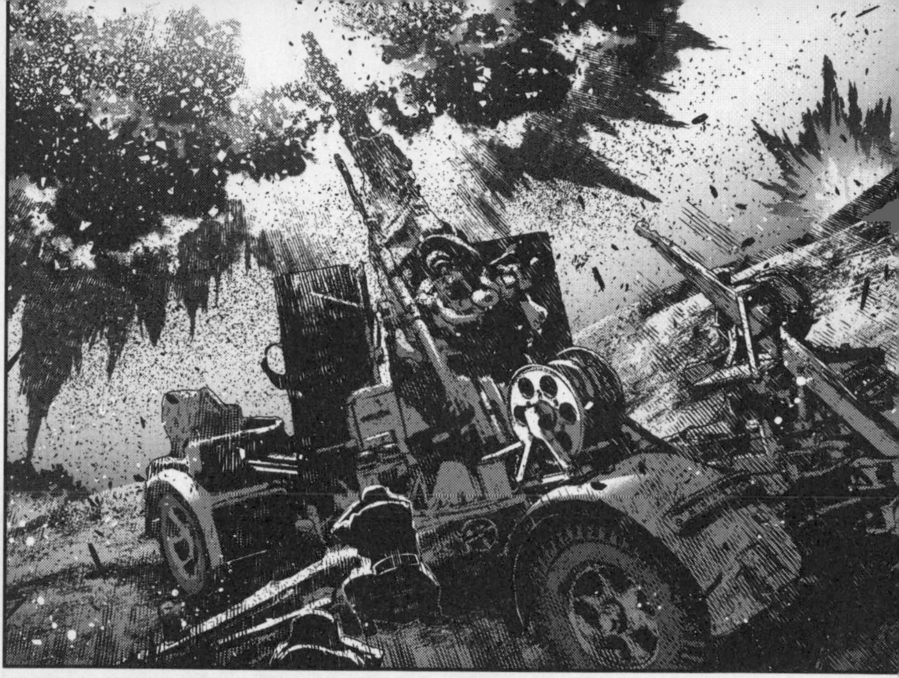
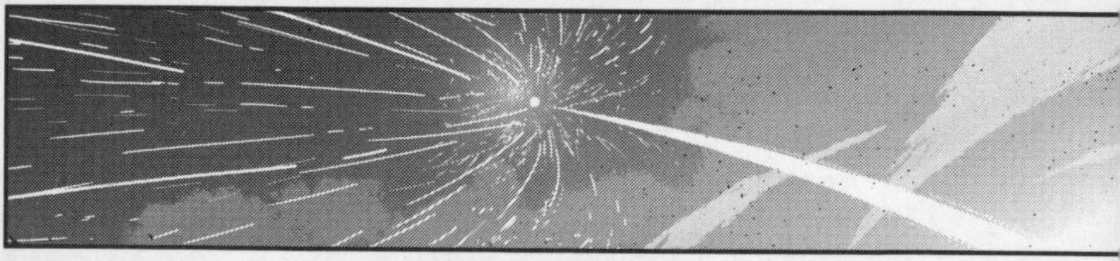
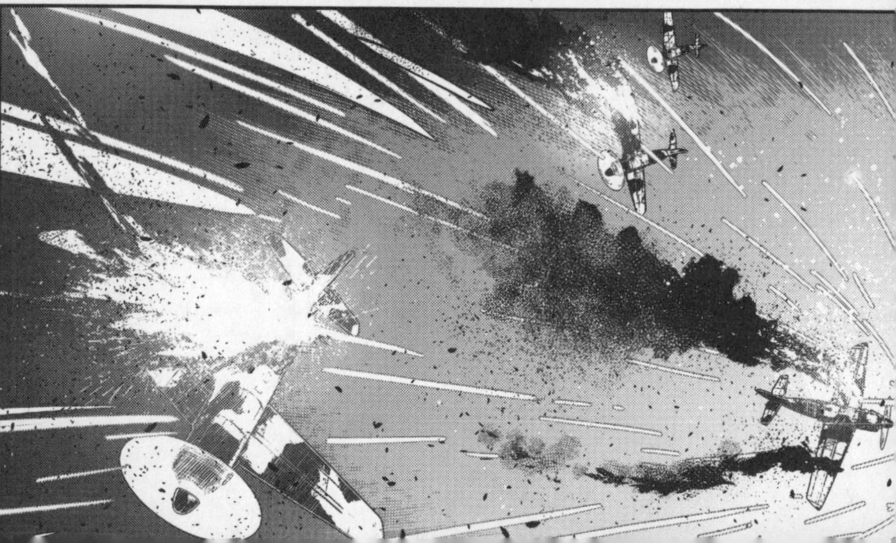

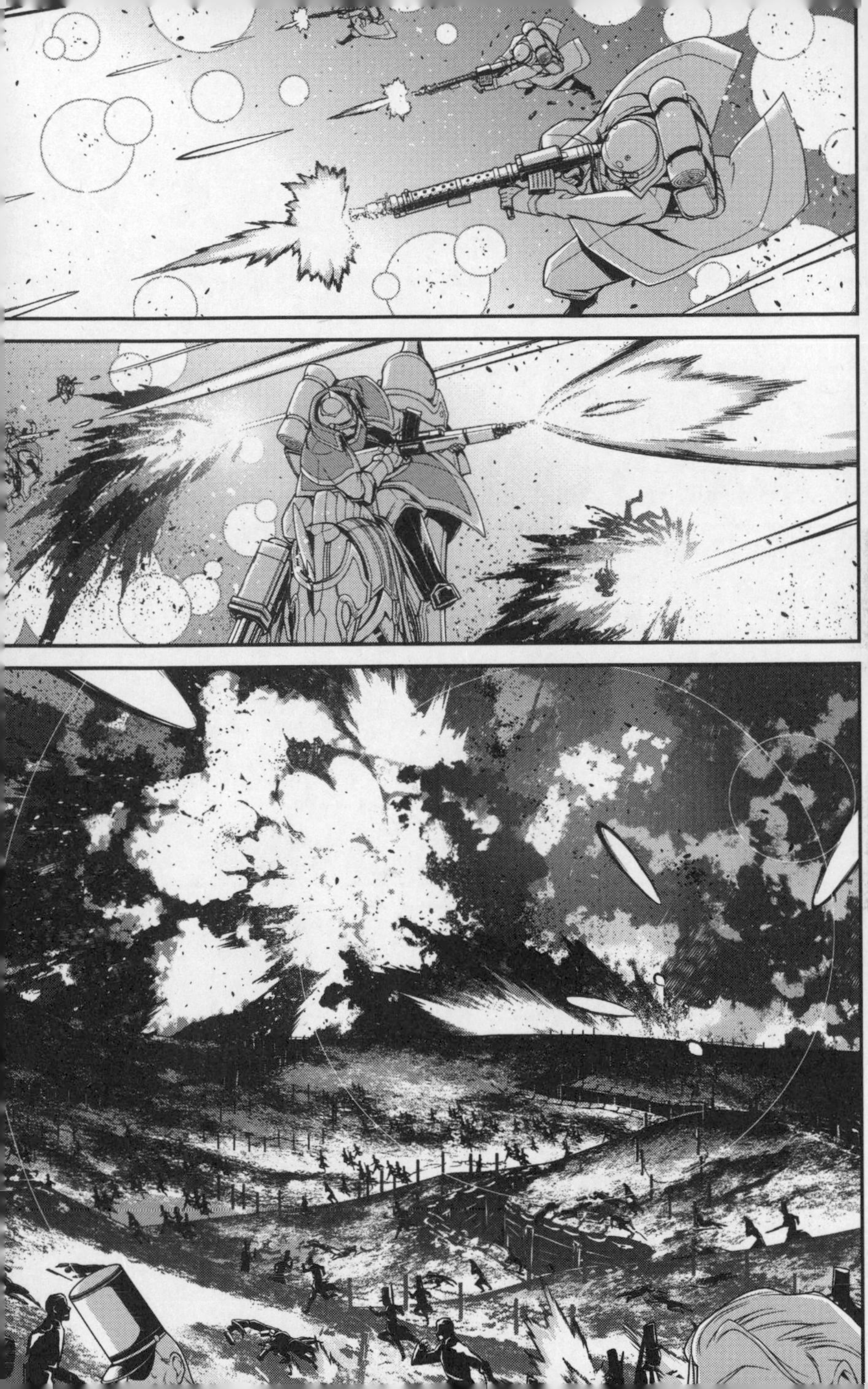

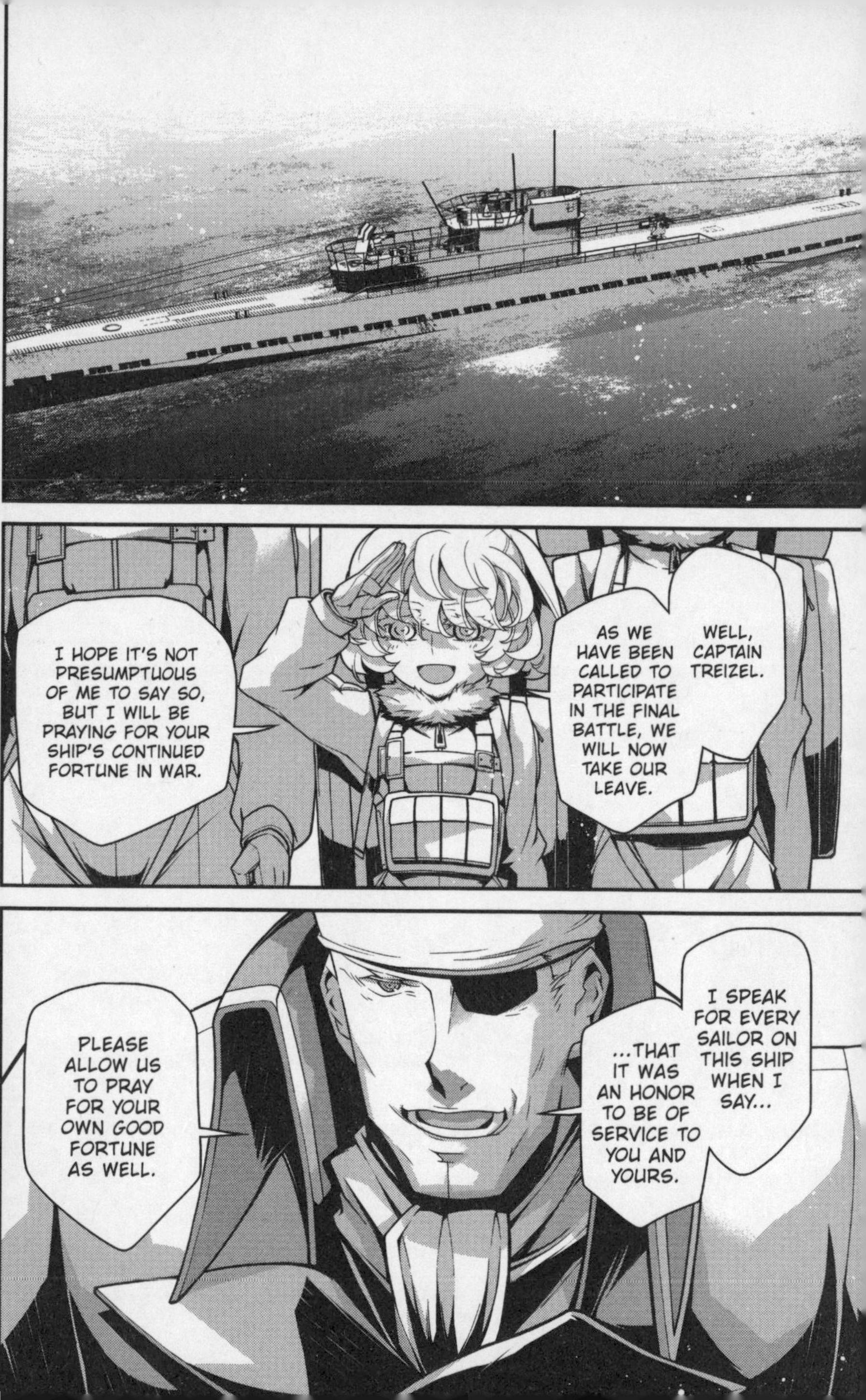
WELL, CAPTAIN TREIZEL.
AS WE HAVE BEEN CALLED TO PARTICIPATE IN THE FINAL BATTLE, WE WILL NOW TAKE OUR LEAVE.
I HOPE IT'S NOT PRESUMPTUOUS OF ME TO SAY SO, BUT I WILL BE PRAYING FOR YOUR SHIP'S CONTINUED FORTUNE IN WAR.
I SPEAK FOR EVERY SAILOR ON THIS SHIP WHEN I SAY...
...THAT IT WAS AN HONOR TO BE OF SERVICE TO YOU AND YOURS.
PLEASE ALLOW US TO PRAY FOR YOUR OWN GOOD FORTUNE AS WELL.

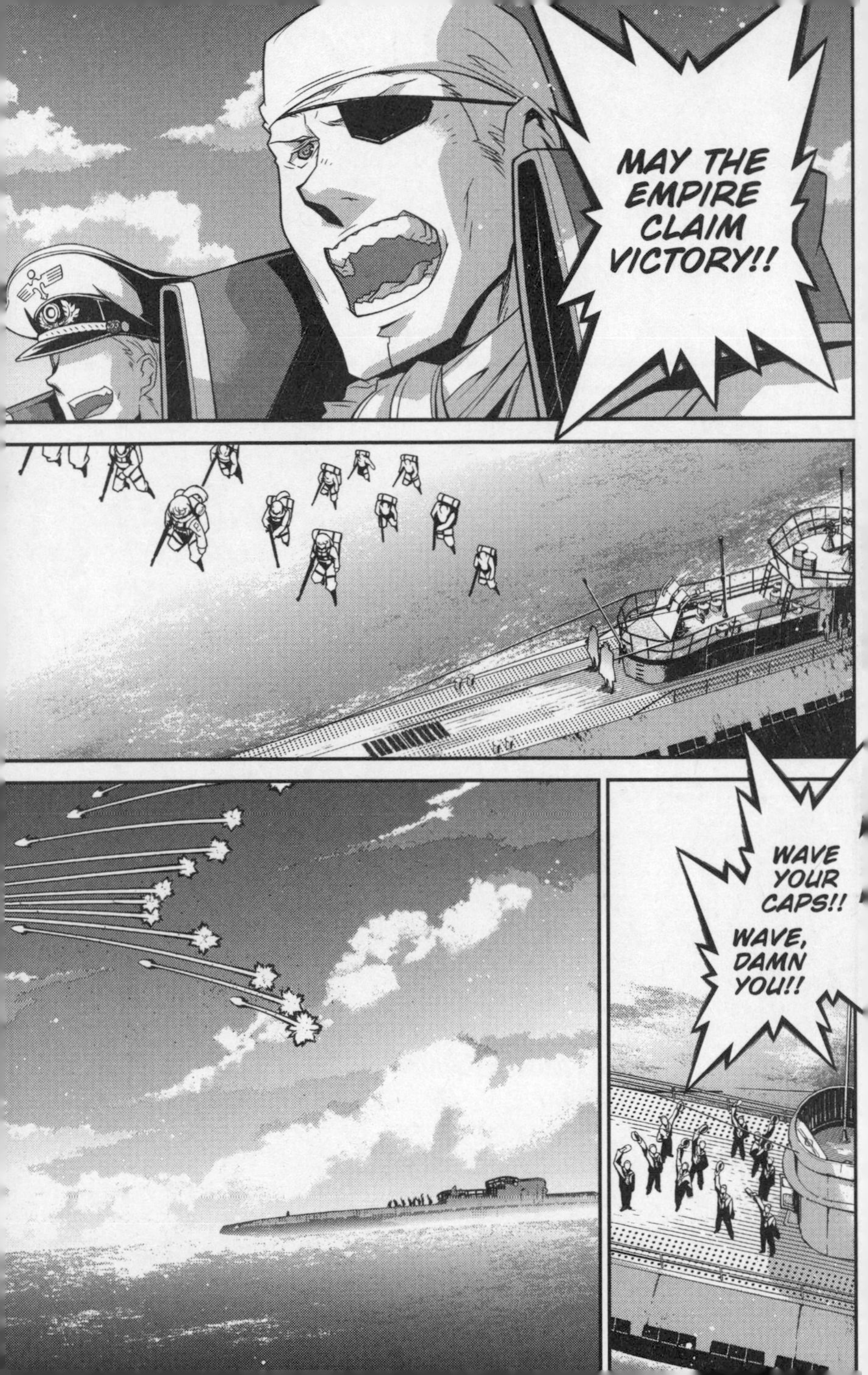
MAY THE EMPIRE CLAIM VICTORY!!
WAVE YOUR CAPS!!
WAVE, DAMN YOU!!

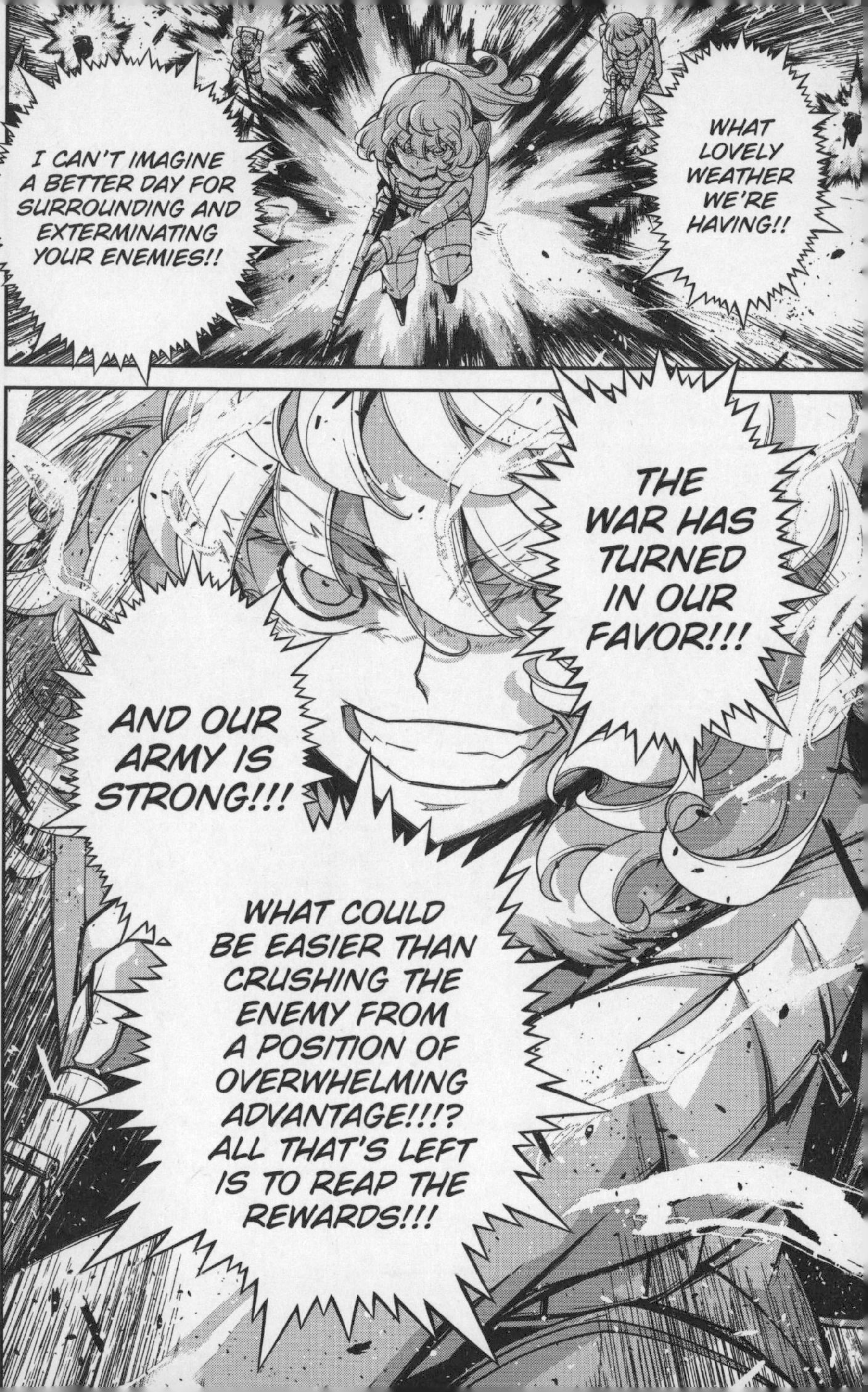
WHAT LOVELY WEATHER WE'RE HAVING!!
I CAN'T IMAGINE A BETTER DAY FOR SURROUNDING AND EXTERMINATING YOUR ENEMIES!!
THE WAR HAS TURNED IN OUR FAVOR!!!
AND OUR ARMY IS STRONG!!!
WHAT COULD BE EASIER THAN CRUSHING THE ENEMY FROM A POSITION OF OVERWHELMING ADVANTAGE!!!? ALL THAT'S LEFT IS TO REAP THE REWARDS!!!

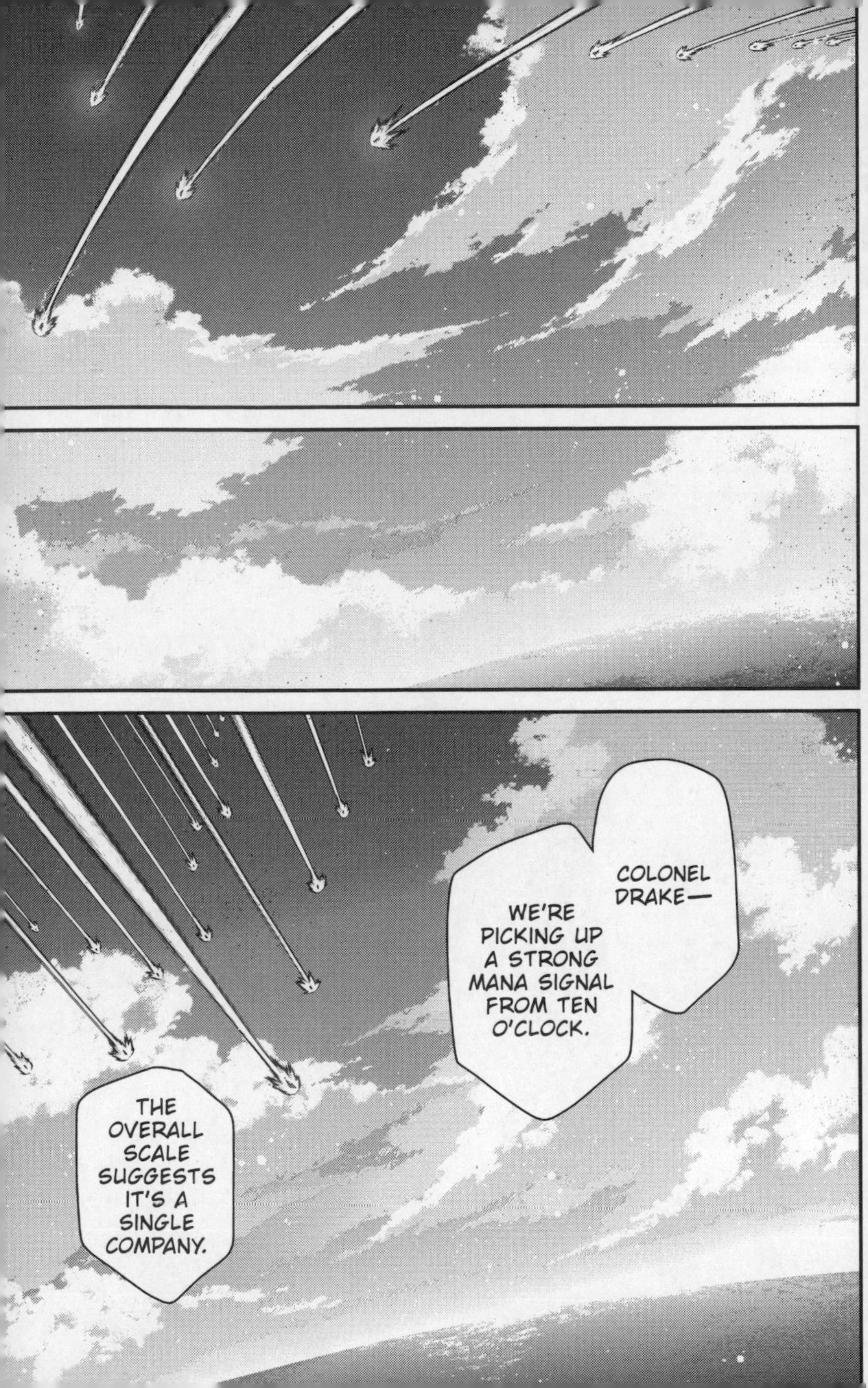
COLONEL DRAKE—
WE'RE PICKING UP A STRONG MANA SIGNAL FROM TEN O'CLOCK.
THE OVERALL SCALE SUGGESTS IT'S A SINGLE COMPANY.

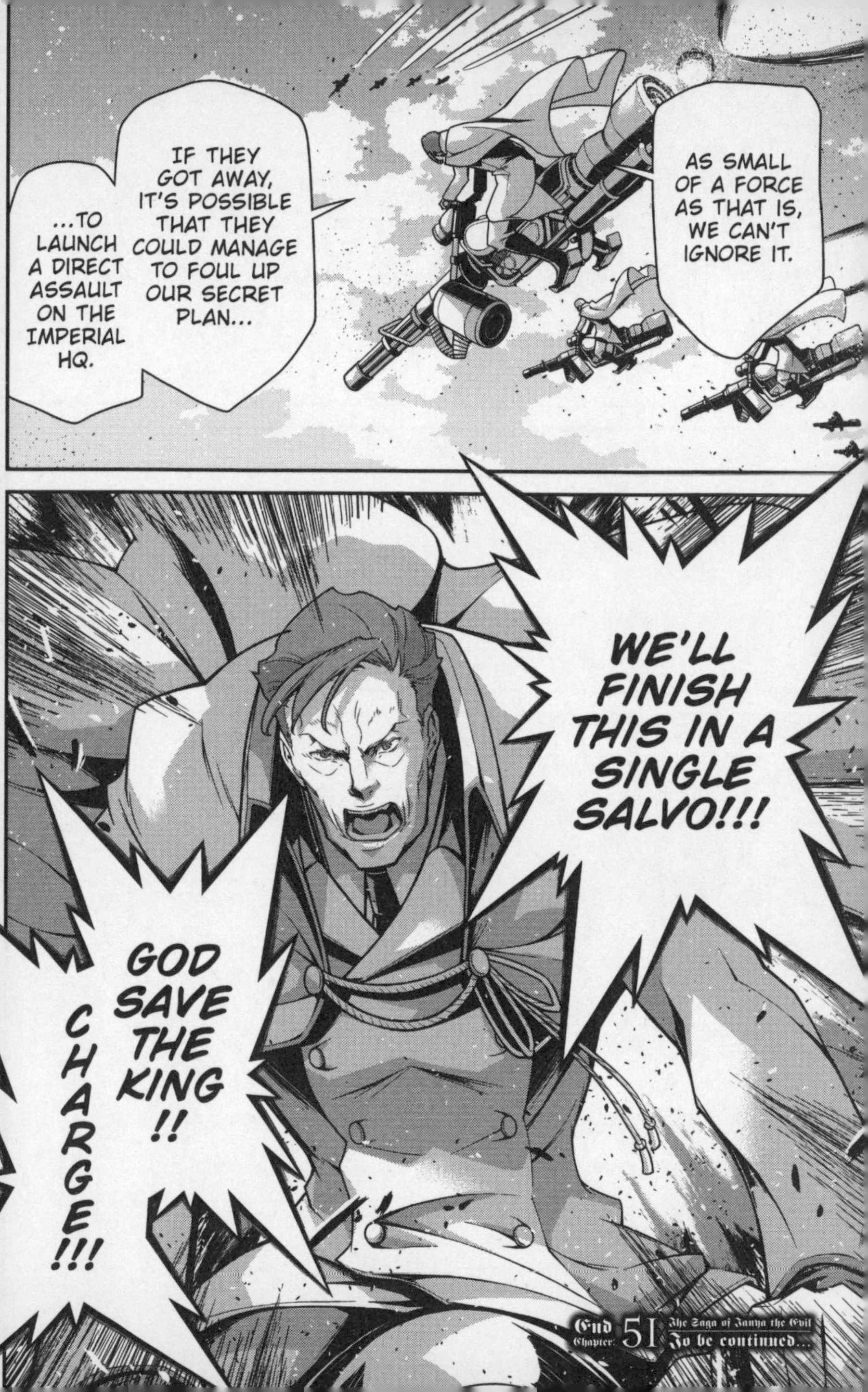
AS SMALL OF A FORCE AS THAT IS, WE CAN'T IGNORE IT.
IF THEY GOT AWAY, IT'S POSSIBLE THAT THEY COULD MANAGE TO FOUL UP OUR SECRET PLAN...
...TO LAUNCH A DIRECT ASSAULT ON THE IMPERIAL HQ.
WE'LL FINISH THIS IN A SINGLE SALVO!!!
GOD SAVE THE KING!!
CHARGE!!!
End Chapter: 51 The Saga of Tanya the Evil To be continued...

Glossary Chapter 60

The Messines Ridge

The location where the Republican Army's right flank was stationed when it was destroyed by massive underground explosions in Operation Lock Pick. A similar tactic was employed at the real-world Messines Ridge during World War I.

The actual Messines Ridge is located on what is currently the border between Belgium and France, but at the time of the war, the ground there was soaked with both German and Allied blood from the meat grinder that is trench warfare. In September 1915, Lieutenant General Sir George Henry Fowke, Chief Engineer of the British Army's Royal Engineers, proposed a plan to break through this deadlock by planting explosives under the Messines Ridge, which would soon be put into action.

After this plan was further refined by geologist and famed Antarctic explorer Edgeworth David, the Royal Engineers set about excavating a main tunnel at a depth of thirty meters—which was so deep that they would have had to dig through clay to go any farther—that would ultimately stretch out over five kilometers. The German Army was actually aware that the Allied forces were attempting to sap their position in this location, so the Allies would periodically detonate shallower, shorter tunnels to launch minor attacks, which kept the full extent of the main tunnel hidden. After two years of digging, Field Marshal Douglas Haig finally gave the order to demolish the Messines Ridge so the Allies could occupy the surrounding area and advance toward the coastline. The day before the operation, General Sir Charles Harington, Chief of Staff of the Second Army, allegedly said, "Gentlemen, I don't know whether we are going to make history tomorrow, but at any rate we shall change geography."

Over 454 tons of explosives were packed into this tunnel and detonated, resulting in an explosion so loud that it was said to have been heard in London and Dublin. Many people in the surrounding area were convinced there had been an earthquake, and witnesses reported that it also formed a massive pillar of fire. War correspondent Philip Gibbs wrote that "enormous volumes of scarlet flame [threw] up high towers of earth and smoke all lighted by the flame, spilling over into fountains of fierce colour, so that many of our soldiers waiting for the assault were thrown to the ground. The German troops were stunned, dazed and horror-stricken if they were not killed outright. Many of them lay dead in the great craters opened by the mines." Over ten thousand soldiers died in the blast, which was the deadliest single nonnuclear planned explosion in recorded history.

This underground explosion began the first of a long series of battles that would become collectively known as the Battle of Passchendaele, which stands out amid even the blood-soaked history of World War I as a particularly brutal conflict. One of the craters formed by the blast became a pond—likely due to an underground spring being exposed to the surface—that is now known as the Pool of Peace and serves as a memorial to the Great War.

Glossary Chapter 61

Whiskey Dog

After suffering an injury in Arene, Lieutenant Colonel Vianto was sent in an official capacity to deliver luxury items, such as cigarettes and alcohol, to the officers on the front lines. (See Vol. 16.)

He likely gave himself this call sign to invite a comparison to the rescue dogs that had small barrels of whiskey attached to their collars to help fortify anyone they found stranded in the mountains. His use of such a facetious call sign presumably stemmed from the common conviction that the François Republic had already won the war.

Jamming

The act of broadcasting radio waves meant to interfere with enemy communications or radar.

To jam radios, high-output, meaningless noise is sent out over a wide range of frequencies used by the enemy to make any attempts at communication within that range unintelligible. A similar technique (known as "noise jamming") can be used to jam radar, but it is also possible to send back false return signals, which is referred to as "deceptive jamming." There are also passive forms of jamming, like stealth technology or decoys, that can keep radar from perceiving a real threat or fool it into detecting one where it does not exist.

In either case, while it is certainly possible to drown out enemy radio communications through this sort of interfering noise, there is no way to silence their actual signals. If there are no transmissions at all on a given frequency, your first thought should be to suspect mechanical issues...or perhaps to wonder whether anybody else is even listening at the other end of the line.

Strategic Reserves

A large quantity of reserve forces held back from battle for strategic purposes. Being able to deploy reserve forces at will to any given battle is a major piece of maintaining a functional war footing. These forces are typically used to counter unpredictable events or attempt to gain numerical superiority in a major offensive. As the name implies, these reserves are dispatched according to strategic-level needs, and as such, the authority to do so resides solely within high command and is not granted to officers on the ground.

Strategic reserve forces are no mere insurance policy—they are essential for being able to respond flexibly to any developments in war. That being said, if reserve forces cannot be deployed en masse with sufficient haste, their utility drops dramatically as the laws of force concentration begin working against them. To paraphrase Clausewitz, "Every reserve which is only intended for use after the final battle is opposed to common sense." Taken conversely, every available reserve troop should be sent to the final battle—should it be lost regardless, you would at least be able to say you had done everything you could.

Glossary Chapter 62

Rubbing Alcohol

Alcohol intended for purposes other than consumption. In some cases, poisonous substances are intentionally mixed in to prevent people from drinking it, so doing so can be very dangerous.

Examples of these industrial-strength alcohols used by the military include ethanol and isopropyl, which are used as disinfectants by medics, as well as methanol, which can be used as fuel. Of these three, pure ethanol—which is, in fact, the active ingredient in all alcoholic beverages—can be safely ingested if sufficiently diluted with water. As such, there are many historical instances of soldiers stealing and drinking their medics' ethanol, but manufacturers would often mix isopropyl or methanol into bottles labeled "ethanol" to avoid having to pay liquor taxes on them or intentionally make them unfit for consumption, so going off the label did not guarantee safety.

Methanol is highly toxic—a fatal dose of it is only a tenth of the volume of a fatal dose of ethanol—and also particularly harmful to the eyes, easily causing blindness in even small quantities. As such, when the Imperial Japanese Army's stockpile of methanol became widely sold on the black market post-WWII to drinkers desperately short on safer options, it acquired the nicknames mechiru alcohol *("eye-destroying alcohol") and* meichiru alcohol *("life-ending alcohol"), both puns on "methyl alcohol," a synonym for methanol. The lesson here is not to fool around with shady, home-brewed liquors and drugs, good boys and girls! (Especially since it's illegal for minors to smoke or drink in any case.)*

Mechanized Infantry

Soldiers who have had body parts or even their entire bodies replaced with machinery, resulting in heavily armored cyborgs with immense strength—okay, just kidding. Actually refers to infantry who ride armored vehicles into battle for improved mobility. Not the same as (but often confused with) motorized infantry, who ride unarmored vehicles and are consequently used for entirely different purposes.

The essential purpose of having mechanized infantry is to improve the mobility of foot soldiers to the point that they can accompany tank squadrons. The concept began as an offshoot of motorized infantry, who would ride on trucks or other comparable vehicles that were not equipped with armor or caterpillar treads and as such needed to be dropped off just outside the battleground, which made it difficult to conduct maneuver warfare with the tank squadrons. The need for vehicles that could accompany tanks into battle led to the development of half-tracks (vehicles with wheels in front for steering and caterpillar treads in the back for propulsion) and armored personnel carriers, enabling the transition from motorized to mechanized infantry.

While the ability to quickly and safely move through the battlefield in an armored vehicle is the defining characteristic of mechanized infantry, they can also dismount to engage in combat on foot to establish control over an area. As mechanized infantry is highly mobile, armored, well-suited for meeting engagements, and even capable of establishing control over and occupying territory, the German Army saw fit to pair them with tank squadrons to form their panzer divisions for the purpose of maneuver warfare in WWII.

Glossary Chapter 63

Sapping

The act of digging a tunnel under the enemy position and setting off explosives inside the tunnel to collapse it, destroying the defenses above in the process. Tunneling underground allows one to close distance to the enemy without being susceptible to attack, but the downside is that the excavation process requires significant time investment.

Sapping is a tactic that has been in use as far back as the days of ancient Rome, when the Romans would dig tunnels under the walls of enemy fortresses, then burn the wooden support beams to cave them in, with the goal of bringing down the entire wall above as a result. In more recent eras, the addition of gunpowder made it possible to turn sapped tunnels into something akin to massive land mines, greatly increasing their offensive power and also making it possible to use them as defensive traps.

This new form of sapping proved especially viable during the trench warfare of World War I, as not only had the necessity of constructing miles upon miles of trenches led to innovations in digging technologies and techniques, but the long periods of deadlock also provided the leeway to make undermining the enemy position worthwhile. England, in particular, hired experienced miners to dig tunnels, forming a specialized cadre of sappers within the Royal Engineers. The aforementioned geologist Edgeworth David oversaw two full battalions of these sappers in digging the Western Front's trenches and tunnels, as well as finding underground water sources and building wells to secure drinking water for the troops, and was awarded the Distinguished Service Order for his role in sapping the Messines Ridge.

Meeting Engagement

Combat that occurs when a moving force unexpectedly encounters the enemy, giving neither side time to fully prepare for battle.

Assault forces are prone to encountering this form of combat, especially when advancing along a predetermined route instead of responding to circumstances, and such battles can be extremely chaotic. As the side with initiative generally has the advantage on contact, an assault force's commanding officer should give orders that allow their soldiers to flexibly act on their own initiative, be able to rapidly assess situations based on factors such as terrain and troop distribution, and possess swift and decisive decision-making skills.

Mobile Encirclement

With "mobility" essentially being the ability to position troops where they are needed at will, a mobile encirclement surrounds, redirects, or isolates enemy troops so as to attack from a position of advantage. Encirclement is one of the oldest forms of maneuver warfare and generally works by having auxiliary forces occupy the enemy's front while the main force moves to the enemy's flank or rear to cut off their avenues of escape before destroying them.

An axis of advance to the enemy's flank or rear, the most critical part of such a maneuver, was created on a continental scale by the Empire's bold line consolidation, enabling them to swing through this "revolving door" to encircle the Republican Army.

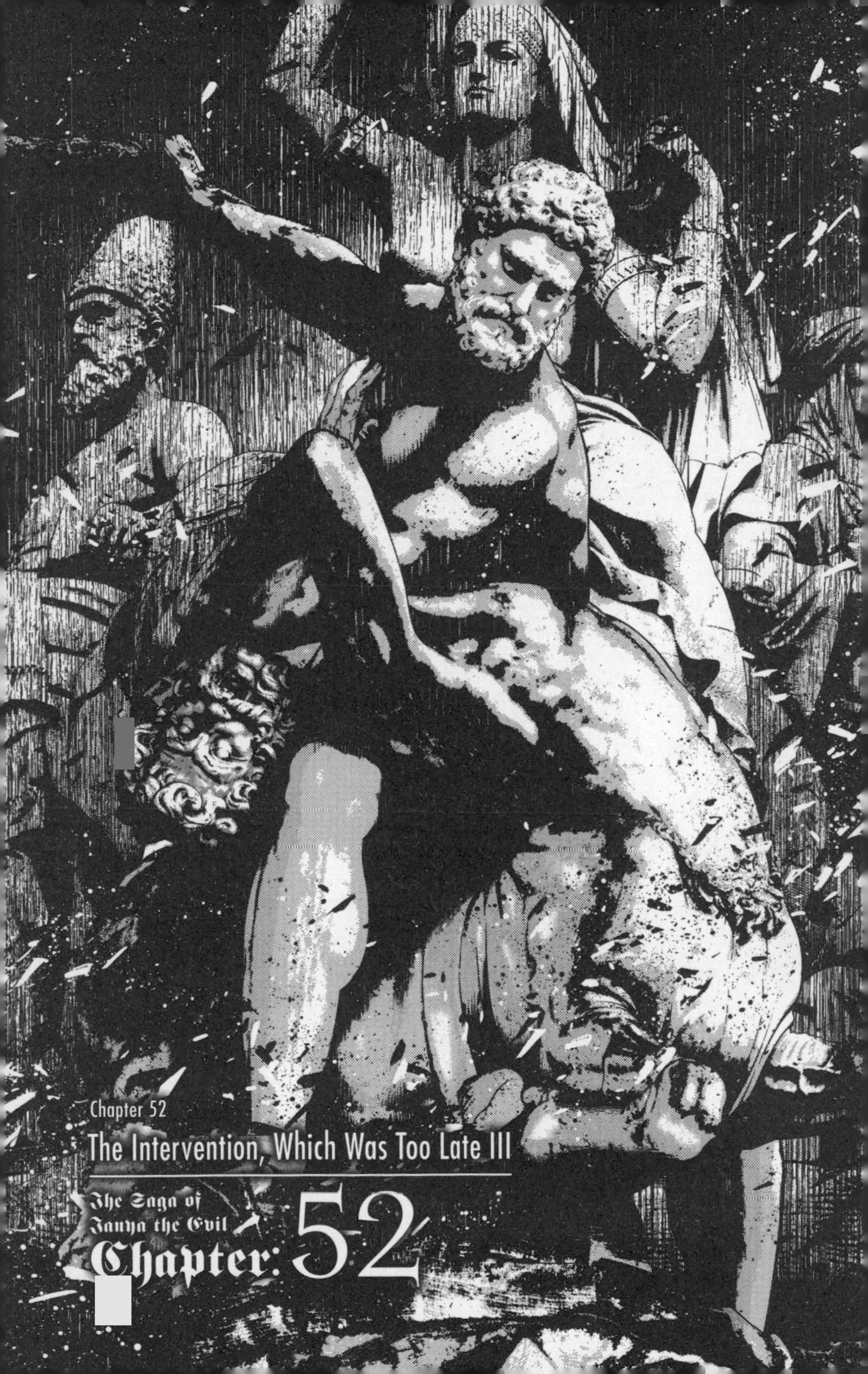
Chapter 52
The Intervention, Which Was Too Late III
The Saga of
Tanya the Evil
Chapter: 52

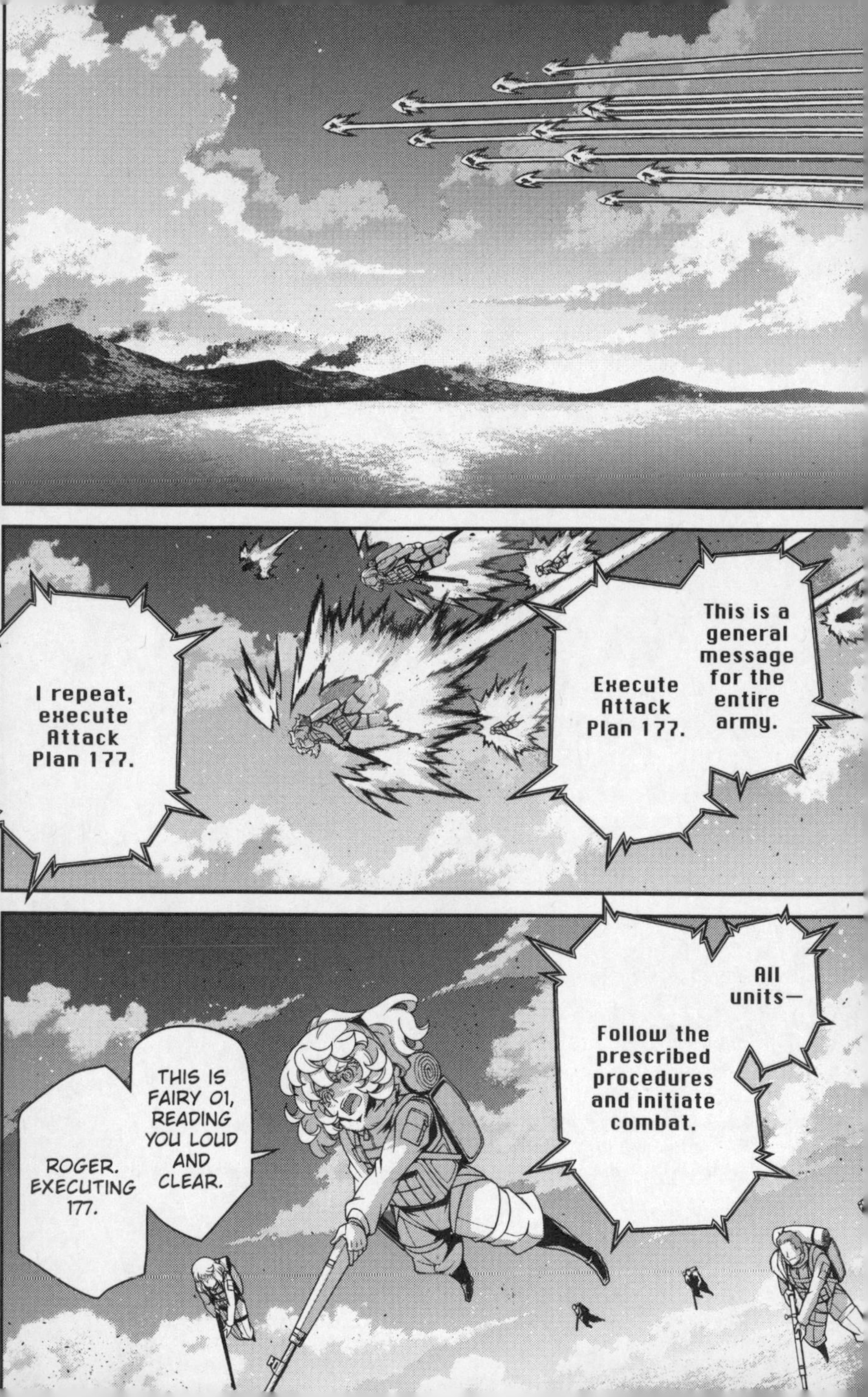

This is a general message for the entire army.
Execute Attack Plan 177.
I repeat, execute Attack Plan 177.
All units—
Follow the prescribed procedures and initiate combat.
THIS IS FAIRY 01, READING YOU LOUD AND CLEAR.
ROGER. EXECUTING 177.

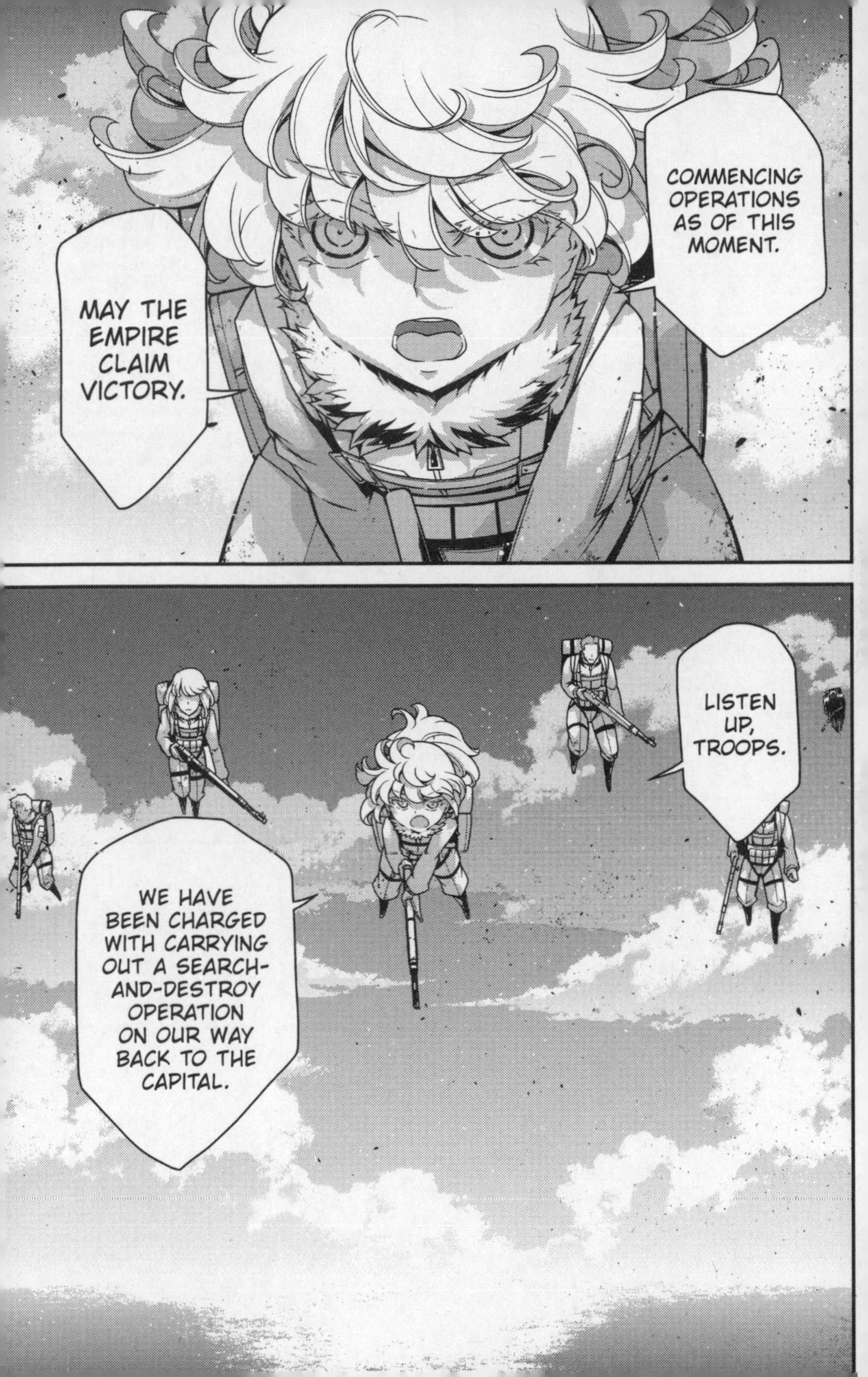
COMMENCING OPERATIONS AS OF THIS MOMENT.
MAY THE EMPIRE CLAIM VICTORY.
LISTEN UP, TROOPS.
WE HAVE BEEN CHARGED WITH CARRYING OUT A SEARCH-AND-DESTROY OPERATION ON OUR WAY BACK TO THE CAPITAL.

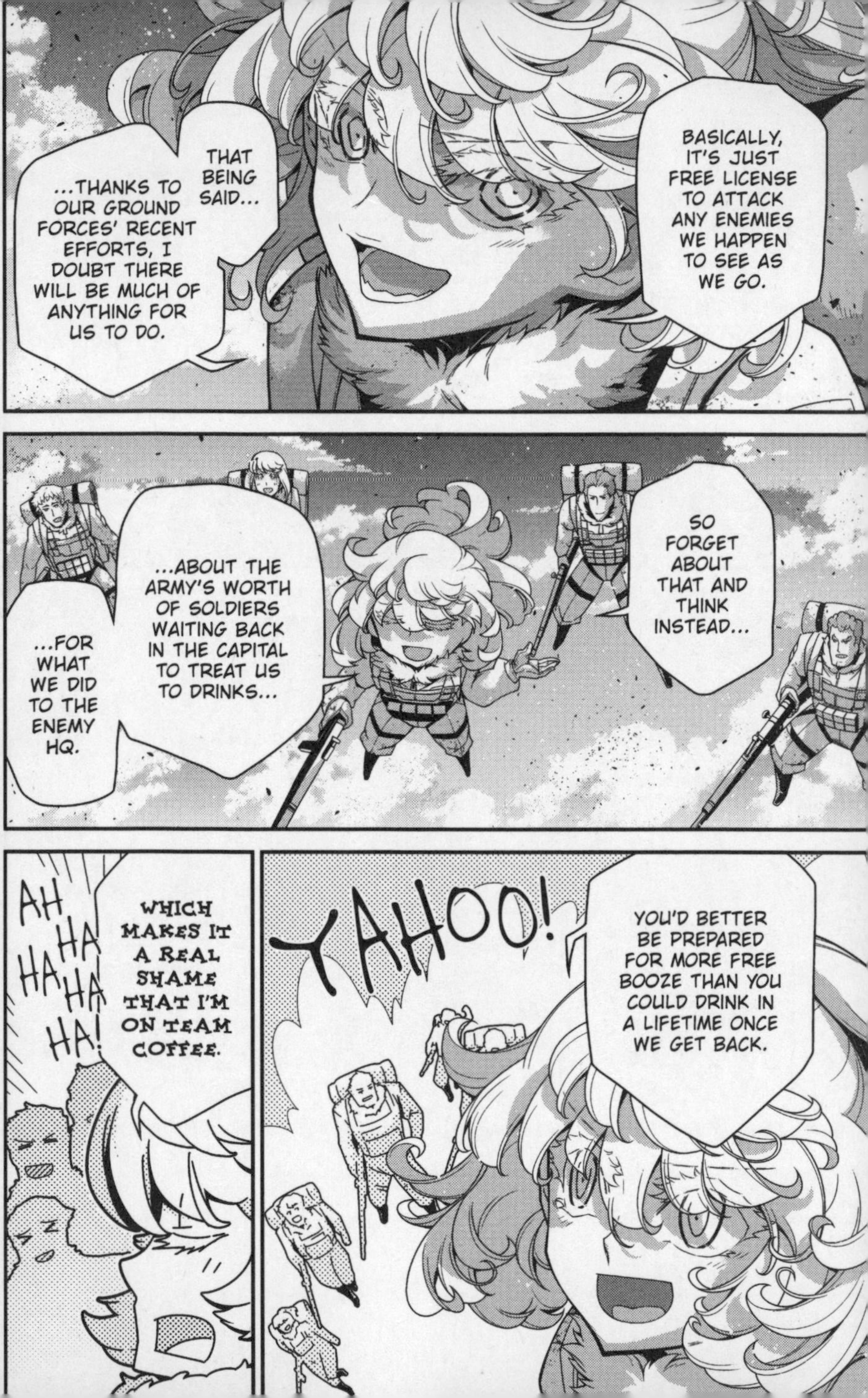
BASICALLY, IT'S JUST FREE LICENSE TO ATTACK ANY ENEMIES WE HAPPEN TO SEE AS WE GO.
THAT BEING SAID...
...THANKS TO OUR GROUND FORCES' RECENT EFFORTS, I DOUBT THERE WILL BE MUCH OF ANYTHING FOR US TO DO.
SO FORGET ABOUT THAT AND THINK INSTEAD...
...ABOUT THE ARMY'S WORTH OF SOLDIERS WAITING BACK IN THE CAPITAL TO TREAT US TO DRINKS...
...FOR WHAT WE DID TO THE ENEMY HQ.
YOU'D BETTER BE PREPARED FOR MORE FREE BOOZE THAN YOU COULD DRINK IN A LIFETIME ONCE WE GET BACK.
YAHOO!
WHICH MAKES IT A REAL SHAME THAT I'M ON TEAM COFFEE.
AH HA HA HA HA HA!

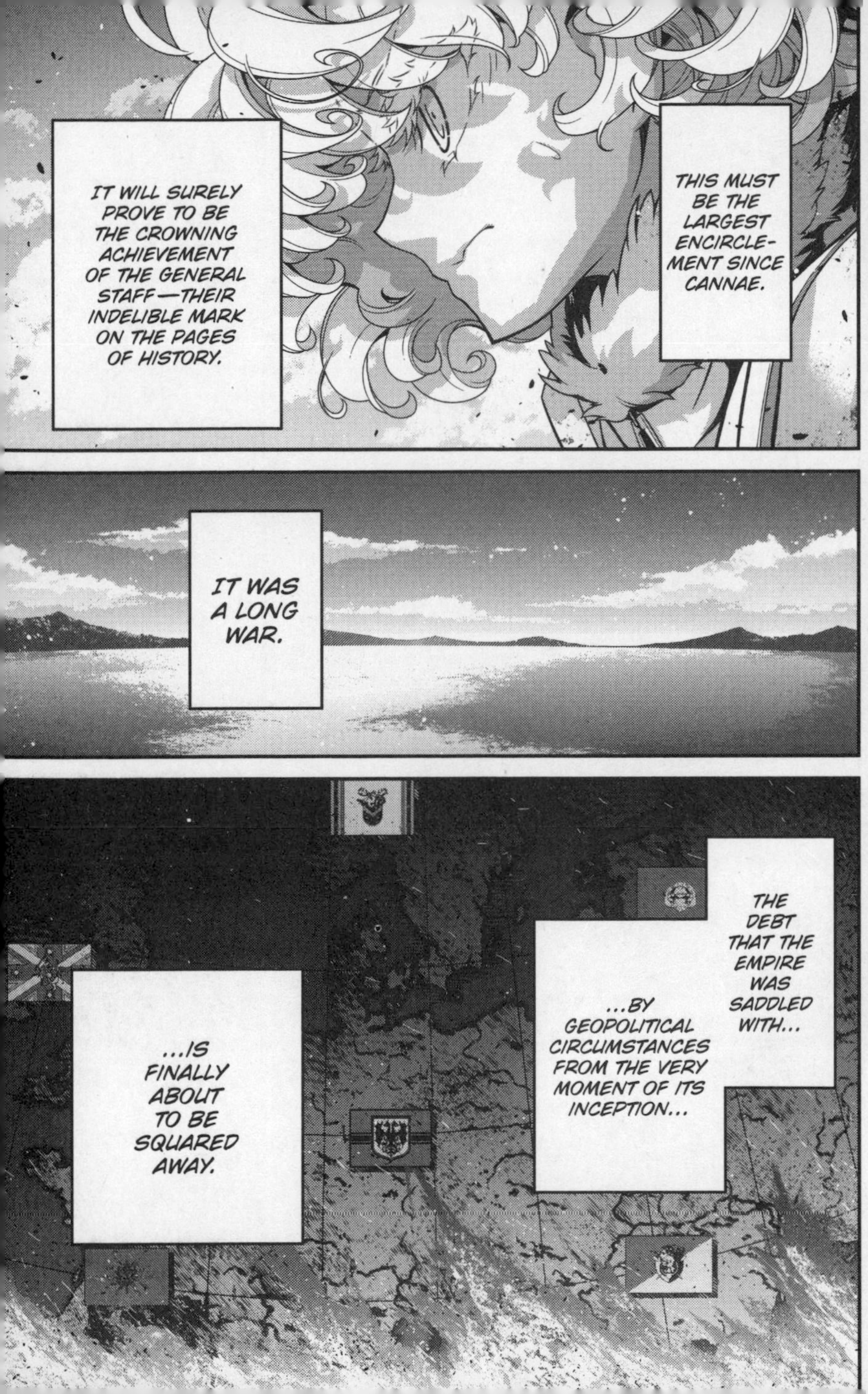
THIS MUST BE THE LARGEST ENCIRCLE-MENT SINCE CANNAE.
IT WILL SURELY PROVE TO BE THE CROWNING ACHIEVEMENT OF THE GENERAL STAFF—THEIR INDELIBLE MARK ON THE PAGES OF HISTORY.
IT WAS A LONG WAR.
THE DEBT THAT THE EMPIRE WAS SADDLED WITH...
...BY GEOPOLITICAL CIRCUMSTANCES FROM THE VERY MOMENT OF ITS INCEPTION...
...IS FINALLY ABOUT TO BE SQUARED AWAY.

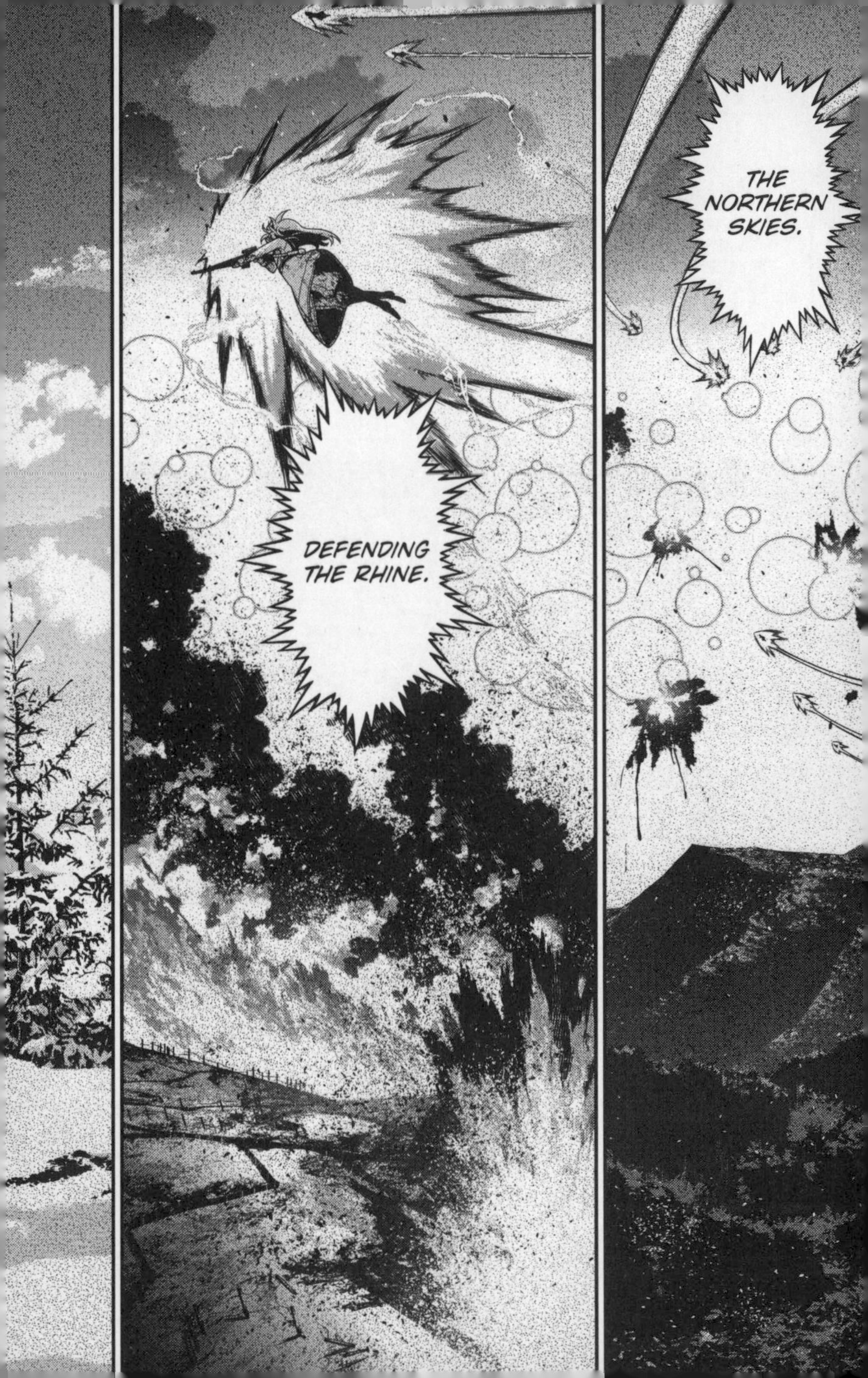
THE NORTHERN SKIES.
DEFENDING THE RHINE.

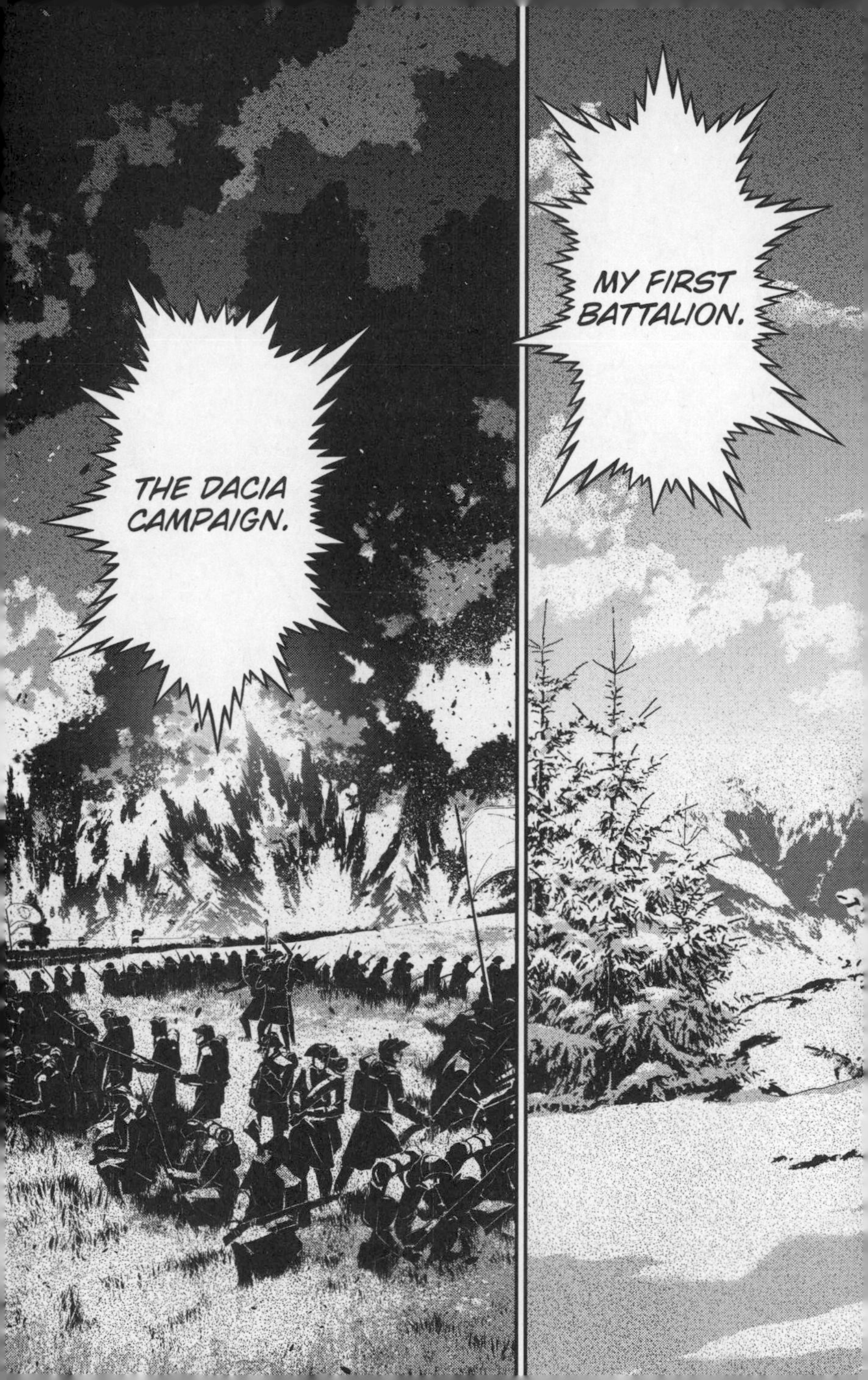
MY FIRST BATTALION.
THE DACIA CAMPAIGN.

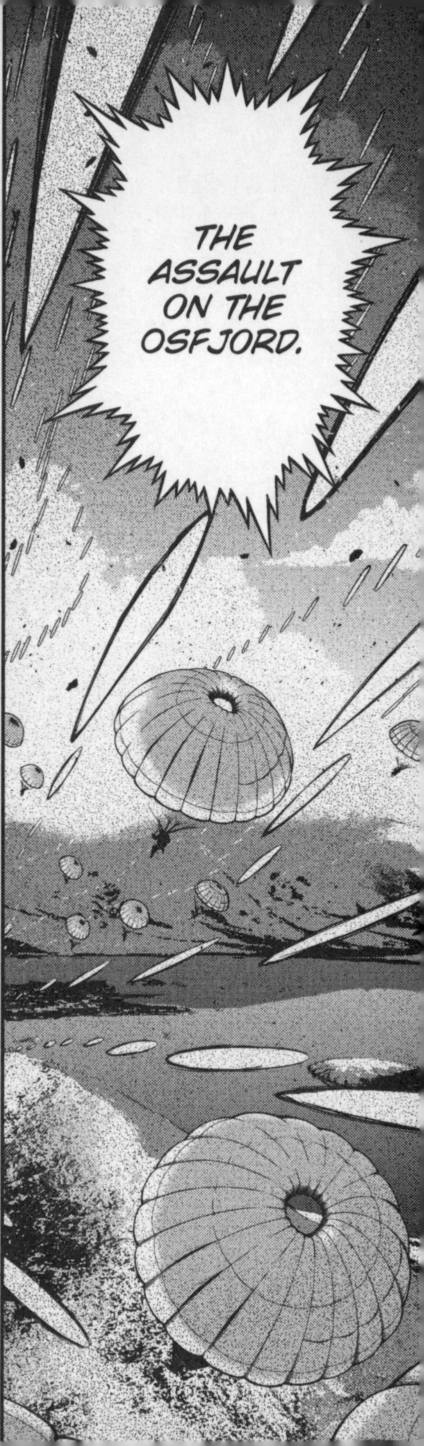
THE ASSAULT ON THE OSFJORD.
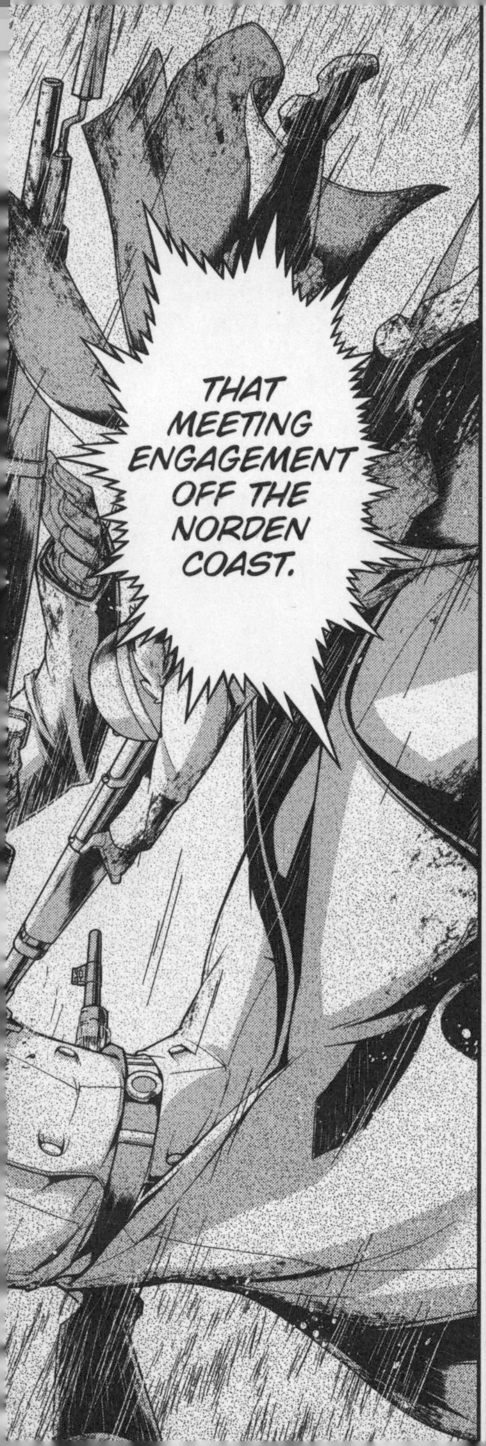
THAT MEETING ENGAGEMENT OFF THE NORDEN COAST.

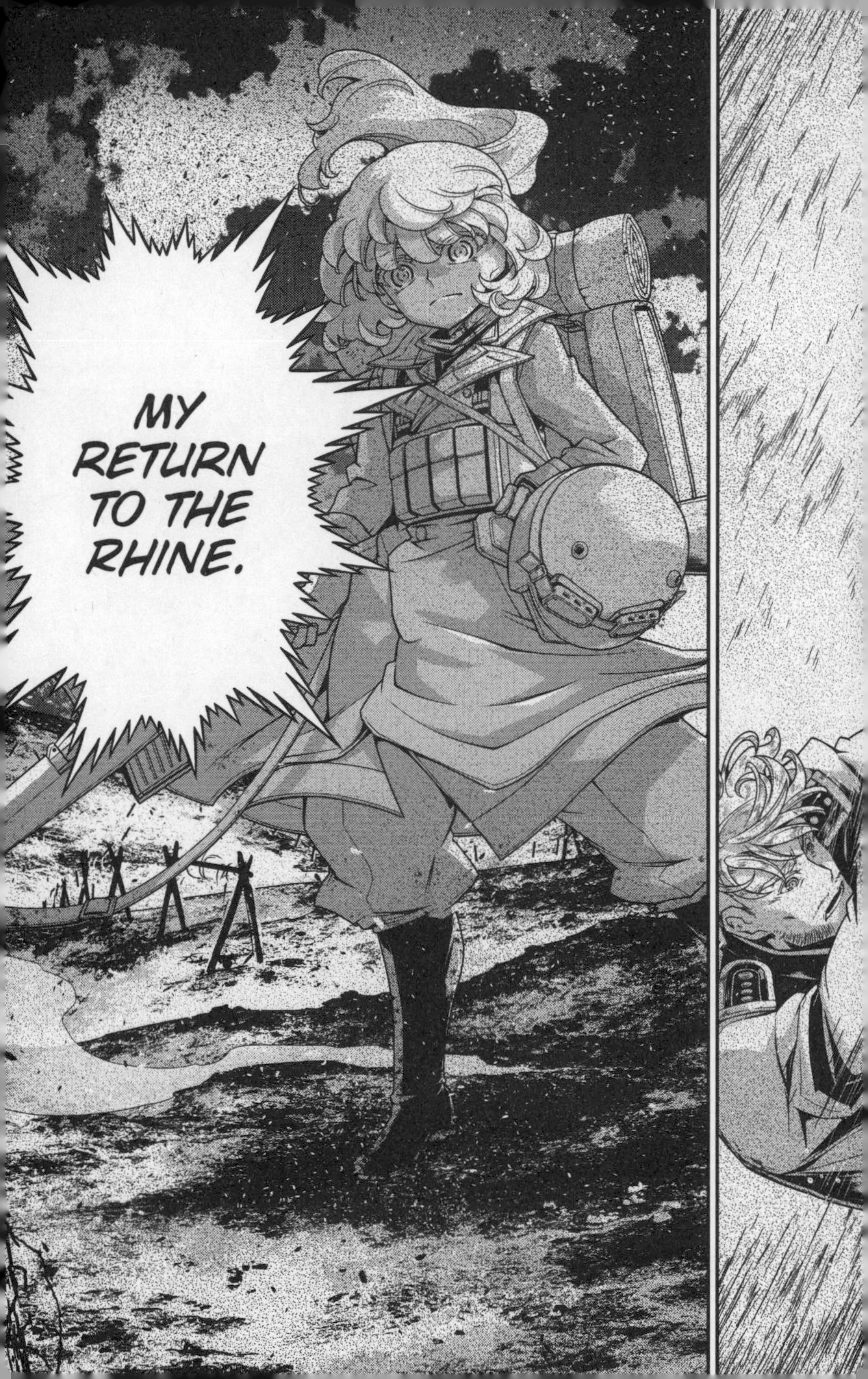
MY RETURN TO THE RHINE.

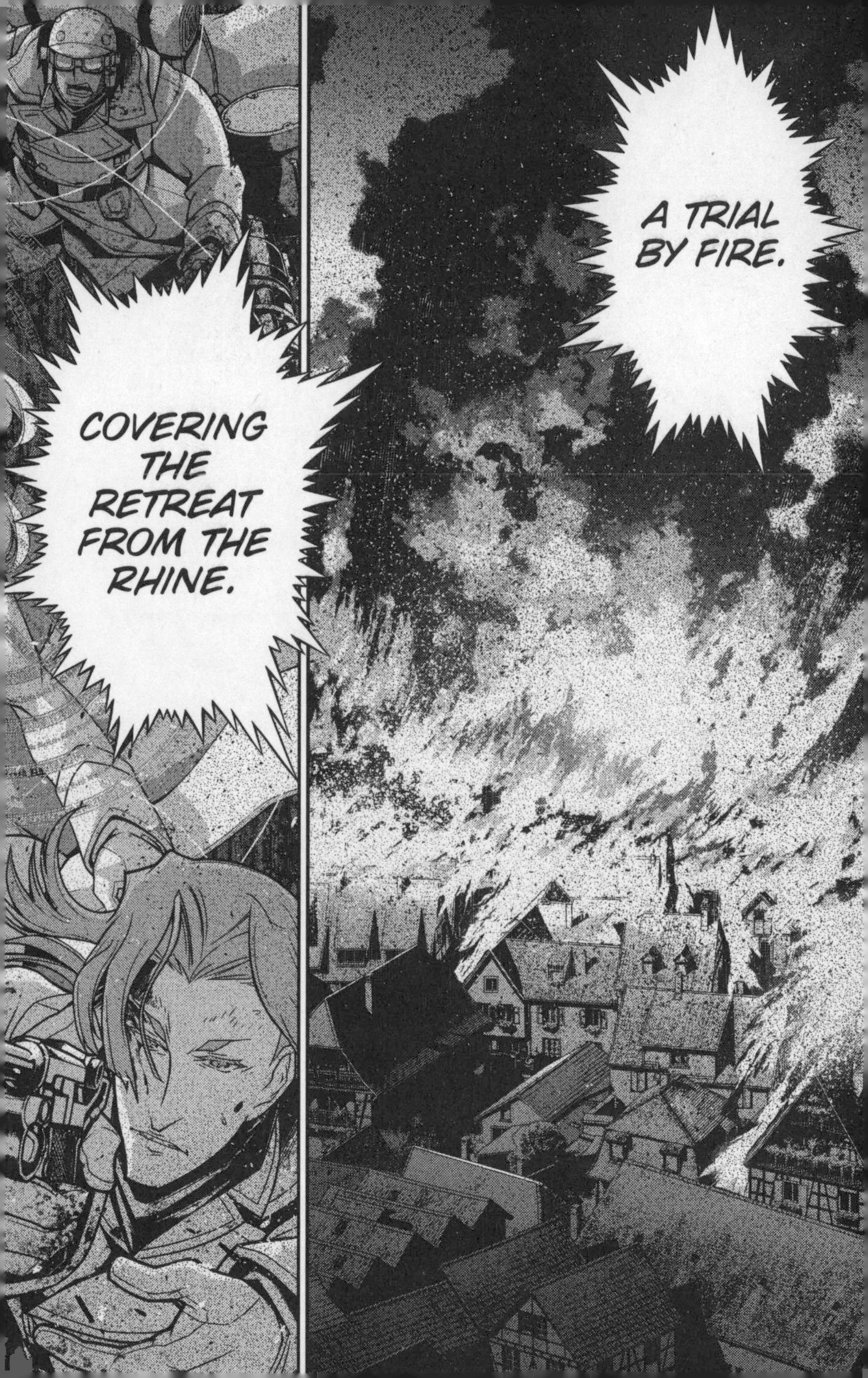
A TRIAL BY FIRE.
COVERING THE RETREAT FROM THE RHINE.

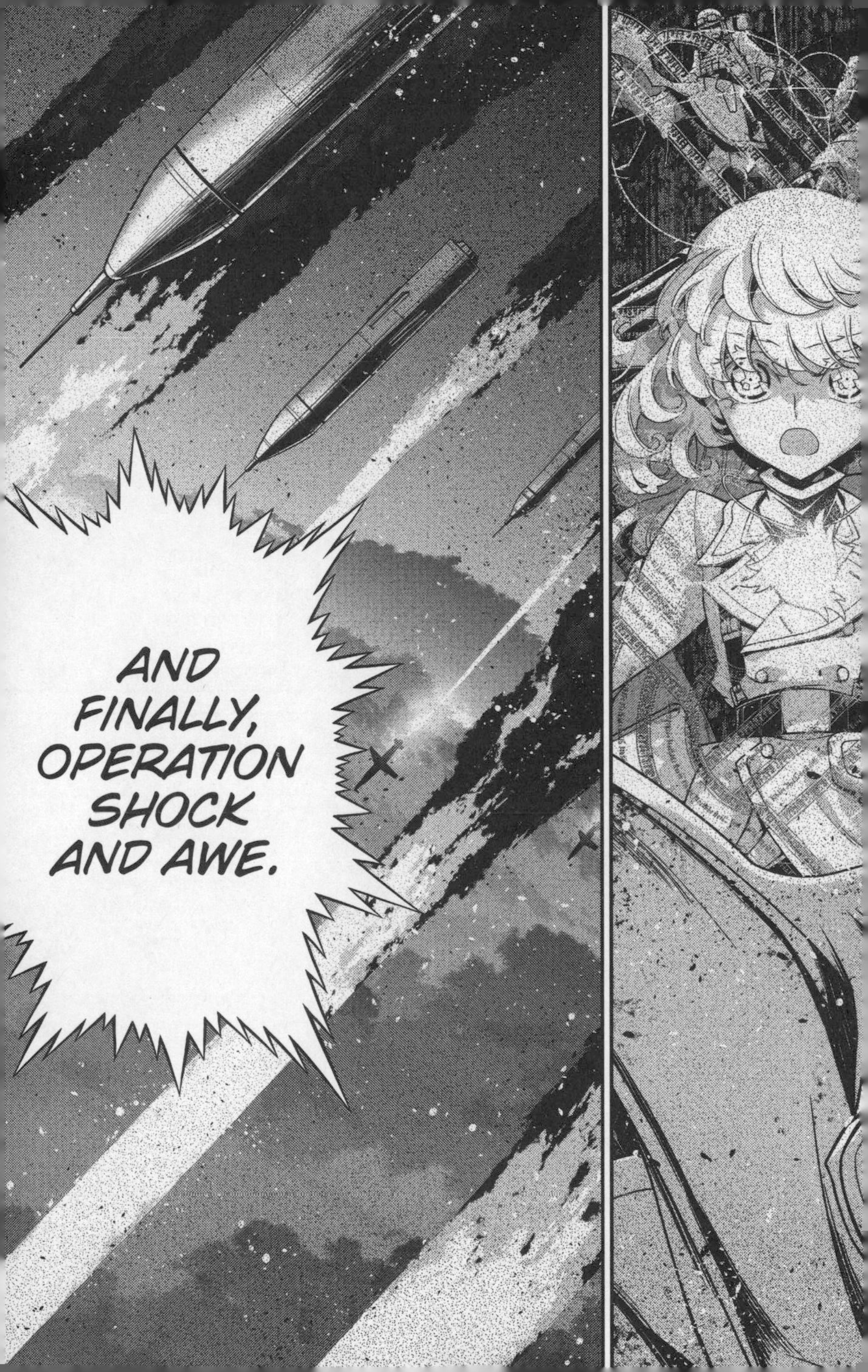
AND FINALLY, OPERATION SHOCK AND AWE.

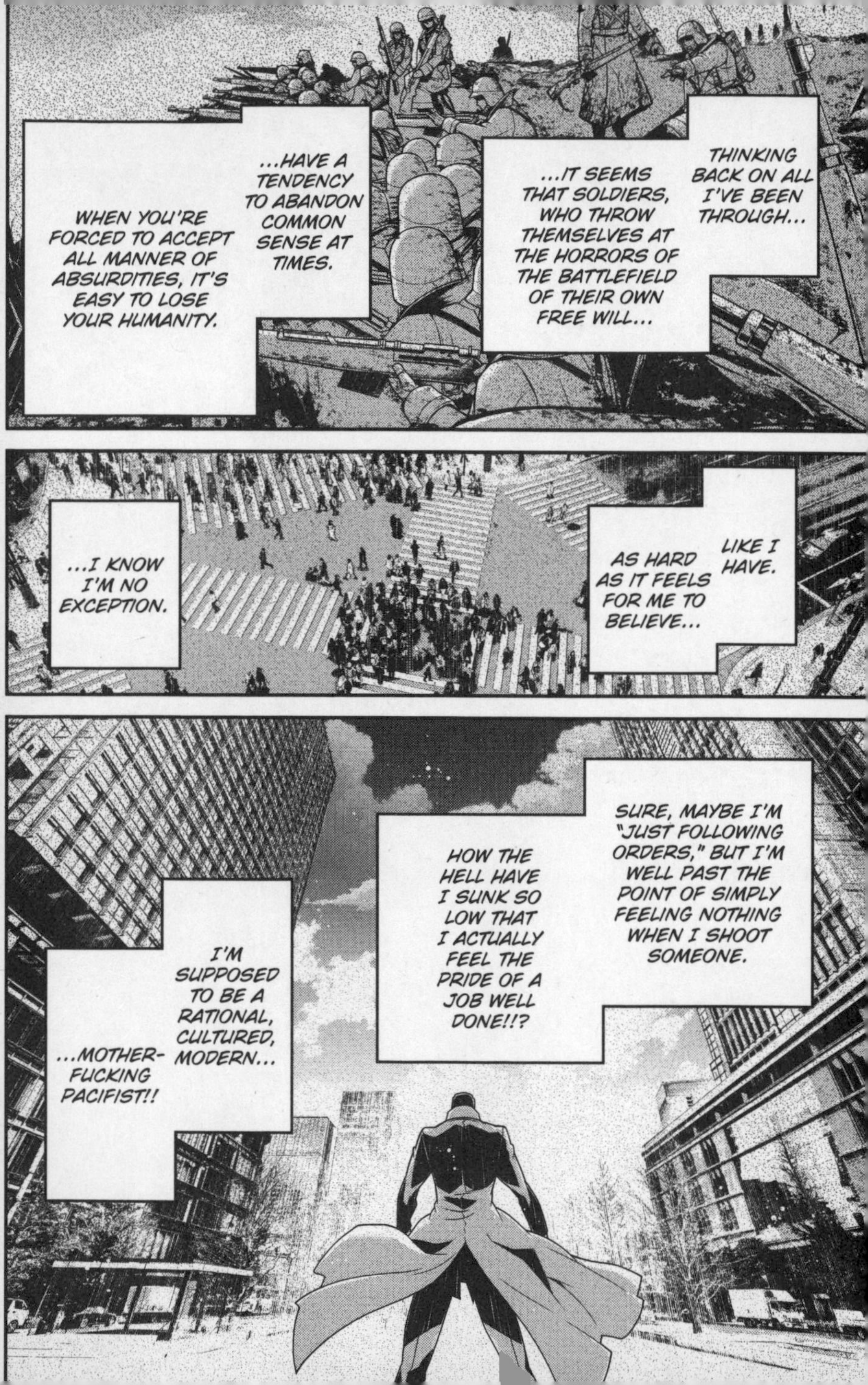
THINKING BACK ON ALL I'VE BEEN THROUGH...
...IT SEEMS THAT SOLDIERS, WHO THROW THEMSELVES AT THE HORRORS OF THE BATTLEFIELD OF THEIR OWN FREE WILL...
...HAVE A TENDENCY TO ABANDON COMMON SENSE AT TIMES.
WHEN YOU'RE FORCED TO ACCEPT ALL MANNER OF ABSURDITIES, IT'S EASY TO LOSE YOUR HUMANITY.
LIKE I HAVE.
AS HARD AS IT FEELS FOR ME TO BELIEVE...
...I KNOW I'M NO EXCEPTION.
SURE, MAYBE I'M "JUST FOLLOWING ORDERS," BUT I'M WELL PAST THE POINT OF SIMPLY FEELING NOTHING WHEN I SHOOT SOMEONE.
HOW THE HELL HAVE I SUNK SO LOW THAT I ACTUALLY FEEL THE PRIDE OF A JOB WELL DONE!!?
I'M SUPPOSED TO BE A RATIONAL, CULTURED, MODERN...
...MOTHER-FUCKING PACIFIST!!

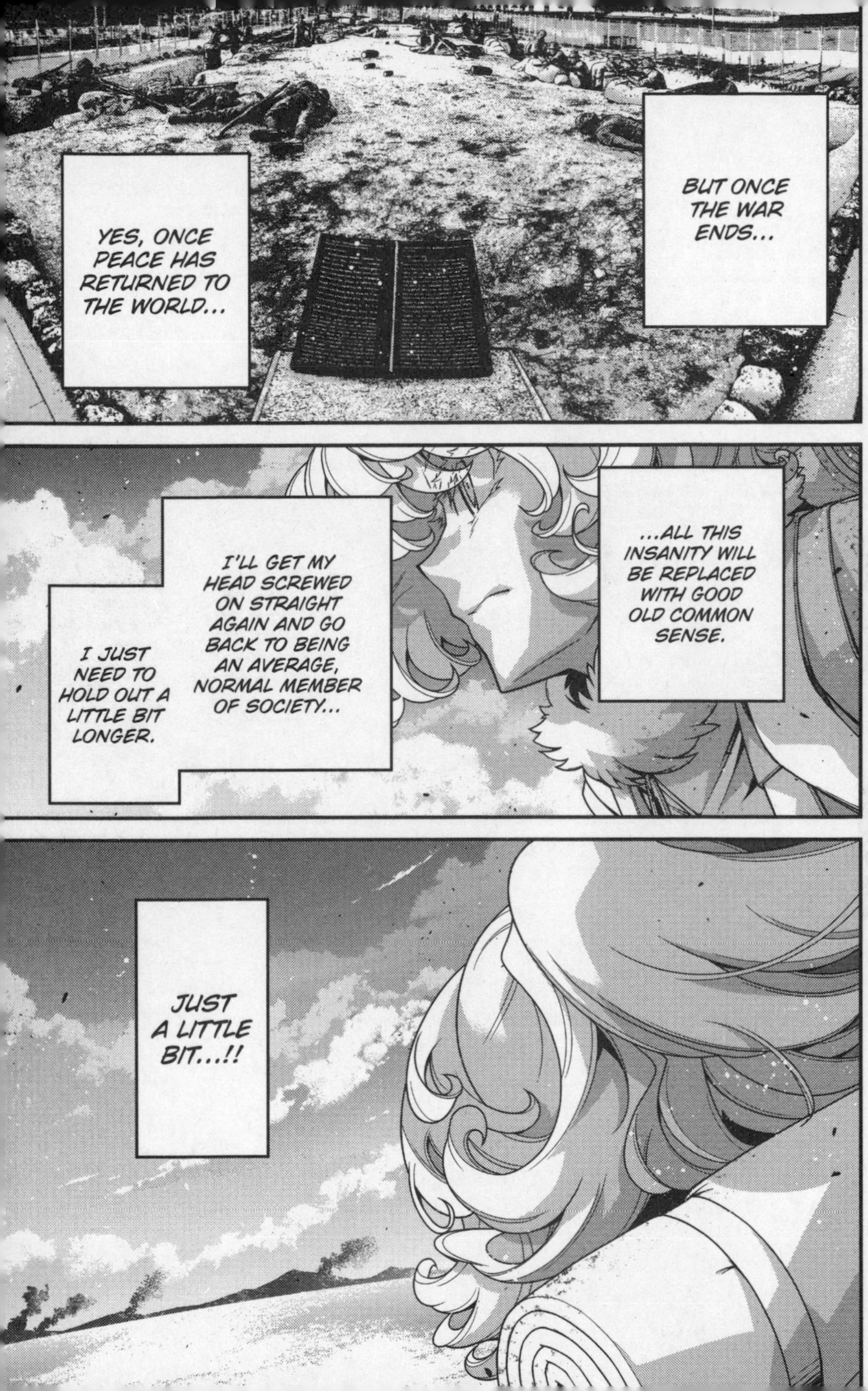
BUT ONCE THE WAR ENDS...
YES, ONCE PEACE HAS RETURNED TO THE WORLD...
...ALL THIS INSANITY WILL BE REPLACED WITH GOOD OLD COMMON SENSE.
I'LL GET MY HEAD SCREWED ON STRAIGHT AGAIN AND GO BACK TO BEING AN AVERAGE, NORMAL MEMBER OF SOCIETY...
I JUST NEED TO HOLD OUT A LITTLE BIT LONGER.
JUST A LITTLE BIT...!!

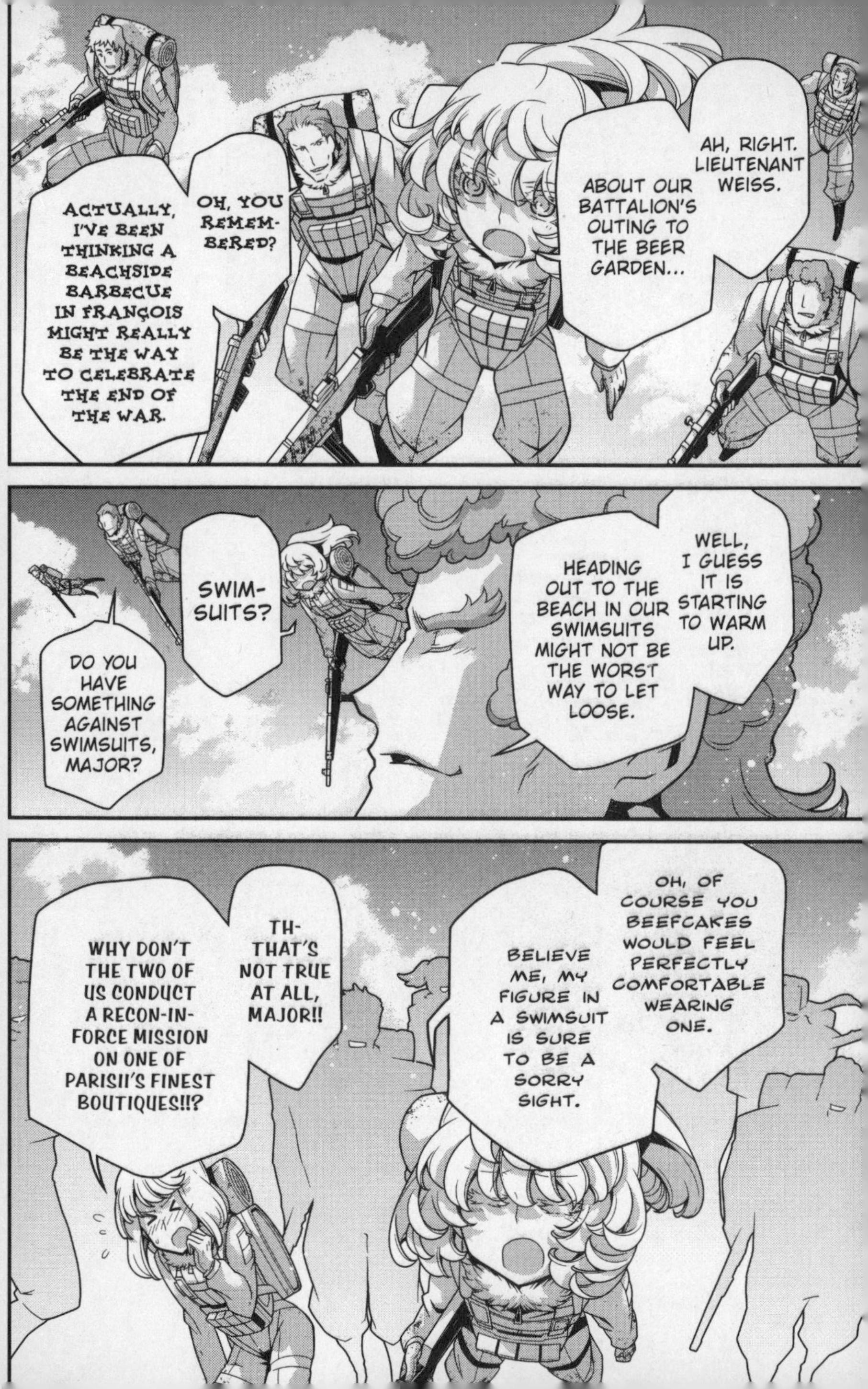
AH, RIGHT. LIEUTENANT WEISS.
ABOUT OUR BATTALION'S OUTING TO THE BEER GARDEN...
OH, YOU REMEMBERED?
ACTUALLY, I'VE BEEN THINKING A BEACHSIDE BARBECUE IN FRANÇOIS MIGHT REALLY BE THE WAY TO CELEBRATE THE END OF THE WAR.
WELL, I GUESS IT IS STARTING TO WARM UP.
HEADING OUT TO THE BEACH IN OUR SWIMSUITS MIGHT NOT BE THE WORST WAY TO LET LOOSE.
SWIMSUITS?
DO YOU HAVE SOMETHING AGAINST SWIMSUITS, MAJOR?
OH, OF COURSE YOU BEEFCAKES WOULD FEEL PERFECTLY COMFORTABLE WEARING ONE.
BELIEVE ME, MY FIGURE IN A SWIMSUIT IS SURE TO BE A SORRY SIGHT.
TH-THAT'S NOT TRUE AT ALL, MAJOR!!
WHY DON'T THE TWO OF US CONDUCT A RECON-IN-FORCE MISSION ON ONE OF PARISII'S FINEST BOUTIQUES!!?

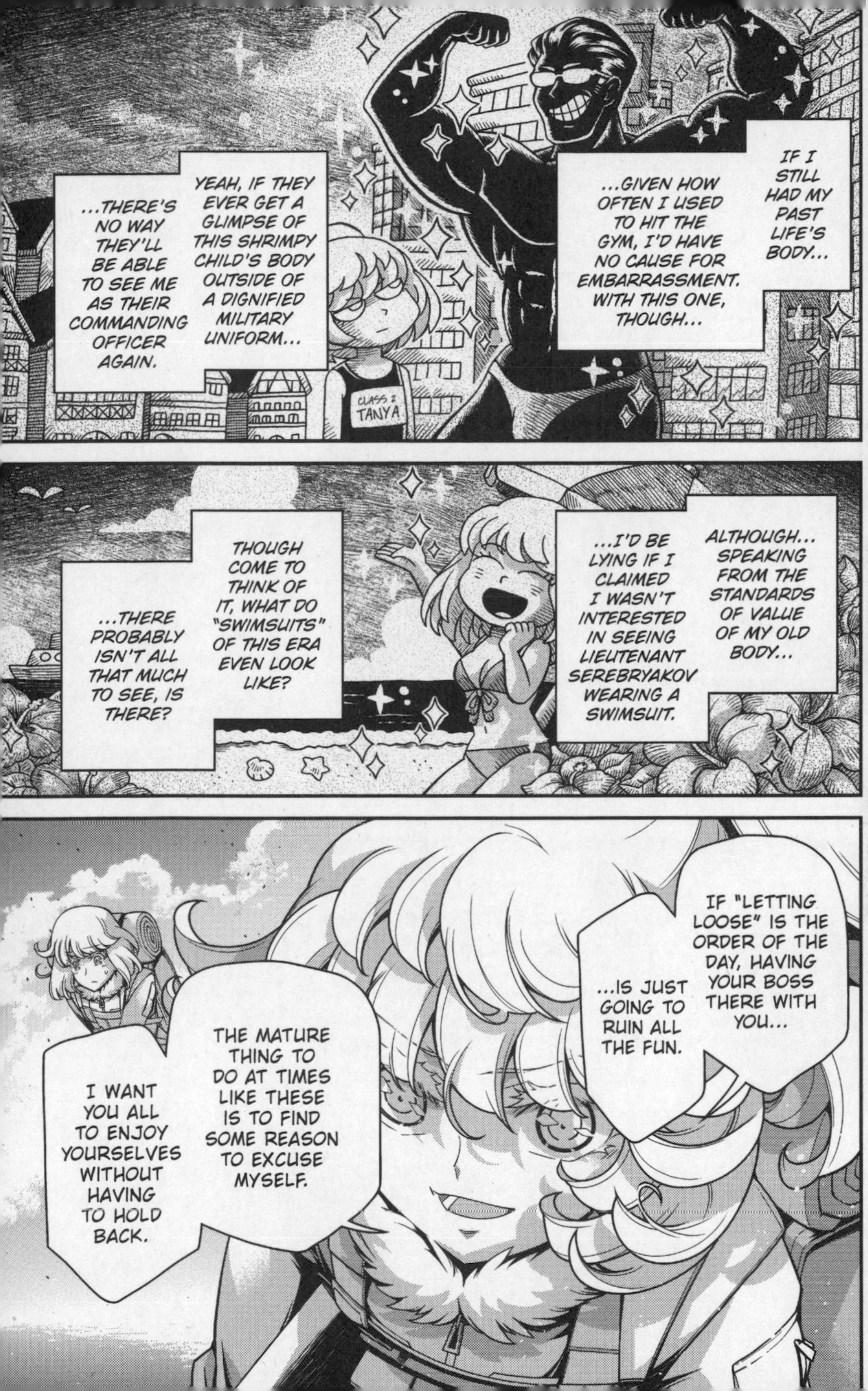
IF I STILL HAD MY PAST LIFE'S BODY...
...GIVEN HOW OFTEN I USED TO HIT THE GYM, I'D HAVE NO CAUSE FOR EMBARRASSMENT. WITH THIS ONE, THOUGH...
YEAH, IF THEY EVER GET A GLIMPSE OF THIS SHRIMPY CHILD'S BODY OUTSIDE OF A DIGNIFIED MILITARY UNIFORM...
...THERE'S NO WAY THEY'LL BE ABLE TO SEE ME AS THEIR COMMANDING OFFICER AGAIN.
CLASS 2 TANYA
ALTHOUGH... SPEAKING FROM THE STANDARDS OF VALUE OF MY OLD BODY...
...I'D BE LYING IF I CLAIMED I WASN'T INTERESTED IN SEEING LIEUTENANT SEREBRYAKOV WEARING A SWIMSUIT.
THOUGH COME TO THINK OF IT, WHAT DO "SWIMSUITS" OF THIS ERA EVEN LOOK LIKE?
...THERE PROBABLY ISN'T ALL THAT MUCH TO SEE, IS THERE?
IF "LETTING LOOSE" IS THE ORDER OF THE DAY, HAVING YOUR BOSS THERE WITH YOU...
...IS JUST GOING TO RUIN ALL THE FUN.
THE MATURE THING TO DO AT TIMES LIKE THESE IS TO FIND SOME REASON TO EXCUSE MYSELF.
I WANT YOU ALL TO ENJOY YOURSELVES WITHOUT HAVING TO HOLD BACK.

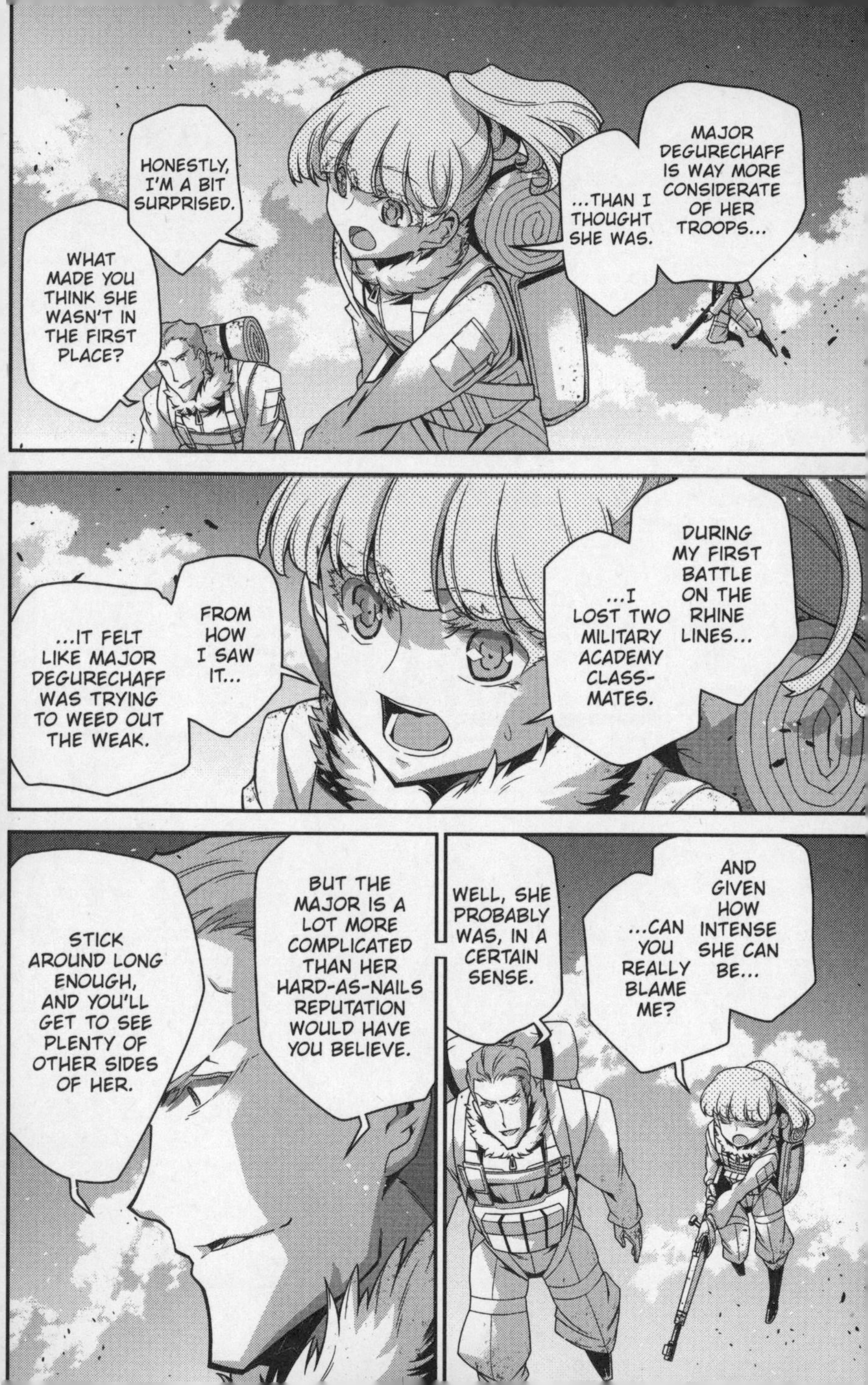
MAJOR DEGURECHAFF IS WAY MORE CONSIDERATE OF HER TROOPS...
...THAN I THOUGHT SHE WAS.
HONESTLY, I'M A BIT SURPRISED.
WHAT MADE YOU THINK SHE WASN'T IN THE FIRST PLACE?
DURING MY FIRST BATTLE ON THE RHINE LINES...
...I LOST TWO MILITARY ACADEMY CLASS-MATES.
FROM HOW I SAW IT...
...IT FELT LIKE MAJOR DEGURECHAFF WAS TRYING TO WEED OUT THE WEAK.
AND GIVEN HOW INTENSE SHE CAN BE...
...CAN YOU REALLY BLAME ME?
WELL, SHE PROBABLY WAS, IN A CERTAIN SENSE.
BUT THE MAJOR IS A LOT MORE COMPLICATED THAN HER HARD-AS-NAILS REPUTATION WOULD HAVE YOU BELIEVE.
STICK AROUND LONG ENOUGH, AND YOU'LL GET TO SEE PLENTY OF OTHER SIDES OF HER.

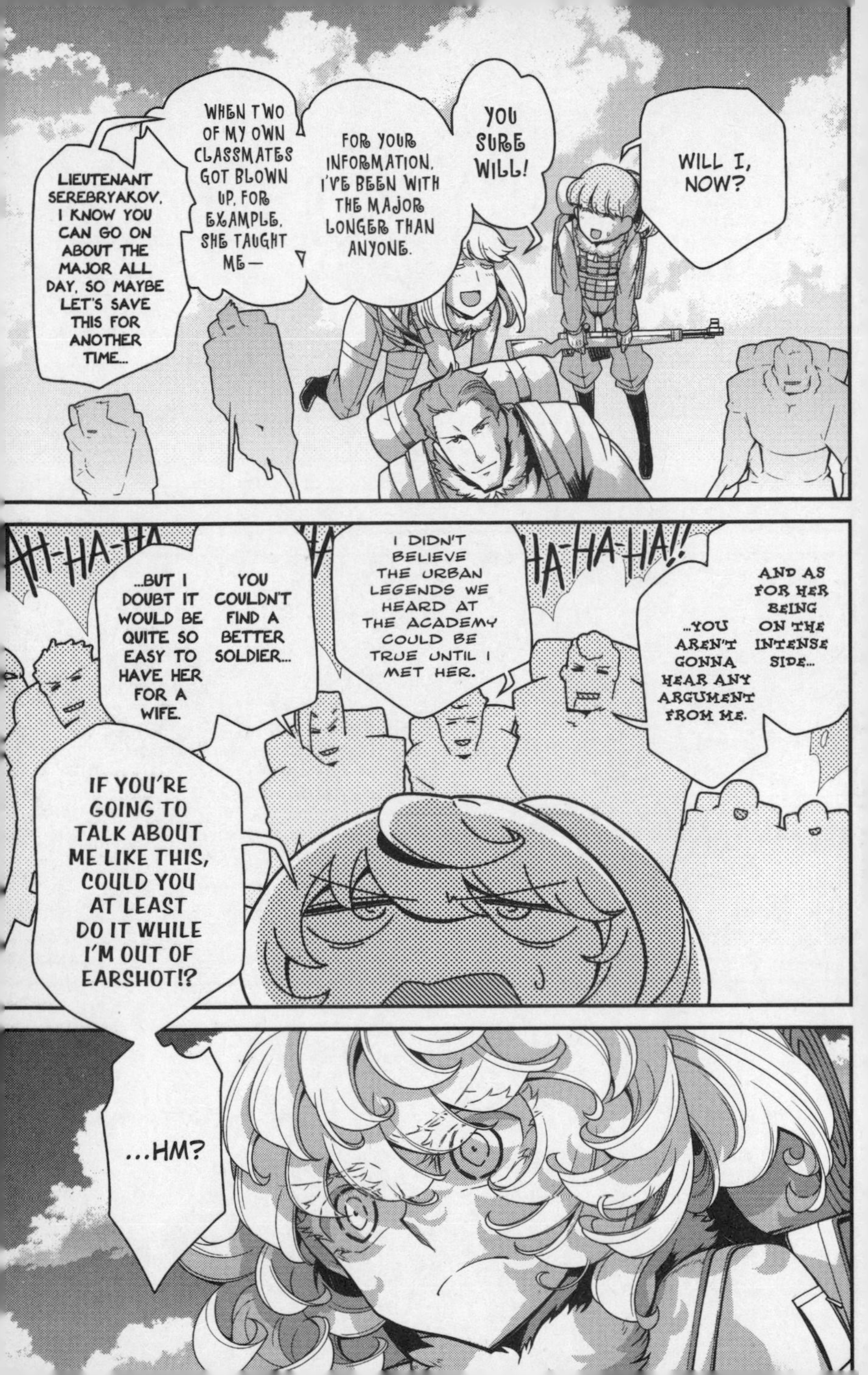
WILL I, NOW?
YOU SURE WILL!
FOR YOUR INFORMATION, I'VE BEEN WITH THE MAJOR LONGER THAN ANYONE.
WHEN TWO OF MY OWN CLASSMATES GOT BLOWN UP, FOR EXAMPLE, SHE TAUGHT ME—
LIEUTENANT SEREBRYAKOV, I KNOW YOU CAN GO ON ABOUT THE MAJOR ALL DAY, SO MAYBE LET'S SAVE THIS FOR ANOTHER TIME...
HA-HA-HA!!
AND AS FOR HER BEING ON THE INTENSE SIDE...
...YOU AREN'T GONNA HEAR ANY ARGUMENT FROM ME.
I DIDN'T BELIEVE THE URBAN LEGENDS WE HEARD AT THE ACADEMY COULD BE TRUE UNTIL I MET HER.
YOU COULDN'T FIND A BETTER SOLDIER...
...BUT I DOUBT IT WOULD BE QUITE SO EASY TO HAVE HER FOR A WIFE.
AH-HA-HA
IF YOU'RE GOING TO TALK ABOUT ME LIKE THIS, COULD YOU AT LEAST DO IT WHILE I'M OUT OF EARSHOT!?
...HM?

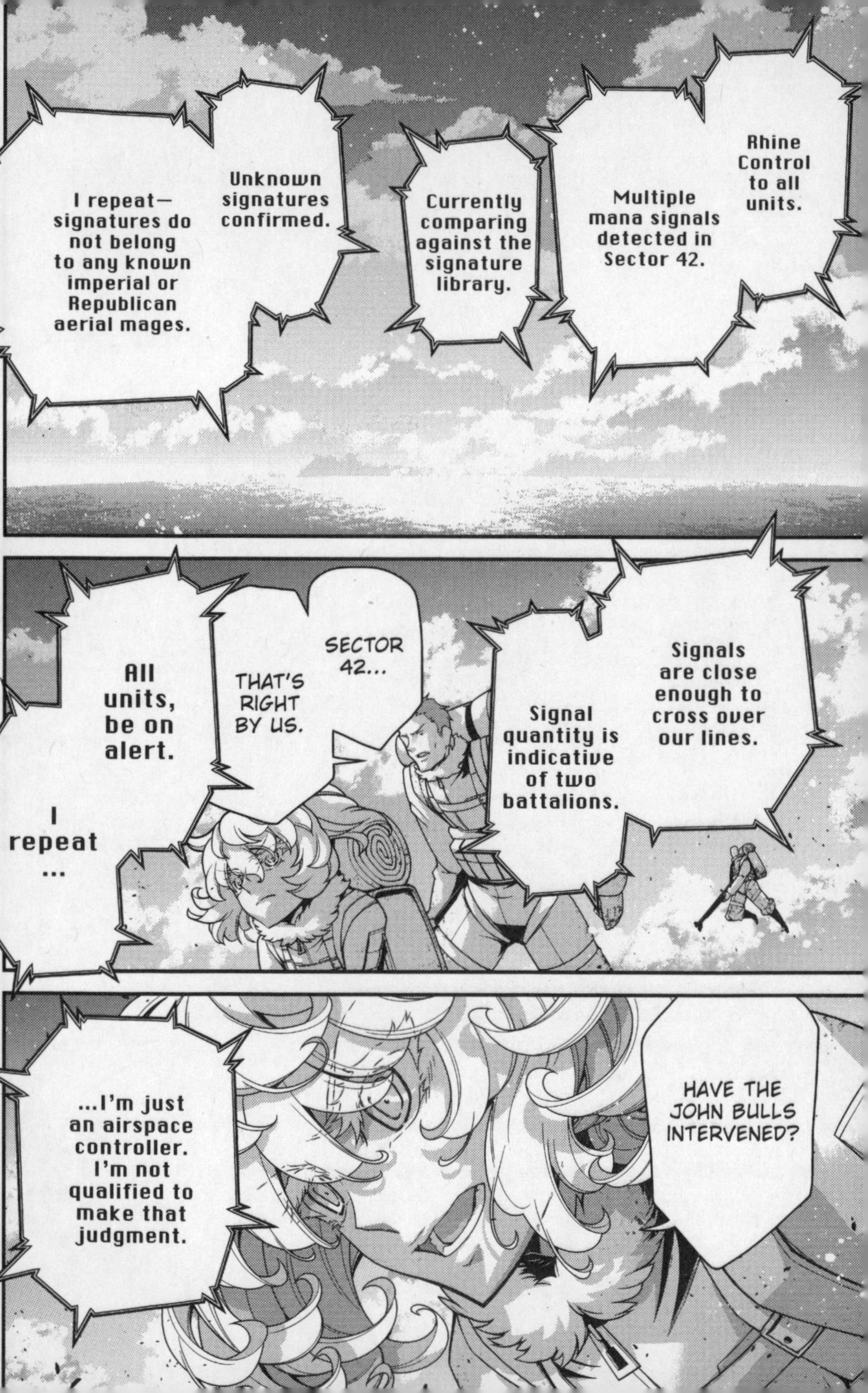
Rhine Control to all units.
Multiple mana signals detected in Sector 42.
Currently comparing against the signature library.
Unknown signatures confirmed.
I repeat—signatures do not belong to any known imperial or Republican aerial mages.
Signals are close enough to cross over our lines.
Signal quantity is indicative of two battalions.
SECTOR 42...
THAT'S RIGHT BY US.
All units, be on alert.
I repeat...
HAVE THE JOHN BULLS INTERVENED?
...I'm just an airspace controller. I'm not qualified to make that judgment.

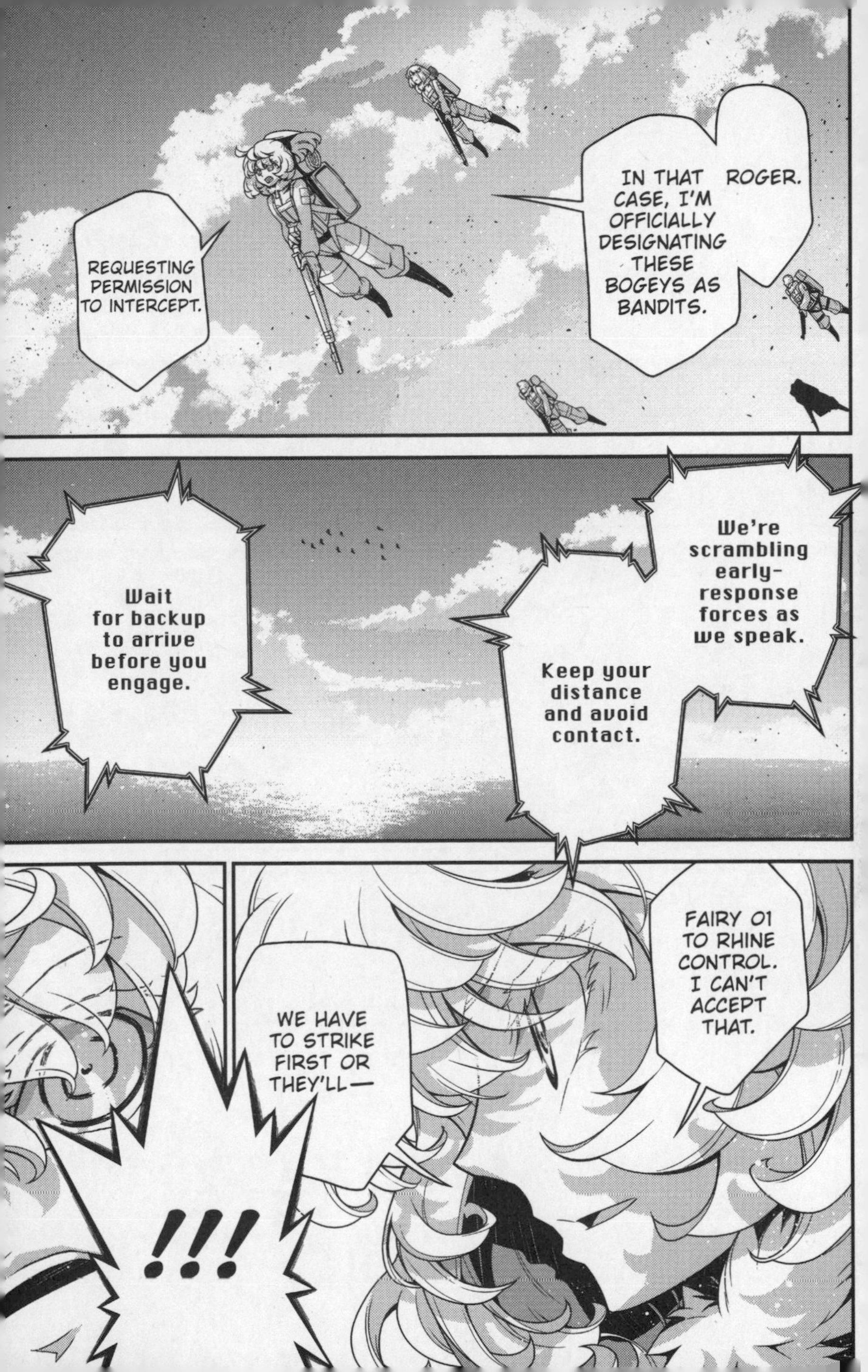
ROGER.
IN THAT CASE, I'M OFFICIALLY DESIGNATING THESE BOGEYS AS BANDITS.
REQUESTING PERMISSION TO INTERCEPT.
We're scrambling early-response forces as we speak.
Keep your distance and avoid contact.
Wait for backup to arrive before you engage.
FAIRY 01 TO RHINE CONTROL. I CAN'T ACCEPT THAT.
WE HAVE TO STRIKE FIRST OR THEY'LL—
!!!

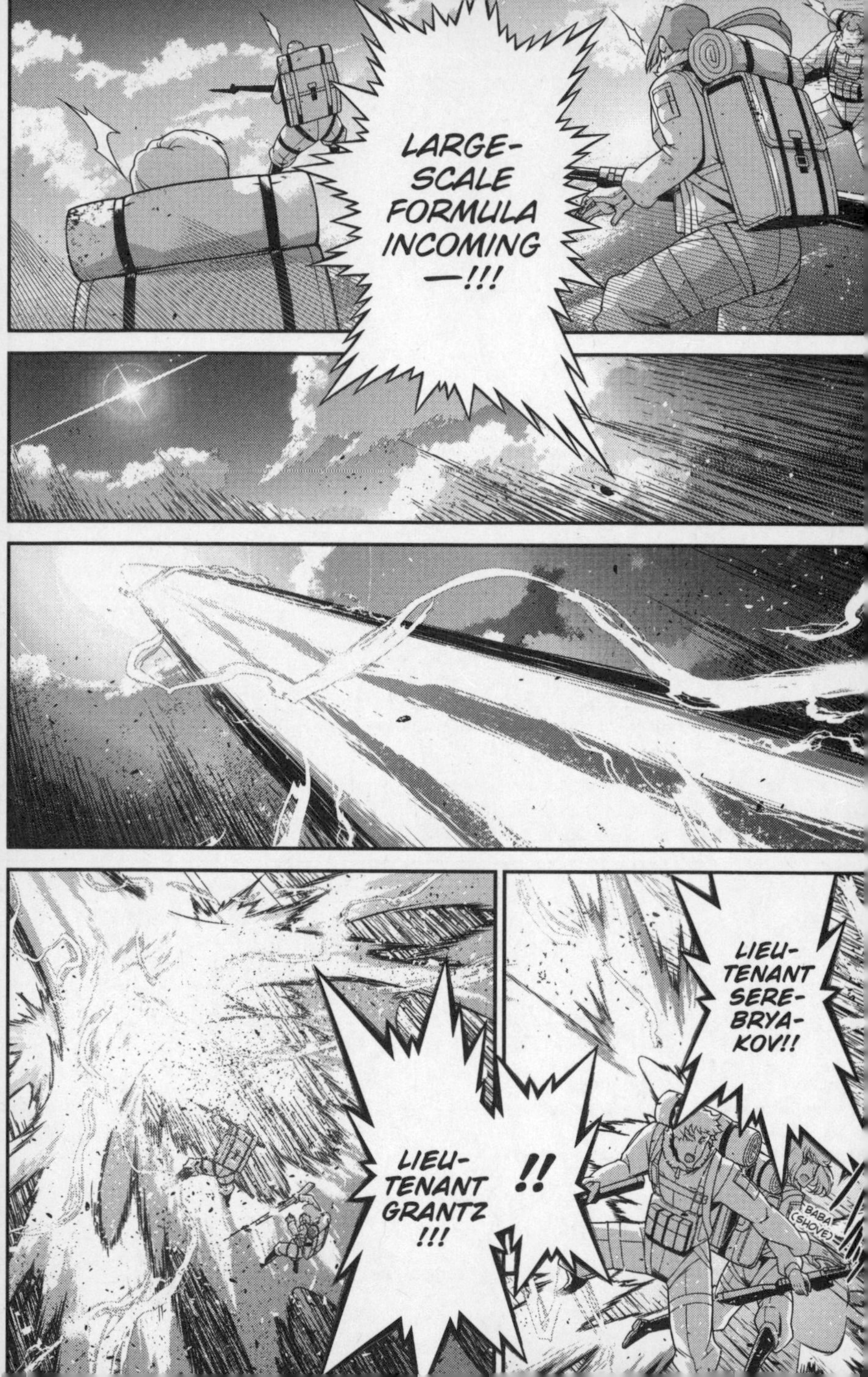
LARGE-SCALE FORMULA INCOMING—!!!
LIEU-TENANT SERE-BRYA-KOV!!
BABA (SHOVE)
LIEU-TENANT GRANTZ!!!
!!

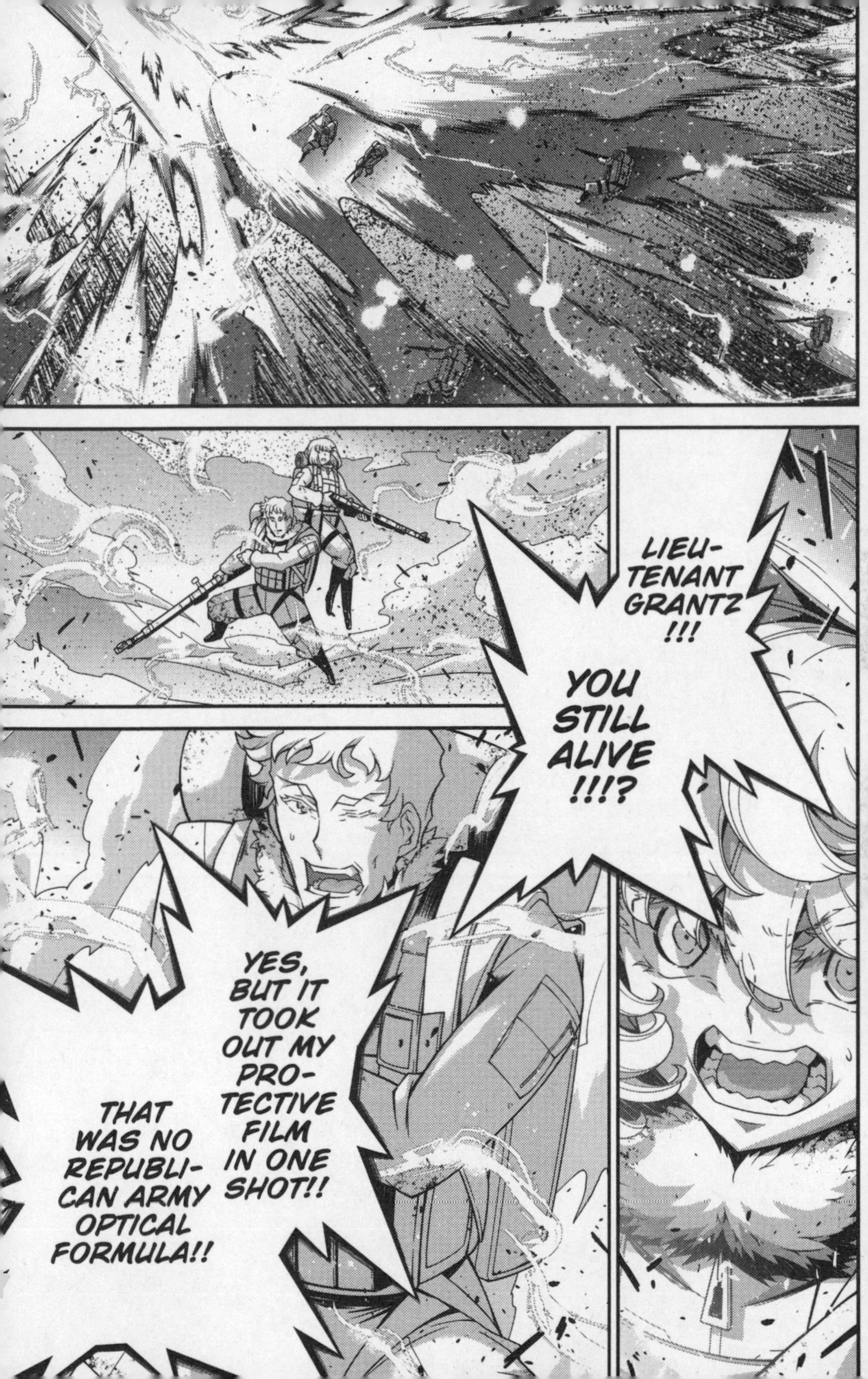
LIEU-TENANT GRANTZ!!!
YOU STILL ALIVE!!!?
YES, BUT IT TOOK OUT MY PRO-TECTIVE FILM IN ONE SHOT!!
THAT WAS NO REPUBLI-CAN ARMY OPTICAL FORMULA!!

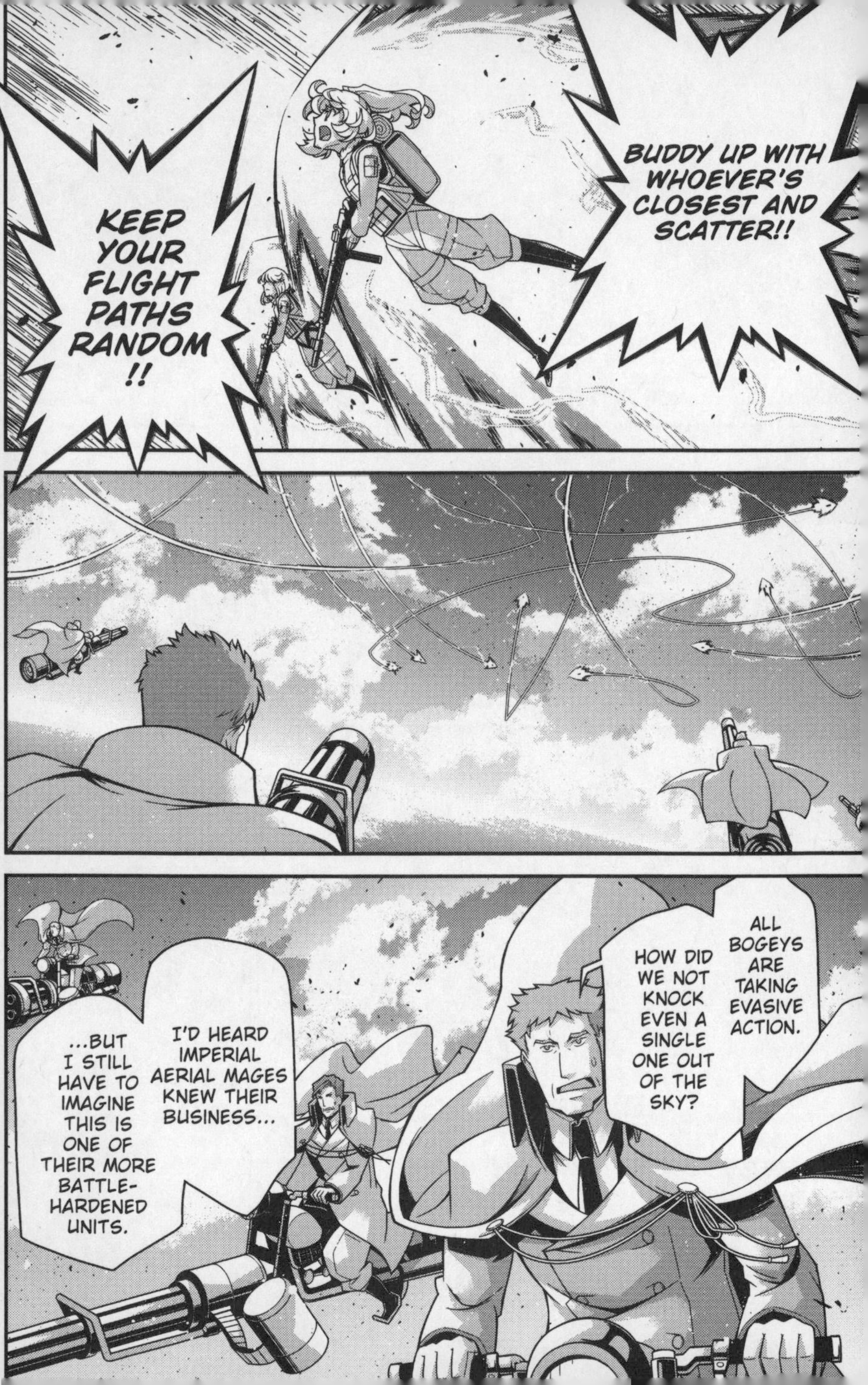
BUDDY UP WITH WHOEVER'S CLOSEST AND SCATTER!!
KEEP YOUR FLIGHT PATHS RANDOM!!
ALL BOGEYS ARE TAKING EVASIVE ACTION.
HOW DID WE NOT KNOCK EVEN A SINGLE ONE OUT OF THE SKY?
I'D HEARD IMPERIAL AERIAL MAGES KNEW THEIR BUSINESS...
...BUT I STILL HAVE TO IMAGINE THIS IS ONE OF THEIR MORE BATTLE-HARDENED UNITS.

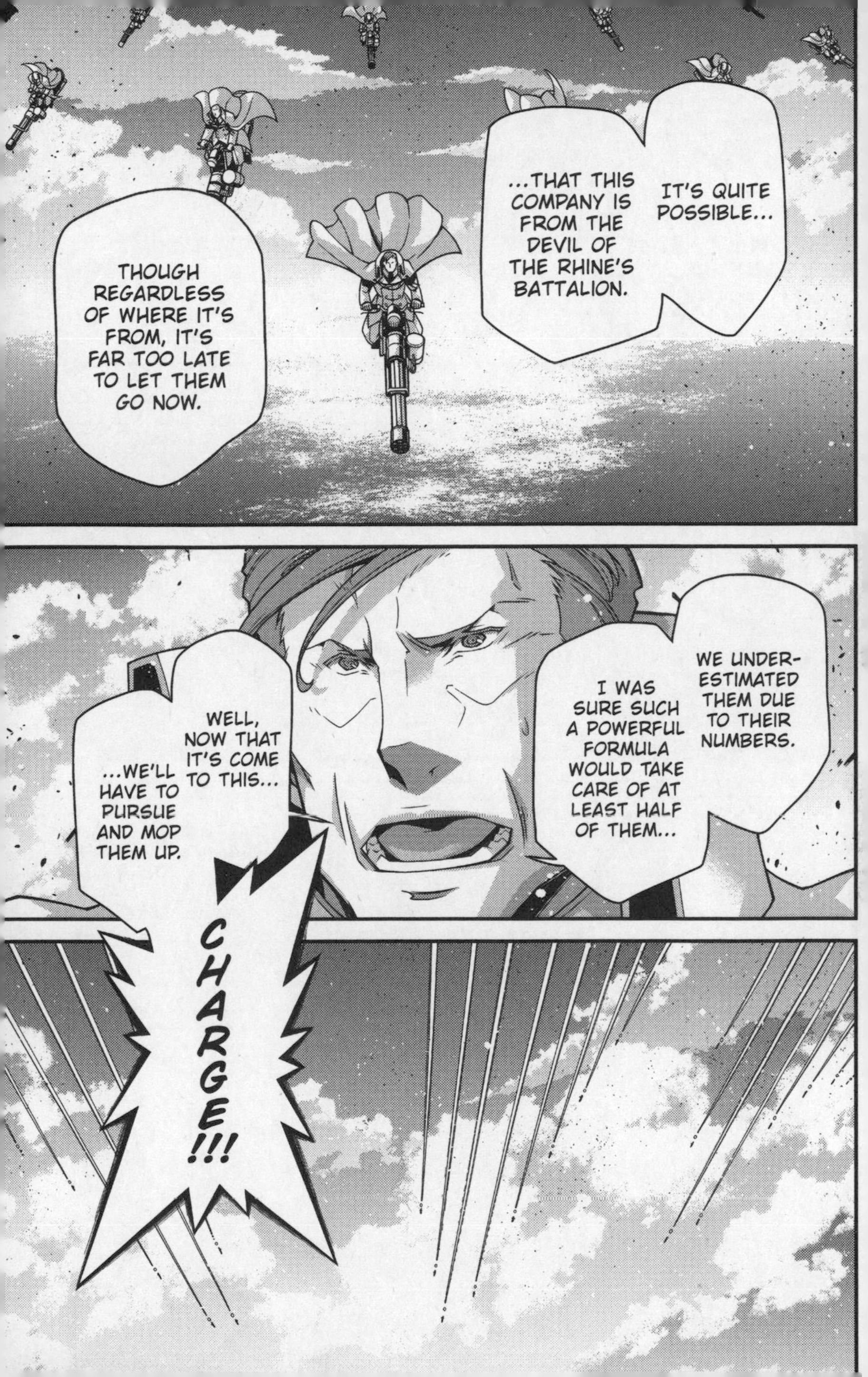
IT'S QUITE POSSIBLE...
...THAT THIS COMPANY IS FROM THE DEVIL OF THE RHINE'S BATTALION.
THOUGH REGARDLESS OF WHERE IT'S FROM, IT'S FAR TOO LATE TO LET THEM GO NOW.
WE UNDER-ESTIMATED THEM DUE TO THEIR NUMBERS.
I WAS SURE SUCH A POWERFUL FORMULA WOULD TAKE CARE OF AT LEAST HALF OF THEM...
WELL, NOW THAT IT'S COME TO THIS...
...WE'LL HAVE TO PURSUE AND MOP THEM UP.
CHARGE!!!

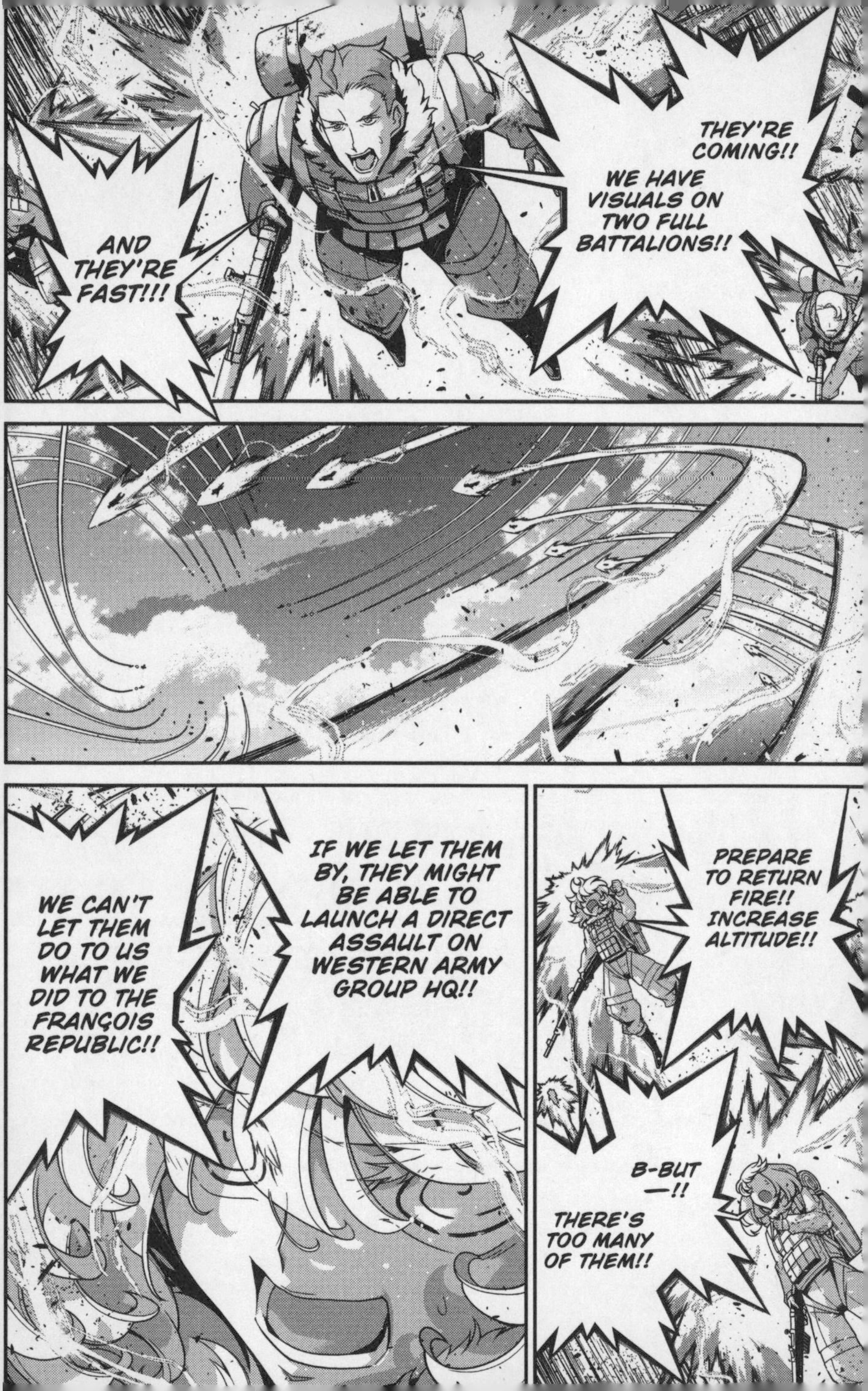
THEY'RE COMING!!
WE HAVE VISUALS ON TWO FULL BATTALIONS!!
AND THEY'RE FAST!!!
PREPARE TO RETURN FIRE!! INCREASE ALTITUDE!!
B-BUT—!!
THERE'S TOO MANY OF THEM!!
IF WE LET THEM BY, THEY MIGHT BE ABLE TO LAUNCH A DIRECT ASSAULT ON WESTERN ARMY GROUP HQ!!
WE CAN'T LET THEM DO TO US WHAT WE DID TO THE FRANÇOIS REPUBLIC!!

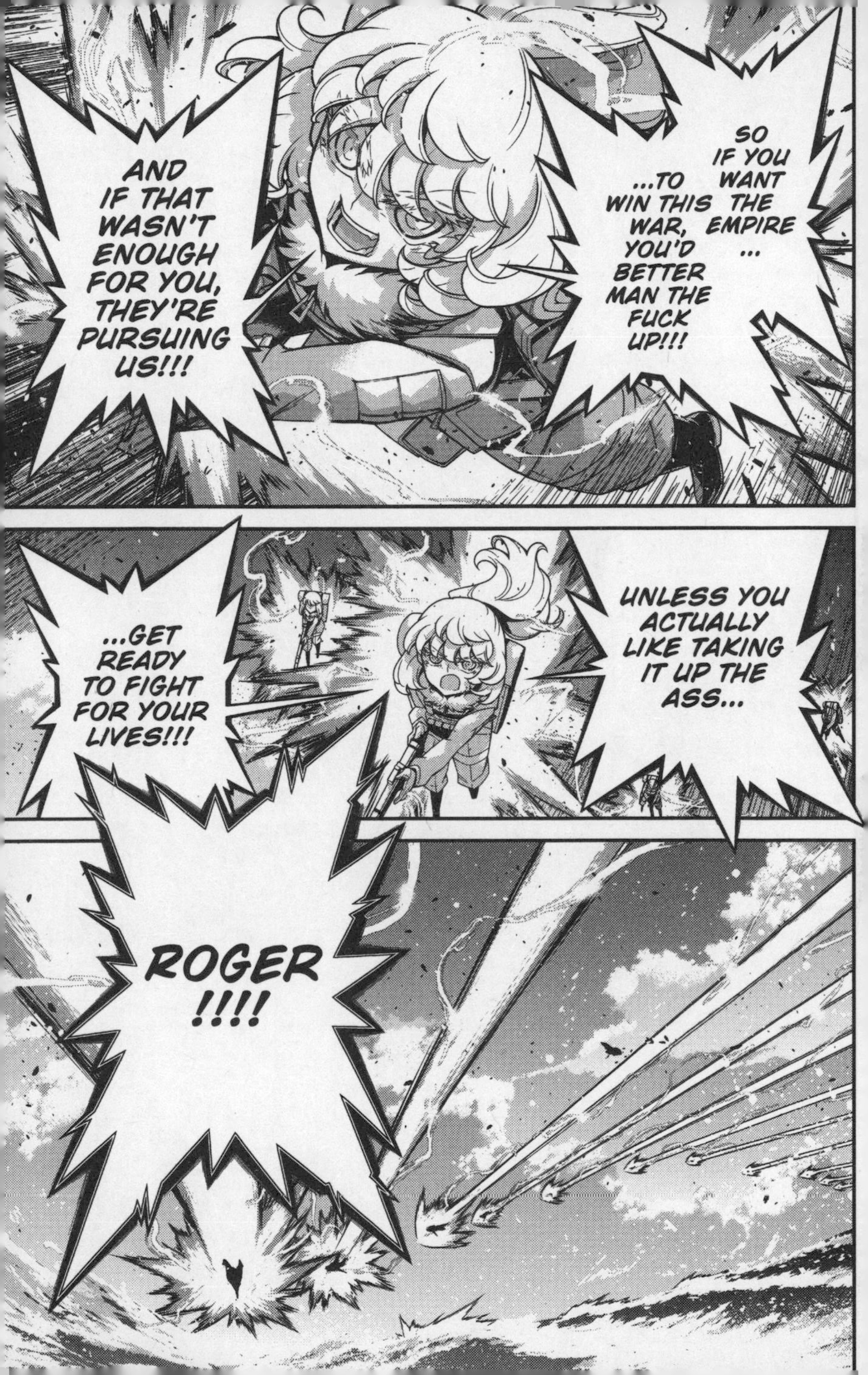
SO IF YOU WANT THE EMPIRE ...
...TO WIN THIS WAR, YOU'D BETTER MAN THE FUCK UP!!!
AND IF THAT WASN'T ENOUGH FOR YOU, THEY'RE PURSUING US!!!
UNLESS YOU ACTUALLY LIKE TAKING IT UP THE ASS...
...GET READY TO FIGHT FOR YOUR LIVES!!!
ROGER !!!!

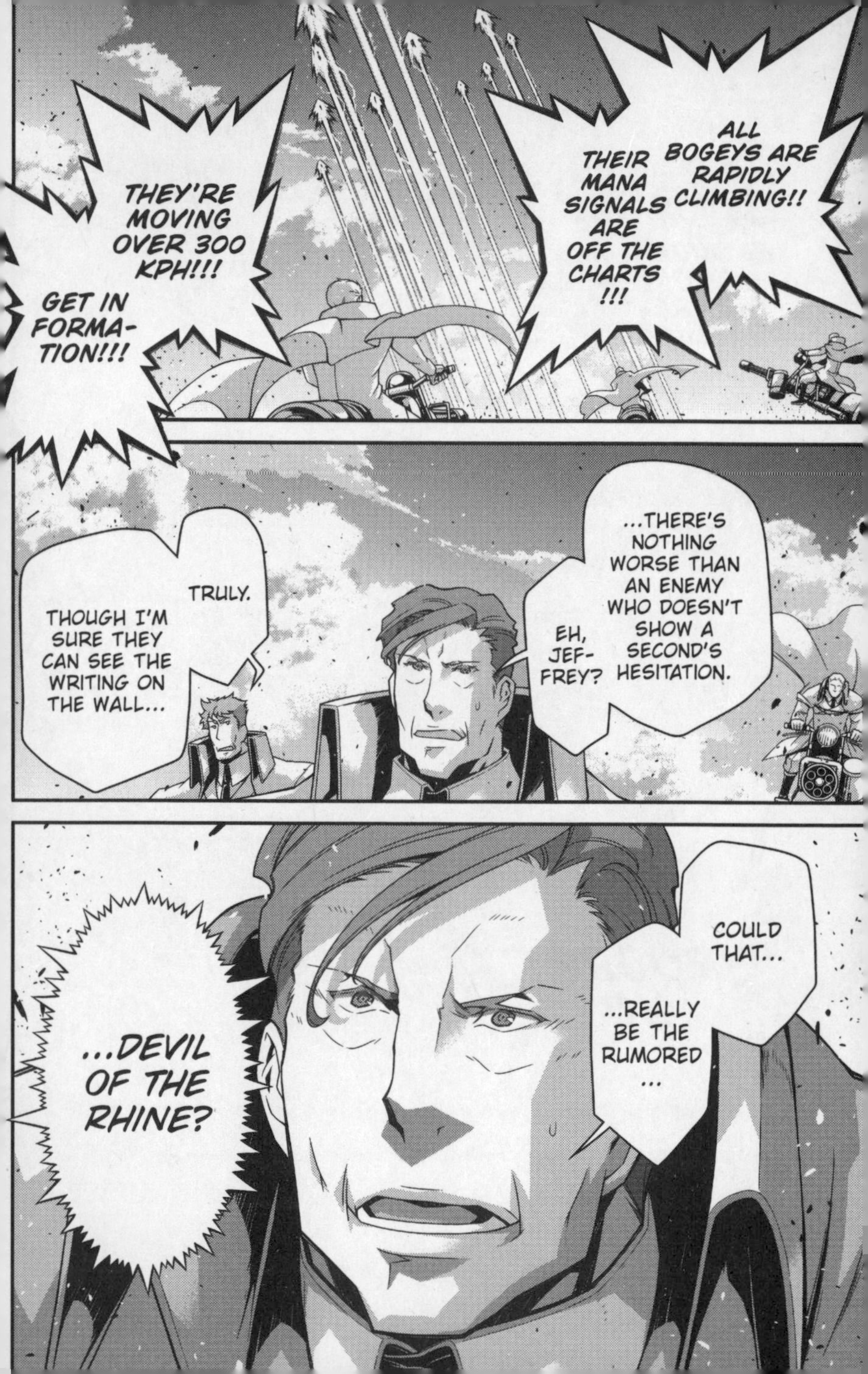
ALL BOGEYS ARE RAPIDLY CLIMBING!!
THEIR MANA SIGNALS ARE OFF THE CHARTS!!!
THEY'RE MOVING OVER 300 KPH!!! GET IN FORMATION!!!
...THERE'S NOTHING WORSE THAN AN ENEMY WHO DOESN'T SHOW A SECOND'S HESITATION.
EH, JEFFREY?
TRULY.
THOUGH I'M SURE THEY CAN SEE THE WRITING ON THE WALL...
COULD THAT...
...REALLY BE THE RUMORED...
...DEVIL OF THE RHINE?

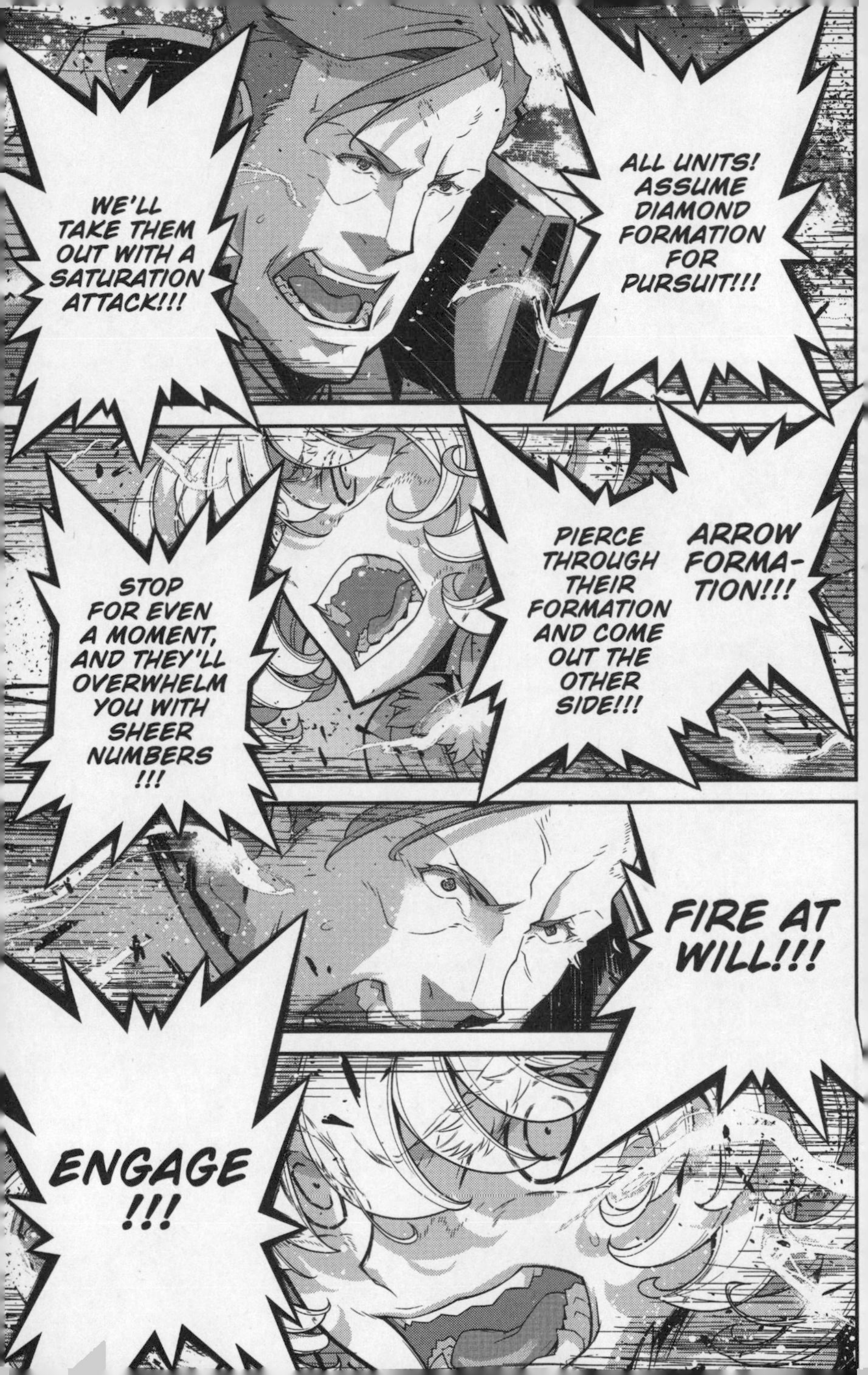
ALL UNITS! ASSUME DIAMOND FORMATION FOR PURSUIT!!!
WE'LL TAKE THEM OUT WITH A SATURATION ATTACK!!!
ARROW FORMATION!!!
PIERCE THROUGH THEIR FORMATION AND COME OUT THE OTHER SIDE!!!
STOP FOR EVEN A MOMENT, AND THEY'LL OVERWHELM YOU WITH SHEER NUMBERS!!!
FIRE AT WILL!!!
ENGAGE!!!

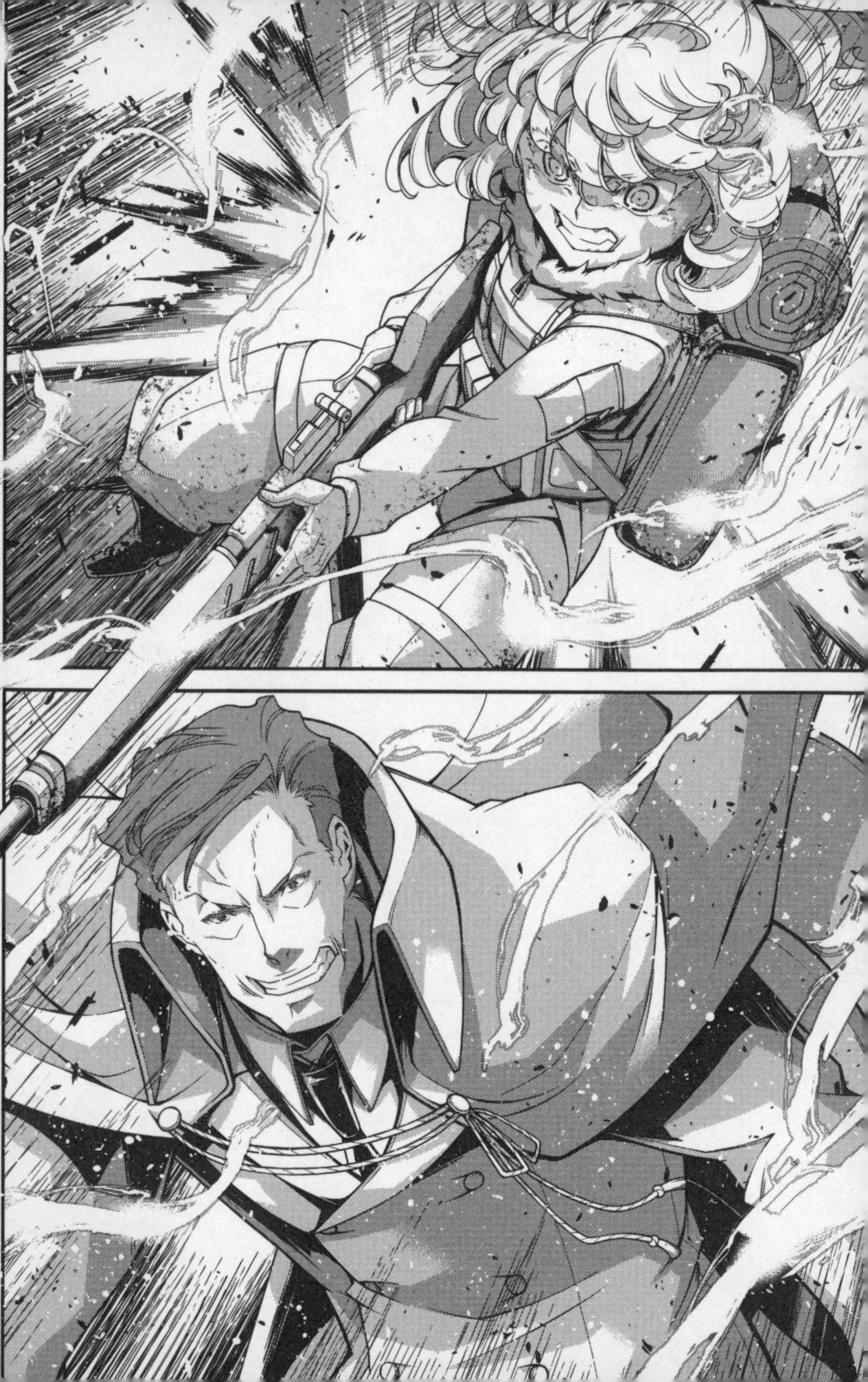

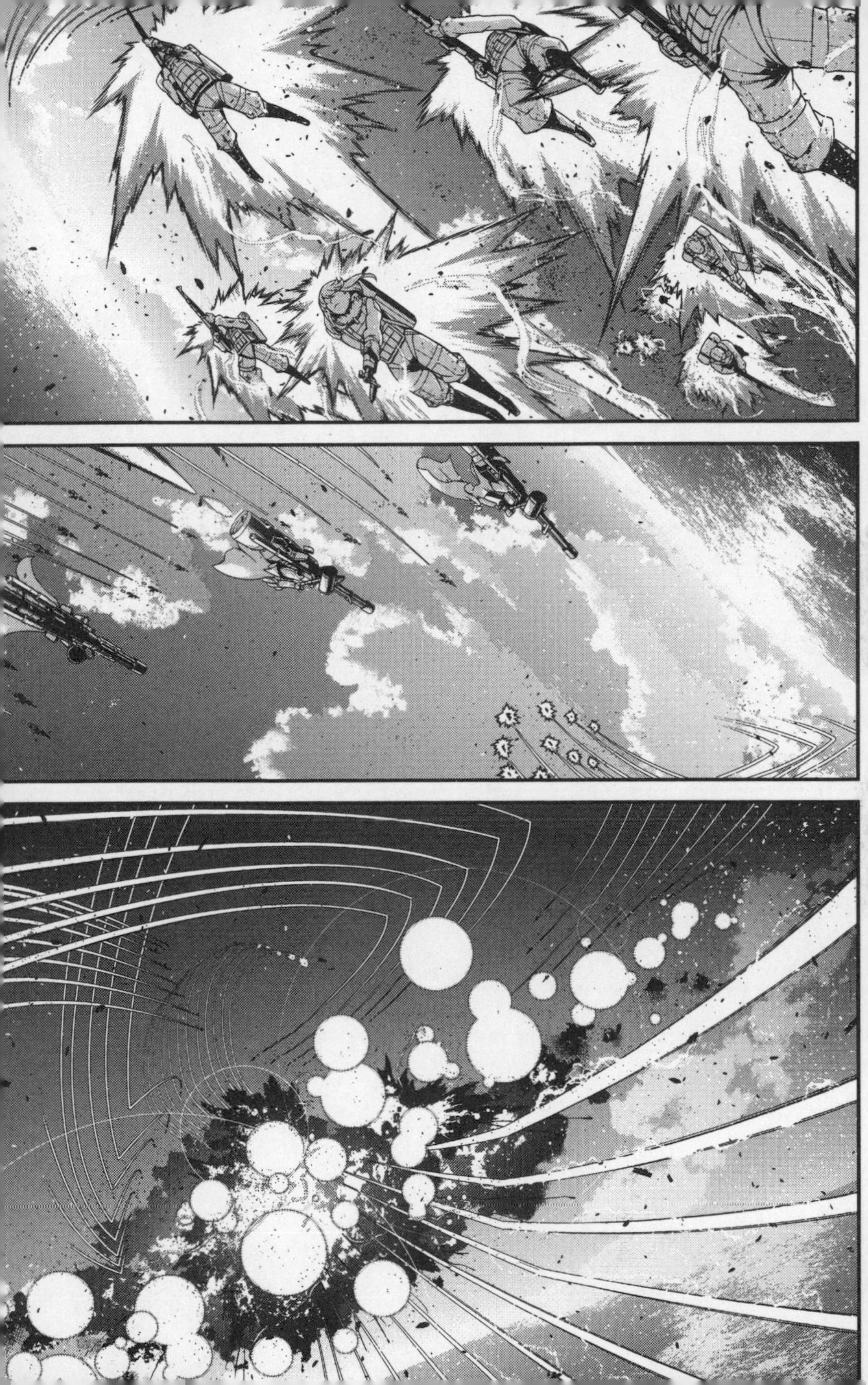

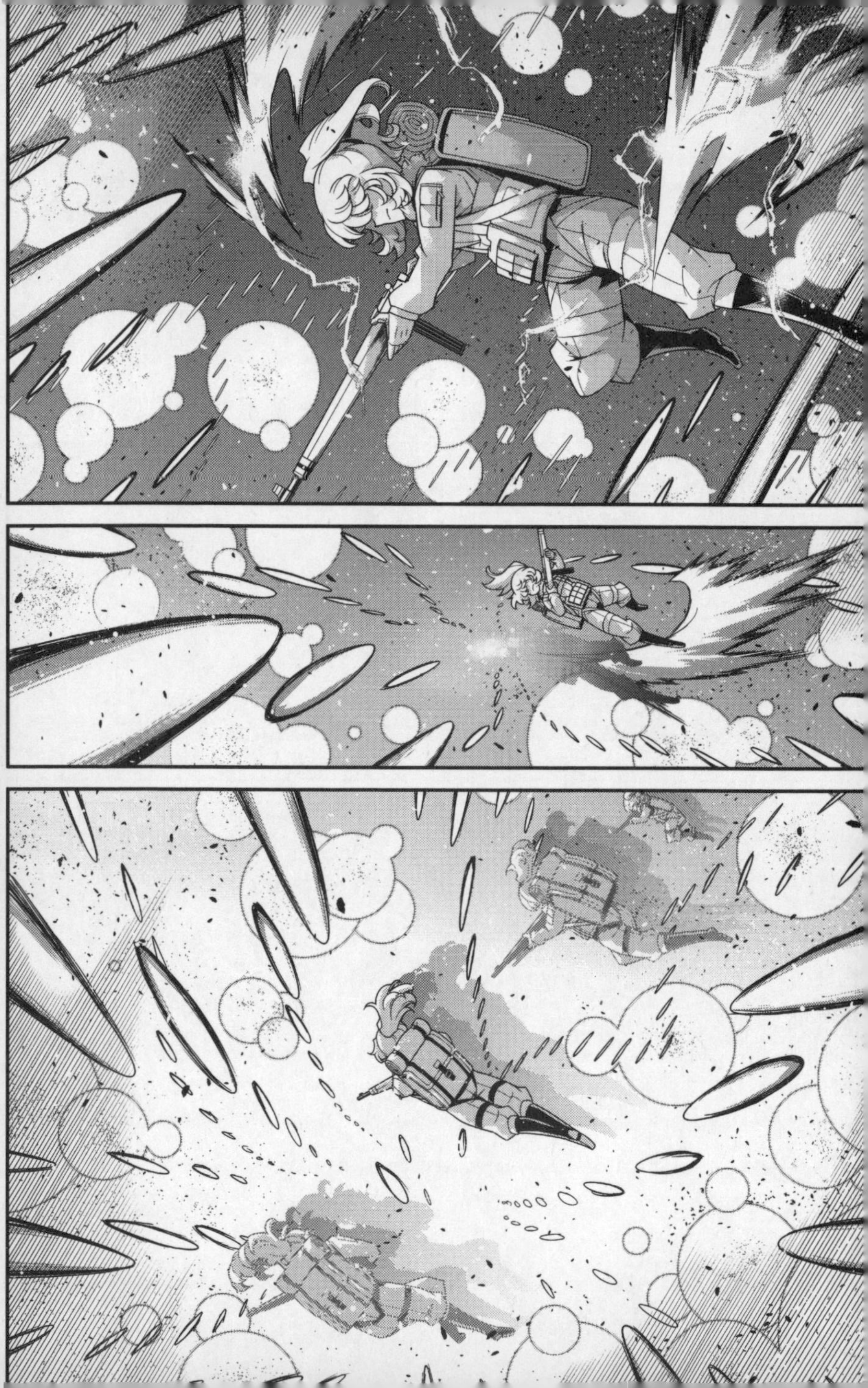

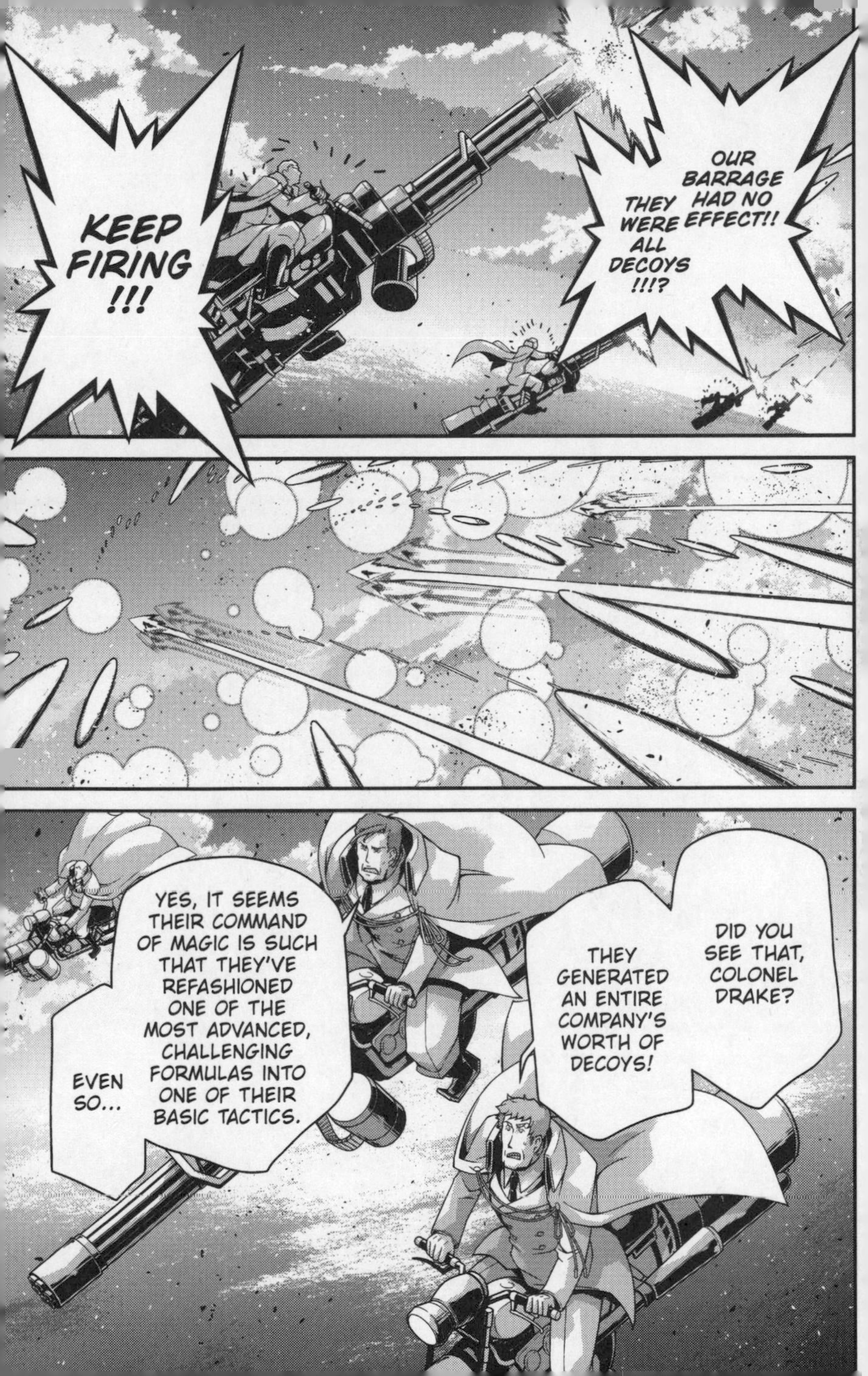
OUR BARRAGE HAD NO EFFECT!!
THEY WERE ALL DECOYS!!!?
KEEP FIRING!!!
DID YOU SEE THAT, COLONEL DRAKE?
THEY GENERATED AN ENTIRE COMPANY'S WORTH OF DECOYS!
YES, IT SEEMS THEIR COMMAND OF MAGIC IS SUCH THAT THEY'VE REFASHIONED ONE OF THE MOST ADVANCED, CHALLENGING FORMULAS INTO ONE OF THEIR BASIC TACTICS.
EVEN SO...

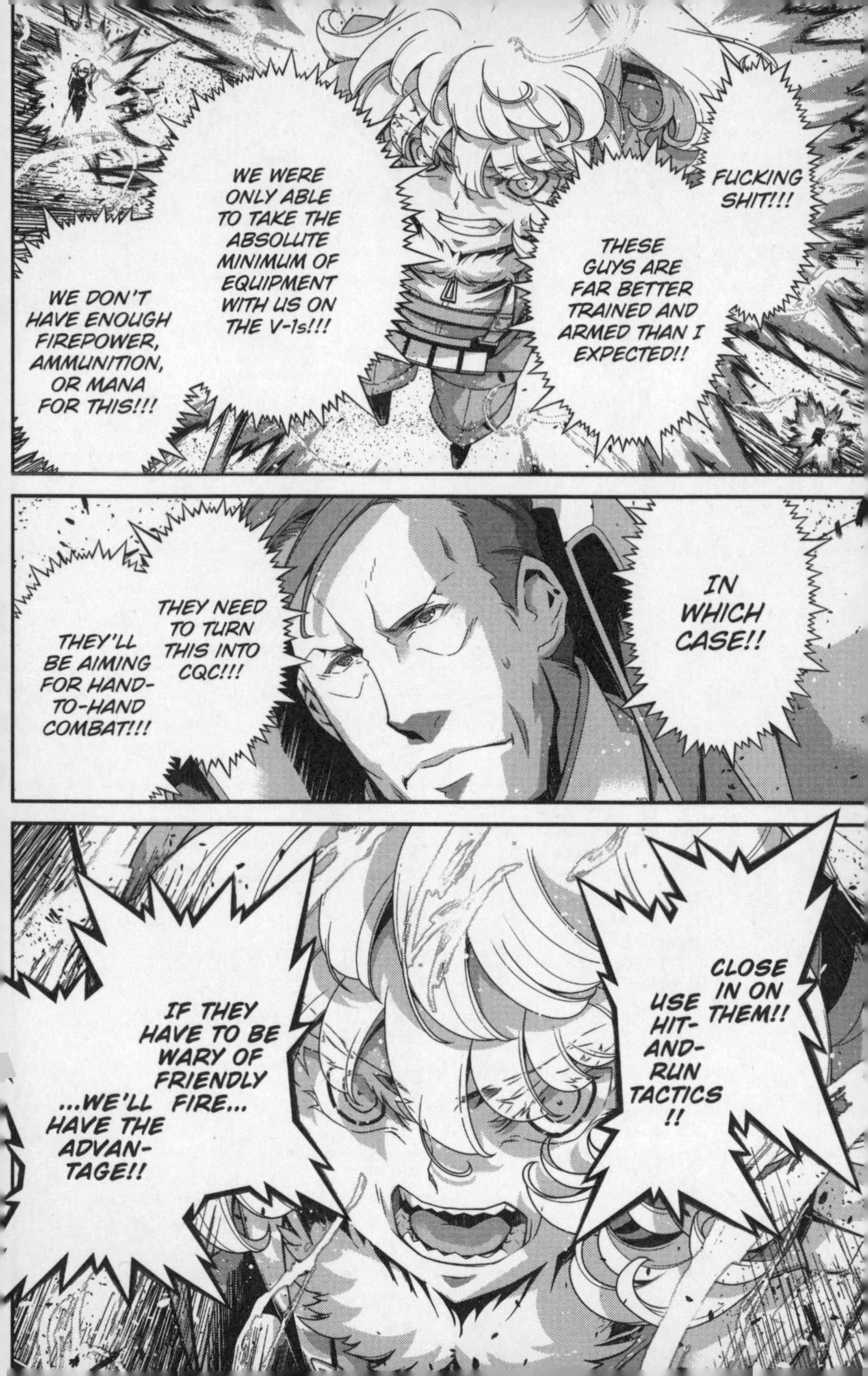
FUCKING SHIT!!!
THESE GUYS ARE FAR BETTER TRAINED AND ARMED THAN I EXPECTED!!
WE WERE ONLY ABLE TO TAKE THE ABSOLUTE MINIMUM OF EQUIPMENT WITH US ON THE V-1s!!!
WE DON'T HAVE ENOUGH FIREPOWER, AMMUNITION, OR MANA FOR THIS!!!
IN WHICH CASE!!
THEY NEED TO TURN THIS INTO CQC!!!
THEY'LL BE AIMING FOR HAND-TO-HAND COMBAT!!!
CLOSE IN ON THEM!!
USE HIT-AND-RUN TACTICS!!
IF THEY HAVE TO BE WARY OF FRIENDLY FIRE...
...WE'LL HAVE THE ADVANTAGE!!

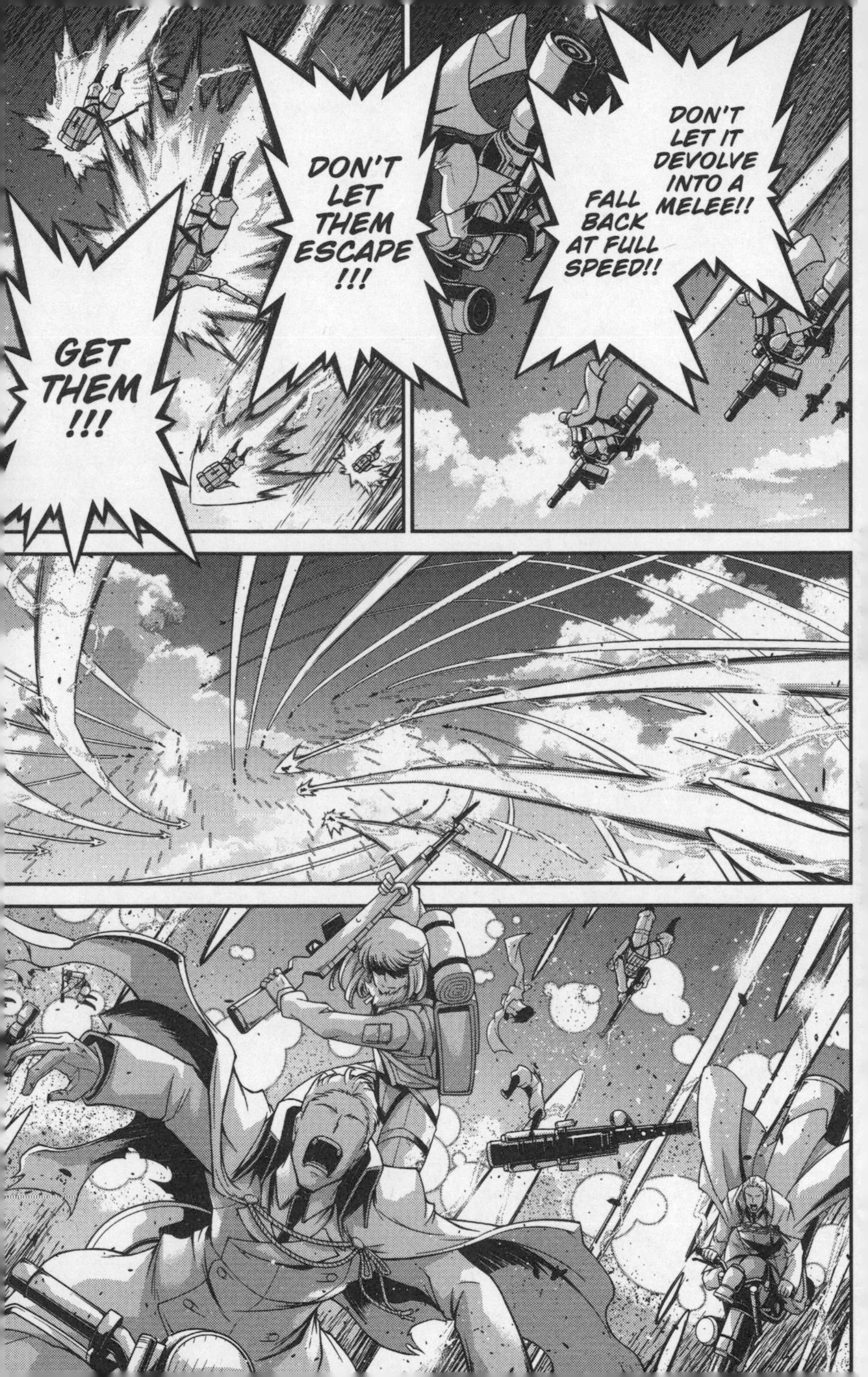
DON'T LET IT DEVOLVE INTO A MELEE!!
FALL BACK AT FULL SPEED!!
DON'T LET THEM ESCAPE!!!
GET THEM!!!

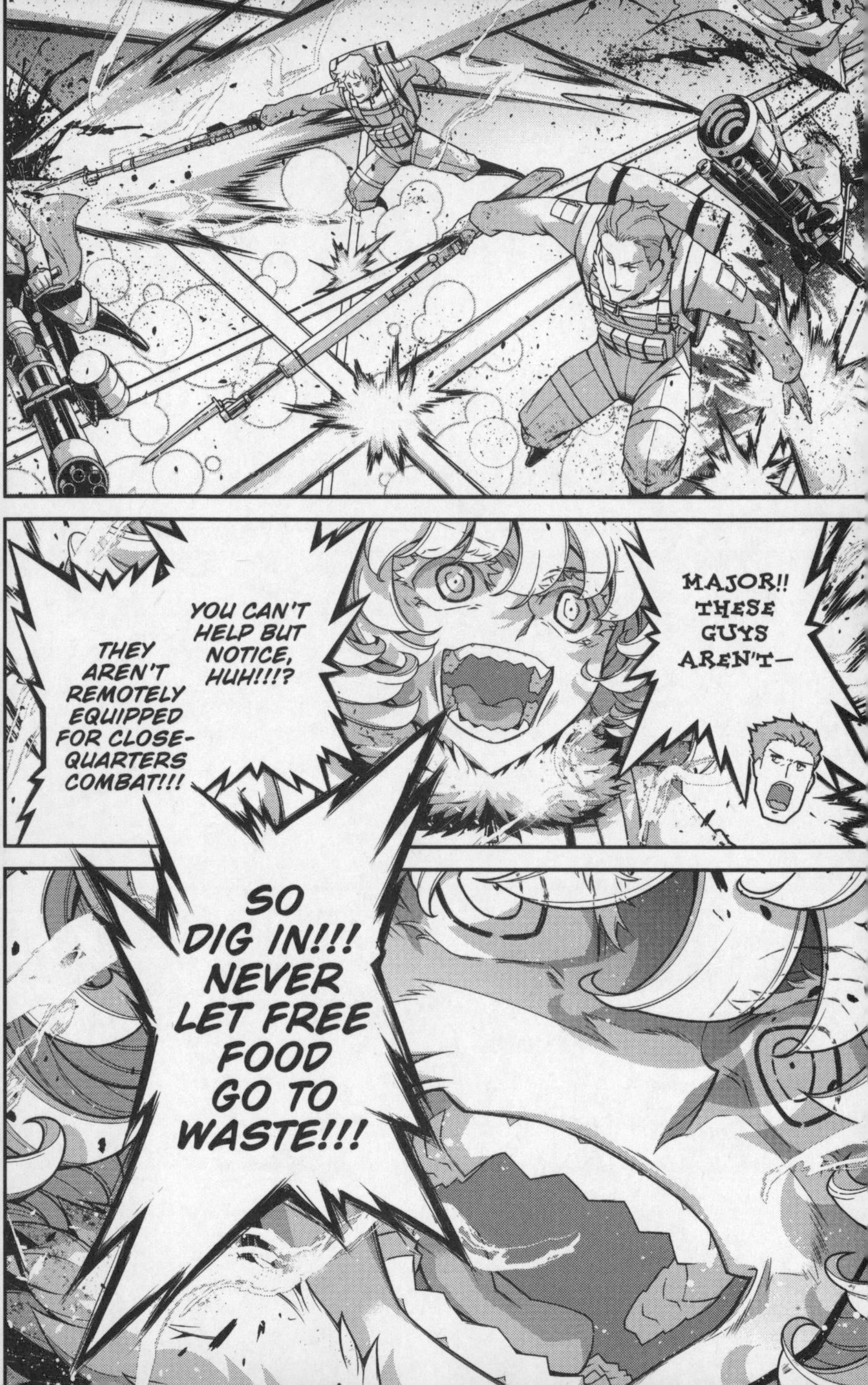
MAJOR!! THESE GUYS AREN'T—
YOU CAN'T HELP BUT NOTICE, HUH!!!?
THEY AREN'T REMOTELY EQUIPPED FOR CLOSE-QUARTERS COMBAT!!!
SO DIG IN!!! NEVER LET FREE FOOD GO TO WASTE!!!

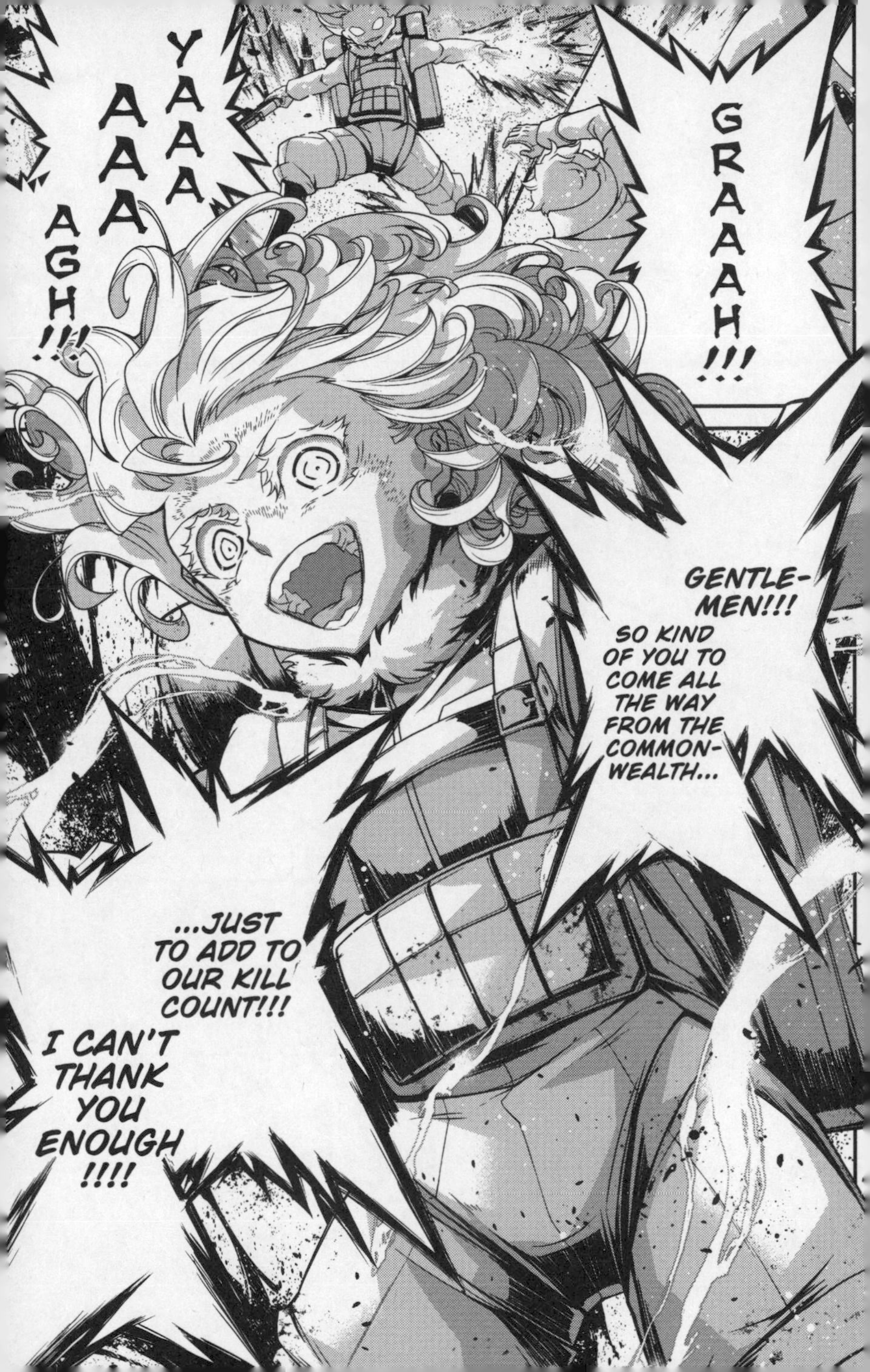
GRAAAH!!!
YAAAAAAAAGH!!!
GENTLE-MEN!!!
SO KIND OF YOU TO COME ALL THE WAY FROM THE COMMON-WEALTH...
...JUST TO ADD TO OUR KILL COUNT!!!
I CAN'T THANK YOU ENOUGH!!!!

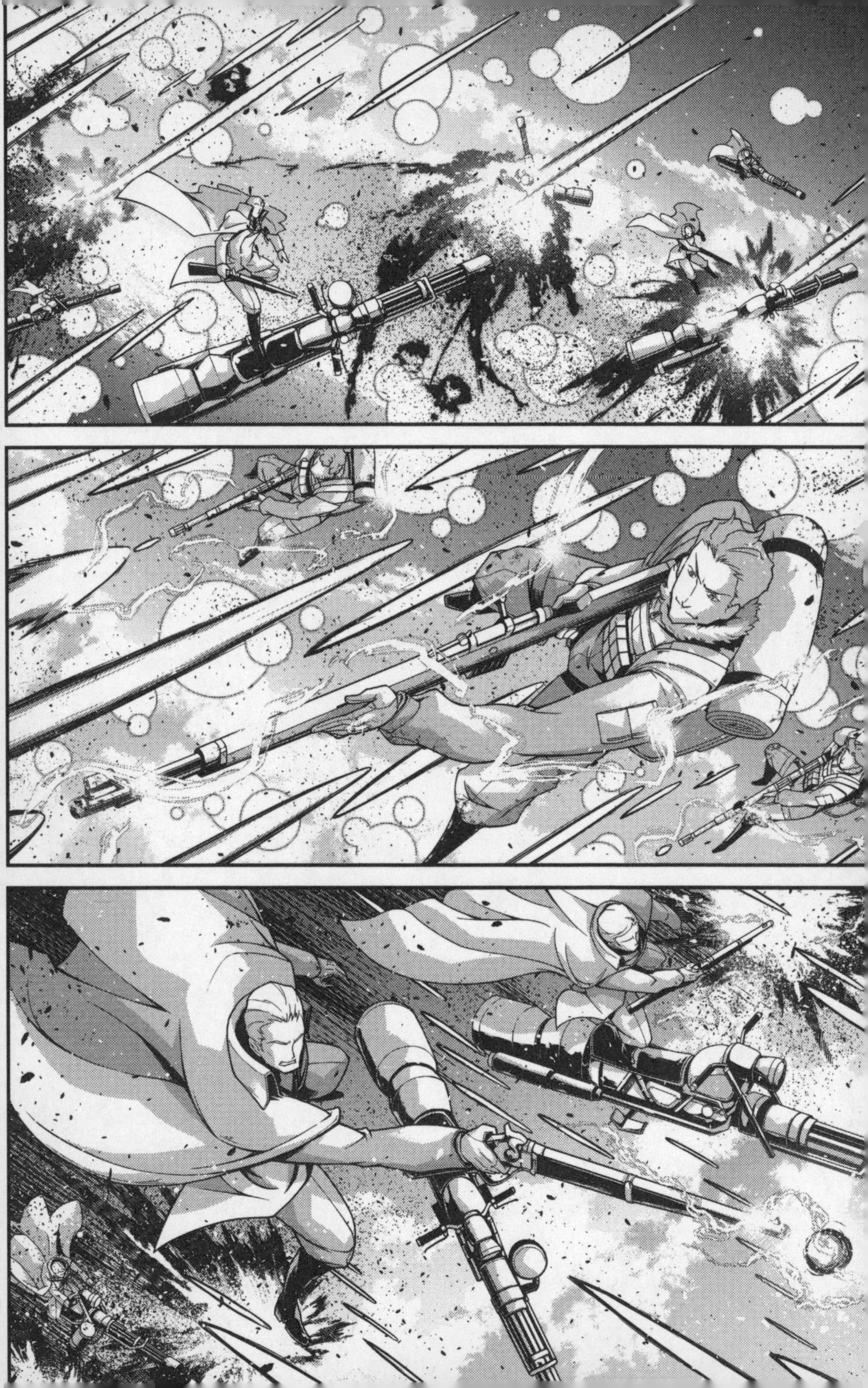

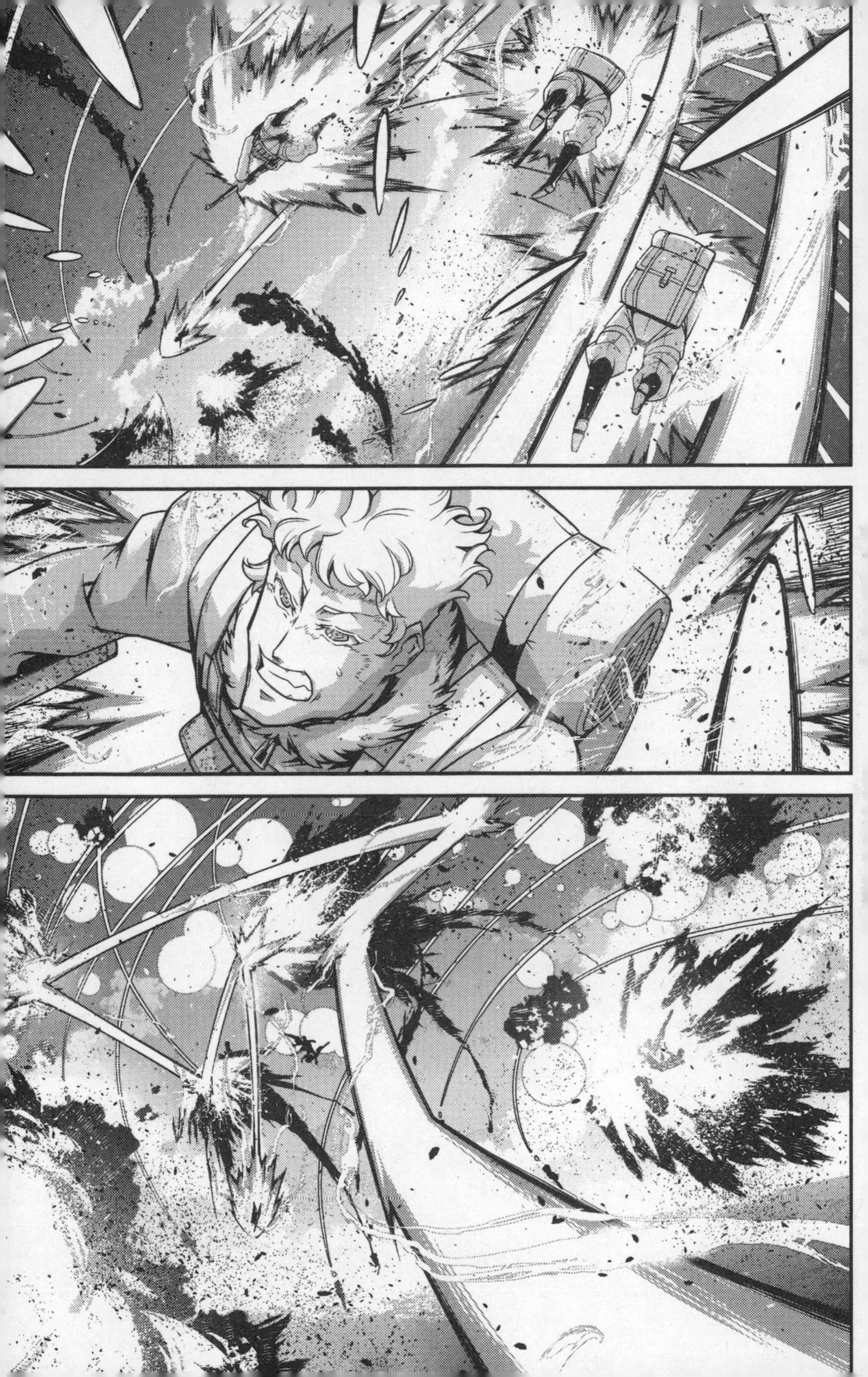

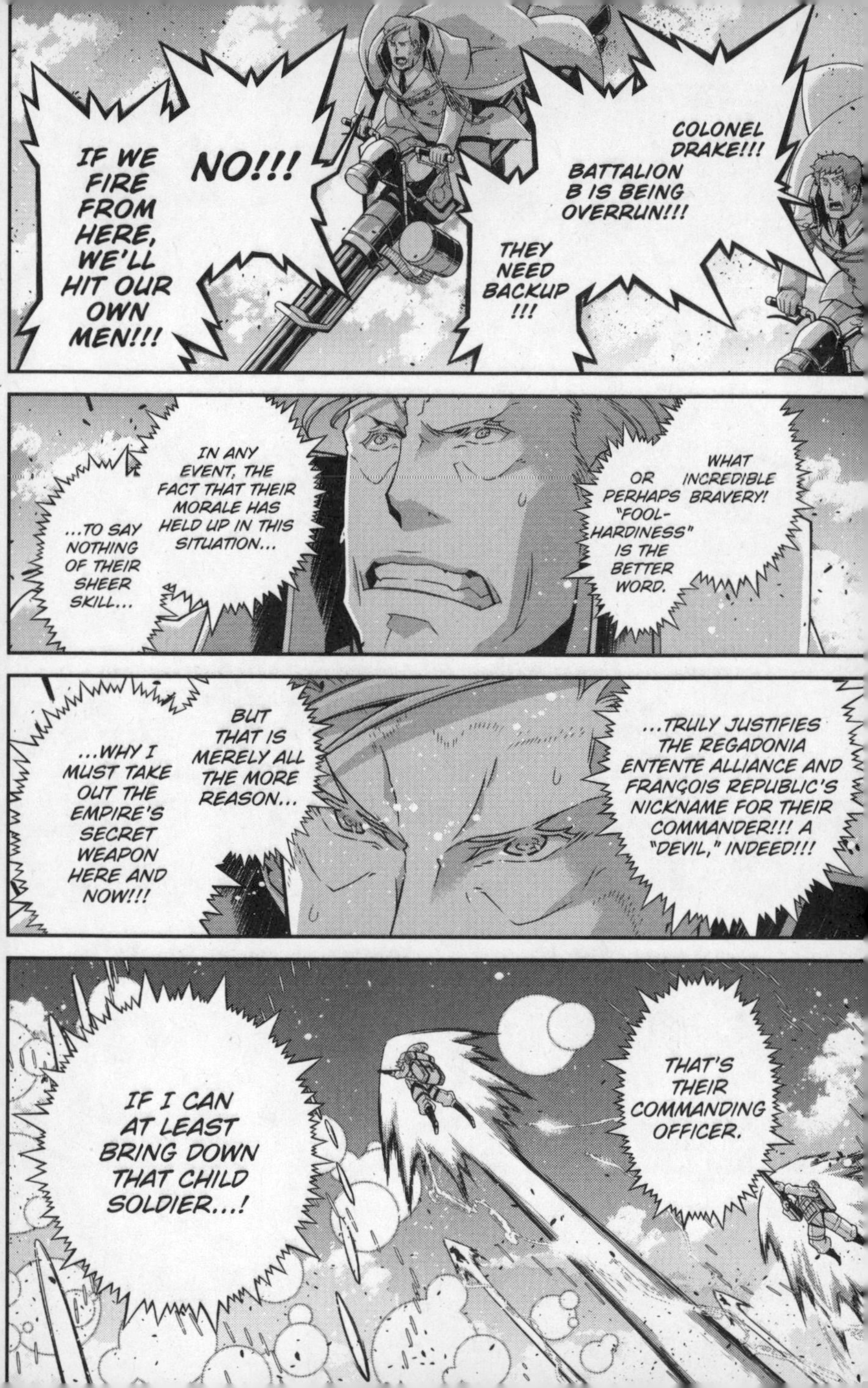
COLONEL DRAKE!!!
BATTALION B IS BEING OVERRUN!!!
THEY NEED BACKUP!!!
NO!!!
IF WE FIRE FROM HERE, WE'LL HIT OUR OWN MEN!!!
WHAT INCREDIBLE BRAVERY!
OR PERHAPS "FOOL-HARDINESS" IS THE BETTER WORD.
IN ANY EVENT, THE FACT THAT THEIR MORALE HAS HELD UP IN THIS SITUATION...
...TO SAY NOTHING OF THEIR SHEER SKILL...
...TRULY JUSTIFIES THE REGADONIA ENTENTE ALLIANCE AND FRANÇOIS REPUBLIC'S NICKNAME FOR THEIR COMMANDER!!! A "DEVIL," INDEED!!!
BUT THAT IS MERELY ALL THE MORE REASON...
...WHY I MUST TAKE OUT THE EMPIRE'S SECRET WEAPON HERE AND NOW!!!
THAT'S THEIR COMMANDING OFFICER.
IF I CAN AT LEAST BRING DOWN THAT CHILD SOLDIER...!

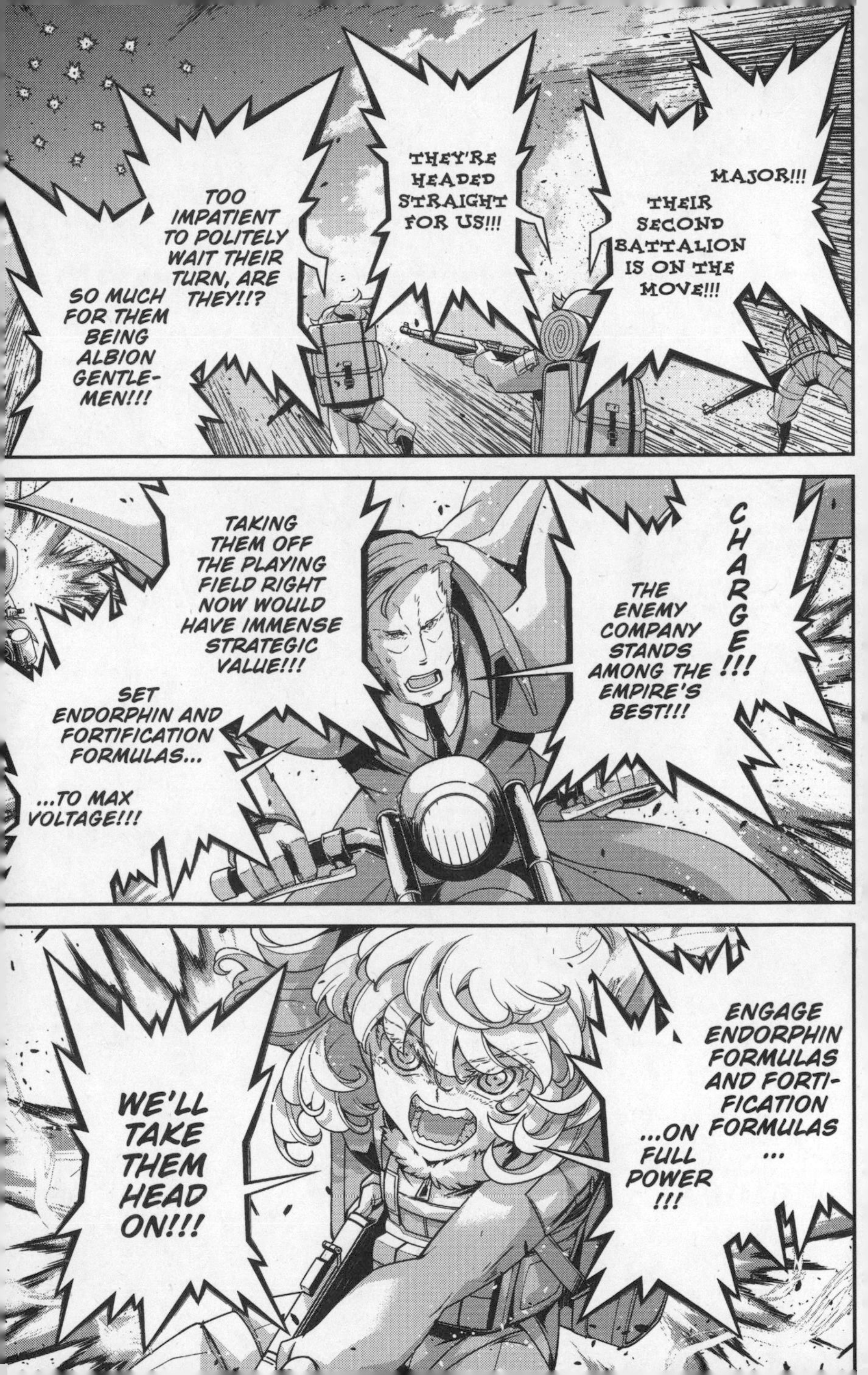
MAJOR!!!
THEIR SECOND BATTALION IS ON THE MOVE!!!
THEY'RE HEADED STRAIGHT FOR US!!!
TOO IMPATIENT TO POLITELY WAIT THEIR TURN, ARE THEY!!?
SO MUCH FOR THEM BEING ALBION GENTLEMEN!!!
CHARGE!!!
THE ENEMY COMPANY STANDS AMONG THE EMPIRE'S BEST!!!
TAKING THEM OFF THE PLAYING FIELD RIGHT NOW WOULD HAVE IMMENSE STRATEGIC VALUE!!!
SET ENDORPHIN AND FORTIFICATION FORMULAS...
...TO MAX VOLTAGE!!!
ENGAGE ENDORPHIN FORMULAS AND FORTIFICATION FORMULAS...
...ON FULL POWER!!!
WE'LL TAKE THEM HEAD ON!!!

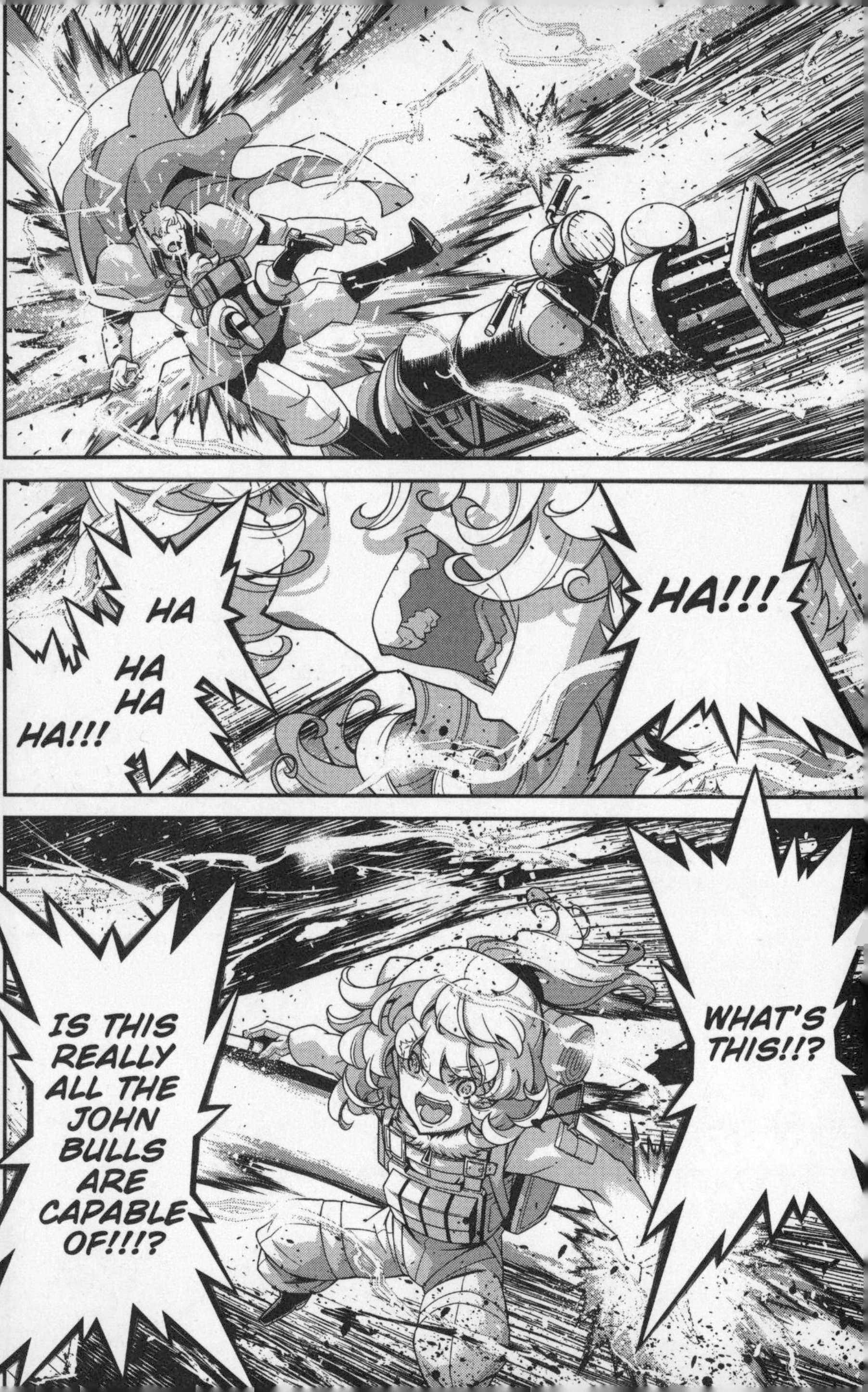
HA!!!
HA HA HA HA!!!
WHAT'S THIS!!?
IS THIS REALLY ALL THE JOHN BULLS ARE CAPABLE OF!!!?

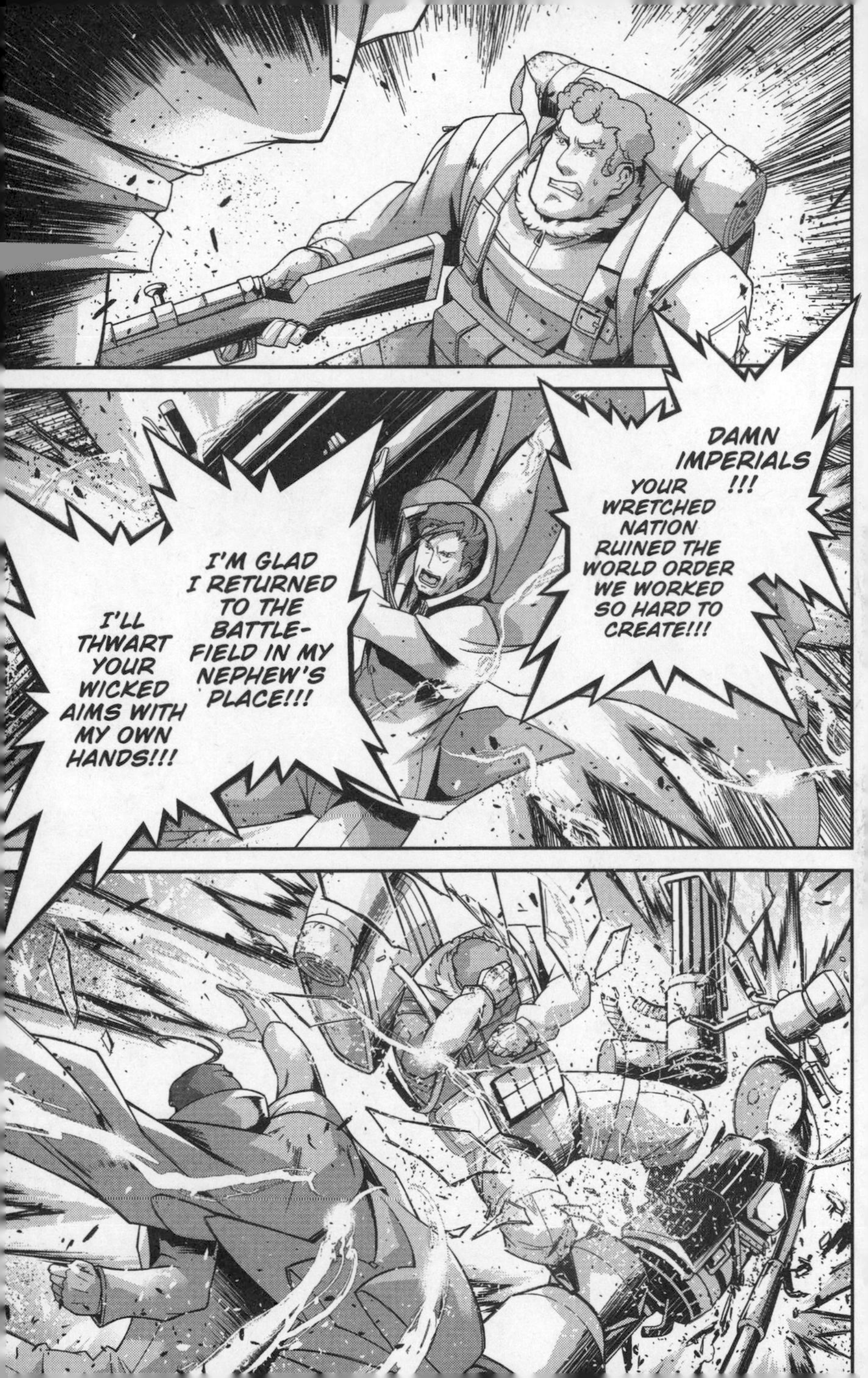
DAMN IMPERIALS!!!
YOUR WRETCHED NATION RUINED THE WORLD ORDER WE WORKED SO HARD TO CREATE!!!
I'M GLAD I RETURNED TO THE BATTLE-FIELD IN MY NEPHEW'S PLACE!!!
I'LL THWART YOUR WICKED AIMS WITH MY OWN HANDS!!!

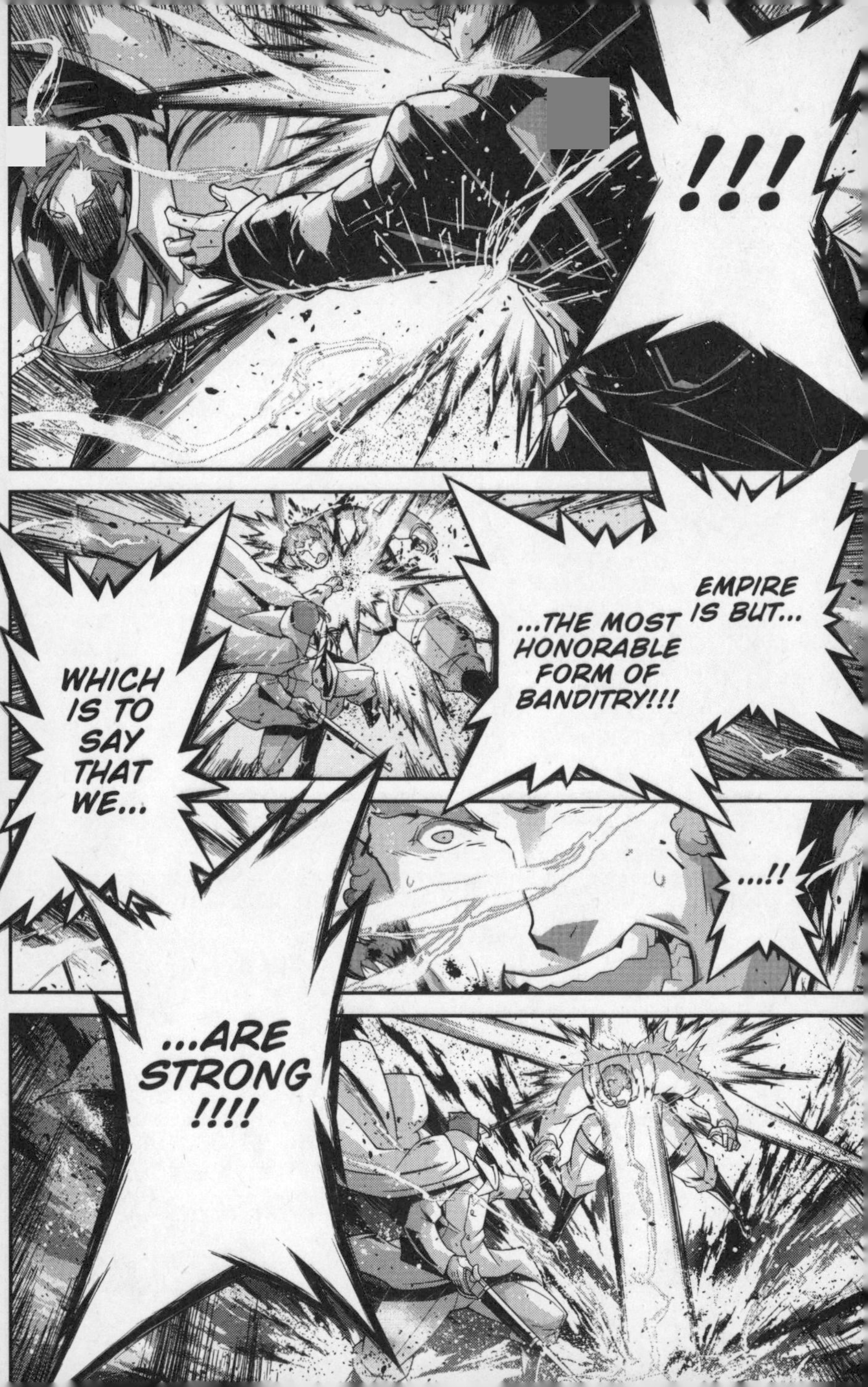
!!!
EMPIRE IS BUT...
...THE MOST HONORABLE FORM OF BANDITRY!!!
WHICH IS TO SAY THAT WE...
...!!
...ARE STRONG !!!!

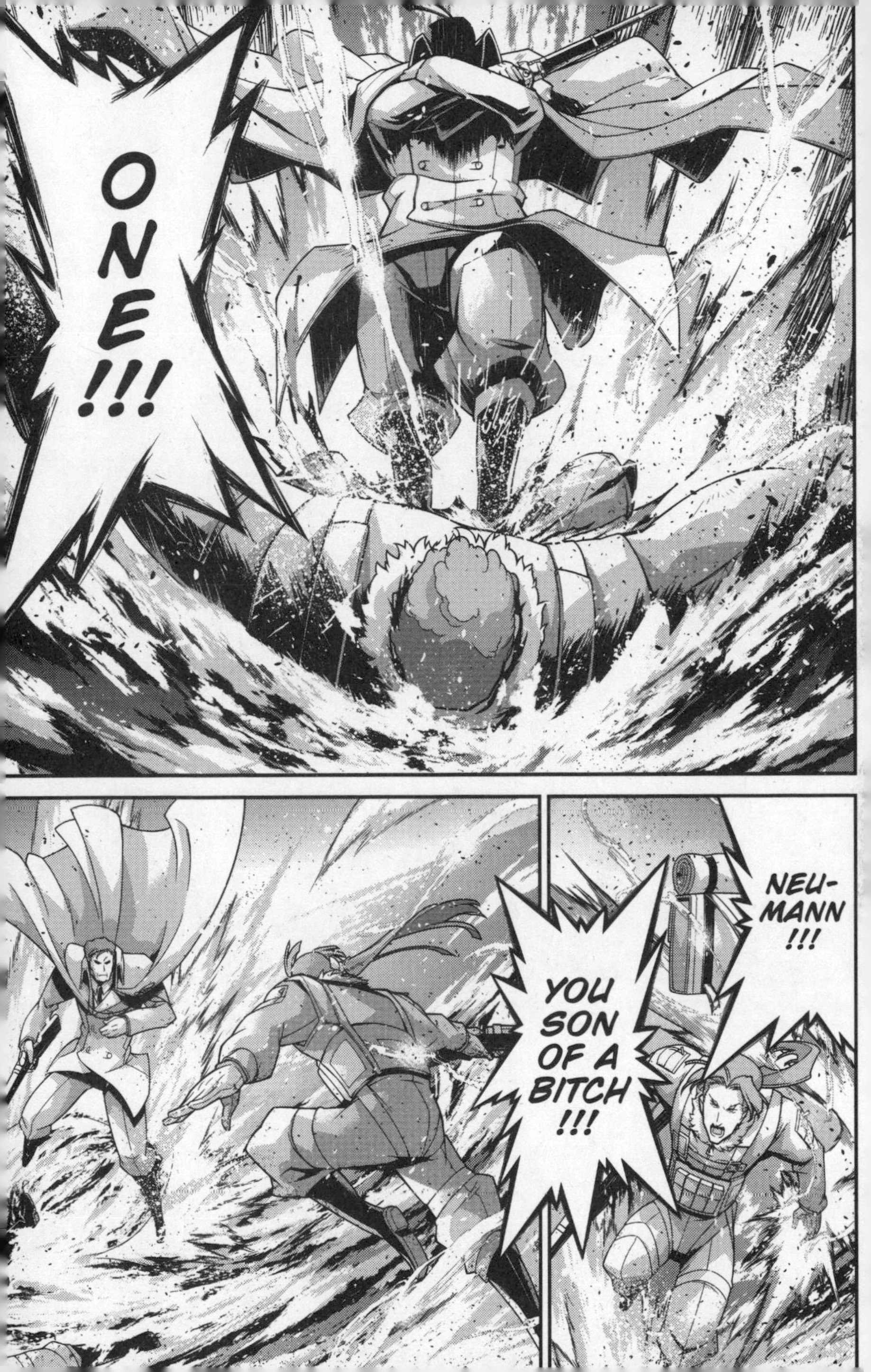
ONE!!!
NEU-MANN!!!
YOU SON OF A BITCH!!!

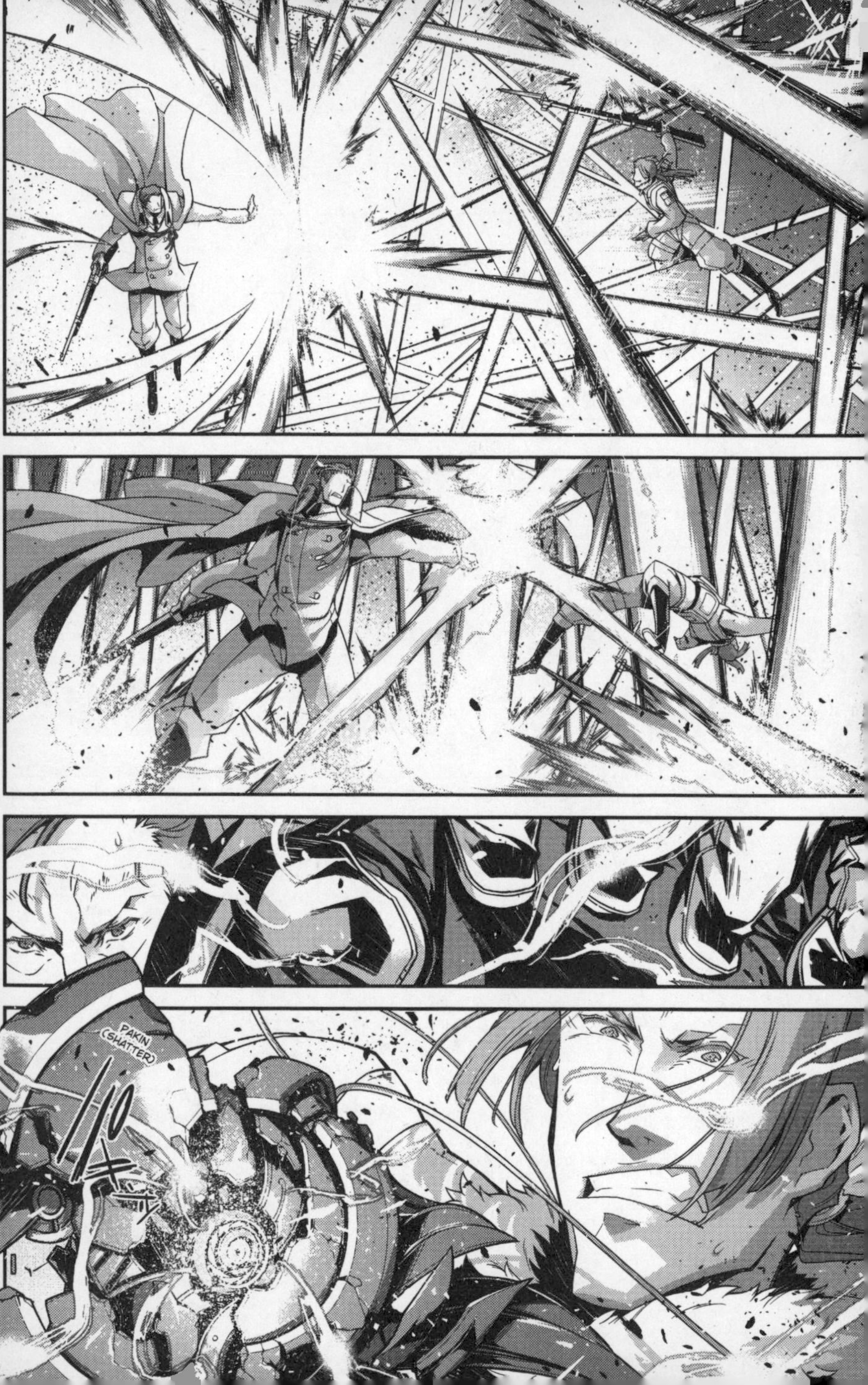
PAKIN (SHATTER)

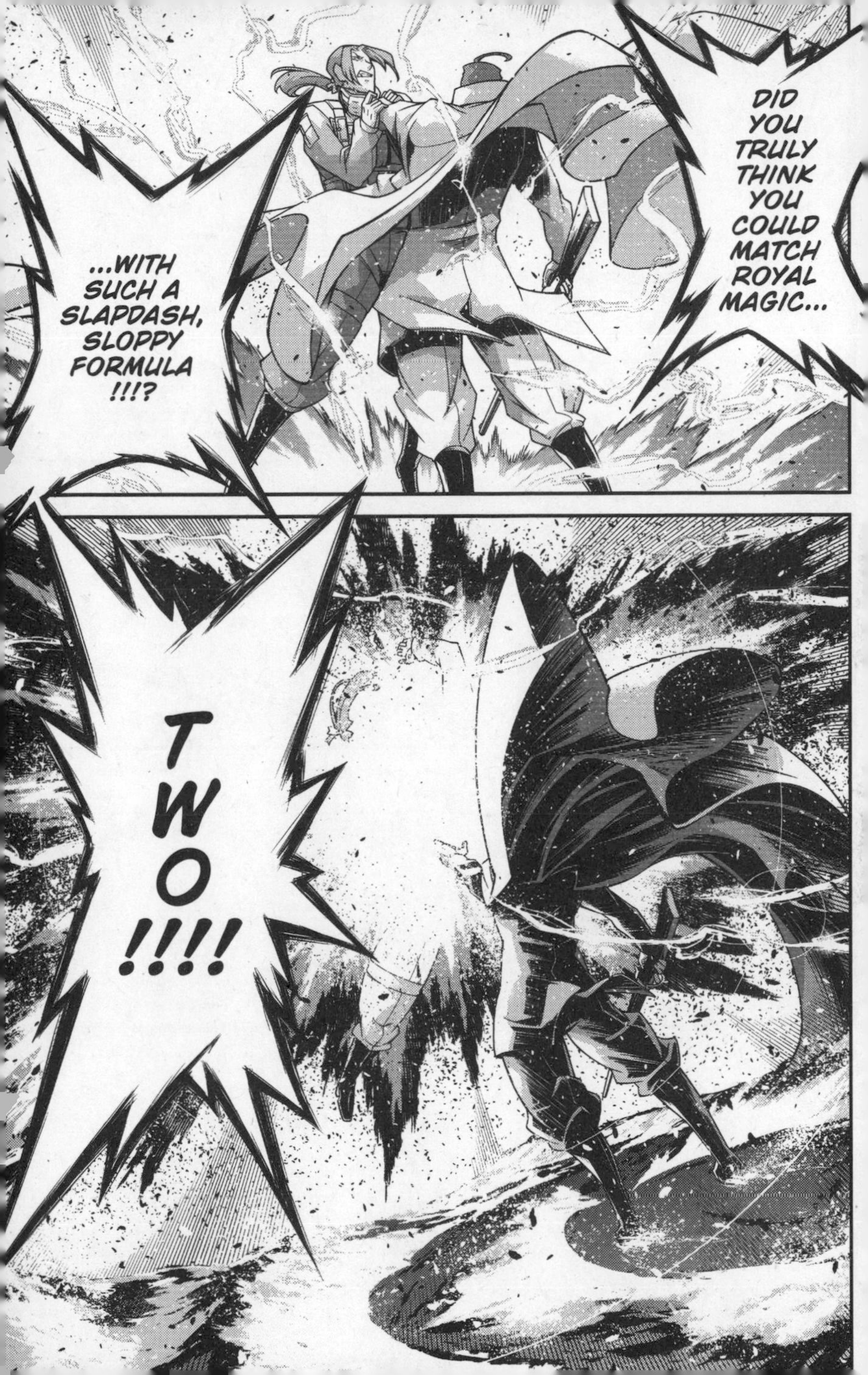
DID YOU TRULY THINK YOU COULD MATCH ROYAL MAGIC...
...WITH SUCH A SLAPDASH, SLOPPY FORMULA !!!?
TWO !!!!

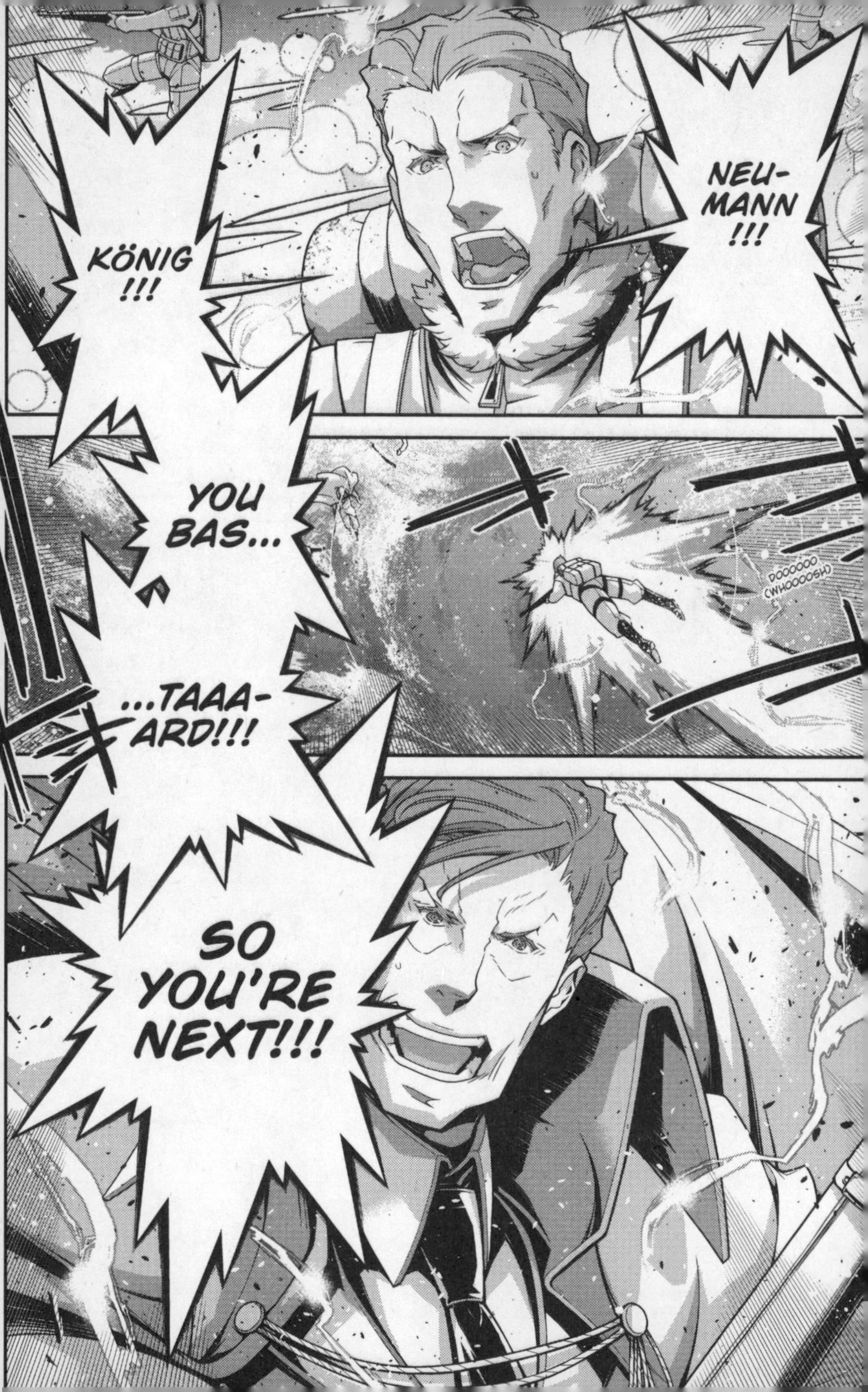
NEU-MANN!!!
KÖNIG!!!
YOU BAS...
DOOOOOO (WHOOOOSH)
...TAAA-ARD!!!
SO YOU'RE NEXT!!!

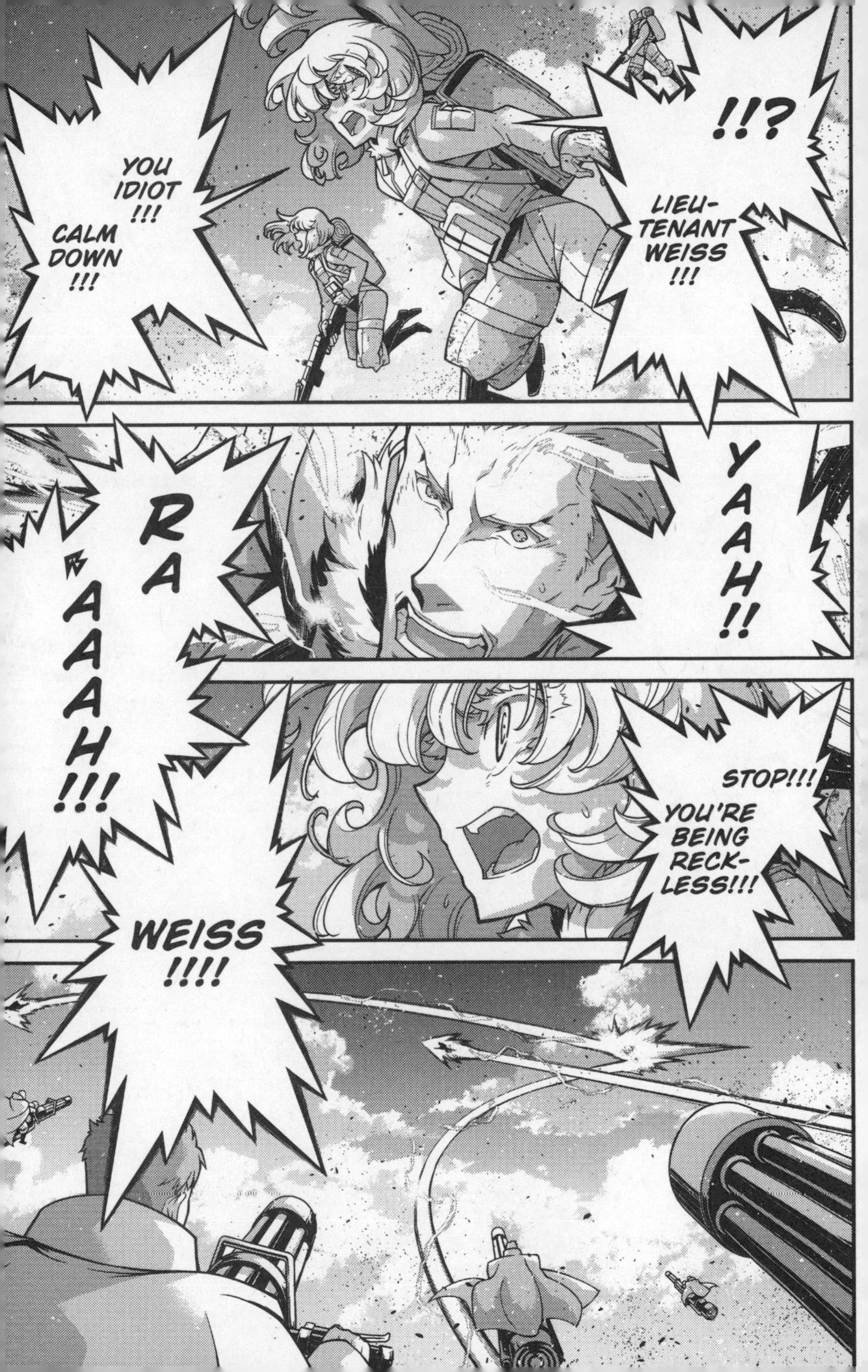
!!?
LIEU-TENANT WEISS!!!
YOU IDIOT!!!
CALM DOWN!!!
YAAAH!!
RA RAAAAH!!!
STOP!!!
YOU'RE BEING RECK-LESS!!!
WEISS!!!!

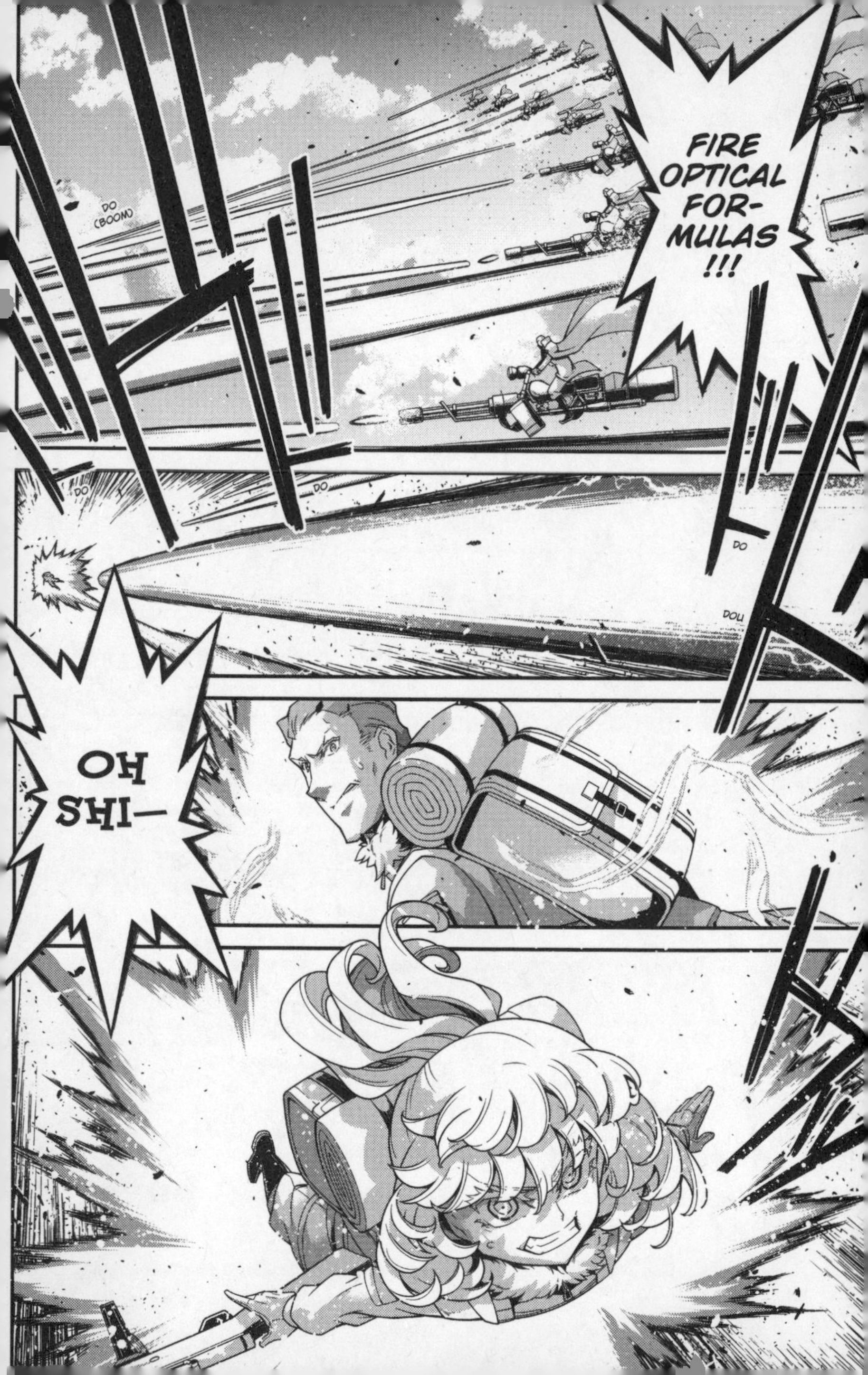

FIRE OPTICAL FOR-MULAS !!!
DO (BOOM)
DO
DO
DO
DOU
OH SHI—

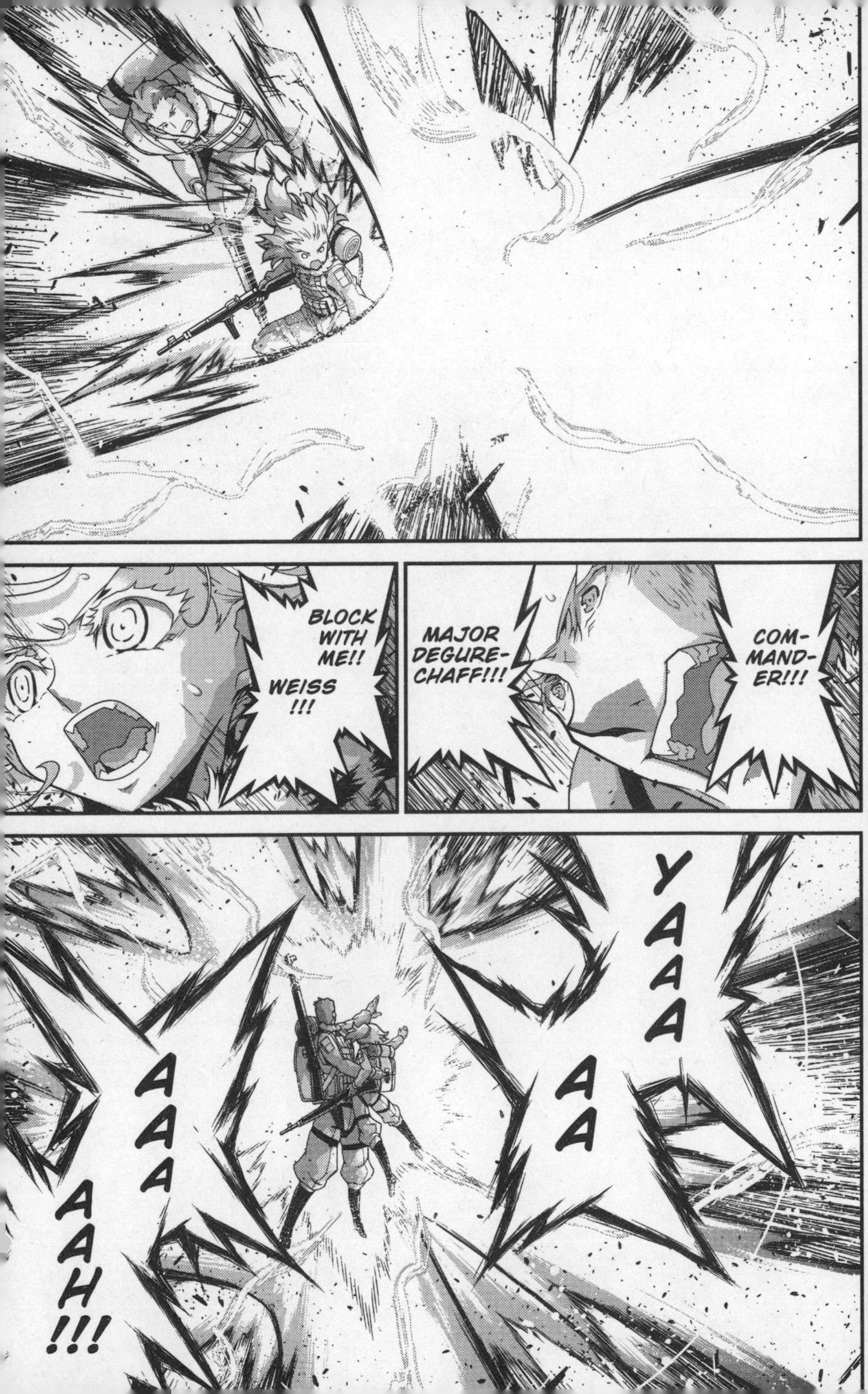
COM-MAND-ER!!!
MAJOR DEGURE-CHAFF!!!
BLOCK WITH ME!!
WEISS!!!
YAAAA
AA
AAA
AAAH!!!

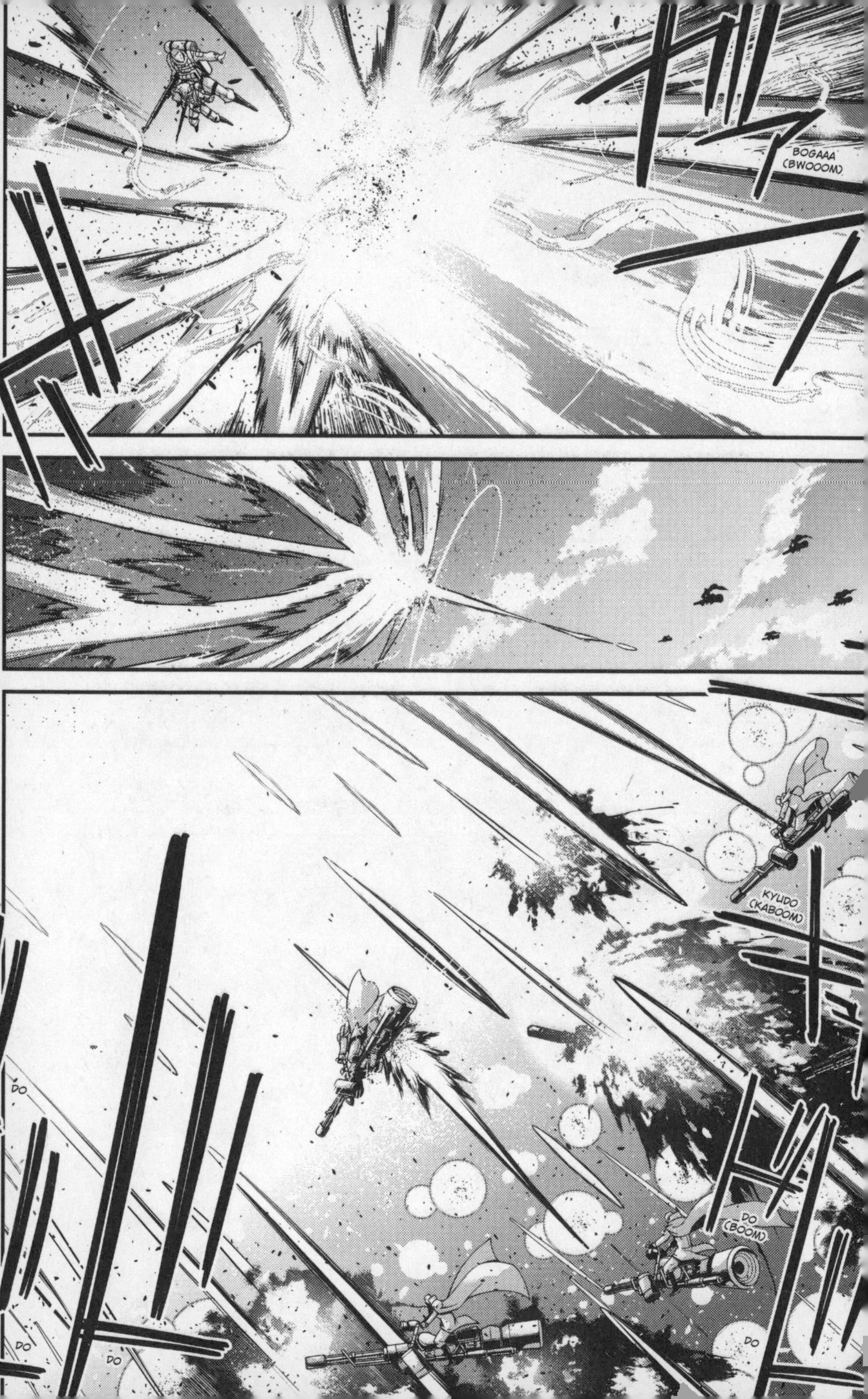
BOGAAA
(BWOOOM)
KYUDO
(KABOOM)
DO
(BOOM)
DO
DO
DO
DO

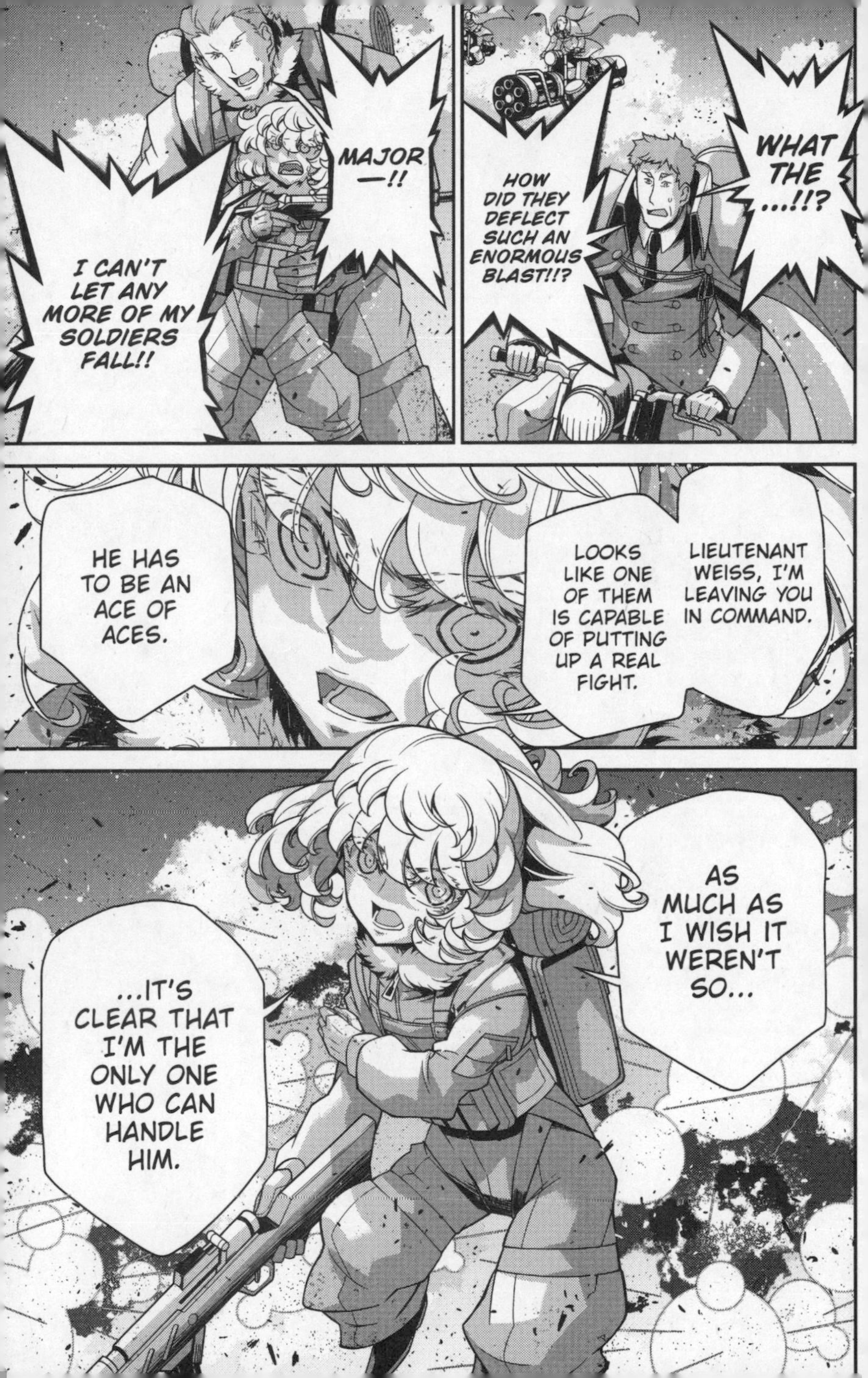
WHAT THE ...!!?
HOW DID THEY DEFLECT SUCH AN ENORMOUS BLAST!!?
MAJOR—!!
I CAN'T LET ANY MORE OF MY SOLDIERS FALL!!
LIEUTENANT WEISS, I'M LEAVING YOU IN COMMAND.
LOOKS LIKE ONE OF THEM IS CAPABLE OF PUTTING UP A REAL FIGHT.
HE HAS TO BE AN ACE OF ACES.
AS MUCH AS I WISH IT WEREN'T SO...
...IT'S CLEAR THAT I'M THE ONLY ONE WHO CAN HANDLE HIM.

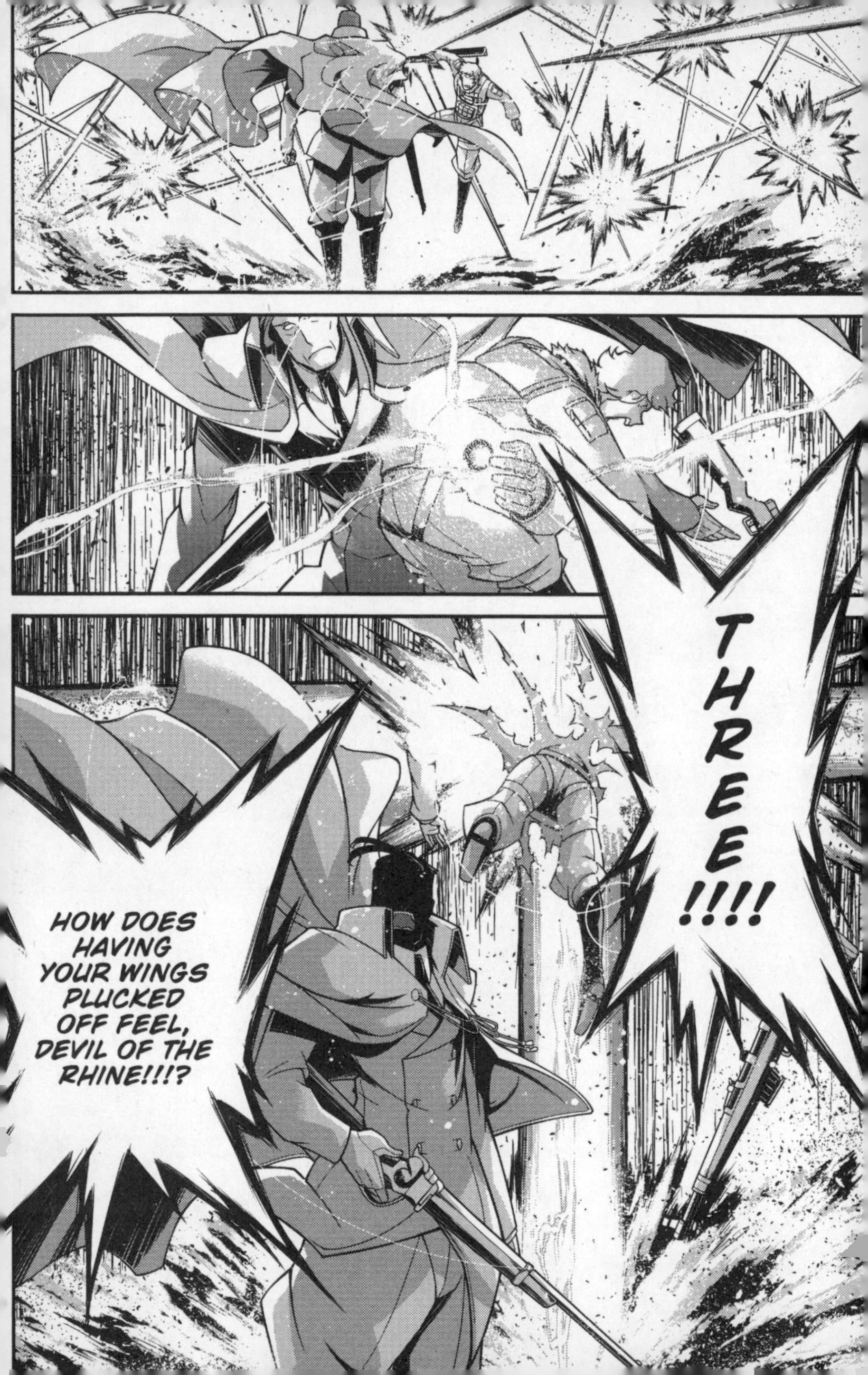
THREE!!!!
HOW DOES HAVING YOUR WINGS PLUCKED OFF FEEL, DEVIL OF THE RHINE!!!?

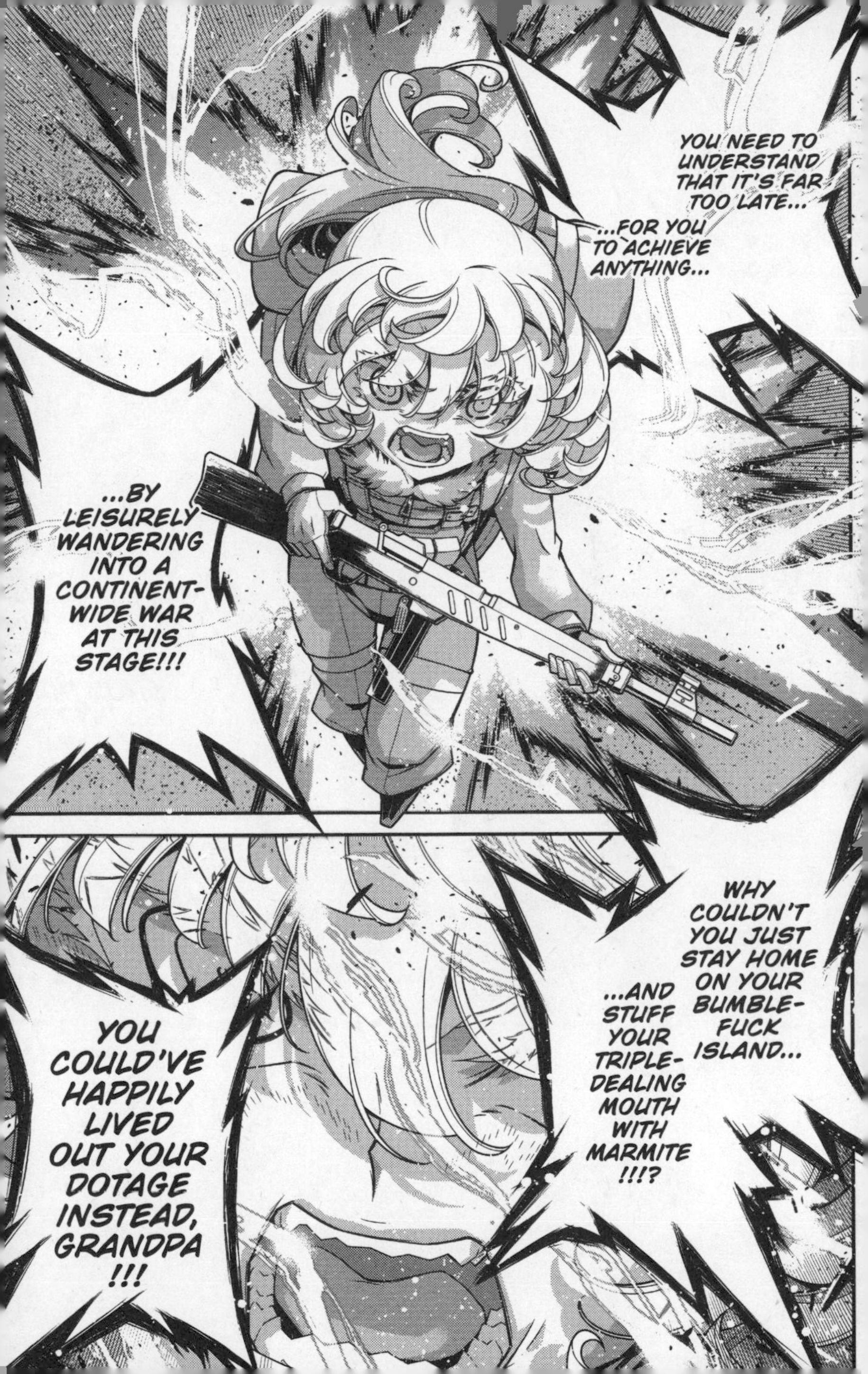
YOU NEED TO UNDERSTAND THAT IT'S FAR TOO LATE...
...FOR YOU TO ACHIEVE ANYTHING...
...BY LEISURELY WANDERING INTO A CONTINENT-WIDE WAR AT THIS STAGE!!!
WHY COULDN'T YOU JUST STAY HOME ON YOUR BUMBLE-FUCK ISLAND...
...AND STUFF YOUR TRIPLE-DEALING MOUTH WITH MARMITE !!!?
YOU COULD'VE HAPPILY LIVED OUT YOUR DOTAGE INSTEAD, GRANDPA !!!

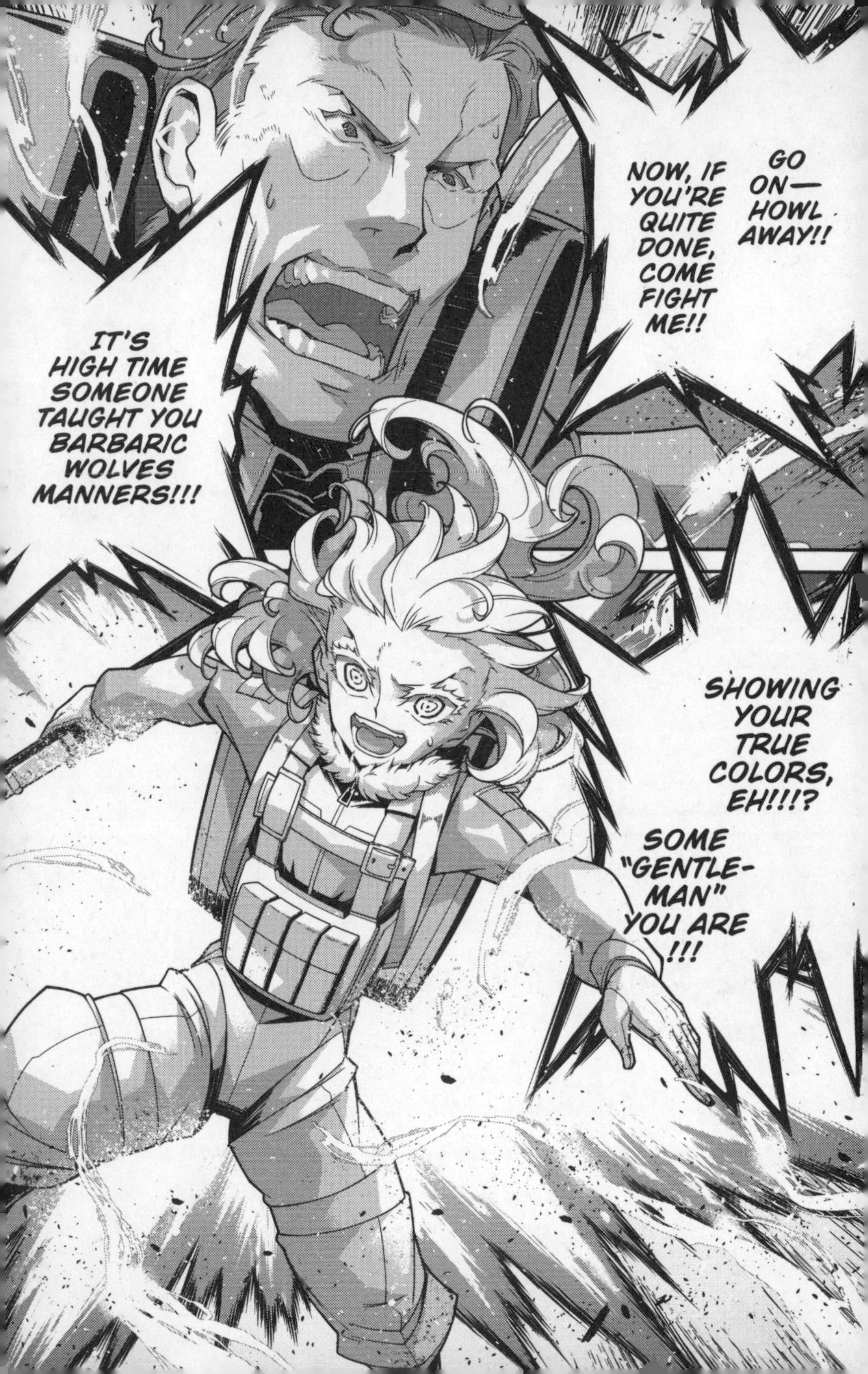
GO ON— HOWL AWAY!!
NOW, IF YOU'RE QUITE DONE, COME FIGHT ME!!
IT'S HIGH TIME SOMEONE TAUGHT YOU BARBARIC WOLVES MANNERS!!!
SHOWING YOUR TRUE COLORS, EH!!!?
SOME "GENTLE-MAN" YOU ARE!!!

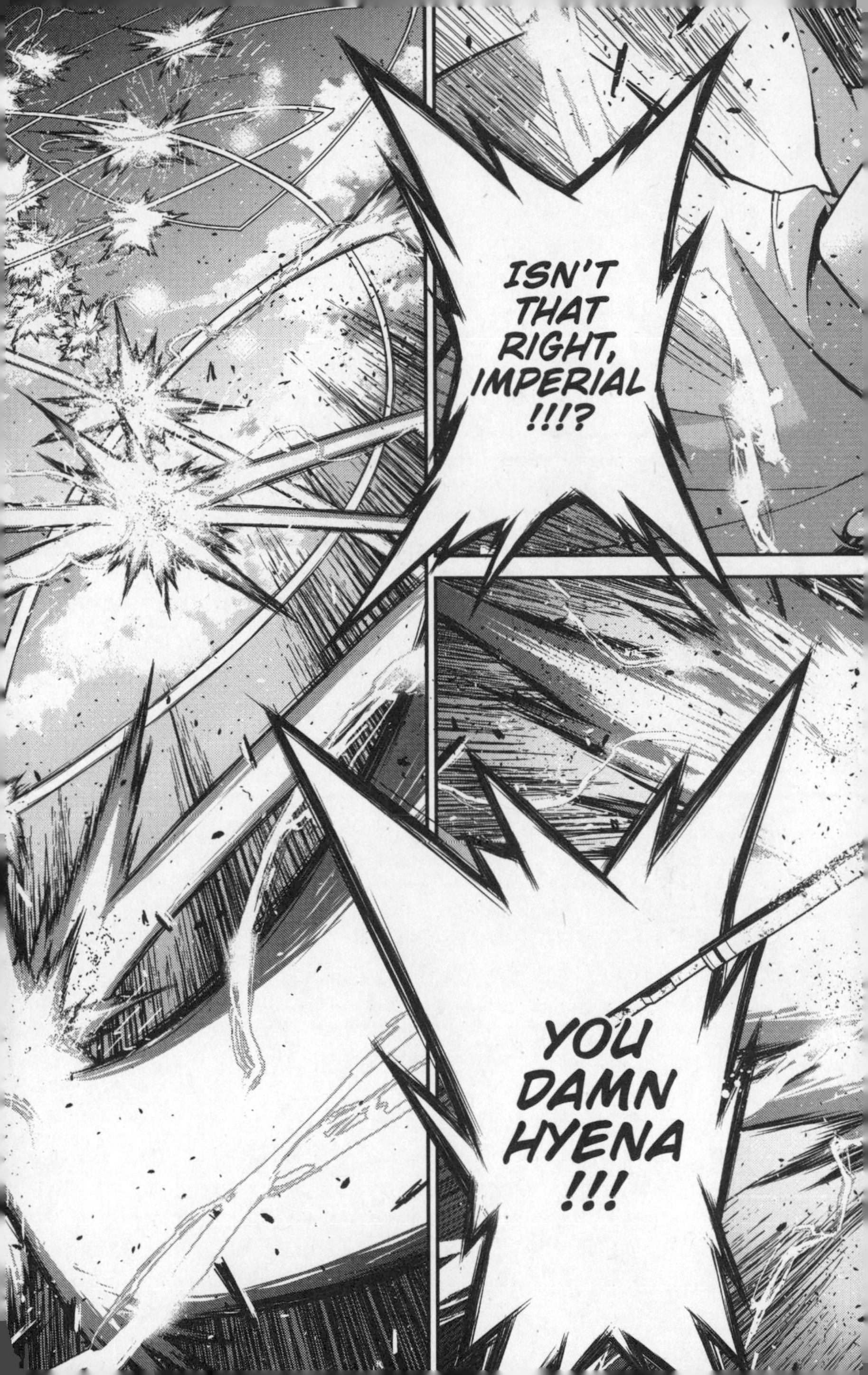
ISN'T THAT RIGHT, IMPERIAL !!!?
YOU DAMN HYENA !!!

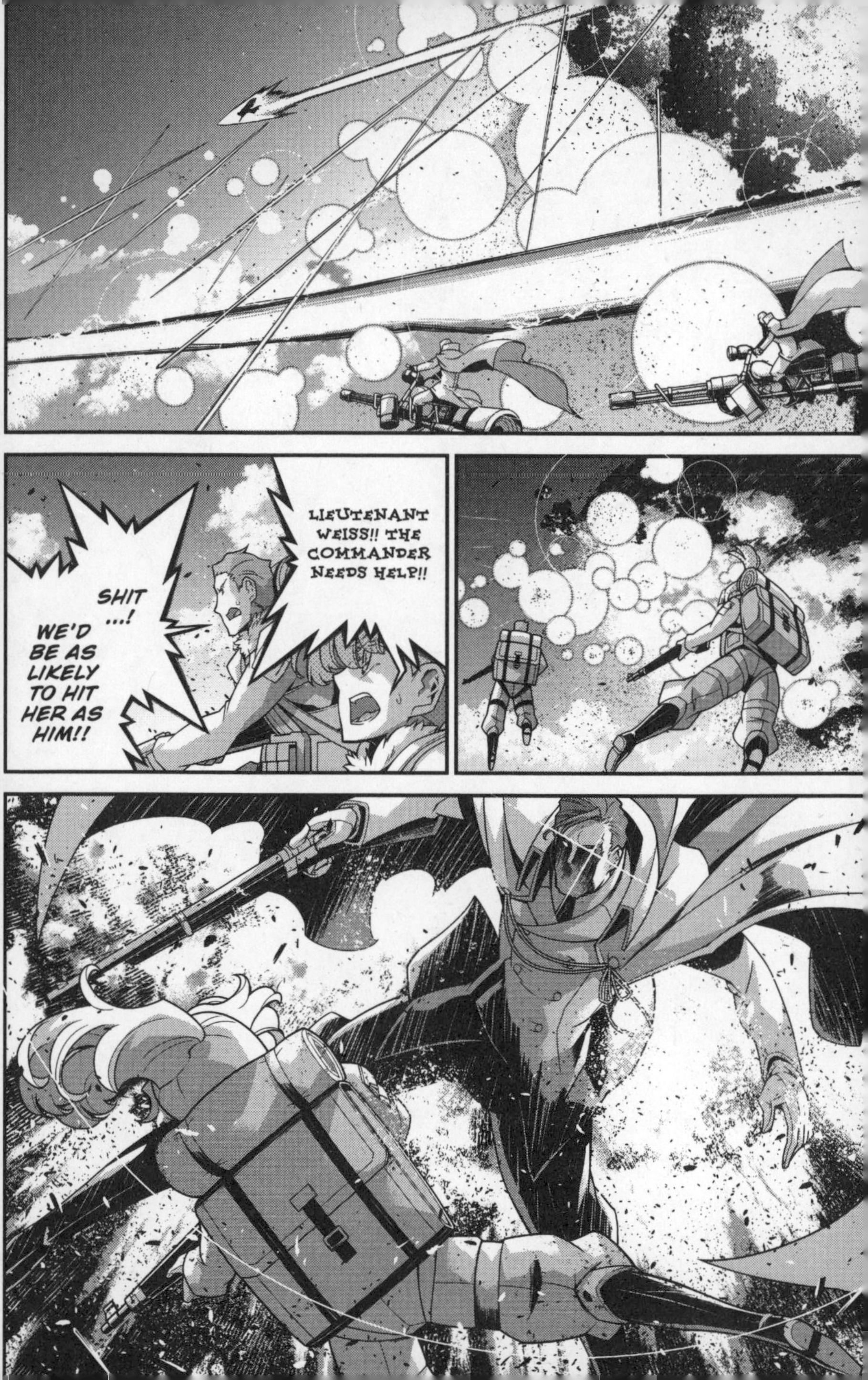
LIEUTENANT WEISS!! THE COMMANDER NEEDS HELP!!
SHIT ...!
WE'D BE AS LIKELY TO HIT HER AS HIM!!

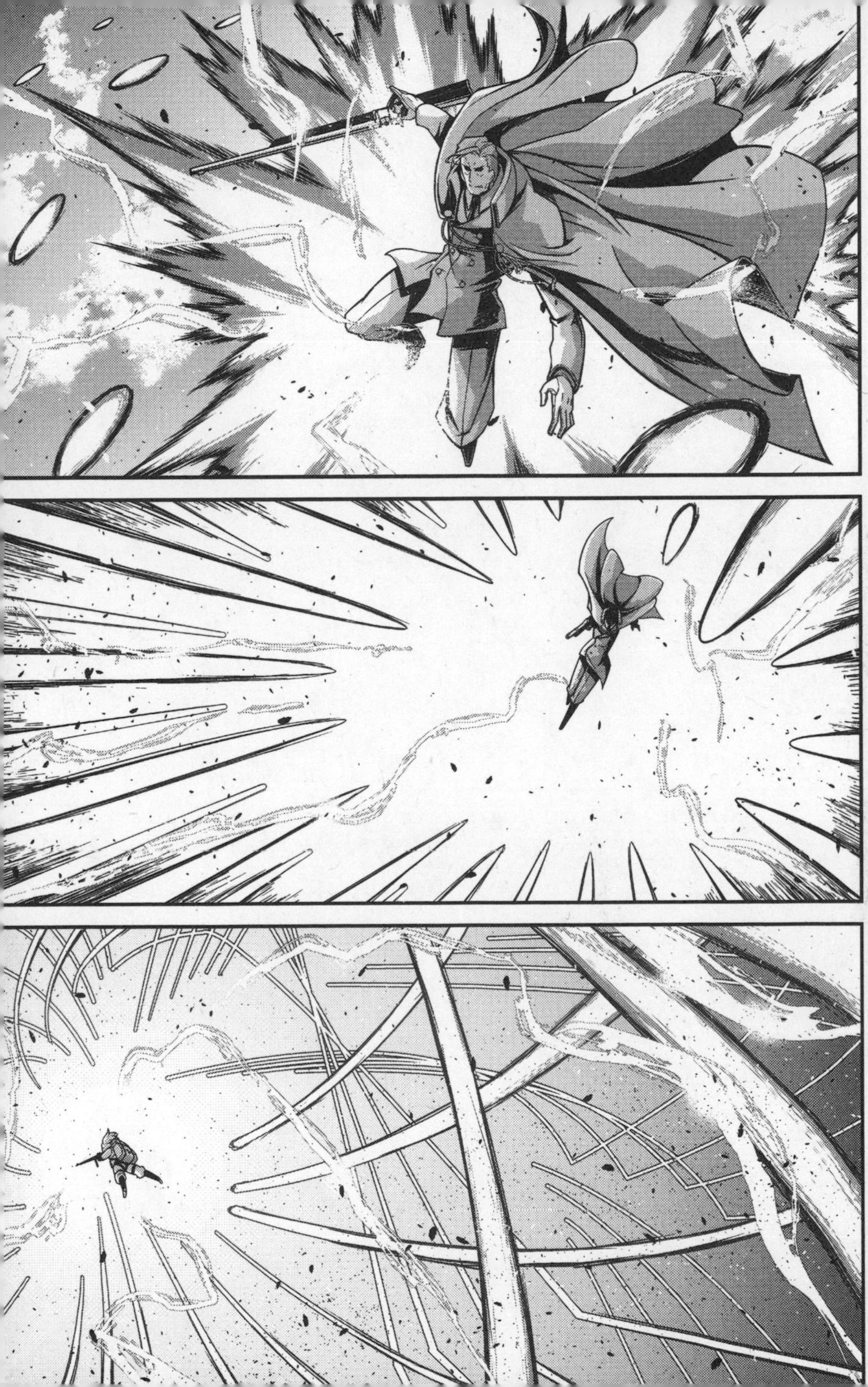

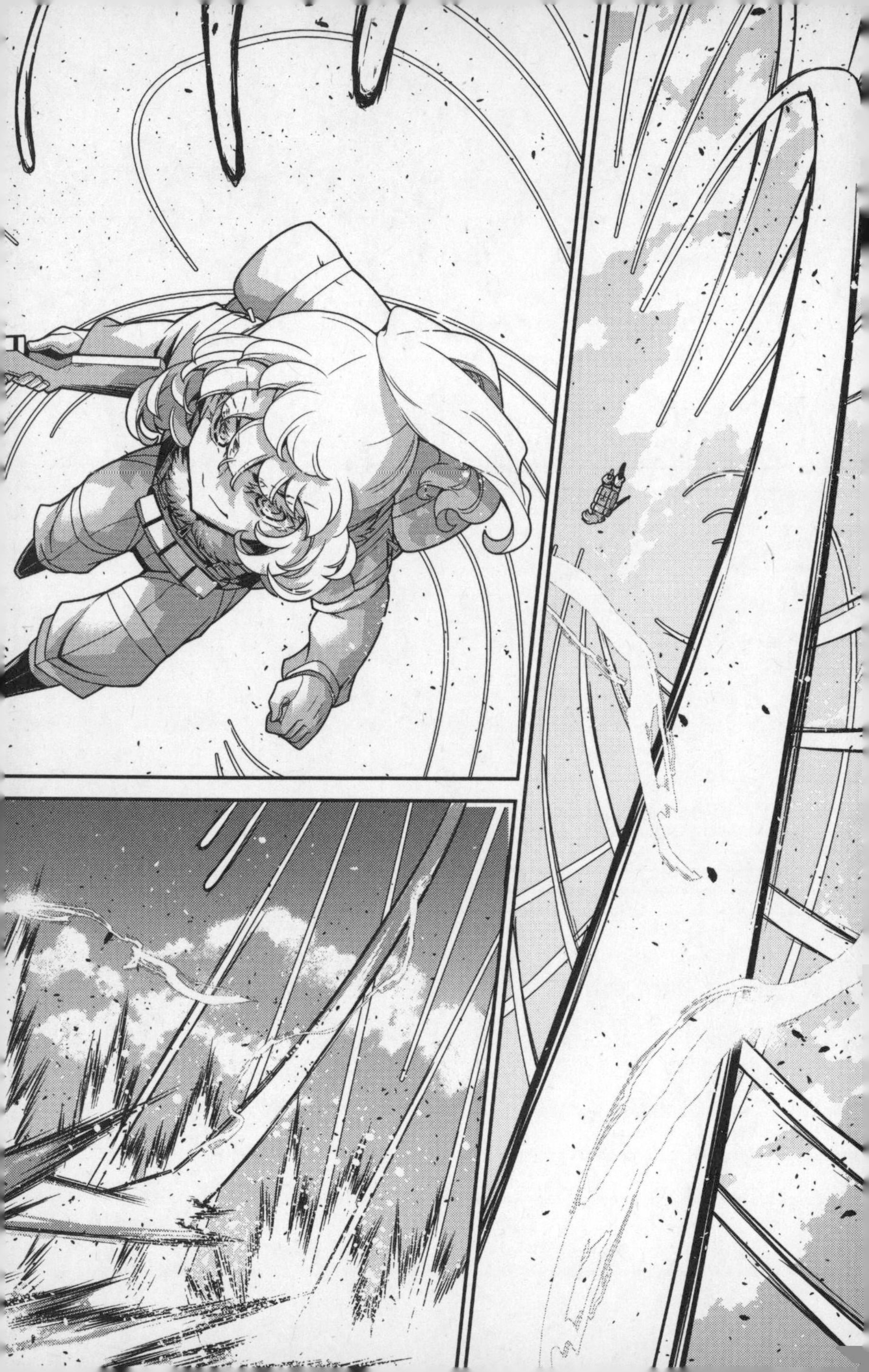

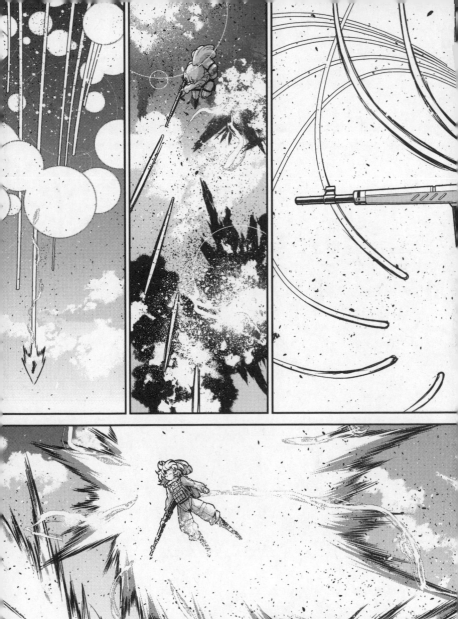
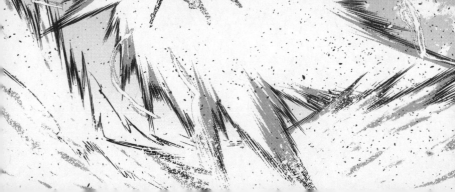

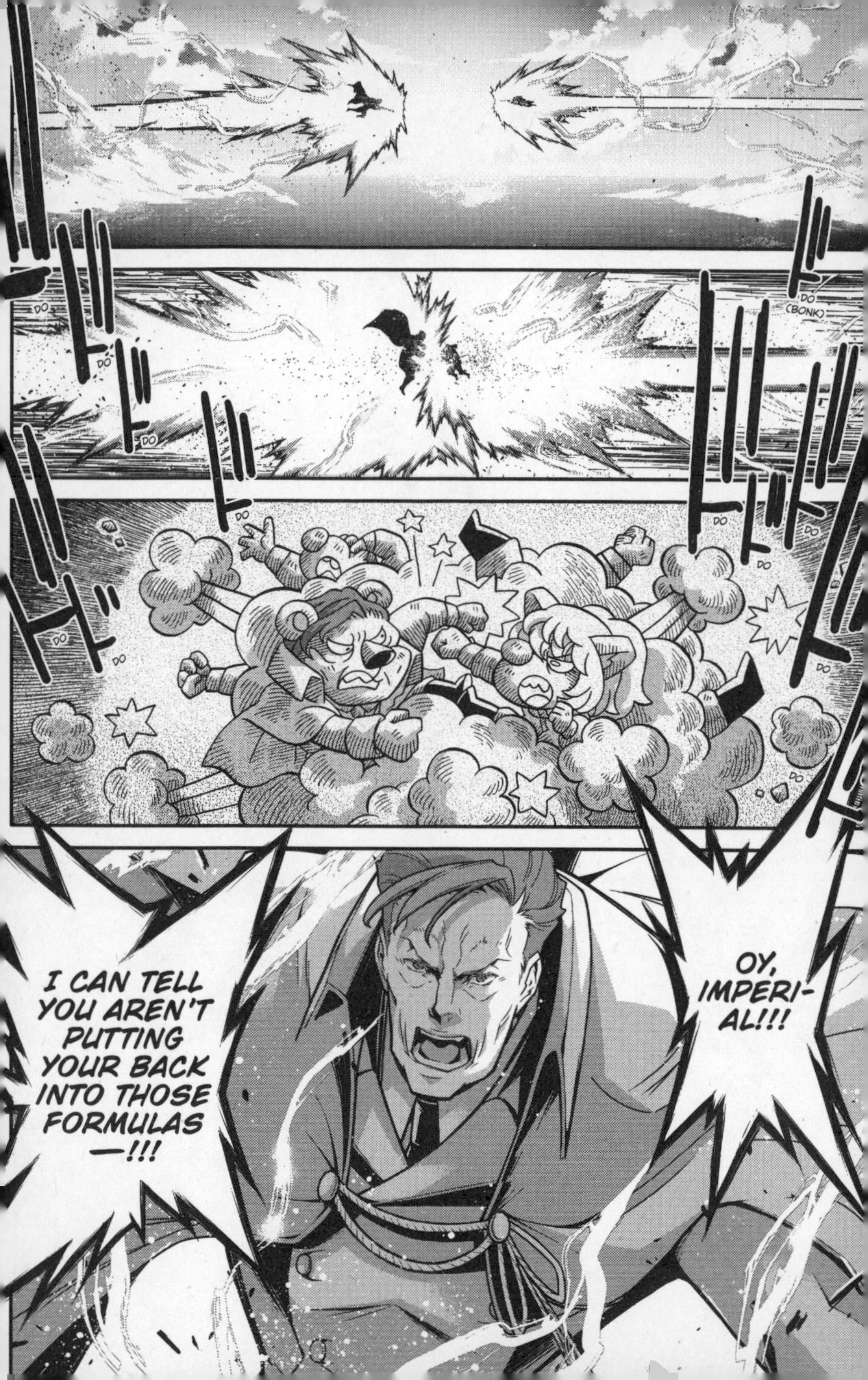
DO
(BONK)
DO
DO
DO
DO
DO
DO
DO
DO
DO
DO
DO
DO
OY, IMPERI-AL!!!
I CAN TELL YOU AREN'T PUTTING YOUR BACK INTO THOSE FORMULAS—!!!

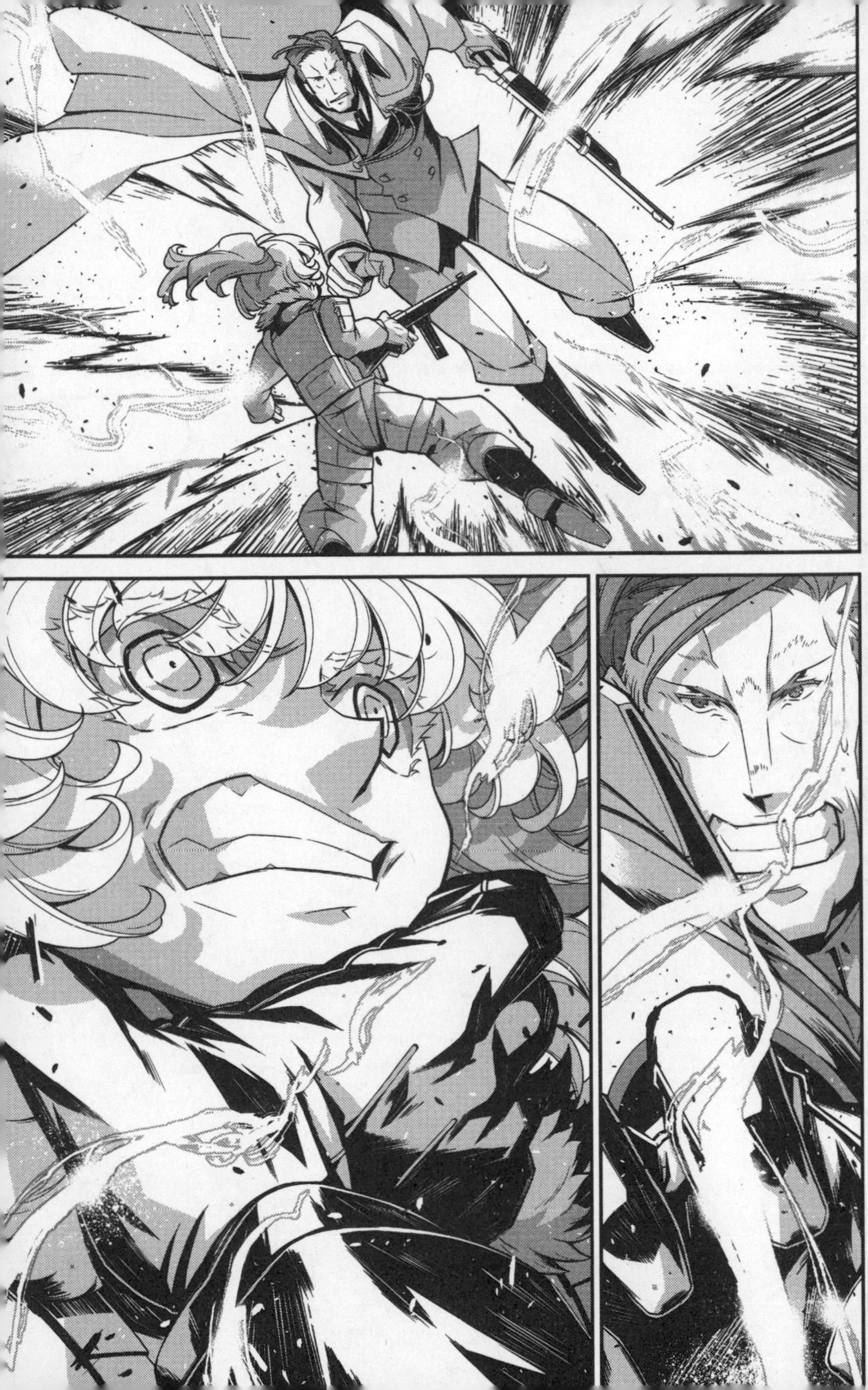

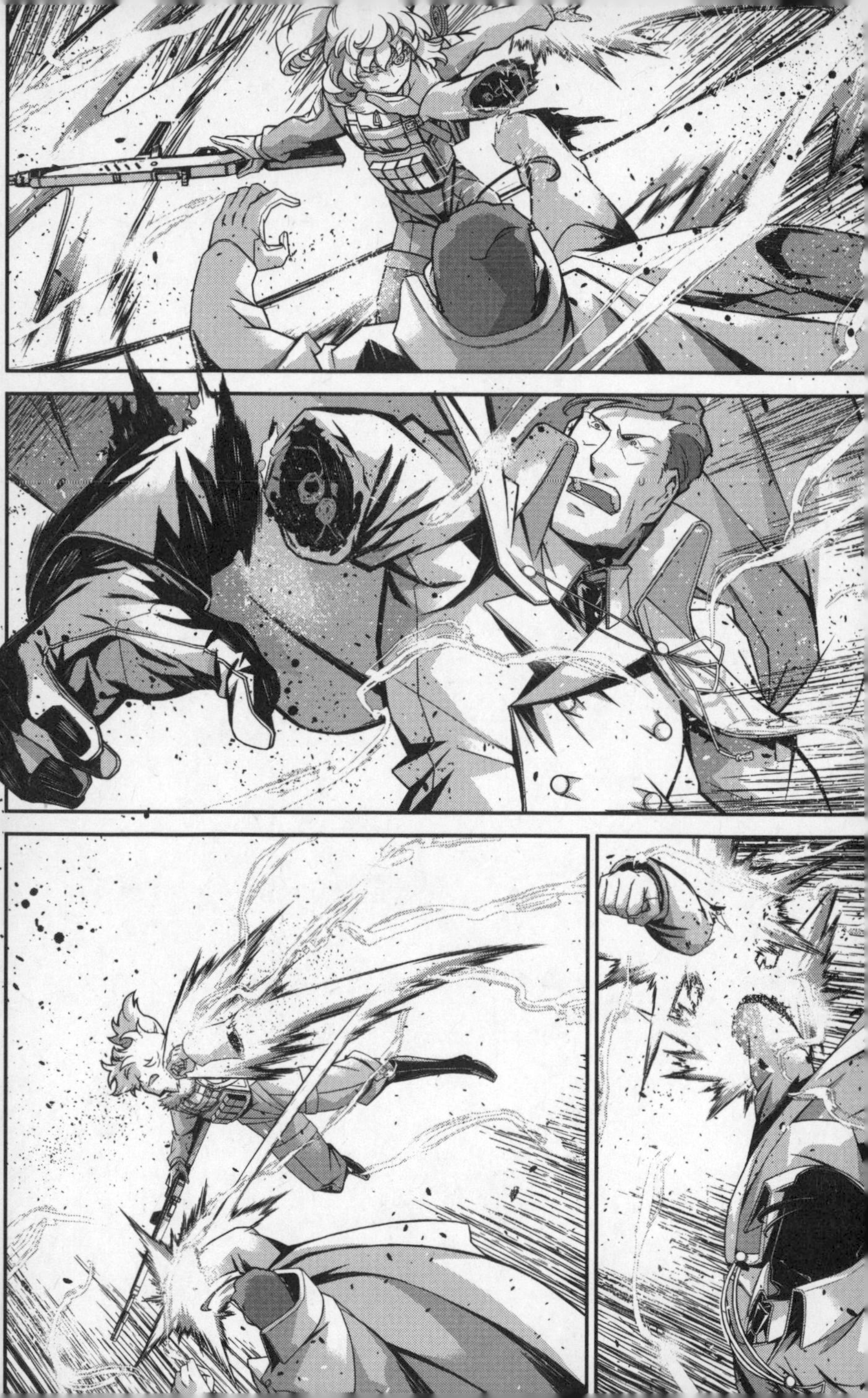

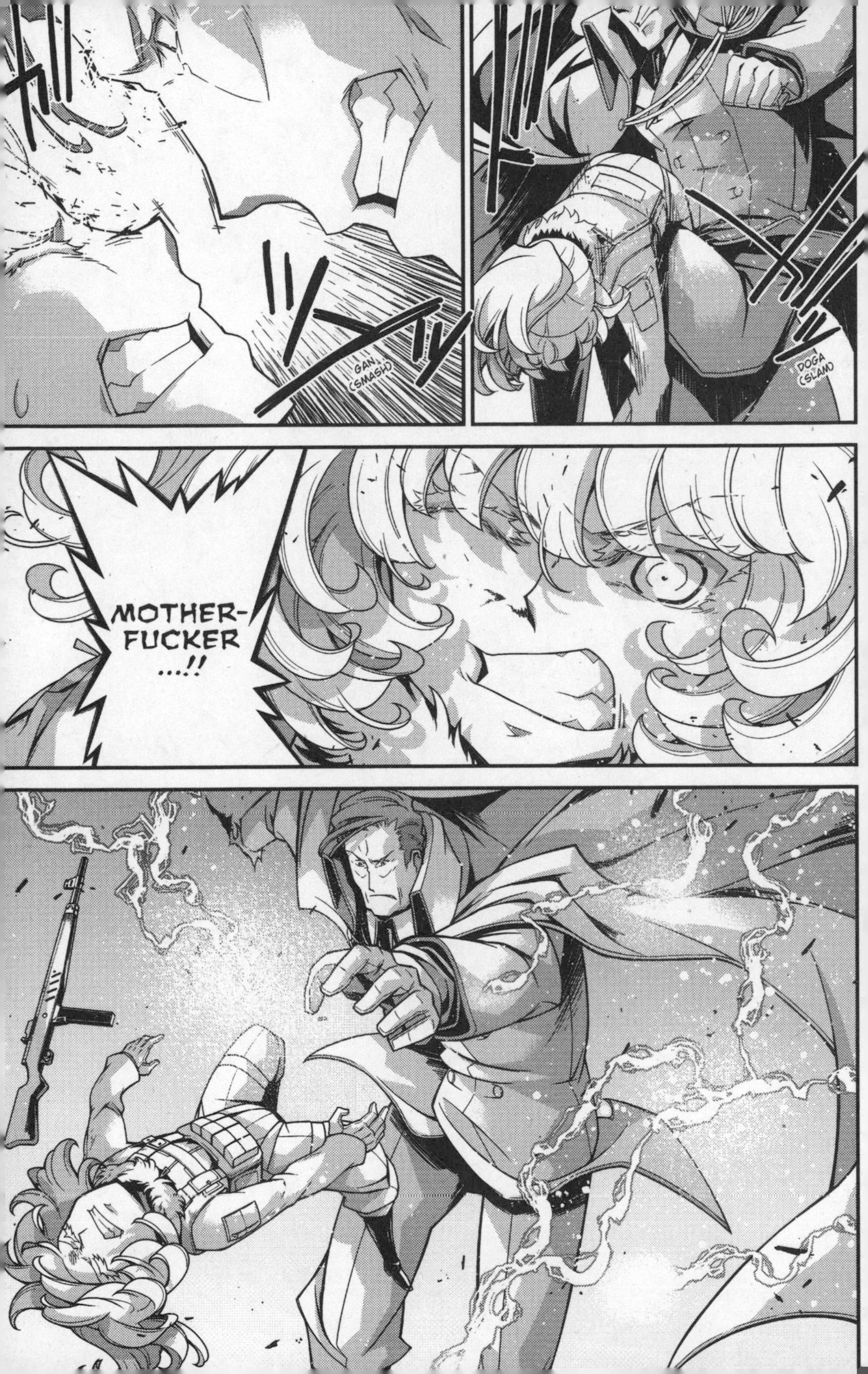
DOGA (SLAM)
GAN (SMASH)
MOTHER-FUCKER ...!!

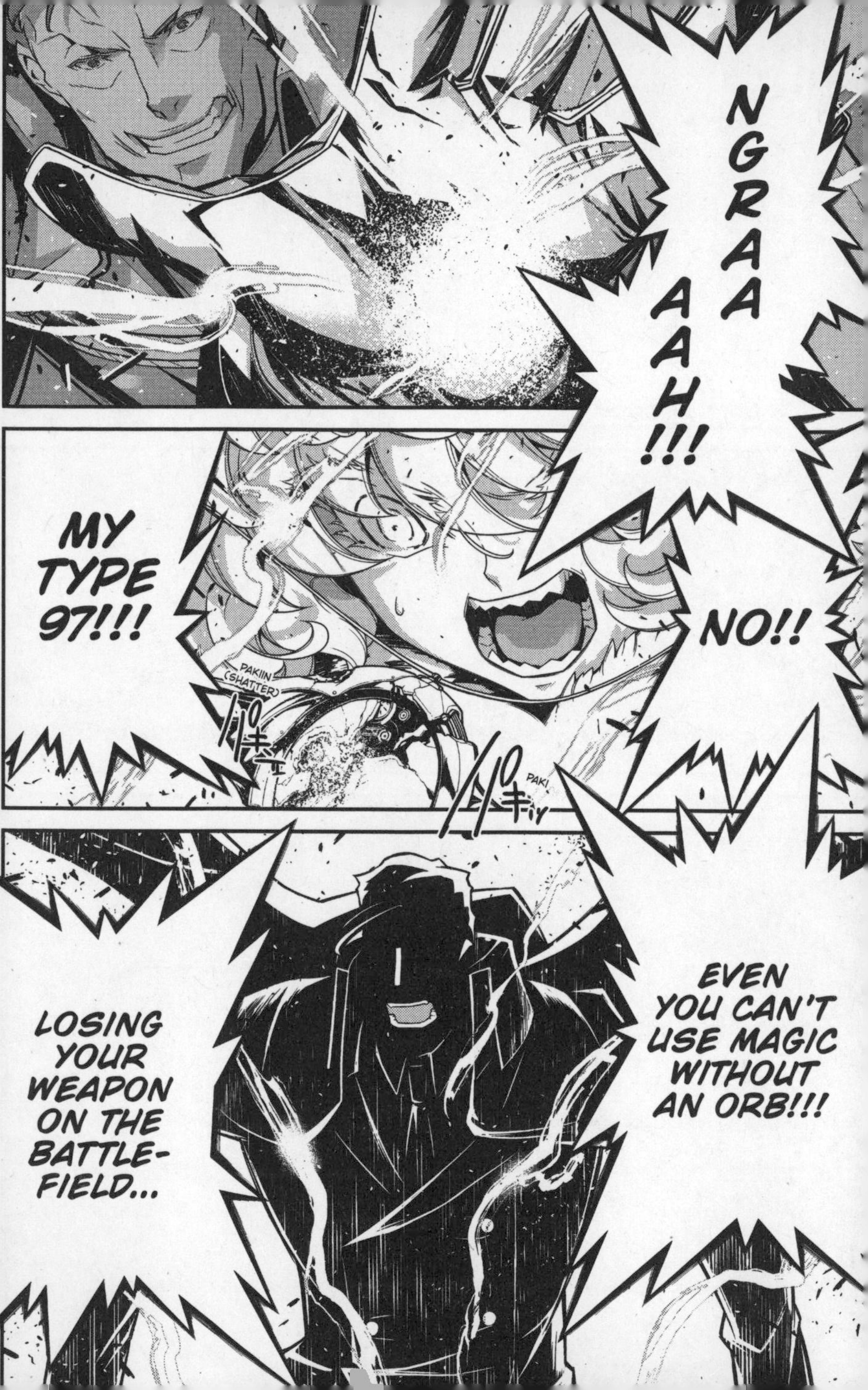
NGRAAAAH!!!
NO!!
MY TYPE 97!!!
PAKIIN (SHATTER)
PAKI
EVEN YOU CAN'T USE MAGIC WITHOUT AN ORB!!!
LOSING YOUR WEAPON ON THE BATTLE-FIELD...

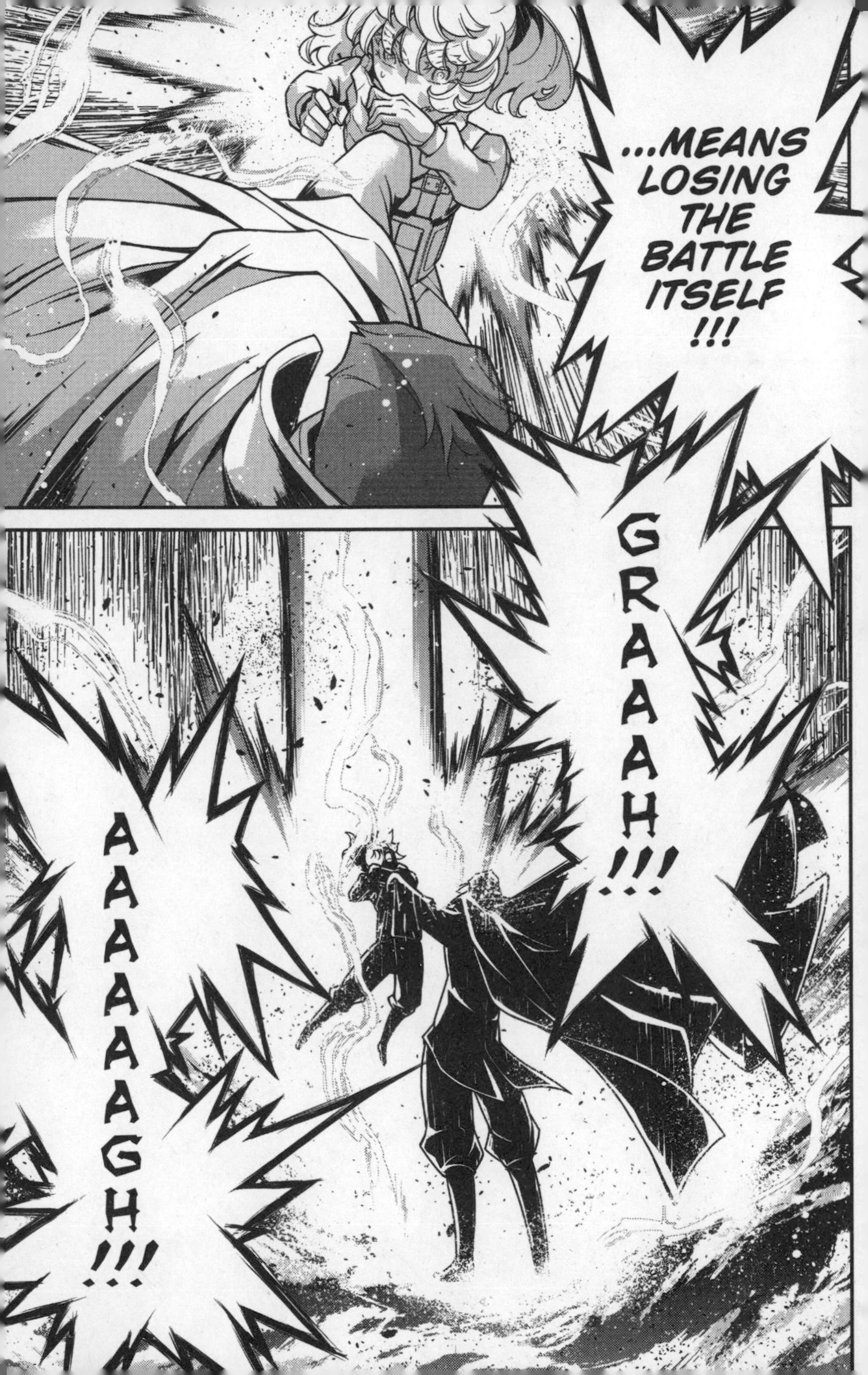
...MEANS LOSING THE BATTLE ITSELF!!!
GRAAAH!!!
AAAAAAGH!!!

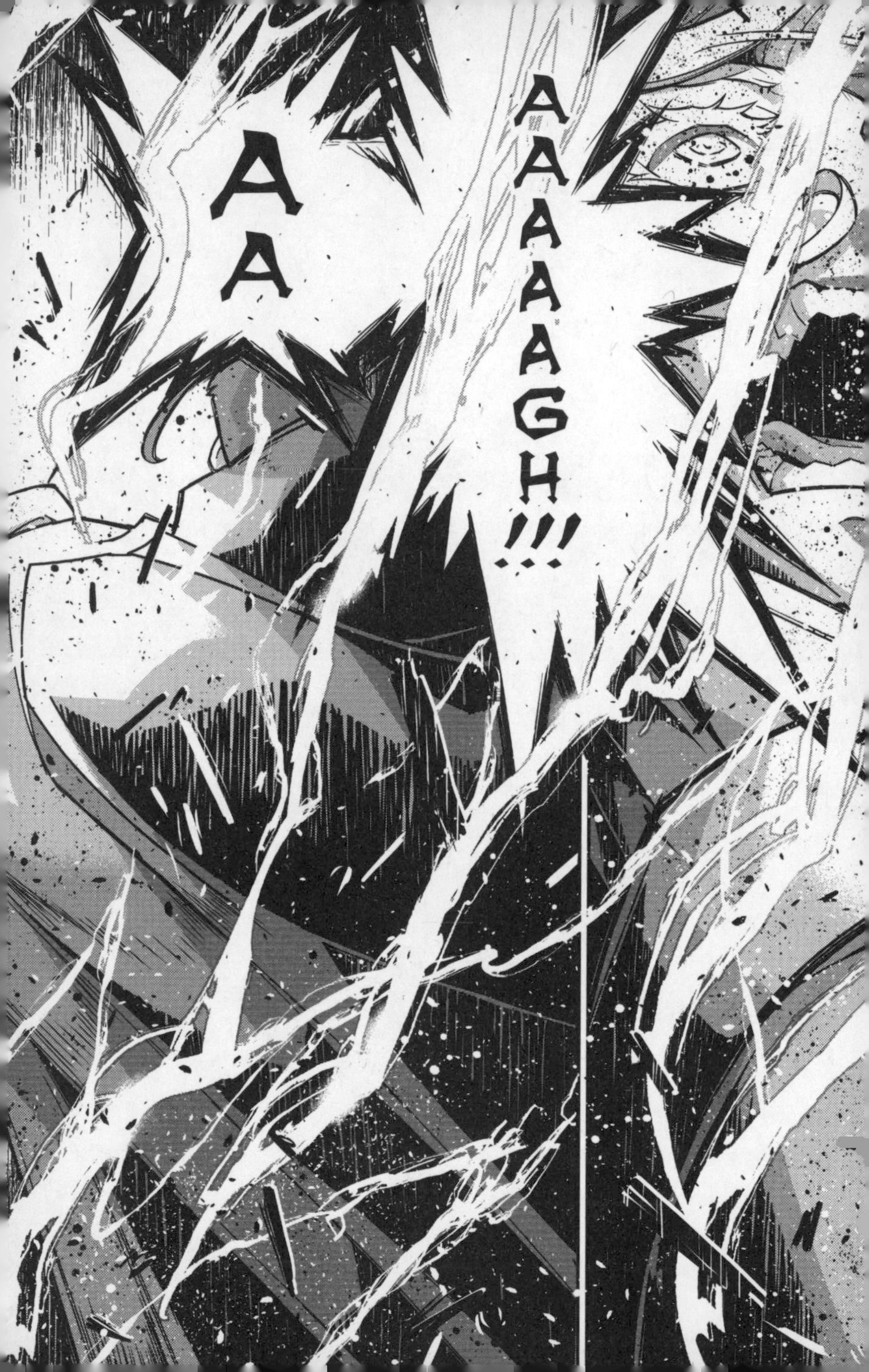
AA
AAAAAAGH!!!

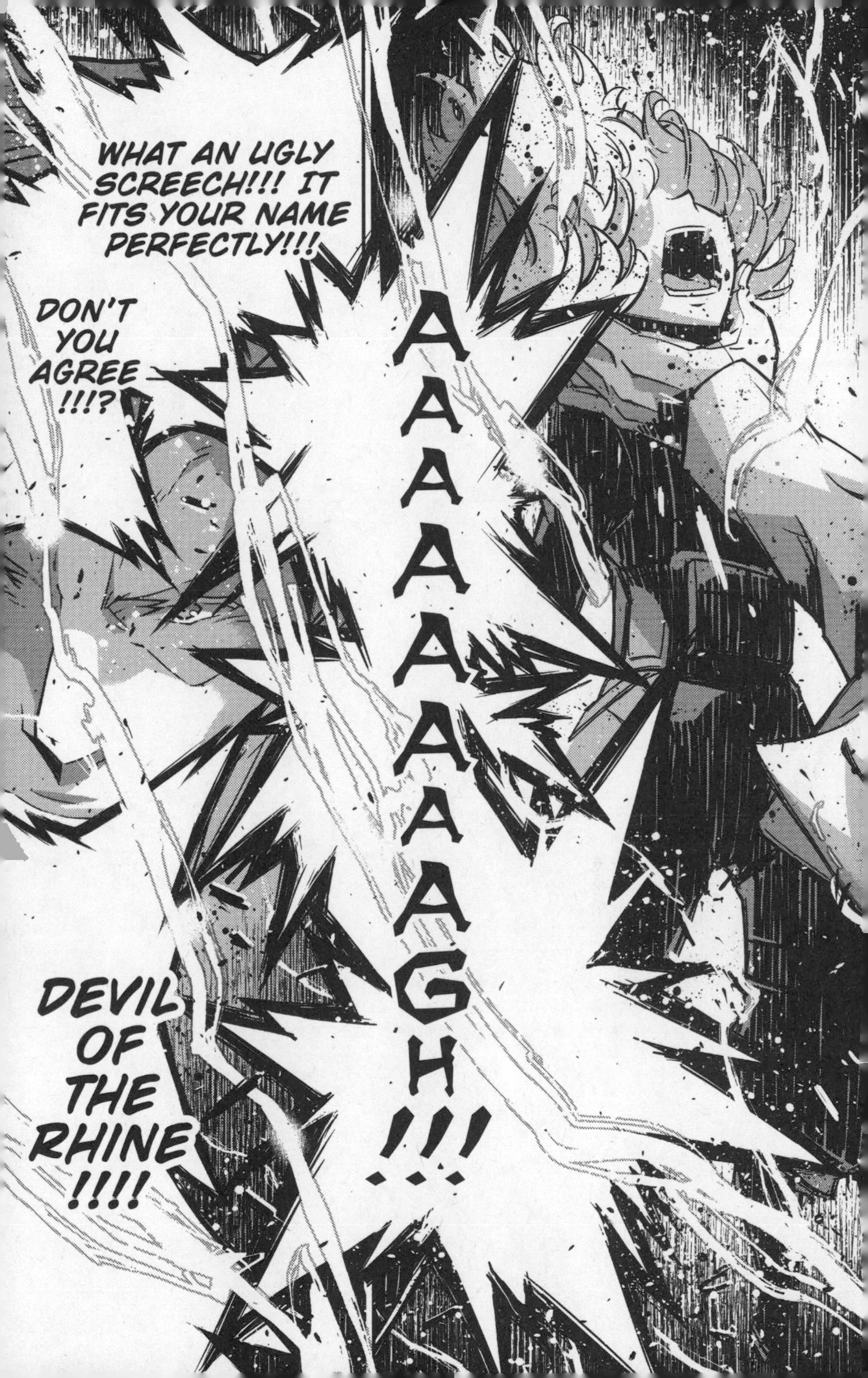
WHAT AN UGLY SCREECH!!! IT FITS YOUR NAME PERFECTLY!!!
DON'T YOU AGREE !!!?
AAAAAAAGH!!!
DEVIL OF THE RHINE!!!!

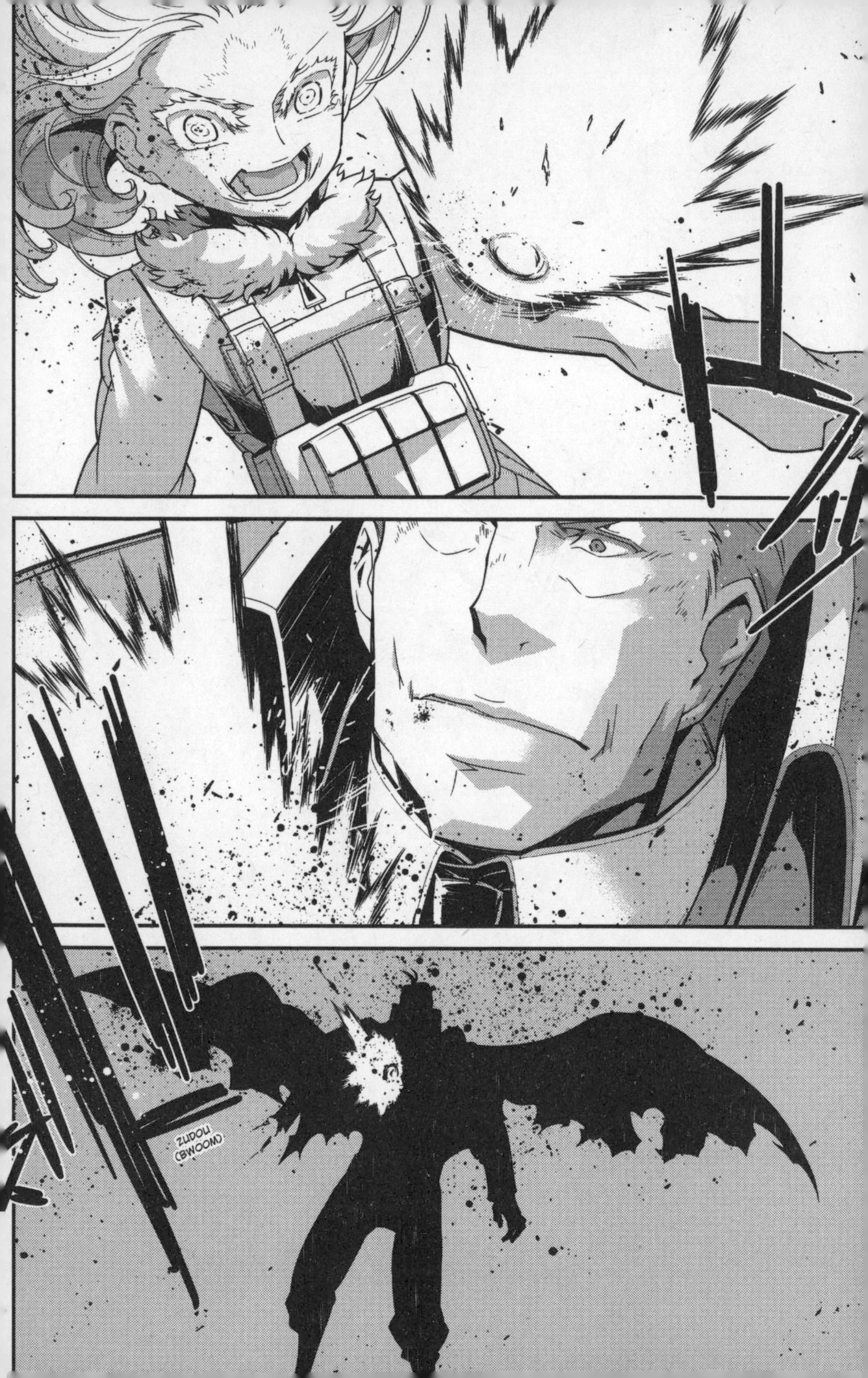
ZUDOU
(BWOOM)

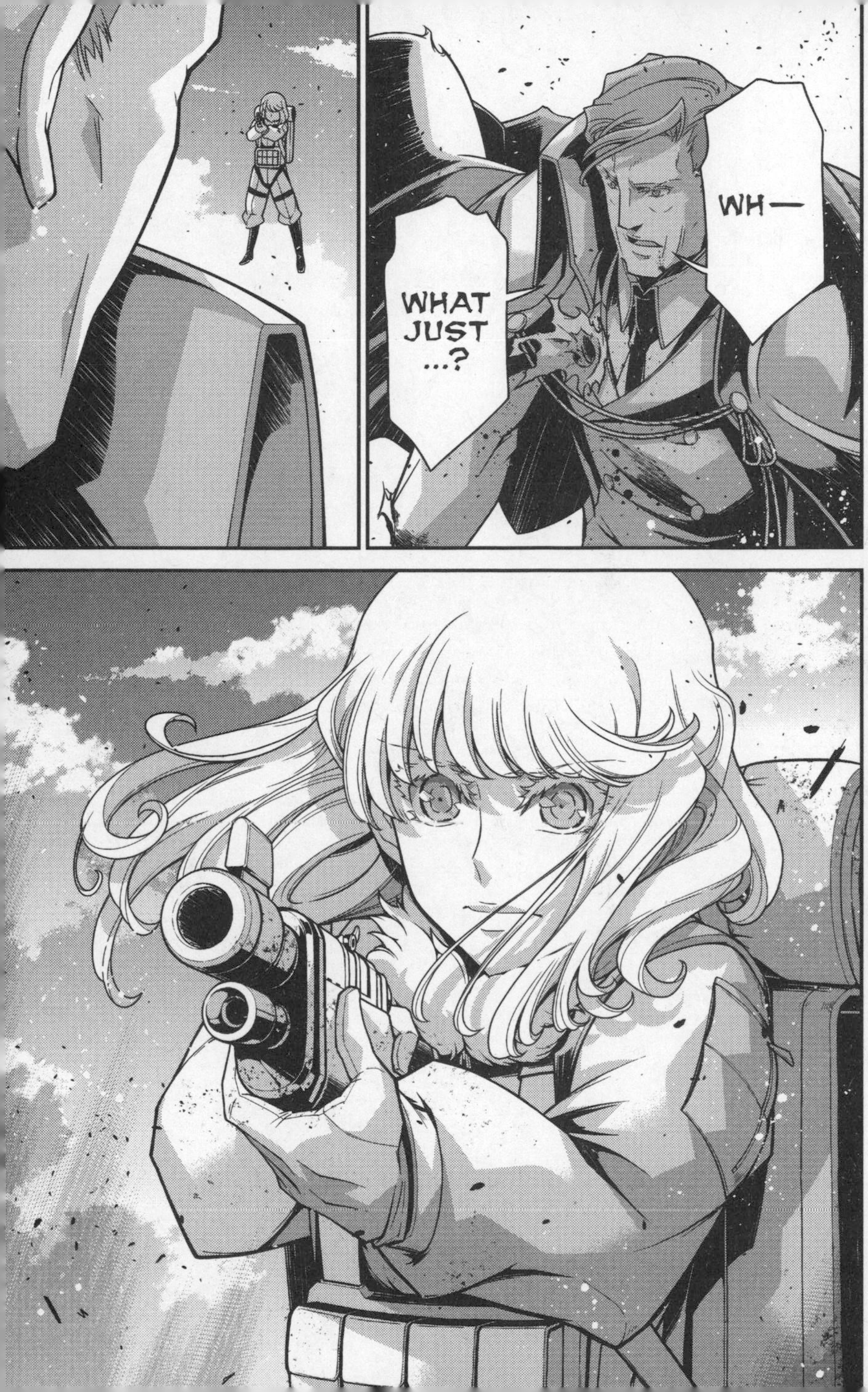
WH—
WHAT JUST ...?

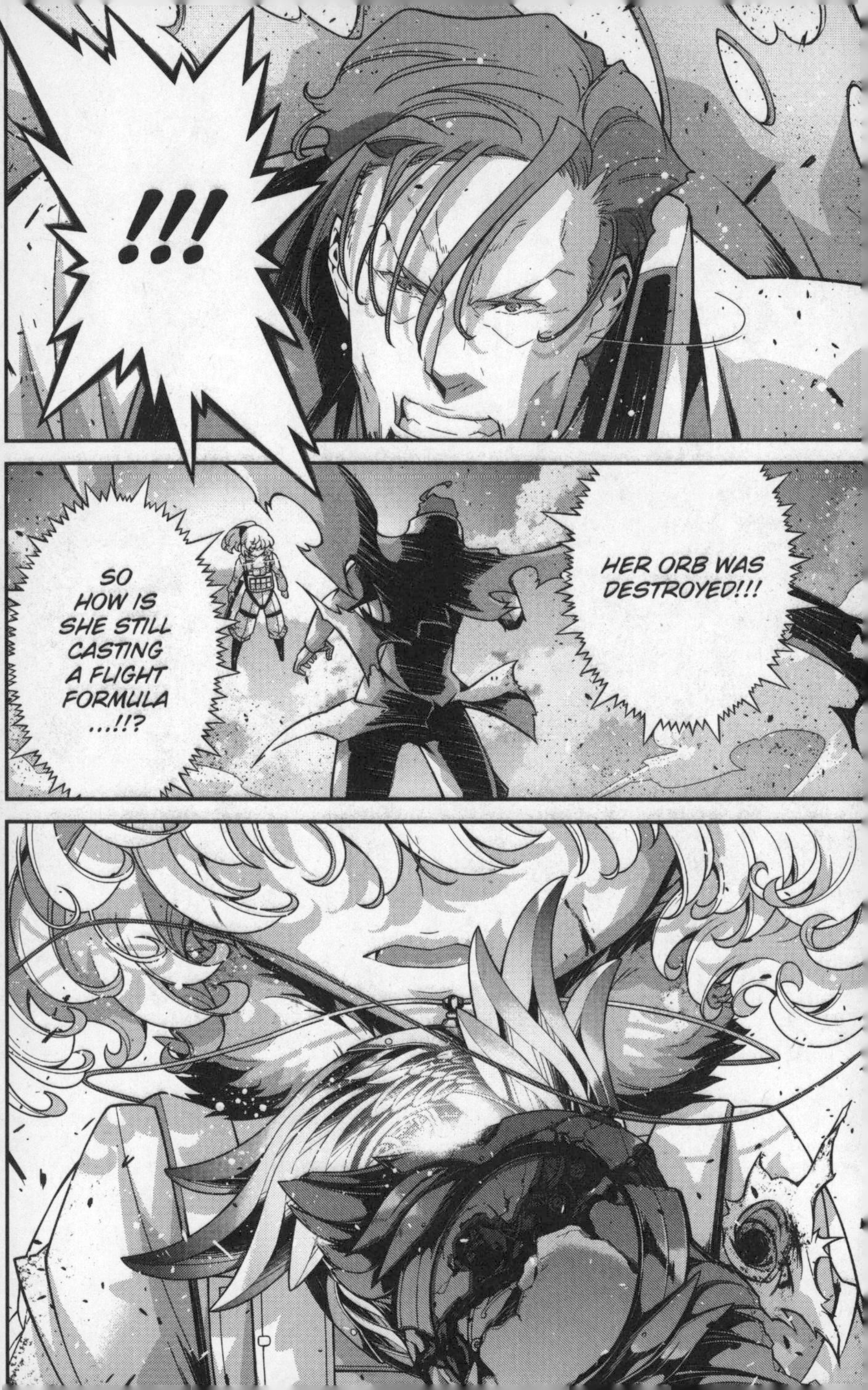
!!!
HER ORB WAS DESTROYED!!!
SO HOW IS SHE STILL CASTING A FLIGHT FORMULA ...!!?

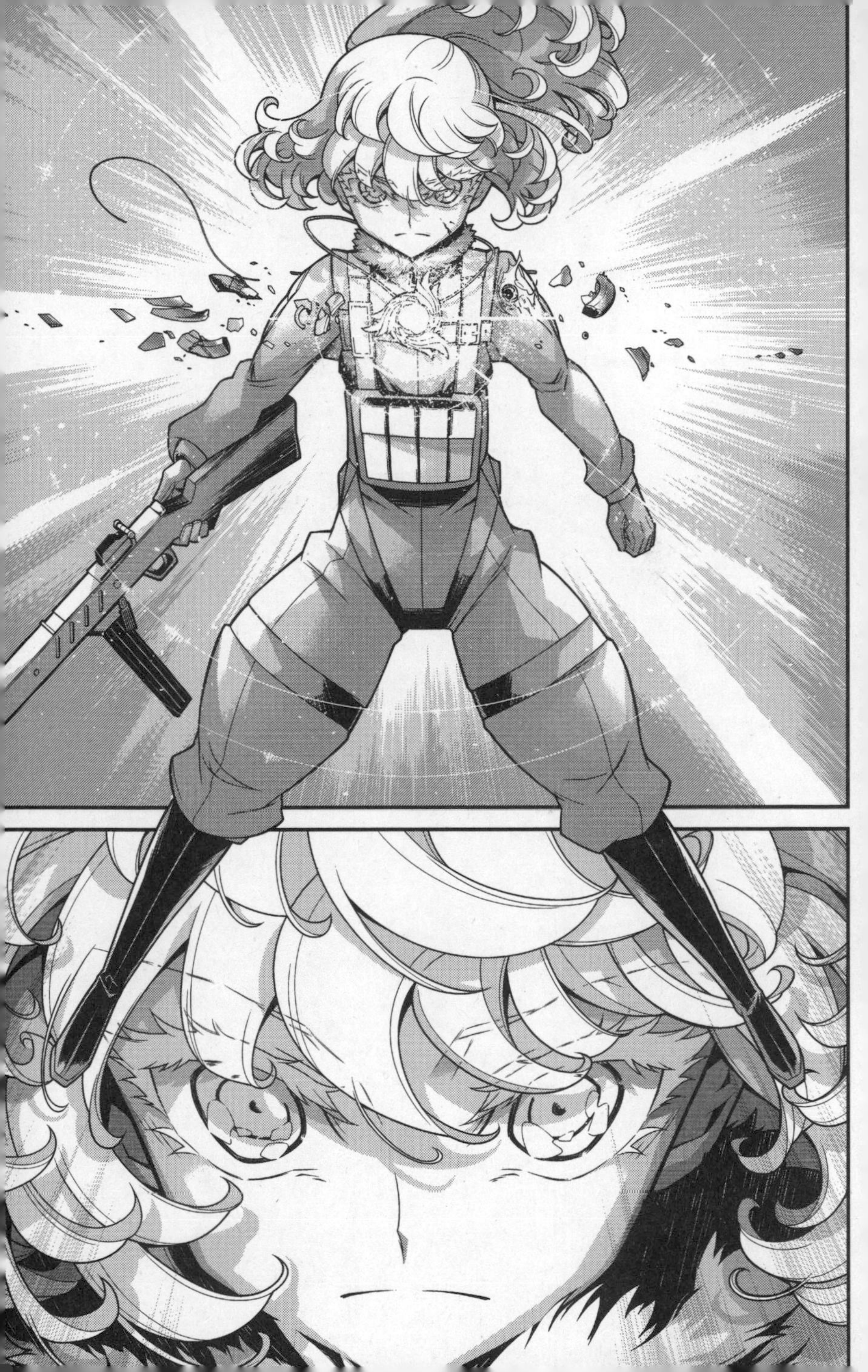

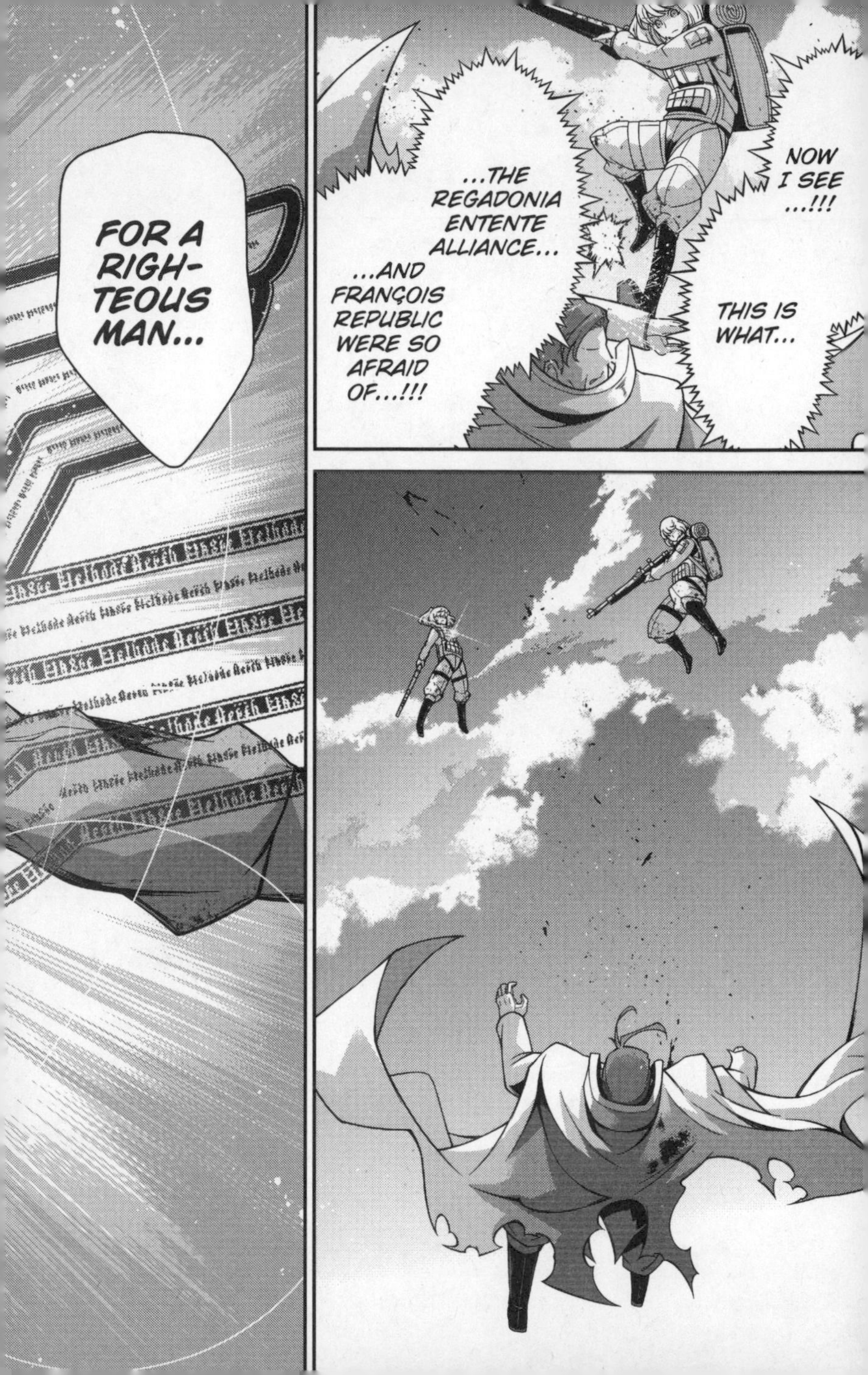
NOW I SEE ...!!!
THIS IS WHAT...
...THE REGADONIA ENTENTE ALLIANCE...
...AND FRANÇOIS REPUBLIC WERE SO AFRAID OF...!!!
FOR A RIGH-TEOUS MAN...

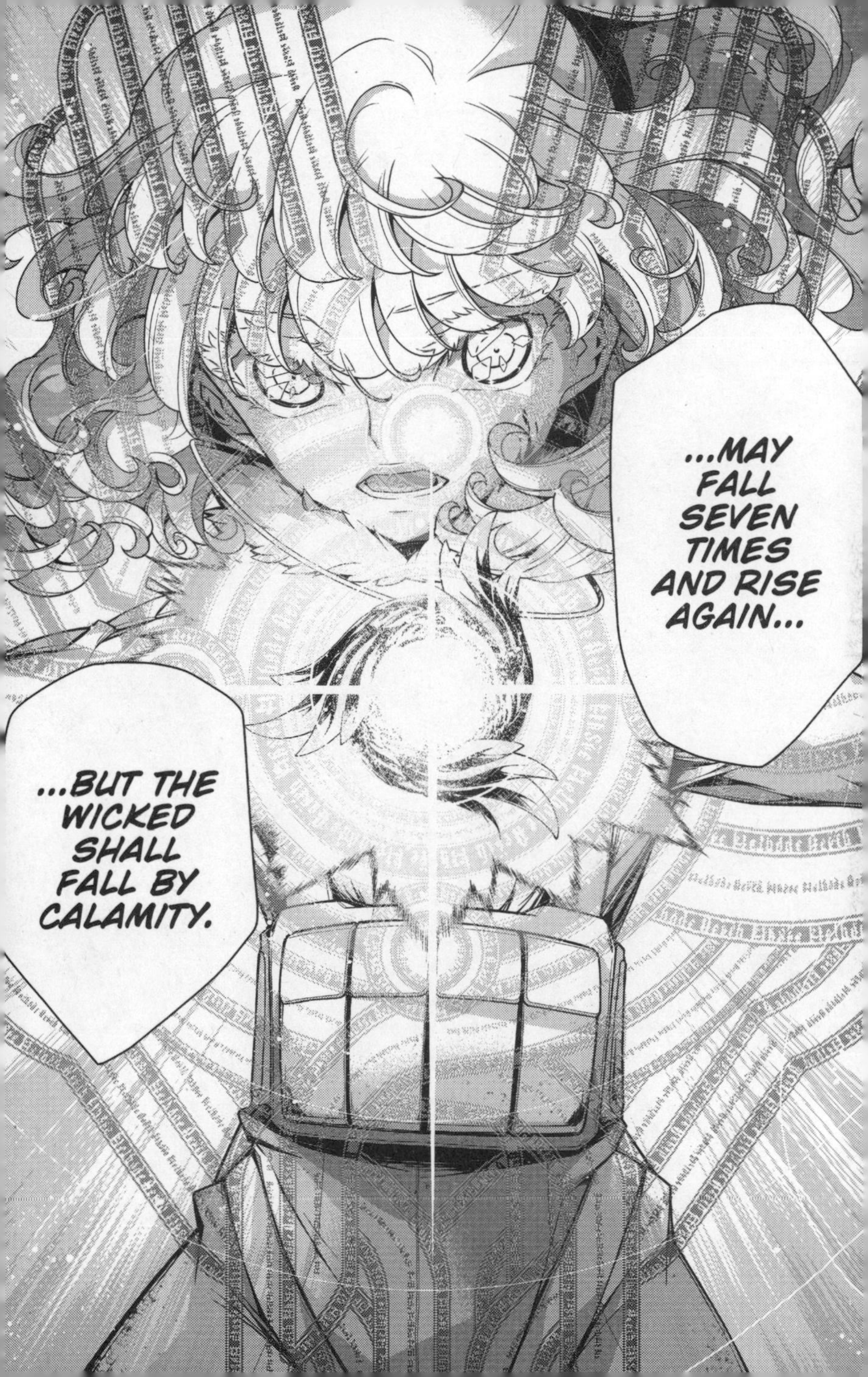
...MAY FALL SEVEN TIMES AND RISE AGAIN...
...BUT THE WICKED SHALL FALL BY CALAMITY.

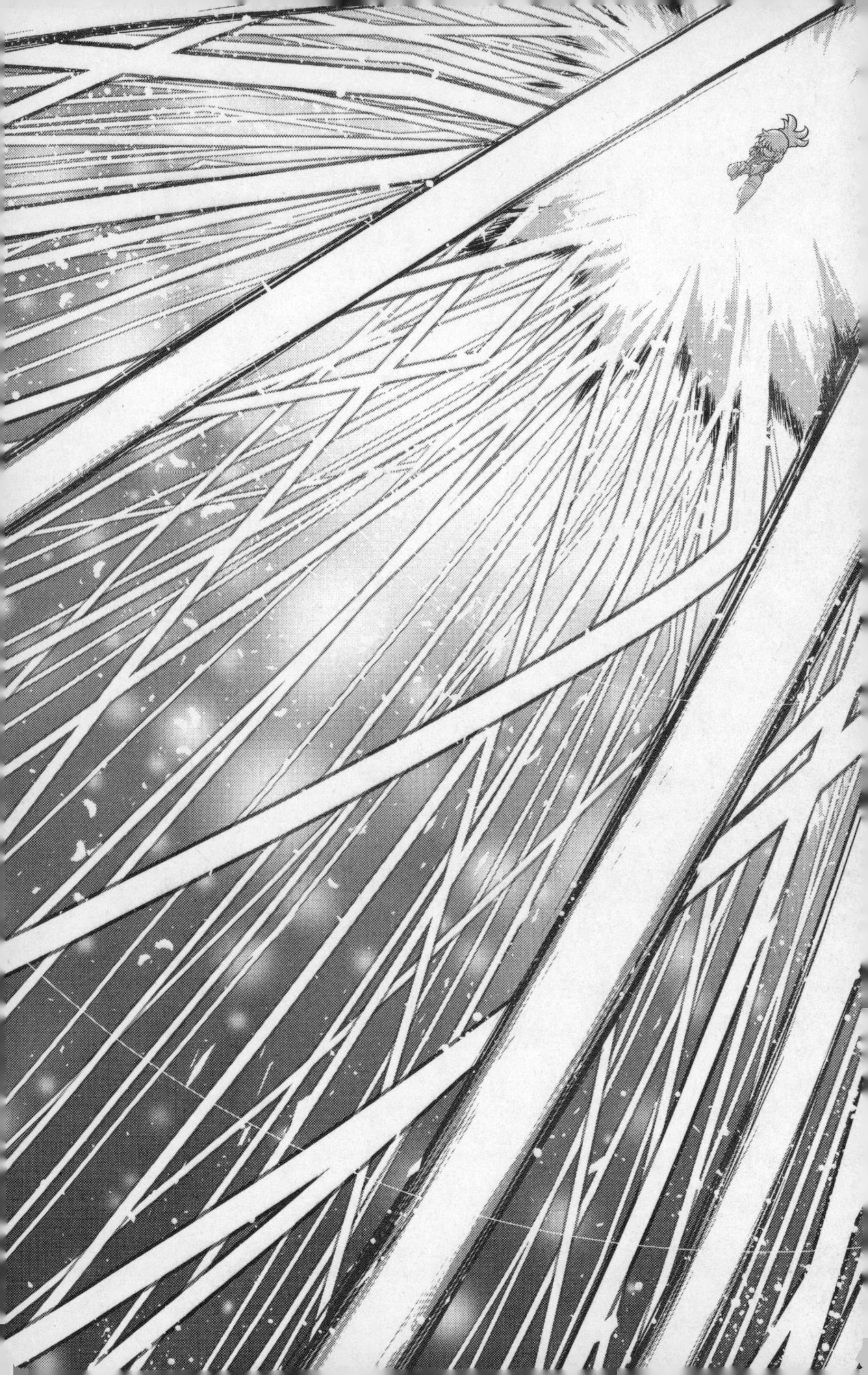

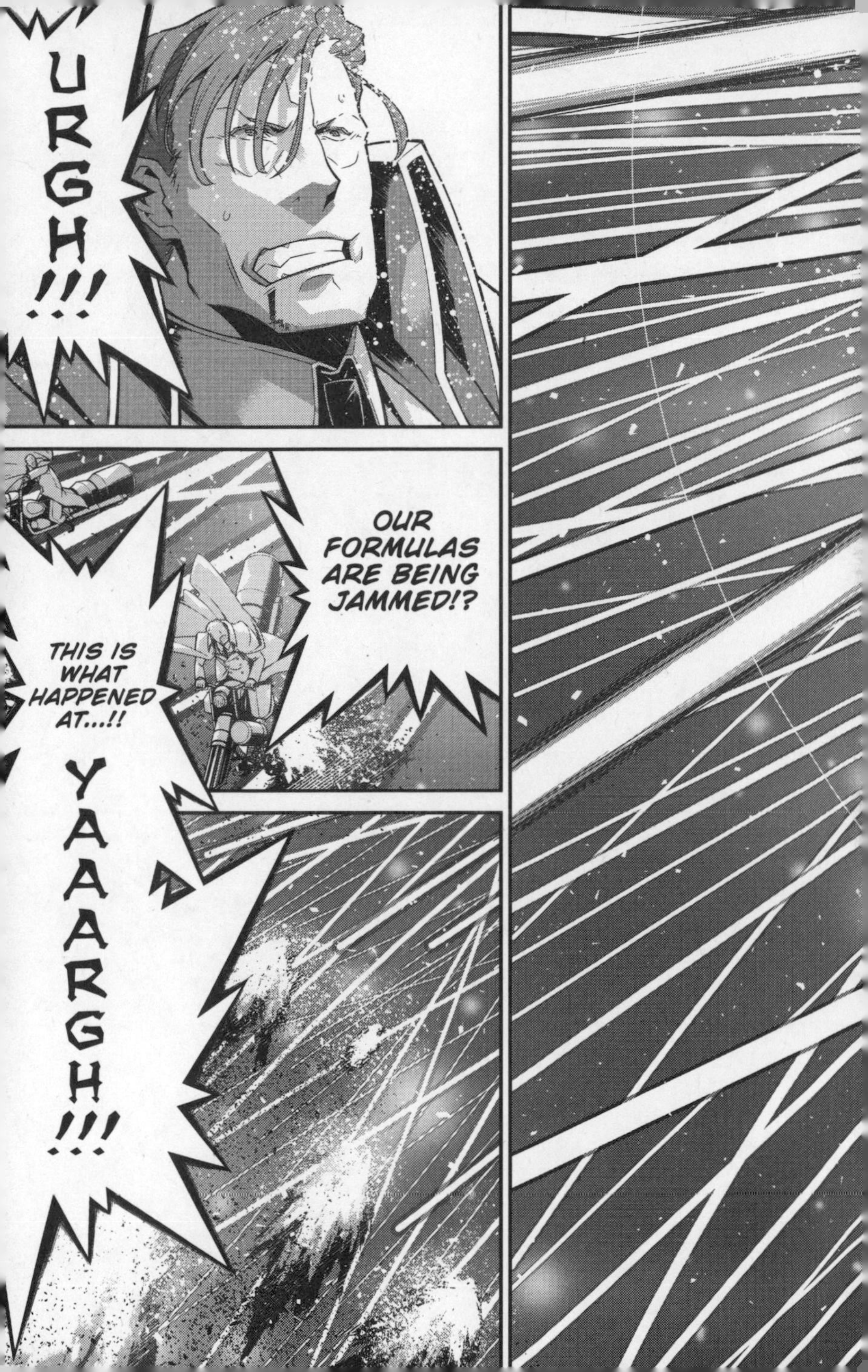
URGH!!!
OUR FORMULAS ARE BEING JAMMED!?
THIS IS WHAT HAPPENED AT...!!
YAAARGH!!!

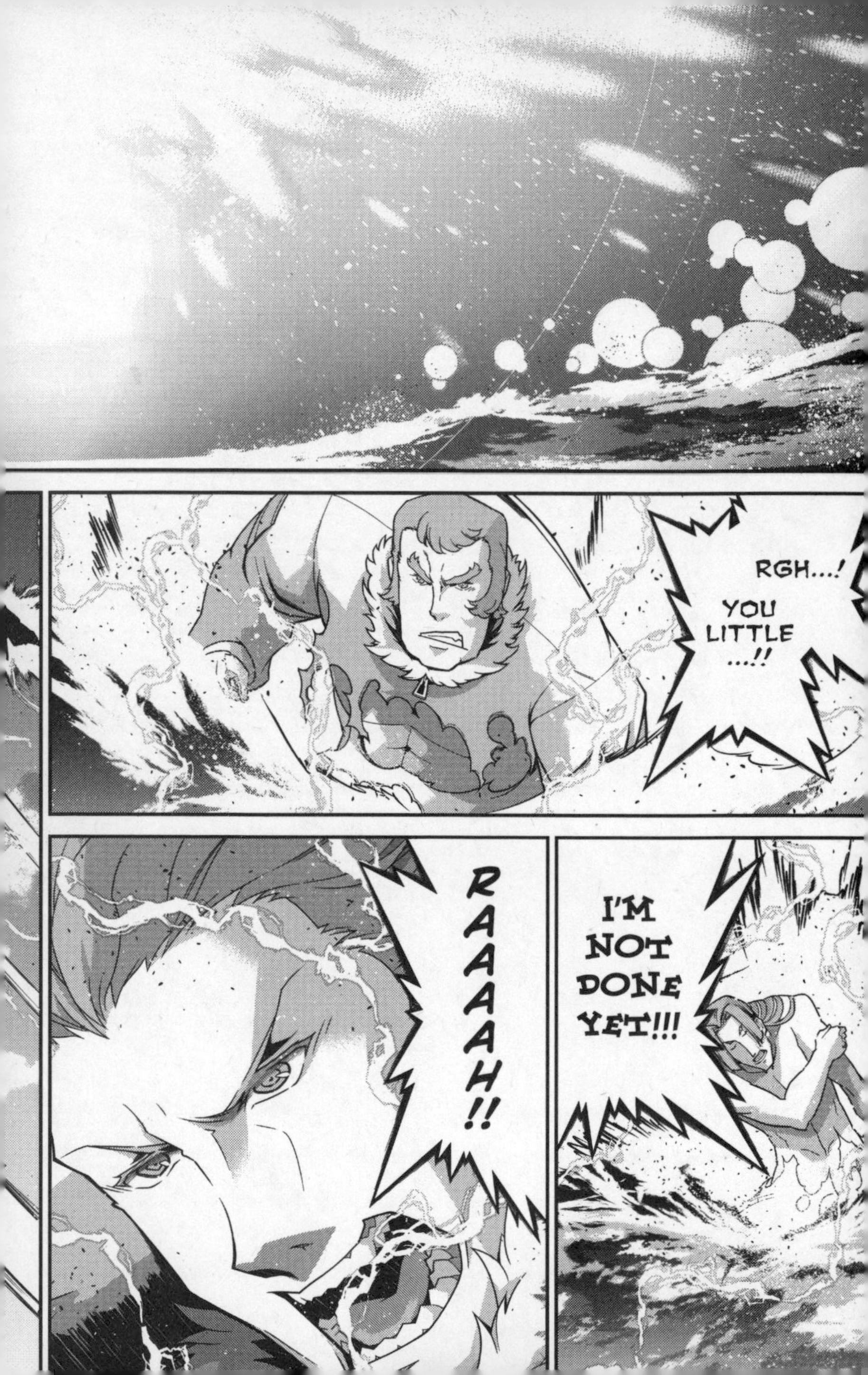
RGH...! YOU LITTLE ...!!
I'M NOT DONE YET!!!
RAAAAAH!!

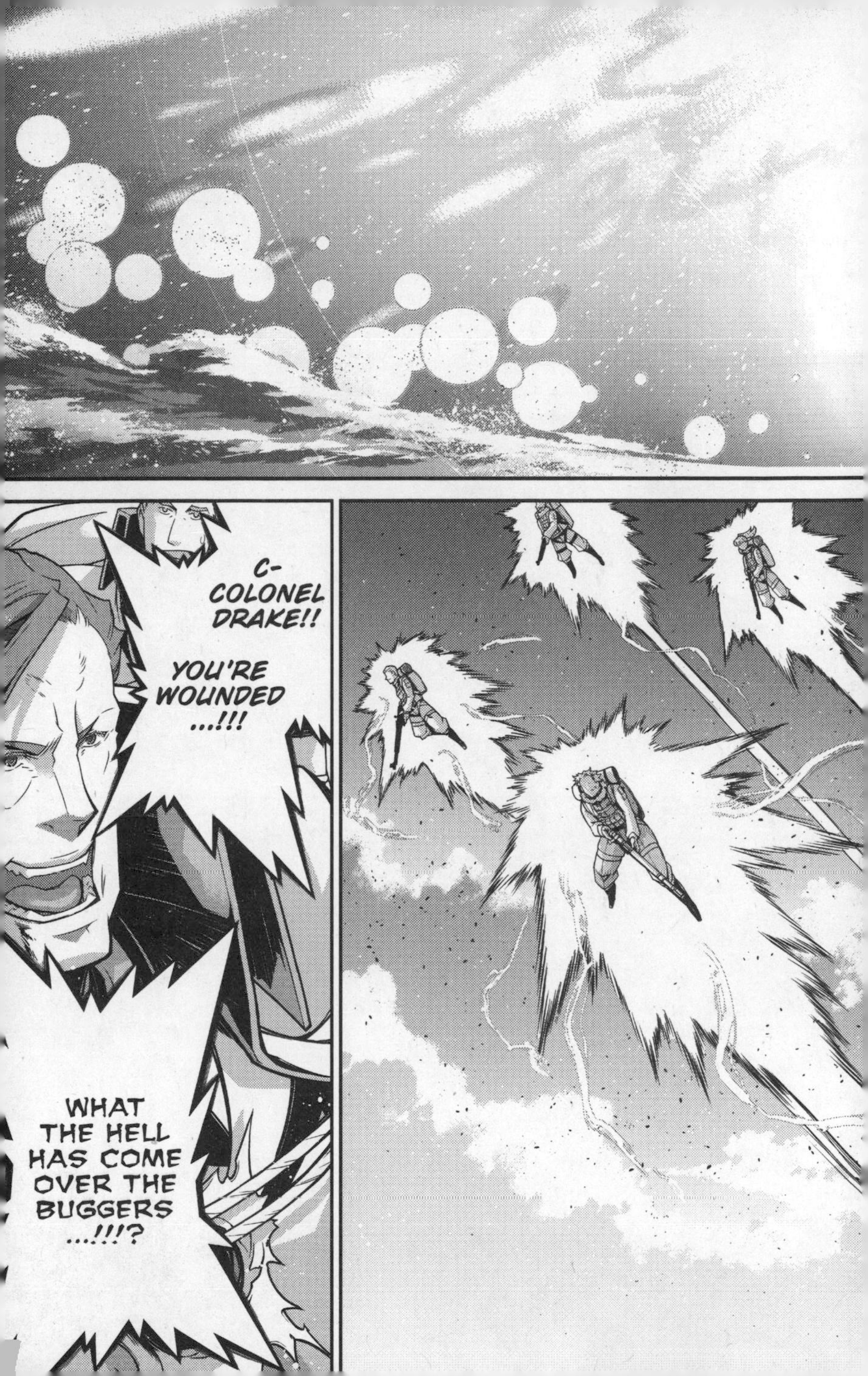
C-COLONEL DRAKE!!
YOU'RE WOUNDED ...!!!
WHAT THE HELL HAS COME OVER THE BUGGERS ...!!!?

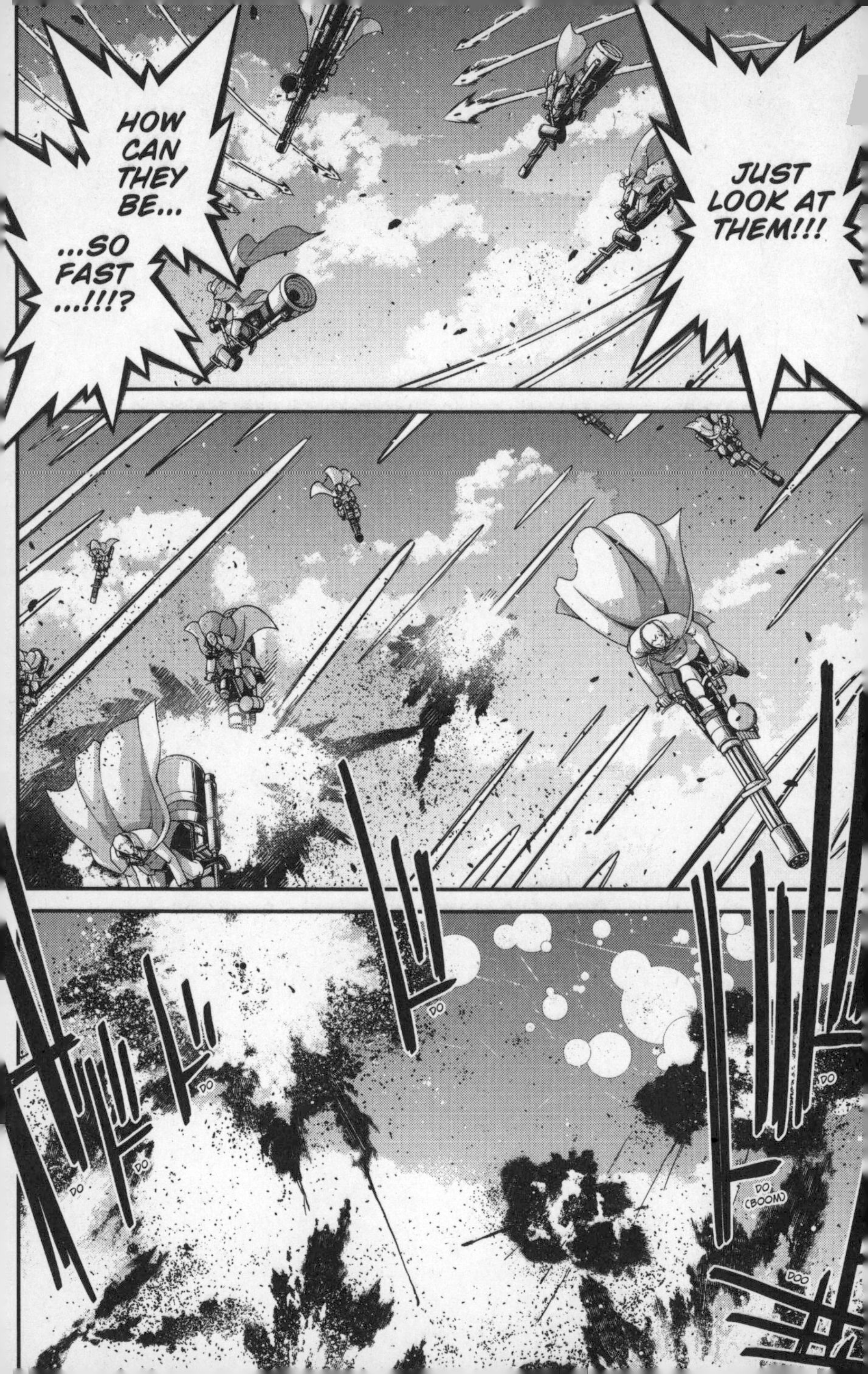
JUST LOOK AT THEM!!!
HOW CAN THEY BE... ...SO FAST ...!!!?
DO
DO
DO
DO
DO
DO (BOOM)
DOO

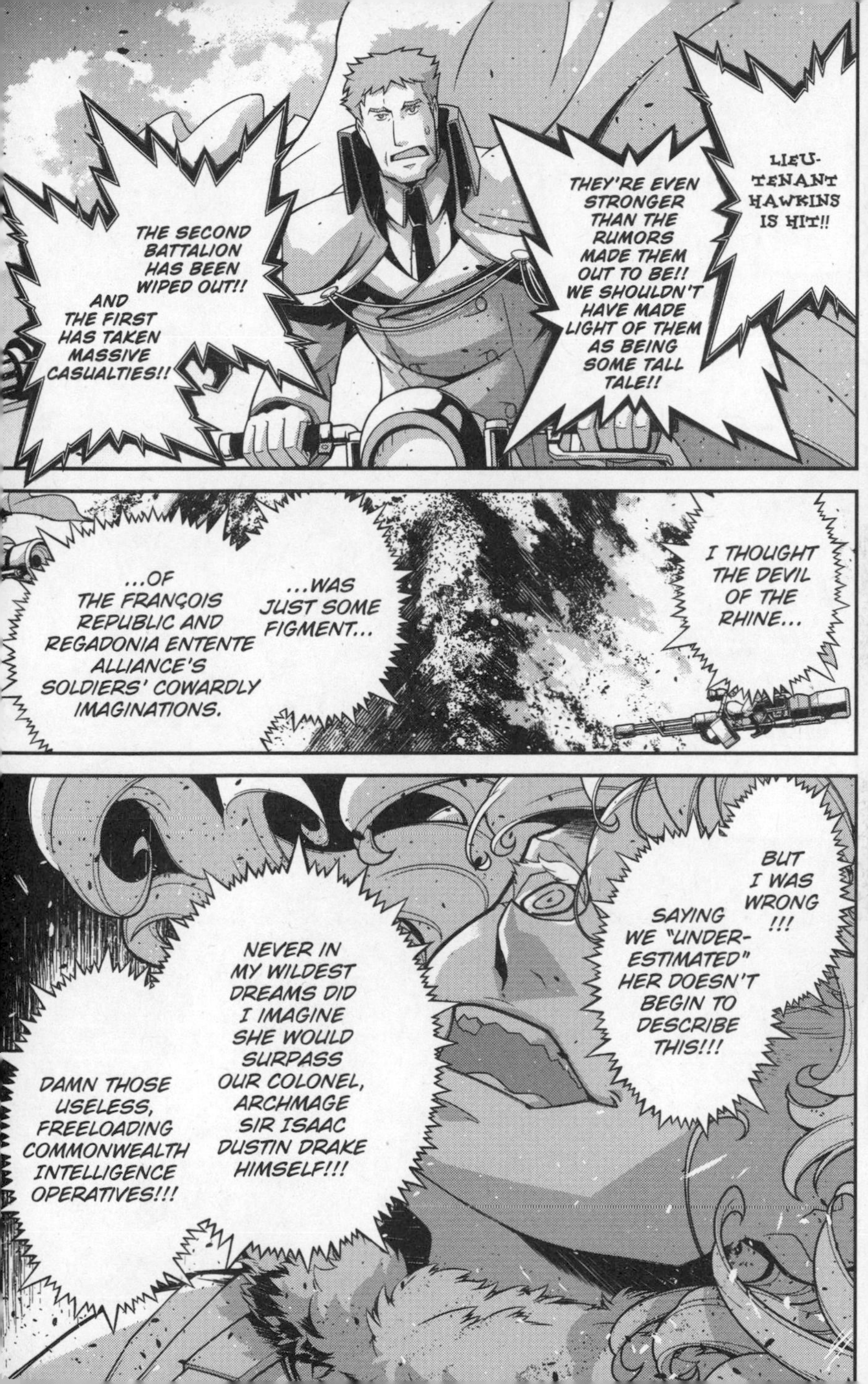
LIEU-TENANT HAWKINS IS HIT!!
THEY'RE EVEN STRONGER THAN THE RUMORS MADE THEM OUT TO BE!! WE SHOULDN'T HAVE MADE LIGHT OF THEM AS BEING SOME TALL TALE!!
THE SECOND BATTALION HAS BEEN WIPED OUT!!
AND THE FIRST HAS TAKEN MASSIVE CASUALTIES!!
I THOUGHT THE DEVIL OF THE RHINE...
...WAS JUST SOME FIGMENT...
...OF THE FRANÇOIS REPUBLIC AND REGADONIA ENTENTE ALLIANCE'S SOLDIERS' COWARDLY IMAGINATIONS.
BUT I WAS WRONG!!!
SAYING WE "UNDER-ESTIMATED" HER DOESN'T BEGIN TO DESCRIBE THIS!!!
NEVER IN MY WILDEST DREAMS DID I IMAGINE SHE WOULD SURPASS OUR COLONEL, ARCHMAGE SIR ISAAC DUSTIN DRAKE HIMSELF!!!
DAMN THOSE USELESS, FREELOADING COMMONWEALTH INTELLIGENCE OPERATIVES!!!

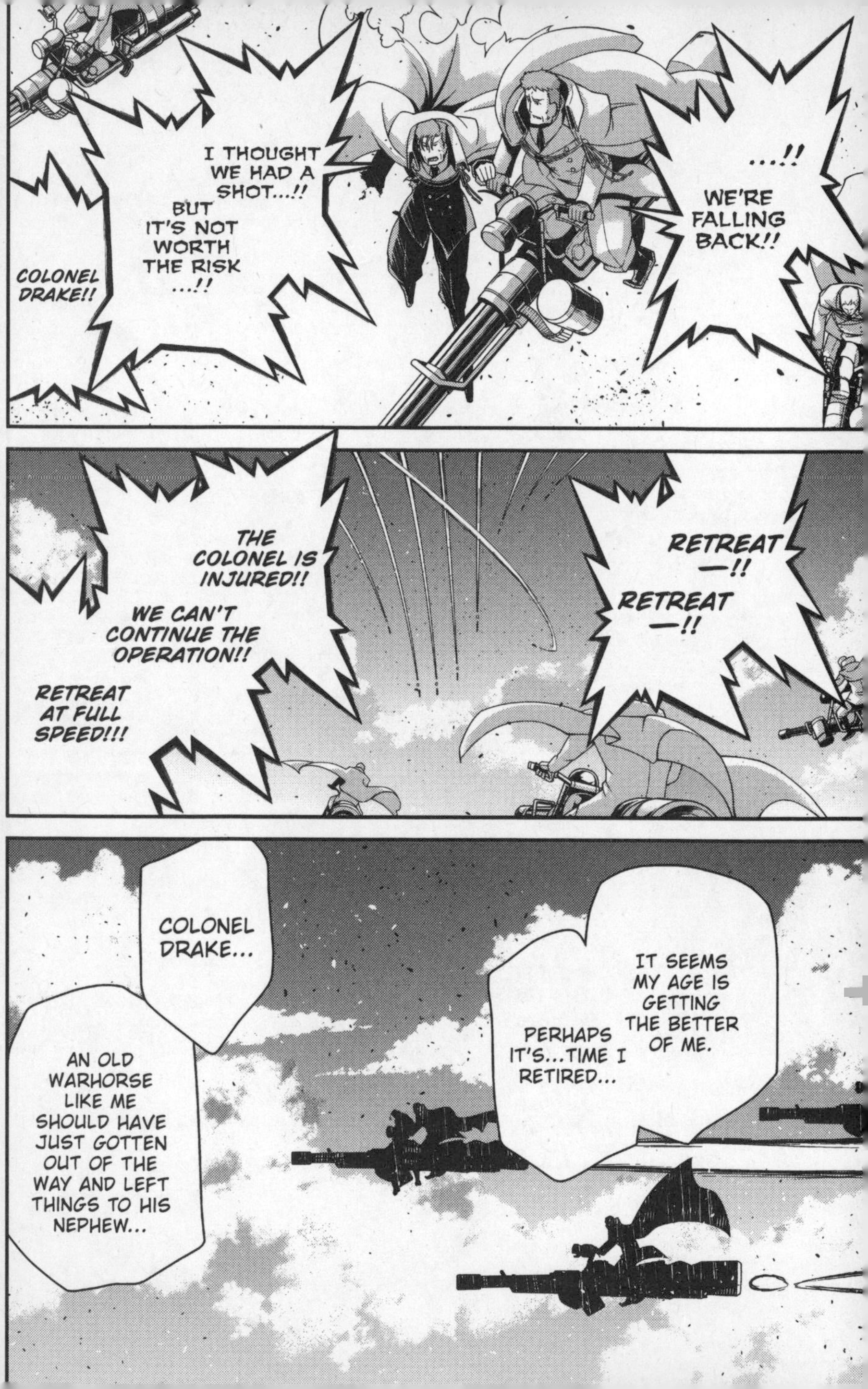

...!!
WE'RE FALLING BACK!!
I THOUGHT WE HAD A SHOT...!!
BUT IT'S NOT WORTH THE RISK ...!!
COLONEL DRAKE!!
RETREAT—!!
RETREAT—!!
THE COLONEL IS INJURED!!
WE CAN'T CONTINUE THE OPERATION!!
RETREAT AT FULL SPEED!!!
COLONEL DRAKE...
IT SEEMS MY AGE IS GETTING THE BETTER OF ME.
PERHAPS IT'S...TIME I RETIRED...
AN OLD WARHORSE LIKE ME SHOULD HAVE JUST GOTTEN OUT OF THE WAY AND LEFT THINGS TO HIS NEPHEW...

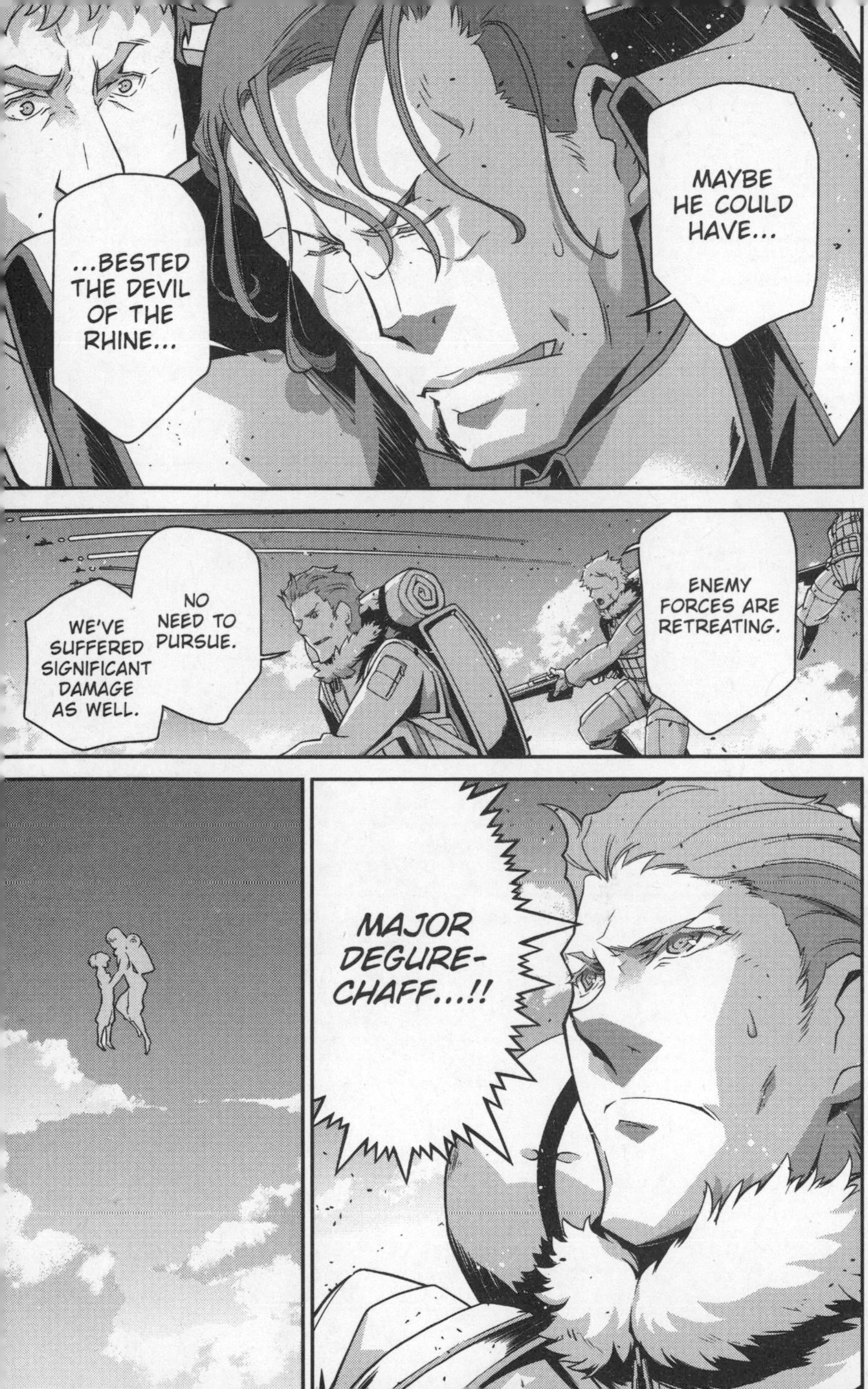
MAYBE HE COULD HAVE...
...BESTED THE DEVIL OF THE RHINE...
ENEMY FORCES ARE RETREATING.
NO NEED TO PURSUE.
WE'VE SUFFERED SIGNIFICANT DAMAGE AS WELL.
MAJOR DEGURE-CHAFF...!!

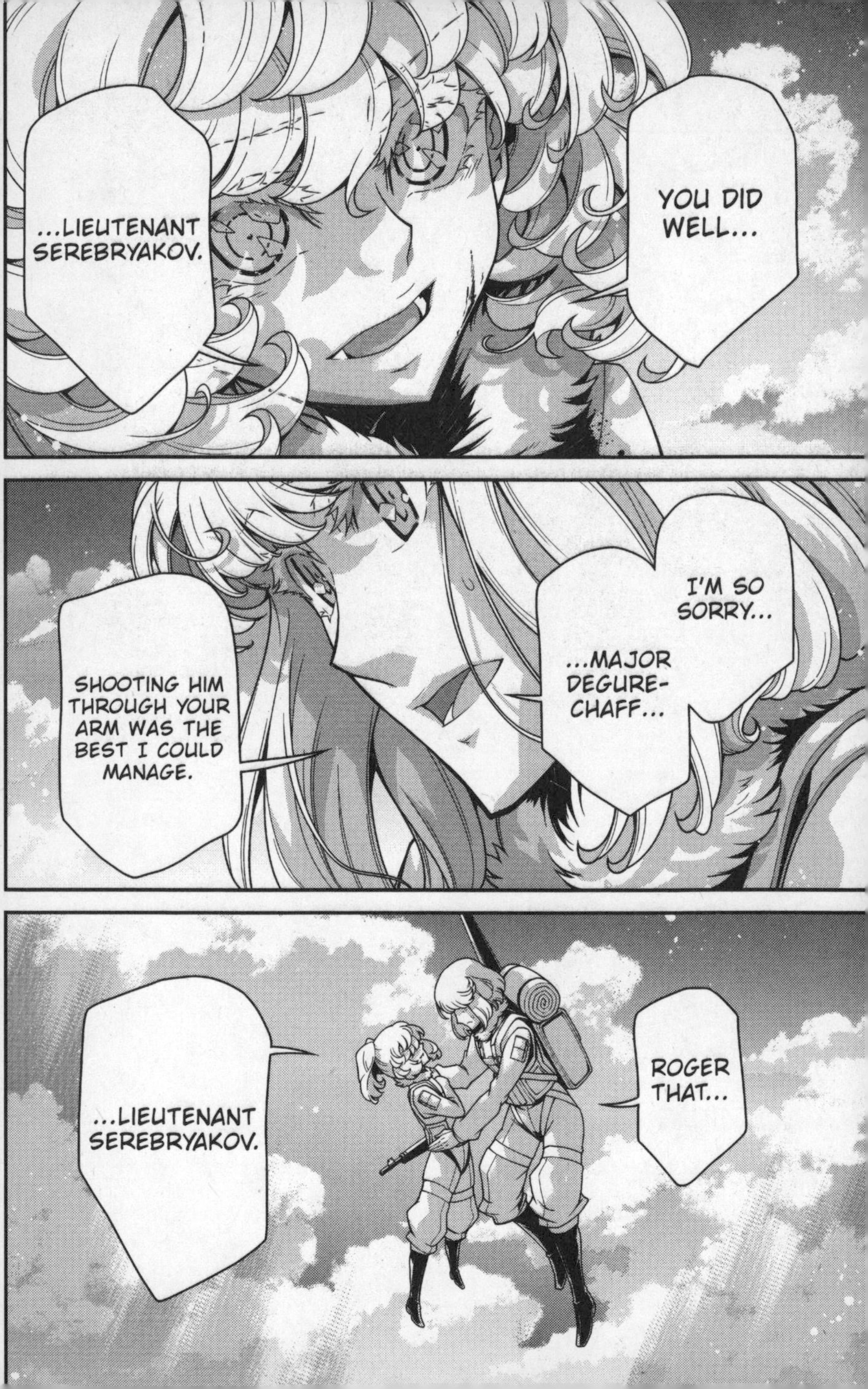
YOU DID WELL...
...LIEUTENANT SEREBRYAKOV.
I'M SO SORRY... ...MAJOR DEGURE-CHAFF...
SHOOTING HIM THROUGH YOUR ARM WAS THE BEST I COULD MANAGE.
ROGER THAT...
...LIEUTENANT SEREBRYAKOV.

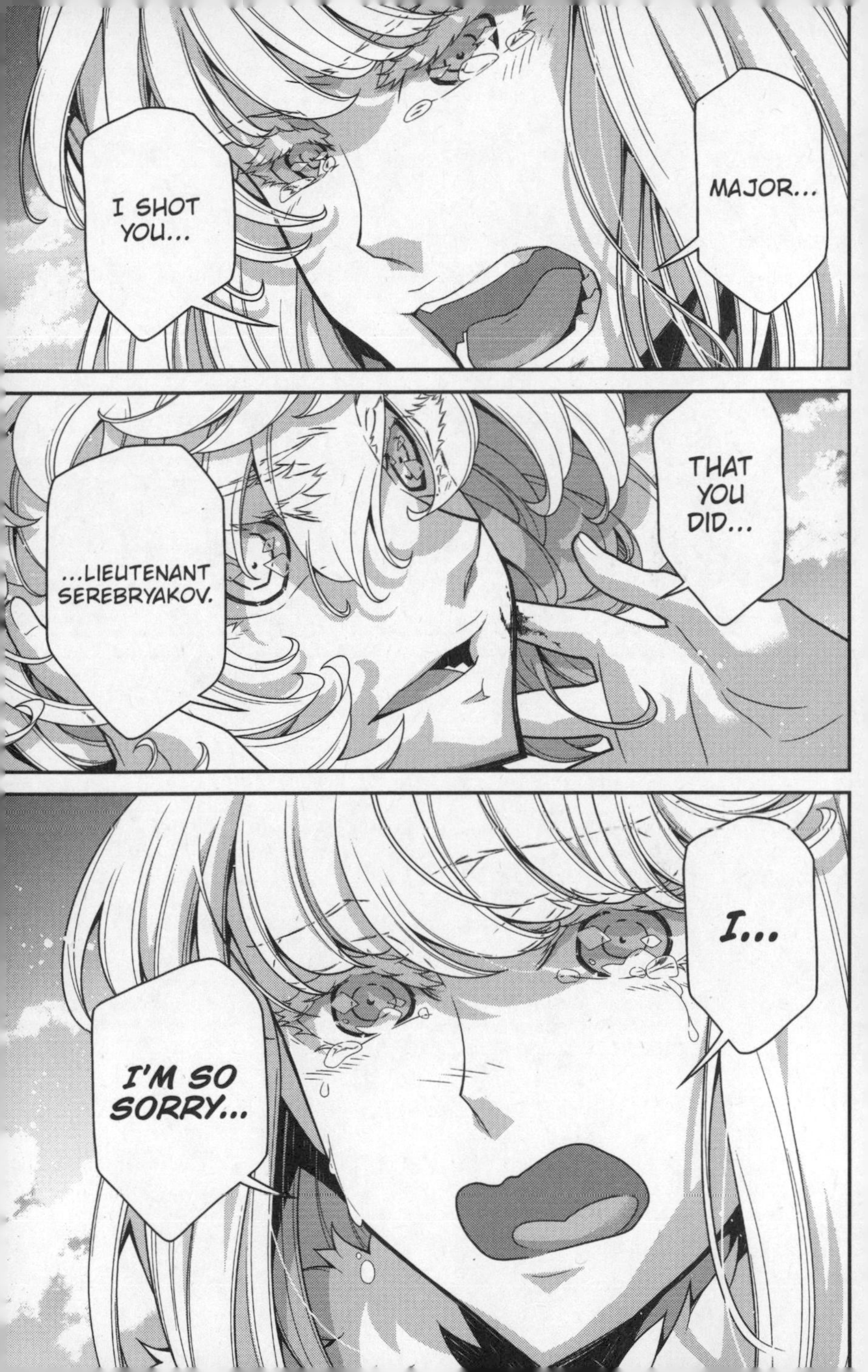
MAJOR...
I SHOT YOU...
THAT YOU DID...
...LIEUTENANT SEREBRYAKOV.
I...
I'M SO SORRY...

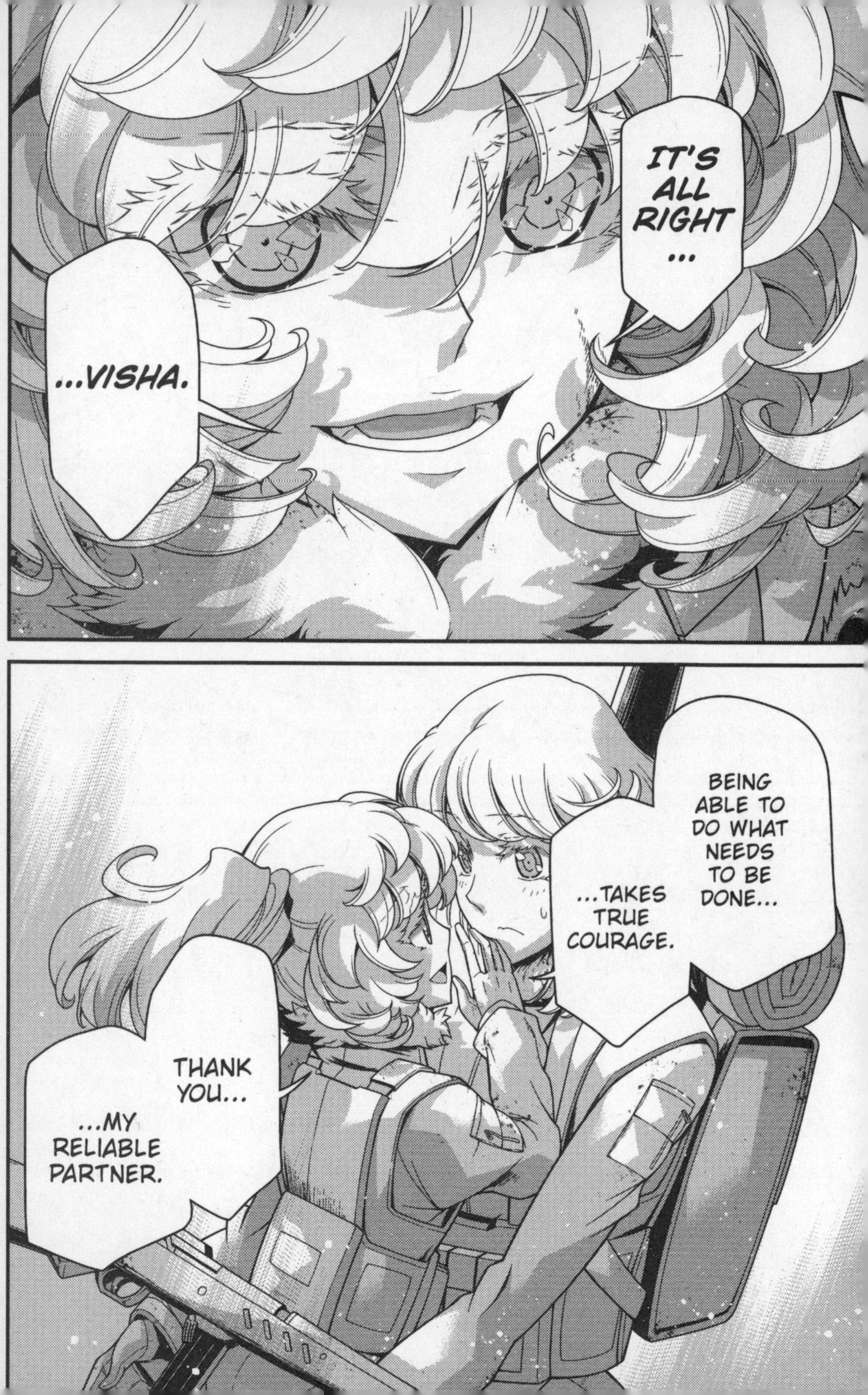
IT'S ALL RIGHT...
...VISHA.
BEING ABLE TO DO WHAT NEEDS TO BE DONE...
...TAKES TRUE COURAGE.
THANK YOU...
...MY RELIABLE PARTNER.

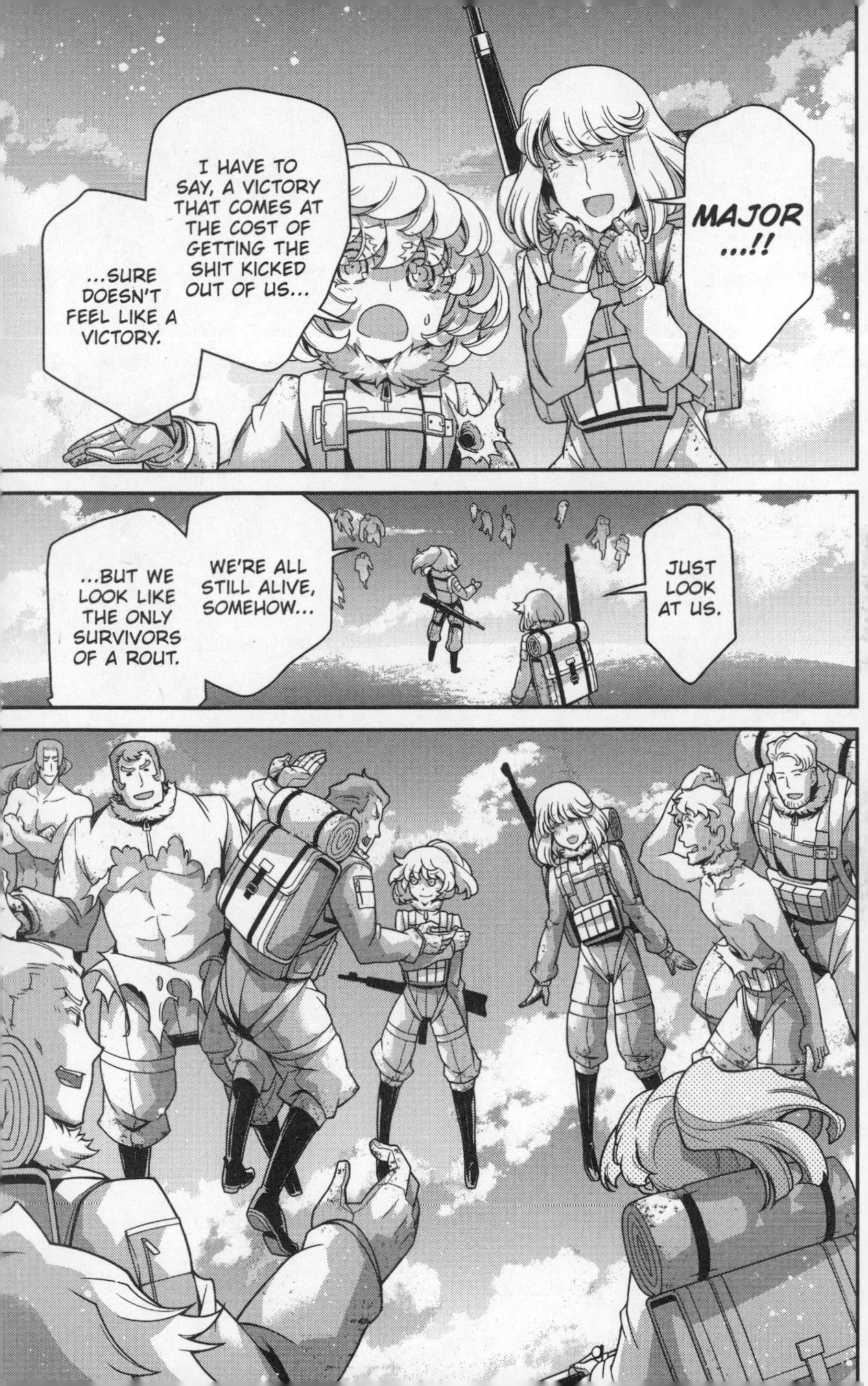
MAJOR ...!!
I HAVE TO SAY, A VICTORY THAT COMES AT THE COST OF GETTING THE SHIT KICKED OUT OF US...
...SURE DOESN'T FEEL LIKE A VICTORY.
JUST LOOK AT US.
WE'RE ALL STILL ALIVE, SOMEHOW...
...BUT WE LOOK LIKE THE ONLY SURVIVORS OF A ROUT.

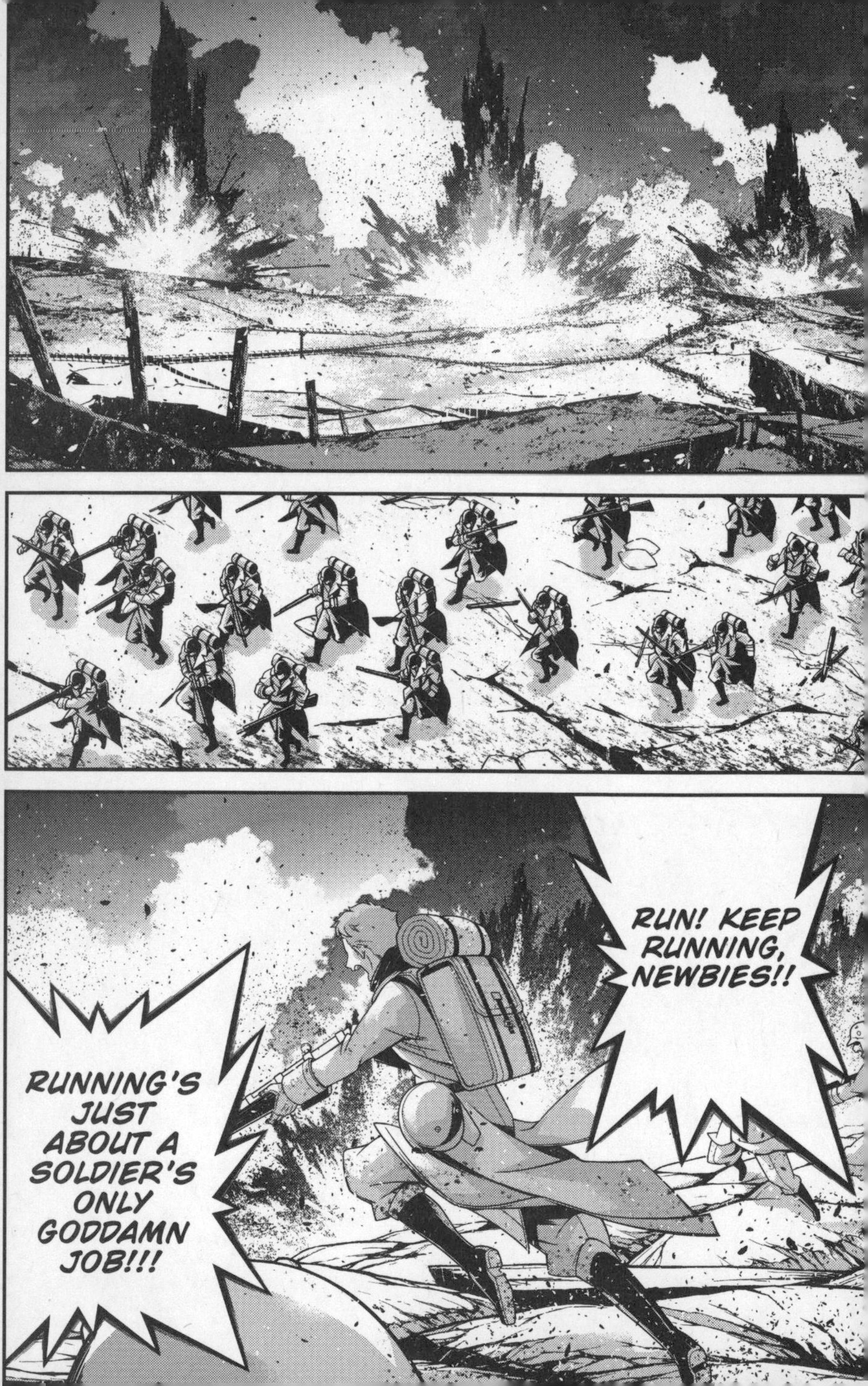
RUN! KEEP RUNNING, NEWBIES!!
RUNNING'S JUST ABOUT A SOLDIER'S ONLY GODDAMN JOB!!!

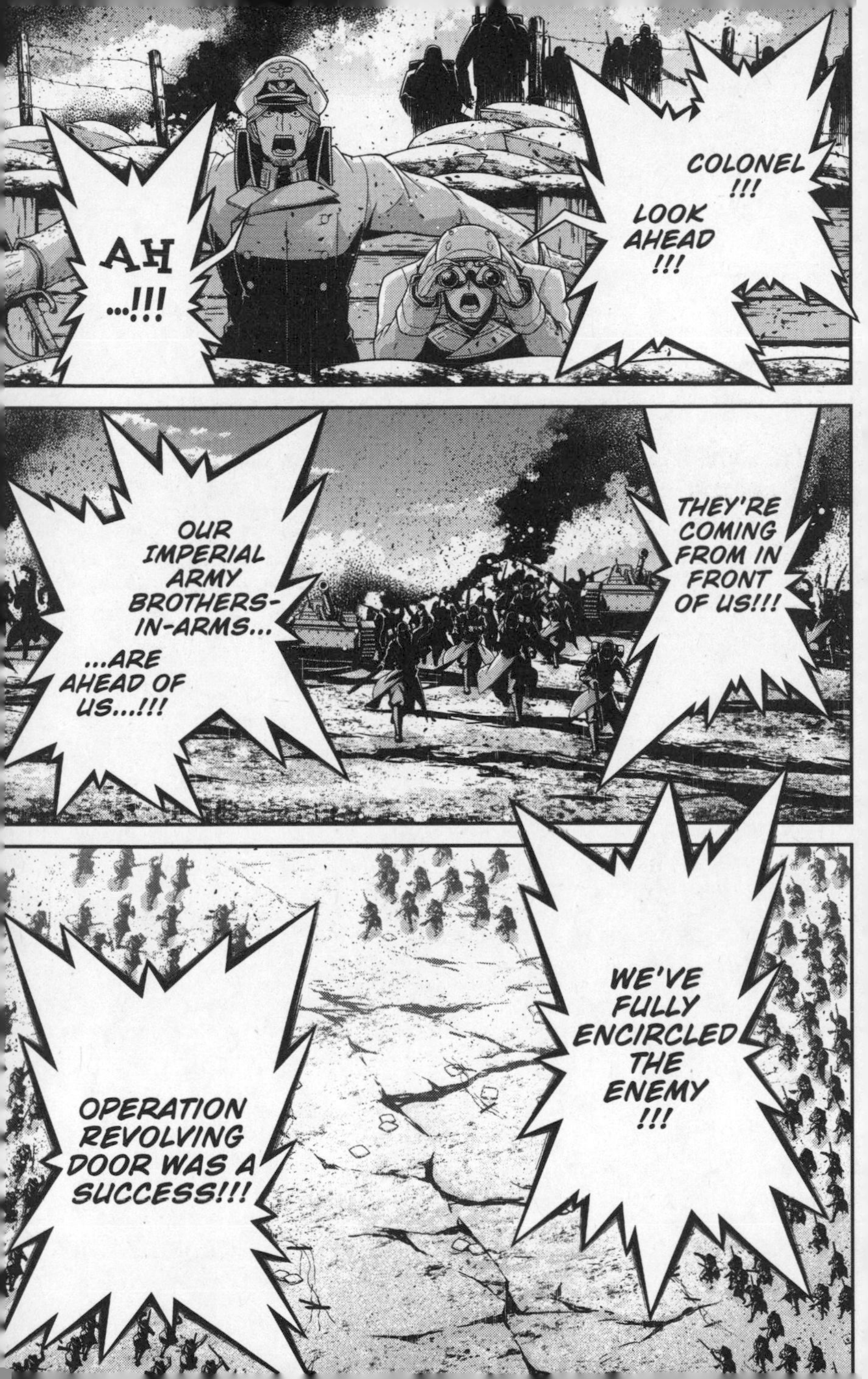
COLONEL!!!
LOOK AHEAD!!!
AH...!!!
THEY'RE COMING FROM IN FRONT OF US!!!
OUR IMPERIAL ARMY BROTHERS-IN-ARMS...
...ARE AHEAD OF US...!!!
WE'VE FULLY ENCIRCLED THE ENEMY!!!
OPERATION REVOLVING DOOR WAS A SUCCESS!!!

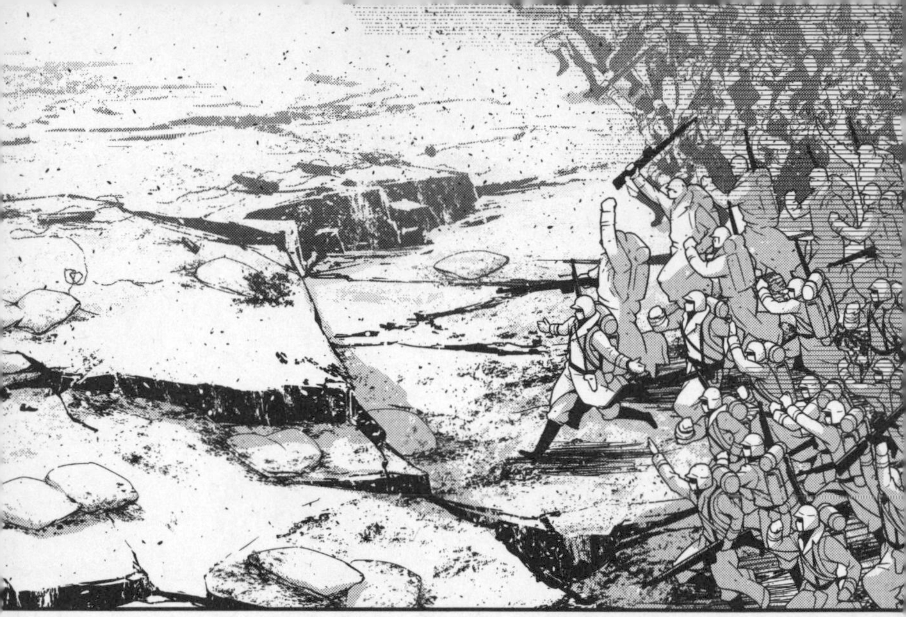
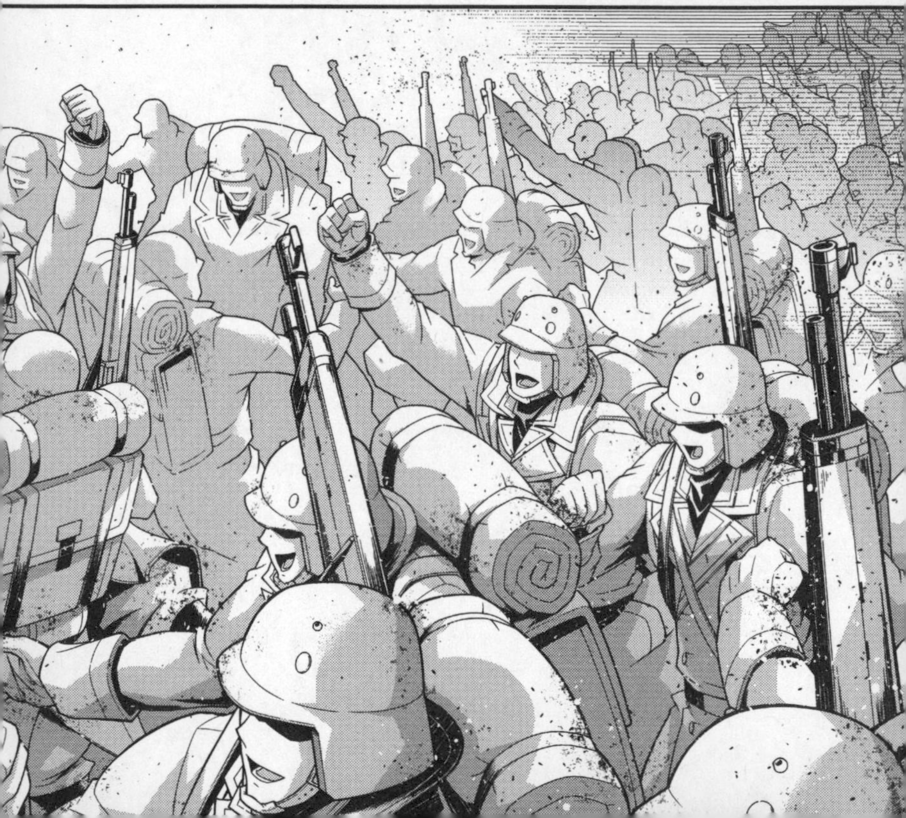

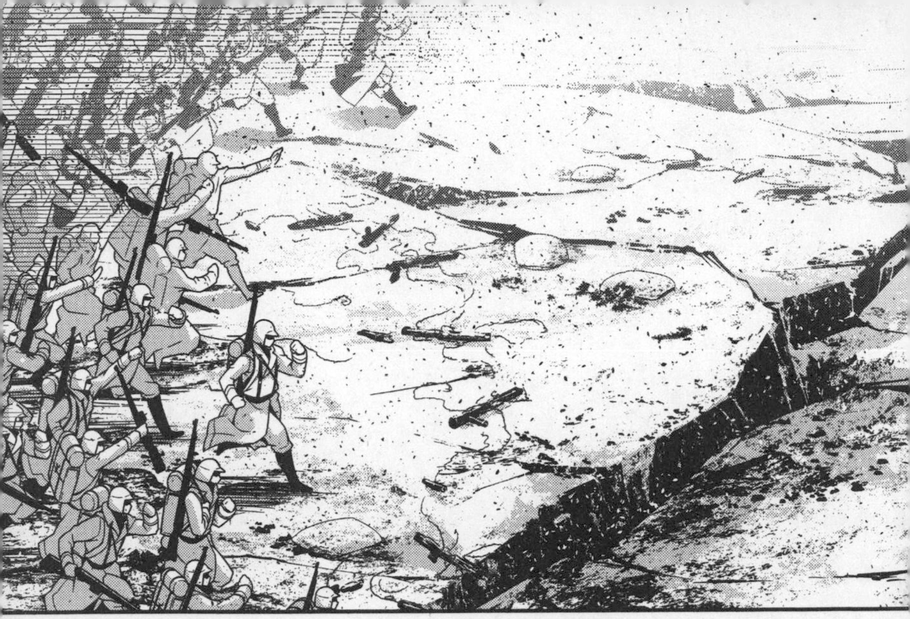
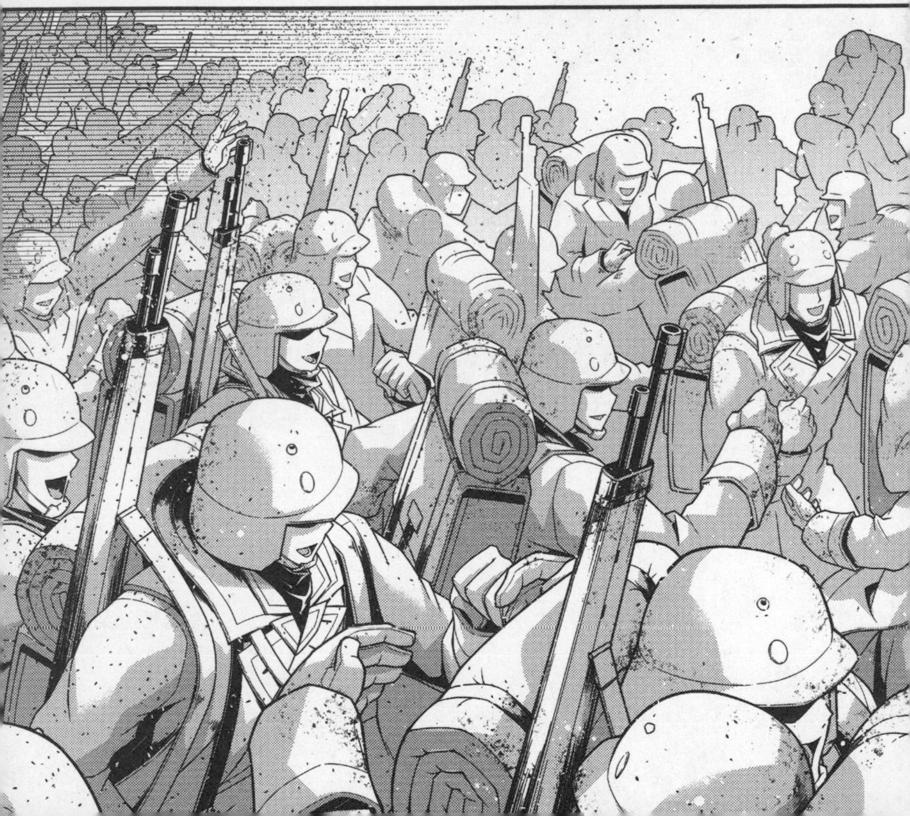

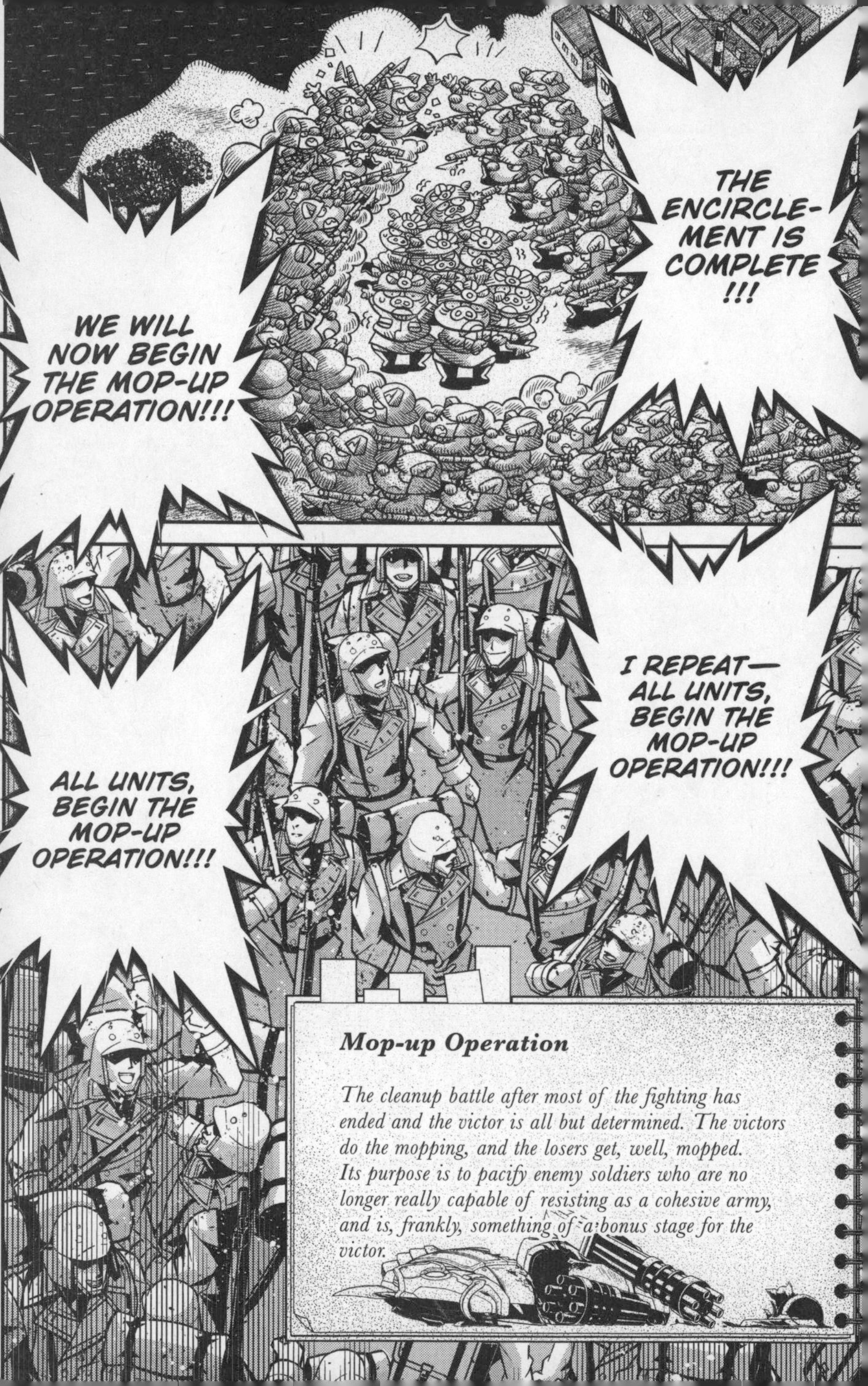
THE ENCIRCLEMENT IS COMPLETE!!!
WE WILL NOW BEGIN THE MOP-UP OPERATION!!!
I REPEAT—ALL UNITS, BEGIN THE MOP-UP OPERATION!!!
ALL UNITS, BEGIN THE MOP-UP OPERATION!!!

Mop-up Operation

The cleanup battle after most of the fighting has ended and the victor is all but determined. The victors do the mopping, and the losers get, well, mopped. Its purpose is to pacify enemy soldiers who are no longer really capable of resisting as a cohesive army, and is, frankly, something of a bonus stage for the victor.

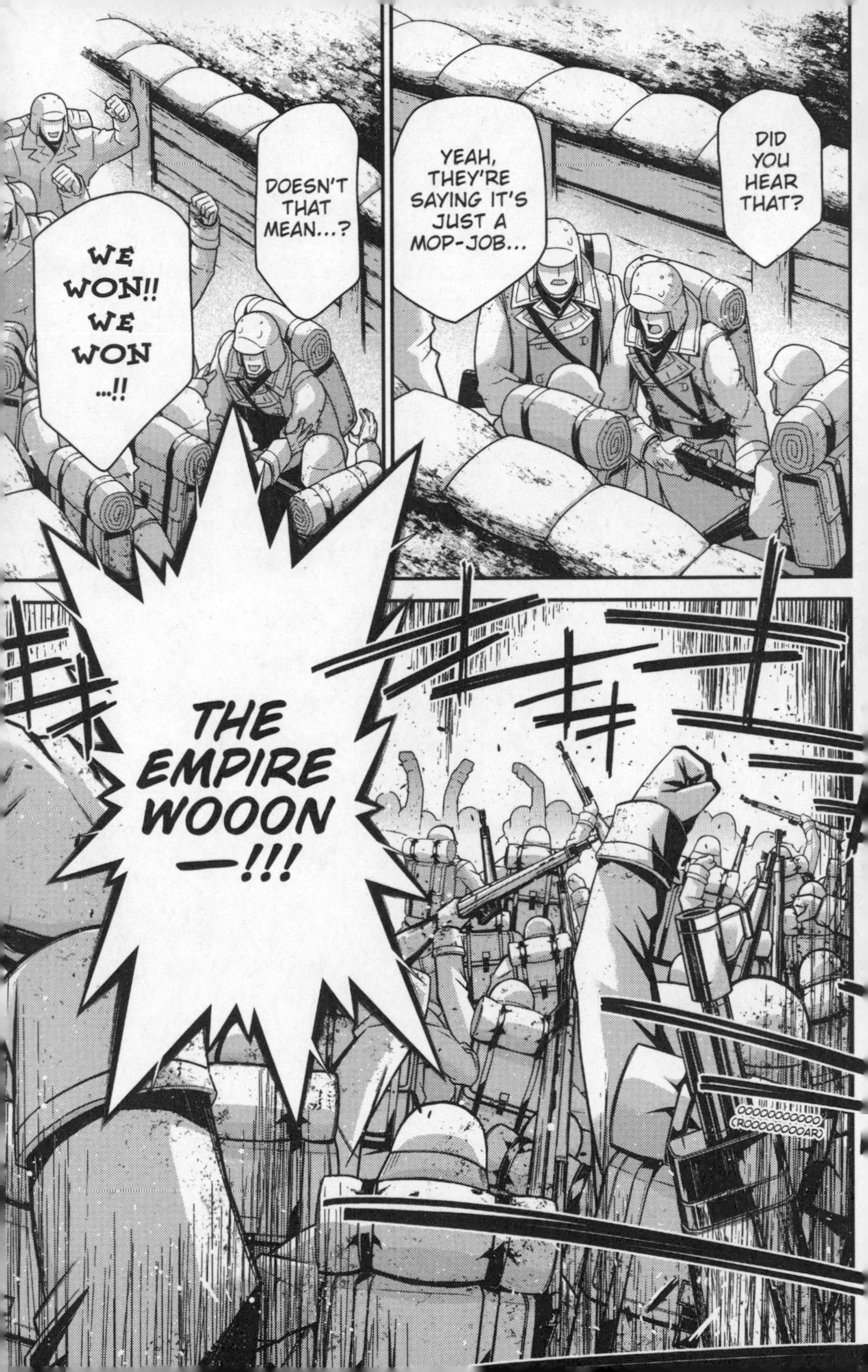
DID YOU HEAR THAT?
YEAH, THEY'RE SAYING IT'S JUST A MOP-JOB...
DOESN'T THAT MEAN...?
WE WON!! WE WON...!!
THE EMPIRE WOOON—!!!
OOOOOOOOOOO (ROOOOOOOOOAR)

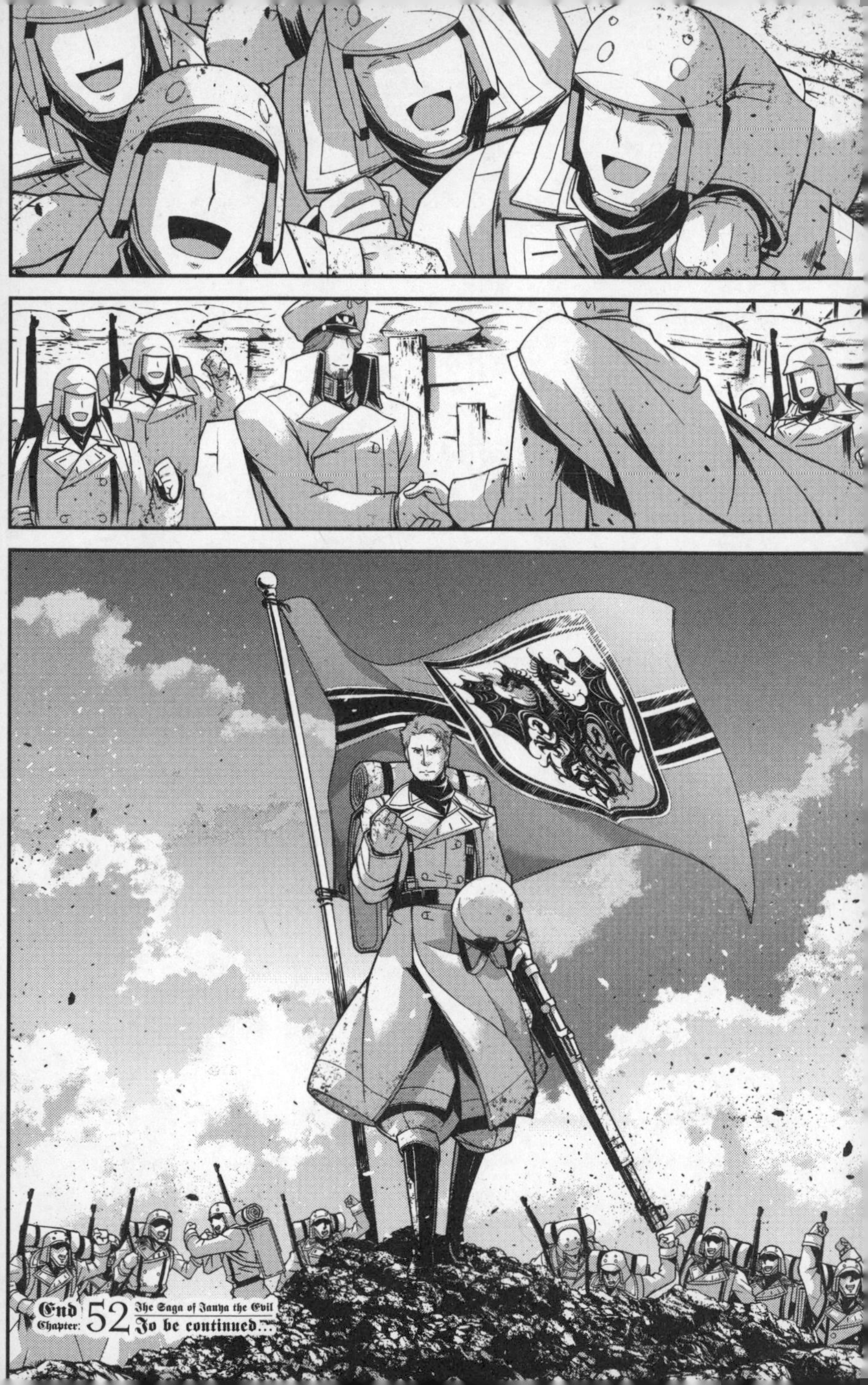
End Chapter: 52
The Saga of Tanya the Evil
To be continued...

Glossary Chapter 64

The Battle of Cannae

A third century BCE battle between Rome and Carthage in which the Carthaginian forces, led by the legendary general Hannibal, crushed the much larger Roman army in history's most famous encirclement.

At the time, Carthage was a flourishing country, located in northern Africa in what is now Tunisia, and also maintained control over the islands of Sardinia and Corsica, the southern Iberian Peninsula, and other surrounding territories. It and the former city-state of Rome, which had gone on to unify the whole Italian Peninsula, would clash with each other in what would ultimately become known as the three Punic Wars.

During the second of these Punic Wars, the Carthaginian general Hannibal traversed the seemingly impassible Alps to invade the Italian Peninsula and attack Rome. In response, Consul Varro dispatched a seventy-thousand-strong Roman army to meet the fifty thousand Carthaginian troops in battle on the plains of Cannae, beginning what is perhaps the greatest battle of ancient history.

Varro positioned the Roman troops with infantry in the center of their formation and cavalry on both flanks, with the objective of breaking straight through the center of Hannibal's line. Meanwhile, Hannibal similarly placed infantry in the center and cavalry on the flanks, making sure that his weakest forces, the Gaulish and Hispanian soldiers, were positioned in the very middle, surrounded by his well-trained Carthaginian soldiers on all sides. The Carthaginian army's flanks were also slightly pulled back, resulting in a bow-shaped formation.

When the battle began, the Roman army made quick work of the Gaulish and Hispanian soldiers, just as Hannibal had predicted, and penetrated the Carthaginian lines. However, the Carthaginian elites stationed around these weaker troops resisted the Romans' attempts to push any farther in, essentially turning their entire infantry formation into a giant bag that simultaneously softened the Roman infantry's blow and captured it whole.

At the same time, the cavalry on the left flank of the Carthaginian cavalry managed to rout their counterparts on the Roman army's right flank. Instead of pursuing the retreating cavalrymen, they circled around to take the enemies attacking their own army's right flank from behind, routing them as well. With both flanks of Carthaginian cavalry free to act at will, they continued to ignore the escaping Roman cavalry and fell upon the enemy infantry from the rear, resulting in one of the few complete encirclements in all of military history.

The Roman infantry soon deteriorated into panic and, unable to break through the Carthaginian lines, were swiftly and soundly defeated. Of particular note is the fact that sixty thousand of the seventy thousand Roman soldiers died in the battle, making this a true "battle of annihilation." It would be the most deaths in any single battle until the first World War.

Many military strategists, including Napoleon and Clausewitz, would study and devise stratagems based on Hannibal's tactics in this battle, which would go on to be considered the prime example of an encirclement. The German strategist Schlieffen would become a particular devotee of Hannibal, resulting in the Schlieffen Plan used in the invasion of France during World War I.

Glossary Chapter 65

Swimsuits of This Era

Major Degurechaff, in spite of becoming a young girl, still seems to be a healthy (?) young man on the inside, given her interest in seeing Lieutenant Serebryakov in a swimsuit. That being said, she was probably right to give up on the idea almost immediately, as the female swimsuits from this era are unlikely to be very stimulating for a man used to more contemporary designs.

To begin with, the very concept of a swimsuit, an article of clothing one wears to swim in the ocean, is itself not particularly old, only becoming prevalent after the invention of the railroad made it possible for people from all walks of life to easily visit the beach. These first-generation swimsuits were, in fact, fairly similar to normal clothes—unlike the thin, tight-fitting swimwear of the modern era, they had to be made out of thick fabric to prevent them from turning see-through when wet.

Obviously, it was something of a challenge to actually swim in this style of swimsuit, so newer iterations came with shorter sleeves, pantaloons that didn't extend all the way to the ankle, and more open collars. In Victorian-era England, where social norms prohibited women from showing skin, mobile changing stations that could be pulled all the way to the coastline grew commonplace. Women would enter one door facing the coast fully dressed in their normal clothes, change into their swimsuits inside, and exit straight into the sea from the opposing door.

In this manner, women's swimsuits gradually began to show more skin, but during the 1900s (the decade, not the century), they still largely resembled normal clothes, complete with long skirts and fairly high collars. During this period, the Australian professional swimmer Annette Kellerman caused an uproar by wearing a swimsuit that only went down to her thighs and fully exposed her shoulders. Most shocking of all was the fact that it was skin-tight, similar to contemporary swimsuits. Despite being arrested for public indecency for wearing such an outfit, Kellerman's arguments that it was purely intended to be practical for swimming and that women had the right to wear what they chose found support, and most female athletes would be wearing similar swimsuits by the time of the 1912 Olympics.

Finally, by the 1920s, skintight swimsuits made out of a material called rayon had become normalized. It was also becoming common for swimsuits to be worn outside of the water for sunbathing and the like, and with the issue of functionality largely resolved, their fashionability began to grow in importance.

So if Lieutenant Serebryakov were to wear a swimsuit, it would likely be one of those one-piece rayon affairs. Though two-piece swimsuits did exist at the time, they had only been worn at individual fashion shows and were not yet in popular usage.

However, women should be able to wear whatever they please, just as Kellerman fought for, so rather than being disappointed at the lack of exposed skin, perhaps Tanya should simply be happy to see her subordinate enjoying herself.

Glossary Chapter 66

John Bull

A personification of the nation of England. He's portrayed as a "quintessential Englishman," which, in this context, usually means depicting him as an upstanding, middle-aged man who, despite being a rural landowner, is less a figure of authority and more a slightly conservative gent fond of a good beer.

The character was originally penned by the Scottish nobleman John Arbuthnot in 1712 in a pamphlet meant to lampoon England's participation in the War of the Spanish Succession. After that, portrayals of John Bull in the work of the American political cartoonist Thomas Nast, as well as in playwright George Bernard Shaw's John Bull's Other Island, helped further popularize the character.

As there is no set model for the character, his depiction is subject to some variation, but most of the time, he is dressed formally in a vest embroidered with the Union Jack, a blue frock coat or tailcoat, and a short top hat. He also has a beer belly, carries a walking stick, and is often accompanied by a bulldog.

Diamond Formation

A diamond-shaped troop formation famously used by Thessalian cavalry, contemporaries of ancient Romans. Allows easy response to attacks from any direction.

Arrow Formation

An arrowhead-shaped troop formation, just as the name suggests. The specific distribution of troops varies by country or unit, but generally speaking, the soldiers or vehicles in an arrow formation will be laid out in a "<" shape.

The arrow formation was likely first brought to Japan in the Wuzi, a classic Chinese work on military strategy, and often used in Japan's own Warring States period. Infantry in an arrow formation would often be followed by a column of cavalry, forming a "←" shape, with the latter charging forward once the infantry had created a gap in the enemy line, which proved to be a highly effective offensive tactic.

Friendly Fire

Attacking an ally on accident or due to misidentification.

The concept has existed since antiquity, but the primary cause used to be mistaking an ally for the enemy. After the development of more advanced firearms, such as machine guns and artillery, however, cases of friendly fire from missed shots due to poor aim or the imprecision inherent to firing at range grew far more common. This was a particular issue with trench warfare, as enemy lines would typically be bombarded with suppressive artillery fire before the infantry charged in. Since this tactic was more effective if less time passed between the bombardment and the charge, many soldiers ended up losing their lives to their own army's artillery fire.

Some data suggest that as many as seventy-five thousand French soldiers may have been killed by friendly artillery fire during World War I.

Glossary Chapter 67

Endorphins

A class of neurotransmitters with analgesic and euphoric effects similar to those of certain illegal drugs.

Neurotransmitters are substances naturally produced and released by the brain that bind to specific receptors found in the nervous system to produce various physiological effects. These include opioids, which are released when the body receives an external wound to inhibit pain and induce a state of intoxication, and monoamines, which are linked to pleasure and desire. They are essential to the functioning of complex biological life, including humans. All illegal drugs work by mimicking the structure of a naturally occurring neurotransmitter, allowing them to bind to the same receptors to artificially induce states of intoxication or pleasure.

While β-endorphin is the namesake of the magic formula featured in The Saga of Tanya the Evil, all endogenous opioids (a category which includes endorphins) and endocannabinoids, as well as dopamine, a monoamine, are neurotransmitters capable of causing these effects. However, β-endorphin is particularly well-known for being immediately released in large quantities when the body is wounded to temporarily inhibit pain.

Drugs such as heroin and morphine, which are capable of artificially inducing these effects, are made from opium, which is why they and other substances that bind to the same receptors are known as "opioids." Cannabinoids, another class of drugs that produce similar effects, bind to the same receptors as endocannabinoids, the neurotransmitters responsible for runner's high.

Meanwhile, dopamine and other monoamines have been linked to pleasure, desire, and the ability to retain new information. Drugs that essentially hack these functions, such as cocaine and methamphetamines, are called "stimulants." Opioids and cannabinoids are considered "downers" that work by numbing pain or unhappiness, while stimulants are considered "uppers" that induce states of pleasure or desire.

Be warned that drugs which deliberately tamper with the natural functioning of the brain are incredibly addictive, and their abuse can lead to mental or physical damage and even death. Just don't use them. It's illegal.

Thwart

To prevent someone from accomplishing something; to impede them from acting as they desire. The Japanese equivalent, seichuu, literally means "to pull someone's elbow."

According to the classical Chinese text Lüshi Chunqiu (Master Lü's Spring and Autumn Annals), when the Confucian scholar Fu Zijian was asked to help govern his master's county, he held one of the retainers his master had sent to assist him by the elbow and ordered him to attempt to write, jostling him all the while. The retainer returned to his master and informed him of Fu Zijian's object lesson that "whatever you may try to achieve, you will be unable to accomplish your aims with someone pulling on your elbow," meaning that he would be unable to effectively govern if his master attempted to interfere with his efforts. As a result, Fu Zijian was left to his own devices to govern as he pleased, producing incredible results said to astound all who visited.

Glossary Chapter 68

Triple-Dealing Mouths

Likely a tongue-in-cheek reference to England's post-WWI Palestinian foreign policy, known in Japan as sanmaijita gaikou ("triple-dealing diplomacy"; lit. "three-tongued diplomacy," a pun on nimaijita, lit. "two-tongued" but figuratively meaning "duplicitous" or "double-dealing").

After England and the other Allied nations defeated the Central Powers in World War I, the Ottoman Empire—one such Central Power—was dissolved. By this point, in order to best make use of the Ottoman Empire's former territory to its own benefit, England had made three agreements with three different involved parties that ended up stepping all over one another. These treaties were the "Sykes–Picot Agreement" over how to split up the Ottoman territory with the French and Russians; the "Balfour Declaration," which established a "national home" for the Jewish people; and the "McMahon–Hussein Correspondence," a series of letters promising to recognize Arab independence in exchange for a wartime rebellion against the Ottoman Empire.

The Sykes-Picot Agreement was a secret treaty, signed into effect when the end of the war was in sight, in which the participating countries, in the name of avoiding the risk of any of the others ending up with the entire Ottoman territory, defined their areas of interest in the region so that they could divide it up among themselves. Meanwhile, the Jewish people, who were under the impression that Palestine, which was being temporarily governed by the League of Nations, would be given to them as an independent state, thanks to the Balfour Declaration, soon ended up butting heads with the Arabic peoples in the region, who had been promised far more land than they actually received in the McMahon–Hussein Correspondence.

The Balfour Declaration was a public promise to establish a country for the Jewish people, largely as a way to rally the large Jewish community in America to support and fund the American war effort. British officials wrote in a document addressed to Zionist leaders that "His Majesty's Government view with favour the establishment in Palestine of a national home for the Jewish people." The phrase "national home" was widely interpreted in the Jewish community as being an independent state, but was apparently only meant as something akin to the Indian reservations in the United States. In addition, as many Arabs were already living in Palestine at the time, the influx of Jews as the result of the Declaration would ultimately spark an intractable ethnic conflict.

Finally, England had agreed to acknowledge an independent Arab state in exchange for the Arab Revolt against the Ottoman Empire in the McMahon–Hussein Correspondence, which became a lasting source of resentment among the Arabic peoples once it became known that much of the Ottoman Empire's territory had already been divided up among other parties by the Sykes-Picot Agreement.

The end result of England's triple-dealing and drawing of arbitrary borders in the Middle East was the Israeli-Palestinian conflict, which continues to this day.

Glossary Chapter 69

Marmite

A processed paste made primarily of brewer's yeast and largely eaten on toast and crackers. Also referred to as the national dish of England, as it's eaten almost exclusively there and in former British territories.

The British had originally just eaten lees, the deposits of yeast that settle in beer barrels during the fermentation process, but once they figured out how to generate such quantities of yeast extract that it could be turned into a concentrated paste, it was bottled and sold across the country. Yeast extract is so rich in vitamins and minerals, such as folic acid, calcium, iron, and zinc, that it's sold in pill form as a health supplement elsewhere, but for all that it's treated as a plant-based health food, it also contains a whole lot of salt and should be eaten in moderation.

Marmite's unique flavor and smell is something of an acquired taste, making it to England what natto is to Japan. It's a hard taste to describe—both briny and extremely bitter, sort of like burned soy sauce or unsweetened molasses. Even among the English, who have somehow grown to enjoy it, it's never eaten on its own, instead usually being thinly spread on buttered toast. It's also commonly used as seasoning on foods like baked beans or pasta and as a secret ingredient in stews. You can apparently even purchase Marmite-flavored sweets and baby food in England.

In short, it's an extremely divisive flavor—it makes people who hate it want to vomit, while people who like it can't get enough. Many residents of the former British colony of New Zealand are in the latter camp, eating it as a breakfast staple; when a 2011 Christchurch earthquake temporarily halted the country's domestic production of Marmite, the resulting shortage was dubbed "Marmageddon" in the media. Honestly, it's probably not a great idea to stuff your mouth full of Marmite—especially not if you have three tongues to better facilitate triple-dealing (see prev. page). Experiencing the taste of Marmite magnified threefold would probably make you explode into a mushroom cloud of sheer bitterness that would still have people gagging a hundred years from now.

"For a righteous man may fall seven times and rise again, but the wicked shall fall by calamity."

A quote from the Old Testament's Book of Proverbs, a collection of wise sayings supposedly written by King Solomon. Just like in the proverb, the fallen members of Major Tanya Degurechaff's company rose back up, full of vim and vigor, to fight once more.

Also possibly the source of the Japanese idiom nanakoribi yaoki ("Fall down seven times, get back up eight").

The Saga of Tanya the Evil

18

Original Story: Carlo Zen   Art: Chika Tojo
Character Design: Shinobu Shinotsuki

Special Thanks

Carlo Zen

Shinobu Shinotsuki

Takamaru

KURI

Miira

Yamatatsu

Agatha

Kuuko

Shinno Himegami

Yoshitsuki Toyama

Koushi Ketsu

Figurine sales and production
Plabbit

THE SAGA OF TANYA THE EVIL 18

ORIGINAL STORY: Carlo Zen

ART: Chika Tojo ❧ CHARACTER DESIGN: Shinobu Shinotsuki

Translation: Richard Tobin ❧ Lettering: Rochelle Gancio

This book is a work of fiction. Names, characters, places, and incidents are the product of the author's imagination or are used fictitiously. Any resemblance to actual events, locales, or persons, living or dead, is coincidental.

YOJO SENKI Vol. 18
©Chika Tojo 2020
©Carlo Zen
First published in Japan in 2020 by KADOKAWA CORPORATION, Tokyo.
English translation rights arranged with KADOKAWA CORPORATION, Tokyo
through TUTTLE-MORI AGENCY, INC., Tokyo.

English translation © 2023 by Yen Press, LLC

Yen Press
150 West 30th Street, 19th Floor
New York, NY 10001

Visit us at yenpress.com
facebook.com/yenpress
twitter.com/yenpress
yenpress.tumblr.com
instagram.com/yenpress

First Yen Press Edition: January 2023
Edited by Yen Press Editorial: Riley Pearsall
Designed by Yen Press Design: Wendy Chan

Yen Press is an imprint of Yen Press, LLC.
The Yen Press name and logo are trademarks of Yen Press, LLC.

The publisher is not responsible for websites (or their content) that are not owned by the publisher.

Library of Congress Control Number: 2017954161

ISBNs: 978-1-9753-4262-3 (paperback)
978-1-9753-4263-0 (ebook)

1 3 5 7 9 10 8 6 4 2

WOR

Printed in the United States of America